CRAFTING KNOWLEDGE-BASED SYSTEMS

Expert Systems Made ~~Easy~~ *Realistic*

John Walters
Digital Equipment Corporation

Norman R. Nielsen
SRI International

WILEY

A Wiley-Interscience Publication

JOHN WILEY & SONS

New York   Chichester   Brisbane   Toronto   Singapore

Library of Congress Cataloging in Publication Data:

Walters, John R., 1933-
    Crafting knowledge-based systems: expert systems made easy
realistic / John R. Walters, Norman R. Nielsen.
             p.   cm.
    "A Wiley-Interscience publication."
    Bibliography: p. 333
    Includes index.
    ISBN 0-471-62479-9. ISBN 0-471-62480-2 (pbk.)
    1. Expert systems (Computer science) I. Nielsen, N. R.
(Norman R.) II. Title.
QA76.76.E95W36 1988
006.3'3—dc19   87-28055
                                                    CIP

Printed in the United States of America

10 9 8 7 6 5 4 3 2

PREFACE

The craftsman shown here is carefully finishing a section of the galley cabinetry to be fitted into a fine sailing yacht. Because the galley is a major focal point of life below decks, a craftsman pays careful attention to the joinery and finish of the teakwood as well as to the stainless steel sink hardware. This close attention to detail in crafting a high-quality yacht is very similar to the close attention that knowledge crafters pay to domain expertise, end-user needs, assembly, and testing in the development of a well-crafted knowledge-based system. The dedication and pride in the finished product exhibited by craftsmen of yachts and knowledge-based systems are also similar. Accordingly, we have chosen to use the sailing analogy as an introduction to each chapter in this book.

We have spent the past several years at SRI International applying artificial intelligence technology and knowledge-based system tools in a variety of contexts. Throughout this work we have observed a tremendous interest in, as well as a need for, information about the *process* of building knowledge-based systems. Managers and prospective application developers are particularly in need of such information, as are those who have been burned by the prevalent "it's easy, just put together a few if-then rules" philosophy and are seeking to make a fresh start.

Although we have searched, we have not yet found the right book to recommend to these individuals. Most books on knowledge-based systems are oriented toward theory, tools, or descriptions of completed applications. While such books certainly have their place, they usually focus on areas other than those needed by the people responsible for managing and applying the technology. Having received so many requests for this type of information, we decided to write this book for managers, prospective developers, and others concerned about effectively applying knowledge-based system technologies to solve operational problems in business and industry.

We have arranged the book in three parts: Planning and Designing a Knowledge-Based Application, Crafting a Knowledge-Based Application, and Knowledge Representation. Together, the first two parts describe the process of building a knowledge-based application from start to completion, from concept to operational use. This material should be equally of value to managers and developers alike. Part III on knowledge representation techniques is necessary given the current state of the technology. Many of the difficulties that organizations encounter in trying to develop knowledge-based systems can be traced to their failure to understand the scope of the technology they attempted to use. Part III should appeal primarily to system designers and developers.

The title we have chosen for this book reflects our philosophy. We believe that knowledge-based systems are *crafted* rather than *engineered*. The word "engineering" connotes the application of a precise metric to an area of knowledge, but our understanding of knowledge acquisition and representation has not yet reached the point that we can "engineer" these processes in the same way. Even the science of psychology, which is presumably much farther advanced than knowledge-based systems, has not yet been "engineered."[1] In contrast, "crafting" connotes to us the process by which an artist creates a work of art by hand. Therefore, we have used the term "knowledge crafting," rather than the more traditional but misleading term "knowledge engineering," throughout this book.

We have become keenly sensitive to the differences among those who research, apply, or sell artificial intelligence. Considerable theory underlies the applications that are being built, but trying to build an application on the basis of theory alone is a painful task. On the other hand, despite the sales pitches and media hype, crafting a high-quality knowledge-based system is neither simple nor easy. Fortunately, the middle

---

[1]Although we have met chemical, electrical, and civil engineers, we know of no one professing to be a "mental engineer"!

ground between the trivial and the impossible is vast; many applications have quite favorable benefit-cost and risk-reward ratios. The subtitle for this book[2] reflects our desire to portray the process of crafting an expert system with realism rather than with either impractical theory or unrealizable idealism.

The planning, designing, building, and testing of a high-quality knowledge-based system is analogous to the planning, designing, building, and testing of a fine sailing yacht. Although the techniques are clearly different, the methodology is similar. Further, the developers must have the same dedication, the same attention to detail, and the same pride in the finished product. Accordingly, we have carried this analogy throughout the book, using pictures of the crafting of sailing yachts to illustrate the less picturesque process of crafting a knowledge-based system. The motto of Sabre Yachts,[3] "Crafted with Fierce Pride," matches the development philosophy that the knowledge crafter should have.

We would like to gratefully acknowledge the wholehearted cooperation we have received from Sabre Yachts (South Casco, Maine), which furnished the yachting pictures we have used to illustrate this book. We would also like to thank our colleagues for their help and forbearance while we were writing the book. Special thanks are due to Connie Brede and Barbara Stevens, whose critical comments and detailed suggestions have contributed significantly to the book's content and readability.

John Walters
Norman R. Nielsen

---

[2]Expert systems made realistic (rather than easy).
[3]Sabre Yachts, South Casco, Maine 04077.

C O N T E N T S

OVERVIEW   1
>   Definition of Terms   3
>   Who Are the Players?   8
>   The Knowledge-Based System Life Cycle   9

PART I

Planning and Designing a Knowledge-Based Application   11

Chapter 1   Getting Started   13
>   The Development Cycle of a Knowledge-Based Application   14
>   Ways That Knowledge-Based Technology Can Help   18
>   Good Programming Practices   20
>   Embedding Knowledge-Based Systems in Existing Systems   21
>   General Human and Organizational Constraints   22

Chapter 2   Forming the Development Team   25
>   Management   26
>   Staffing   28
>   The Knowledge-Crafting Team   29
>   An Apprenticeship Program   30

Chapter 3   Acquiring Knowledge   34
>   Interviewing   35
>   Problems with Experts   39
>   Preparing for Interviews   42
>   Early Interview Sessions   43
>   Ongoing Interviews   44
>   Testing Interviews   44
>   Role of Apprentices in Interviewing   45

Chapter 4   Developing the Requirements   46
>   The Design Process   47
>   Understanding the Application Environment   48
>   Establishing the Requirements   48
>   Whose Requirements?   50
>   Formulating the Requirement Set   52
>   Summary   56

Chapter 5   Conducting the Feasibility Study   57
>   Overview   58
>   Technical Issues   60
>   Suitability of the Problem   60
>   Characteristics of the Knowledge   63

Characteristics of the Experts   66
Interfaces   69
Validation and Testing   71
Economic Issues   72
Cultural Issues   75
Constraints   76
Pulling It All Together   77
References   78

Chapter 6   Crafting a System Design   79
Crafting the Design   80
The Representation of Knowledge   82
Selecting Appropriate Knowledge Representations   83
Selecting Development Tools   87
Hardware   88
Software   90
Delivery Considerations   91
Approaches   92
Environment   97
Interfaces   99
Developing an Initial Design   102

PART II

Crafting a Knowledge-Based Application   107

Chapter 7   Crafting the Prototype Application   109
General Prototyping Considerations   110
Strategies for Prototyping   112
Prototyping Using the First Development Strategy   113
Prototyping Using the Second Development Strategy   117
Prototyping Using the Third Development Strategy   119
Perspective   120

Chapter 8   Evaluating the Prototypes   121
The Evaluation Process   122
Testing   124
Testing Techniques   129
Debugging   136
Validation   140

Chapter 9   Crafting the Pilot Application   144
Illustrative Applications   145
Application 1: The Architectural Advisor   147
Application 2: The Mortgage Loan Advisor   148
Application 3: The Transaction Validator   150

Application 4: A Built-In Diagnostic System   151
Summary   151

Chapter 10   Conducting the Operational Phases   152
Pilot Operation Phase   153
Operational Phase   162

Chapter 11   Preparing a Project Schedule   166
Scheduling a Study to Select Among Candidate Applications   167
Scheduling the Feasibility Study for a Preselected Application   169
Scheduling the Design Effort   171
Scheduling Prototype Development   173
Scheduling Pilot Versions   176

Chapter 12   Crafting Successful Knowledge-Based Systems   180
Design   181
Knowledge Crafting   184
Operations   189
Summary   191

PART III

Knowledge Representation   193

Chapter 13   Knowledge Crafting with Rule-Based Representations   195
Backward-Chaining   196
Forward-Chaining   197
A Simple Example   197
Attributes of Rule-Based Applications Development Tools   200
Problems with Rule-Based Systems   204
Selecting an Appropriate Representation   206
References   208

Chapter 14   Knowledge Crafting with Frame-Based Reasoning   209
Frames   210
Structure   218
Inheritance   228
Relationship Knowledge   233
Other Types of Slot Contents   237
Object-Oriented Programming   243
Advantages of Frame-Based Reasoning   246
Problems with Frame-Based Reasoning   247
Summary   251
References   252

Chapter 15   Knowledge Crafting with Multiple Contexts   253
Introduction   254
The Concept of Multiple Contexts   255
Reasoning with Multiple Contexts   258
Truth Maintenance Systems   264
Search Mechanisms   272
Deciding How to Use Multiple Contexts   279
References   284

Chapter 16   Knowledge Crafting with Model-Based Representations   285
Model-Based Representations   286
Static Model Representations   289
Dynamic Model Representations   295
Advantages of a Model-Based Representation   297
Disadvantages of Incorporating Model-Based Structures   299
Summary   301
References   301

Chapter 17   Knowledge Crafting with Blackboard Representations   302
The Blackboard Concept   303
Components   304
An Analogy   310
Assumptions   312
Hierarchical Structure   314
When to Use a Blackboard Representation   317
References   318

Chapter 18   Selecting Appropriate Knowledge Representation Techniques   320
Select the Representation to Fit the Problem   321
Decompose the Problem   323
Plan for the Needed Representations   325
Work to the Strengths of the Representations   326
Keep the Problem Structure Visible   328
Understand the System Being Used   329
Summary   332

BIBLIOGRAPHY   333

INDEX   335

O V E R V I E W

One way to examine a yacht's sailing plan is to view the yacht from the very top of the mast. This overview shows the overall sailing arrangement of the vessel and the placement of the mast, boom, shrouds, stays, and halyards. With such a layout in mind, the yachtsman can then examine the details of the keel, hull, and deck structures. Similarly, our overview chapter presents the layout and arrangement of this book. With such a layout in mind, the reader can then examine details of individual chapters as appropriate.

We have divided this book into three major sections:

1. Part I deals with the design of a knowledge-based system. It covers the organization, preparation, evaluation, planning, initial knowledge acquisition, and designing processes that lead to a documented overall design for a knowledge-based system.

2. Part II discusses the implementation of the system design. It covers acquiring further knowledge, developing, testing, and validating a succession of prototype and pilot versions, as well as conducting the operational phases that lead to the successful deployment of the system.

3. Part III describes knowledge representation techniques. It covers some of the major knowledge representation techniques and their application to various types of knowledge representation situations.

Thus, the book can be regarded as a matrix, such as indicated in Figure 1, where Part I and Part II form a development axis describing the system's development from inception to deployment, while Part III forms a technology axis indicating how various knowledge representation techniques can be used to support the various phases of development.

For some readers the first few planning chapters may seem overly simple and of little use. We have deliberately included this material, however, both because we want to provide a comprehensive description of the knowledge-based system development process for persons new to the subject, and more importantly because we repeatedly see people courting disaster by not following these principles.

Some ordinary system developers have discovered that they can cut a few corners here and there and still produce a reasonably good system

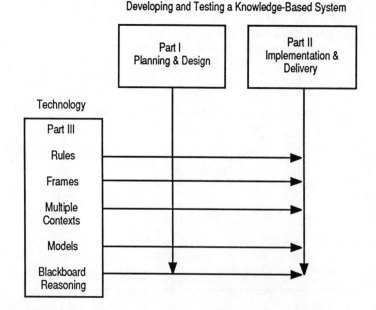

Developing and Testing a Knowledge-Based System

Figure 1 The Organization of the Book

without having to pay for their sloppiness. Knowledge-based systems, however, allow much less latitude for such sloppiness. Therefore, we feel justified in emphasizing the planning, preparation, evaluation, testing, and validation activities we describe.

Definition of Terms

Computers: Numeric and Symbolic Processing

Typically, computers and computer programs are designed to process a wealth of *numeric* information. If a problem can be reduced to numbers and an algorithm exists for processing those numbers, then the problem can likely be solved with a computer.

Computers can also be used to process information *symbolically*,[1] in which case the atom of information is not a number but a symbol for which most numerical operations are undefined.[2] By representing information in various structures of symbols (e.g., lists), analysts can define and solve an entirely different category of problems using digital computers.

Artificial Intelligence

For roughly the last 30 years researchers have been working in *artificial intelligence (AI)*, an interdisciplinary subfield of computer science that typically involves symbolic problem solving to approximate human behavior with a computer. Within the field of AI, special attention has been focused on the areas of:

- Natural language understanding
- Robotics
- Planning systems
- Speech
- Image understanding
- Knowledge-based systems.[3]

While significant research results have been achieved in each of these areas, progress in the commercialization of knowledge-based systems has been the most pronounced. Although much research remains to be performed,[4] a considerable amount of the technology has progressed

---

[1] Since digital computers record all information as numbers, a symbol is actually encoded as a number in the computer; however, in the context of this programming environment, the symbol remains an atomic unit and is not manipulated arithmetically.

[2] The only "numeric" operations defined for symbols are EQUAL and NOT EQUAL.

[3] These systems have been popularly called "expert systems," and sometimes "knowledge systems" and "knowledge-based systems." Although people have tried to distinguish between these terms to indicate various levels of complexity, no widely accepted definitions have evolved. Because these systems maintain their knowledge in the form of a separate knowledge base, the authors have chosen to use the term "knowledge-based systems" throughout this book.

[4] Research is currently being conducted on the problems presented by evidential, spatial, and temporal reasoning as well as on the topics of common sense reasoning and learning.

from the research laboratories to the commercial world where it is being applied to the successful solution of problems that heretofore had not been solved with a computer.

Knowledge-Based Systems

In the simplest of terms, the notion behind knowledge-based systems is to capture the problem-solving *expertise* of a human being—an *expert* in a highly constrained problem area, called a *problem domain*—and *represent* this person's knowledge or expertise in a computer in such a way that the computer can approximate the expert's ability to solve a particular class of problems. Examples of such knowledge-based systems are found in:

- Medical diagnosis
- Faultfinding or troubleshooting of complex electronic or mechanical systems
- Equipment configuration
- Scheduling of nonhomogeneous resources
- Parameter estimation for complex systems.

Because such knowledge-based systems do contain some portion of an expert's knowledge that can be used to solve well-defined problems in the problem domain, many knowledge-based systems have been constructed as *advisory* systems, in which the user (who is typically not an expert but rather a person who would consult an expert) interacts with the system in a dialog much in the same way that the user might interact with the real expert. Thus, the subject matter of various knowledge-based systems can be quite diverse, and the expert can be anyone from a highly trained physician to a skilled automotive mechanic.

Types of Expertise and Knowledge

Just what kind of expertise or knowledge goes into these systems? Clearly, a wealth of published information can be found in textbooks, journals, and articles on various subjects, and formal high school, college, and university training can be used for the more academic subjects. This type of information, called *public knowledge*, is more or less generally available to anyone who wants it.

Is this typically the kind of information that makes someone an expert? No, but it is a prerequisite. Normally, though, people become experts when they apply public information to a problem domain. Because the public knowledge inadequately covers the problem domain, these people become experts as they discover various rules-of-thumb, hints, and experiences that are obtained and refined over time. The true expert is the one who has an especially good collection of this information for the problem domain. A knowledge-based system is an attempt to capture this knowledge, which is called *private knowledge* or *heuristics*, and make it available to others lacking this degree of understanding.

Anyone can obtain a road map of San Francisco, for instance, and study the location of the various streets and landmarks; this is public knowledge. However, knowing the traffic patterns, which streets are hilly, what roads are well paved or presently under construction, and which are good and bad alternate routes when traffic is congested on a certain street cannot be determined from the map. For this knowledge, one would need an experienced cab driver, pizza deliverer, or fireman, a person who has learned this information from experience obtained over time.

Acquiring and Crafting Knowledge

The process of obtaining the public and private knowledge used by an expert skillful in solving problems in a constrained and restricted domain is called *knowledge acquisition*.

People who are skilled in analyzing problems, acquiring knowledge, and structuring that knowledge in a computer for solving the class of problems at hand have often been termed "knowledge engineers," supposedly indicating that they can "engineer" the knowledge into a form suitable for use in a knowledge-based system. However, we believe the current level of understanding about the process of acquiring and representing knowledge is a long way from engineering; therefore, we have chosen to use the term *knowledge crafting* throughout this book in the hope that the term *crafting* will convey more accurately the real nature of the work these people do when they select the appropriate pieces of knowledge and place and adjust those pieces in a knowledge-based system to solve a particular class of problems.

The Structure of a Knowledge-Based System

A knowledge-based system is typically arranged into three sections as follows:

1. The *knowledge base*, containing the expert's factual and relationship knowledge represented in one or more different ways

2. A knowledge-independent *inference engine*, containing the computer instructions to reason with the information contained in the knowledge base

3. A group of *interfaces*, connecting the inference engine to the user, to external data bases, as well as to other computers or computer programs.

The Knowledge Base

The knowledge base contains all the application-specific information. This information can be in the form of simple facts (e.g., data names and values), relationships (e.g., parent-child class memberships), or procedural information (e.g., sequential code for printing a report or drawing a graph).

The knowledge base is the major component of a knowledge-based system, and it is the building of this knowledge base that lies at the heart of knowledge crafting. In most applications, even after the development is complete, this knowledge base must be regularly modified to reflect changes in the problem domain. Although self-repairing or self-learning knowledge bases would be extremely useful, today's technology does not permit the automatic refinement or updating of such knowledge bases. Hence, knowledge crafters must plan for continued maintenance and updating of the knowledge base.

The Inference Engine

The inference engine is a general-purpose software "machine" that draws on information in the application knowledge base to deduce a solution to a query or to infer all consequences from a new piece of information.

Many different types of inference engines exist, each one using one or more forms of inferencing techniques. Presently, each inference engine requires that the associated application knowledge base be encoded in a form unique to that inference engine type; therefore, a knowledge base for one inference engine cannot be readily used with a different inference engine. This situation is similar to the problem of compilers and programming languages where functionally equivalent COBOL and PASCAL programs can only be compiled by their respective compilers.

The Interfaces

Knowledge-based systems typically employ two kinds of interfaces: one interface to the user, and another interface to data bases, operating systems, etc. The user interface needs to be carefully designed, since many knowledge-based systems are beginning to interface directly with users who have very little, if any, understanding of computers and require an easy-to-use interface (e.g., one that is problem oriented). Examples of such interfaces are architectural drawings for architects and circuit drawings for electronics designers. Even more severe interface requirements are posed by shop floor workers who may be wearing gloves or by customers in a bank who may not be able to type.

Many knowledge-based systems also have nonhuman interfaces to data bases, other programs in the computer, or other computers. In some cases a human interface may not even exist. Some knowledge-based systems are being embedded within the context and framework of much larger systems, so that the knowledge-based application may be invoked as a component of the larger system. In such cases a computer-encoded request is passed across the interface to the knowledge-based application, which in turn produces a computer-encoded response that is passed back across the interface to the requesting system.

Knowledge-Based System Applications

Knowledge-based systems provide a mechanism to share *existing* but *scarce* expertise:

- When the expert is *unavailable*
- When the *qualitative performance* of nonexperts needs to be enhanced

- When the *efficiency and consistency* of the expert need to be enhanced
- When others need to be *trained* to understand the expert's thought processes.

Because knowledge-based systems deal with heuristic knowledge in a very limited domain of expertise, these systems can infer or reason from a set of facts that may be incomplete or uncertain.

General problem types for which knowledge-based systems have been used include: diagnosis or classification, evaluation, selection, parameter estimation, design, and configuration. Application domains have included bioengineering, chemistry, computer configuration, design, education, engineering, finance, geology, law, equipment maintenance, management science, manufacturing, medicine, and petroleum engineering.

In the material that follows, we will use the term *knowledge-based system* to refer to system-building tools and generic knowledge-based reasoning capabilities. We will use the term *knowledge-based application* to refer to specific systems that have been developed to address specific problems.

Prerequisites

As a prerequisite for creating a knowledge-based application, the following general criteria should be met:

- No known algorithmic solution exists, thereby forcing consideration of the use of heuristic knowledge.
- The expert's solution to the problem is satisfactory (but may suffer from procedural difficulties such as timeliness).
- Decisions made by persons other than the experts are likely to be different from those of the expert and to have a significant impact on the organization in terms of:
  - financial cost
  - resource consumption
  - delay
  - risk.

These criteria fundamentally describe the economic worth of the intended system. If none of these criteria are met, the system will be of little value. Even though an elegant system could be produced to solve the problem, failing to meet any of these criteria would tend to indicate that the system, when produced, regardless of its quality or sophistication, would have little impact.

Frequently, people try to solve toy problems to "get a feel" for the technology. While solving such problems does produce some proficiency in using a tool, that effort yields very little insight into solving real problems. An analogy would be the writing of a book. Practicing typing provides competence at the keyboard, but it yields no insight to the writer on what to type. Therefore, even the first knowledge-based system application for an organization should be economically feasible, and beginners should seek guidance from experienced knowledge crafters to achieve this goal.

Who Are the Players?

People with several different roles develop a knowledge-based system:

- Management
- End-users
- Project champion
- Experts
- Knowledge crafters
- Apprentice knowledge crafters.

Management

Management's duty is to represent the needs and requirements of the organization for the knowledge-based application. Whether these needs and requirements are met will ultimately determine the overall benefit of the application.

End-Users

These people will actually use the application. In general, they do not have the same training and experience as the expert, and in some cases (e.g., when the system is to be used by customers of the organization) they may not even belong to the organization.

Project Champion

This person champions the cause of the project and facilitates the resolution of problems that may occur in the running of the project. More will be said about the project champion in Chapter 2 and thereafter.

Experts

These people provide the expertise that serves as the fundamental source of knowledge for the system.

Knowledge Crafters

These people study the problem domain, acquire the knowledge, and structure it to solve the class of problems associated with the domain. Knowledge crafters are also concerned with interfacing the knowledge-based system to end-users, data bases, and other computing facilities.

Apprentice Knowledge Crafters

Because trained knowledge crafters are very scarce, many knowledge-based system projects include apprentice knowledge crafters. They work with the knowledge crafters to understand knowledge crafting in general and to learn how to build a specific system so that they can maintain and enhance it as well as build additional ones.

The Knowledge-Based System Life Cycle

Although each knowledge-based system application has a unique set of requirements that dictate certain aspects of the development project, the commonality between projects is nevertheless significant. Figure 2 presents a general overview of the major phases through which development of a typical knowledge-based system will pass.

The Design Phase

Steps that lead to a complete, documented overall system design are:

- Project Inception—This step is devoted to the initial planning and organization of the project.

  Chapter 1 covers this effort.

- Forming the Development Team—Here the members of the project team are selected. The team includes the developers, as well as representatives of management and the end-users.

  Chapter 2 discusses the duties and requirements of various persons on the development team.

- Determining the Requirements—The development team seeks to establish the requirements of the application as seen by management and the end-users.

  Chapter 4 discusses how the development team defines the overall requirements for the system in preparation for the feasibility study.

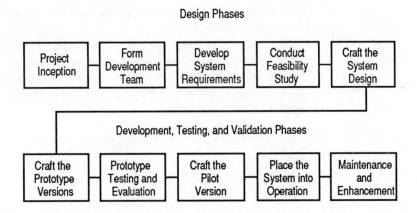

Figure 2 A General Knowledge-Based System Life Cycle

- Conducting a Feasibility Study—The purpose of this step is to determine whether it is feasible to continue developing a knowledge-based system for the proposed application.

  Chapter 5 discusses how a feasibility study can be used to evaluate the technical feasibility of and to derive a benefit-cost analysis for the proposed application.

- Crafting the Overall Design—The developers complete a formal description of the overall application design in this step.

  Chapter 6 is devoted to a discussion of the overall design process for a knowledge-based system.

The Development, Testing, and Validation Phase

Steps that lead to the operation of a successful knowledge-based application are:

- Crafting the Prototype Versions—A series of prototype versions is developed to test and evaluate the knowledge acquired from the expert vis-a-vis the requirements of the system.

  Chapter 7 discusses how the development of a series of prototype versions can result in an application knowledge base that matches the needs and requirements of the end-user with the expert's knowledge of the problem domain. Chapter 3 discusses the knowledge-crafting process.

- Testing and Evaluating the Prototypes—This effort is conducted in conjunction with prototype and pilot version development. Its purpose is to verify that each prototype version performs as intended and to identify problem areas in the development of the knowledge base and overall system.

  This activity is described in detail in Chapter 8.

- Crafting the Pilot Version—This area covers the conversion from the final prototype to a running pilot version.

  This process is described in Chapter 9.

- Placing the System into Operation—This process involves placing the pilot system into operation.

  The activities to be performed during pilot operation are described in Chapter 10.

- Maintenance and Enhancement—This step covers modification of the system over time to reflect changes in the expertise and to provide additional function. These endeavors are assumed to follow a design and development cycle similar to the one used to produce the initial system.

PART I

Planning and Designing a Knowledge-Based Application

CHAPTER 1

Getting Started

Lofting a yacht requires a certain amount of preparation. Floorspace must be cleared, tools arranged, and materials acquired and laid out. The floor shown here will soon be the scene of bustling activity and a clutter of objects. Similarly, crafting a knowledge-based application requires a certain amount of preparation. Chapter 1 sets forth a number of considerations that must be understood before a knowledge-crafting project is undertaken.

Some people have viewed the material that follows as a set of platitudes that, while indisputably nice, has little importance in building knowledge-based systems. Since much of this material has long been touted but not used for developing ordinary software, these same individuals would prefer to ignore this advice and plunge into the project. Unfortunately, while some developers have generally been able to ignore this counsel in building ordinary computer applications, we have found many times over that the dynamics of building a knowledge-based system provide much less room for such shortcuts.

The purpose of this chapter is to introduce you to planning and building knowledge-based system applications. To carry out this process, you should first understand the general way in which such applications are designed, built, and tested, as well as the role that knowledge-based system development technology plays in the process. Although some new tools and techniques have made the development of these applications quite feasible, you should certainly not discard the practices that contributed to the successful development of ordinary computer applications in the past. However, because many of the newer knowledge-based system applications are being designed as a component to fit into larger systems, a series of additional requirements needs to be addressed early in the planning process. Finally, the effect of knowledge-based system applications on existing staffs and systems needs to be understood and dealt with at the outset of any knowledge-based system application project.

The Development Cycle of a Knowledge-Based Application

Developing an application generally involves five steps:

1. Performing a detailed feasibility study
2. Completing an overall system design
3. Developing and testing a series of successively refined prototypes
4. Developing and testing a pilot delivery application based on the final prototype
5. Developing and testing postdelivery versions of the application.

The successful completion of each step in this process should be considered as a major milestone in the development of the application, and work should not proceed with the next step until the current one has been satisfactorily completed. Because assessing the size and complexity of the overall effort is often quite difficult until the first two steps have been completed, major organizational commitments may not be forthcoming until these two milestones have been accomplished.

The Feasibility Study

The primary purpose of the feasibility study is to determine whether a proposed knowledge-based application is both technically and economically feasible. The benefits attributed to the application should outweigh the costs associated with producing and maintaining it. Additionally, a rough design should be done as part of the study to expose various risks that may be associated with producing the application. Such risks include the availability of experts, the ability to test certain assumptions, and the ability of the application to meet various performance criteria. Chapter 4 presents the issues and describes the process of conducting the feasibility study.

The Overall Initial Project Design

Once a proposed application has been found to be feasible, and the organization determines that the perceived benefits, costs, and risks warrant continuing development, a rigorous overall design effort should begin. This activity really addresses two issues—the design concept of the application, and the overall specifications of what the application is to achieve. These issues, which encompass the whole application, are formulated by answering the following questions:

- In what way is the knowledge to be used to solve the problem at hand?
- What types and sources of knowledge are to be contained in the application?
- What are the application interfaces to the users?
- What are the application interfaces to other systems or data bases?
- In what way is the application to be tested, not only with regard to the accuracy of the knowledge and the results it produces, but also with respect to the needs and requirements of the users?
- What is the schedule for producing it?

The purpose of such a design is to provide a central focus for the development of the application, much in the same way that a set of plans and specifications provides the central focus for designing and crafting the yachts illustrated in this book. When used in this fashion, the overall design first serves to calibrate the expectations of management, users, experts, and the application builders. It can and should also serve as a contracting aid to specify what items will be produced, when they will be produced, and how they are to be tested. The nature of the design effort is described in much greater detail in Chapter 6.

Because the system is designed quite early in the development cycle (after completion of the feasibility study), later findings will likely change various assumptions underlying the design. Therefore, the design must be reviewed periodically and updated to reflect these findings. Today, word processing systems and software development tools can assist in this process. Finally, almost everyone involved with the project must understand and accept the design. A number of design reviews and walkthroughs should also be scheduled as the project unfolds to keep people informed.

The Development and Testing of Successively Refined Prototypes

Prototype development is perhaps the most novel aspect of producing a knowledge-based system application. Because the development of ordinary software applications has no familiar counterpart, developers hold many misconceptions about what this effort involves and what it is intended to accomplish.

The main purpose of prototyping is to develop a model of the application in prototype form that is as complete as possible. By developing a successful prototype, knowledge crafters determine the structure of the knowledge base and the reasoning associated with it. This process is explained in much greater detail in Chapter 7.

Strategically, the prototyping process results from the developers' inability to prepare meaningful knowledge representation specifications for a knowledge-based system application in advance. Additionally, some people cannot envision how the final system will appear to the end-user. Thus, prototyping greatly reduces the risk that the application will not perform as logically intended.

Tactically, the prototyping effort permits the development and testing of a knowledge base structure that seems appropriate for the application. The prototyping stage also serves to test the validity of the overall design, especially with respect to its purpose and, to the extent possible, with respect to the ultimate interface with the end-users. These issues and others related to testing, debugging, and validating are covered in greater detail in Chapter 8.

Contrary to what might be imagined, the prototype stage does not normally entail the building of a single, perfect prototype of the application. Rather, it consists of building and testing a succession of more and more accurate and refined prototype versions of the application, until a correct and complete version is obtained. As the knowledge crafters develop a prototype system, they obtain an ever-improving understanding of the problem that permits them to incorporate this understanding in the next prototype version. Thus, by developing a series of prototype versions and evaluating each version carefully, the knowledge crafters can produce a solid, tested knowledge base.

Knowledge crafters frequently develop their prototypes using knowledge-based development software tools, such as ART™, Epitool™, KEE™, Knowledge Craft™, OPS5, or S.1™. These tools typically run either on special-purpose AI (LISP) development hardware, such as that offered by Symbolics, Texas Instruments, and Xerox, or on more general-purpose engineering workstations, such as those offered by Apollo, Digital Equipment Corporation, Hewlett-Packard, IBM, Sun, and Tektronix.

The latter engineering workstations are often specially configured for developing such knowledge-based system applications.

Although smaller knowledge-based system applications can sometimes be developed successfully with various software development tools that run on PC-type computers, these tools have proven to be too weak to support the development of any but the smallest applications. The next generation of PC-type computers (e.g., those built around the Intel-80386 or Motorola-68020 microprocessors) should be adequate for handling a much wider range of knowledge-based system applications.

A succession of application versions exploits the rapid prototyping capabilities offered by many of these development tools. This activity should be viewed much more as the refining, further development, and testing of the overall application design and not as a programming exercise. In fact, many application software development facilities do not require programming per se; rather, they focus on developing the knowledge base and the attendant reasoning. These facilities usually provide extensive graphic display and explanation facilities for use in or with the application.

The Development and Testing of a Pilot Version

The real purpose for producing a pilot version of the application is to be able to test it in the delivery environment on a set of life-like problems. Consequently, the first task in this phase of the project is to move the application to the delivery environment. Because the tools involved in developing the prototype versions of the application are often unsuitable for use with the production version, either due to cost or other factors relating to the final environment of the application, the knowledge-crafting team usually needs to move the final prototype version of the application into an environment suitable for delivery. This process is described in detail in Chapter 9.

Developing the pilot typically entails moving the application to an entirely different computer system (something other than an AI workstation) and frequently implies moving the application to a computer with a different instruction set, especially when the hardware supporting the development is a LISP machine. In some cases, knowledge-based tool support extends to various delivery environments, so that the application can be moved from the development environment to the delivery environment without having to redo the knowledge base and its associated reasoning. Because knowledge-based system software vendors are beginning to provide more delivery system support, loading a prototype version of an application onto one or more delivery environments is expected to become considerably easier in the near future. For some delivery environments, however, especially those involving process control, mainframe subsystems, and special-purpose computer environments, delivery support is likely to be minimal, and the prototype application will likely have to be moved by hand. This process needs to be planned very carefully in advance.

Once produced, the pilot delivery version of the application must be tested extensively to verify:

- That the knowledge base and its associated reasoning are accurate and complete for the application
- That the application meets its design goals
- That the application interfaces properly with other systems
- That the user interfaces match the abilities and expectations of the users.

As the pilot delivery version of the application nears completion, the knowledge-crafting team must begin actual pilot testing of the application in the operational environment and then phase its use into the organization.

Postdelivery Versions

With current technology, knowledge-based system applications cannot correct themselves or extend themselves to handle other areas that were not part of the original development effort. Therefore, an organization must plan for an ongoing effort to maintain the application, to be able to extend it to encompass similar reasoning for other cases, and possibly to enhance it to provide additional functionality. These issues are discussed throughout Parts I and II of this book.

Ways That Knowledge-Based Technology Can Help

The general development cycle that has been described here is quite similar to development cycles used to produce ordinary computer applications. Managing the development of ordinary computer applications is not easy. In fact, serious problems can arise even in pedestrian applications. Because obtaining and representing knowledge in a knowledge-based system application are difficult and complex, rapid prototyping and other tool capabilities provide a way to monitor and measure the development of these applications and avoid some of the pitfalls that can plague the development process.

Rapid Prototyping

By using rapid prototyping techniques, developers can test their understanding of the problem domain and expertise. In this way, they can very quickly build and test a wide range of designs and select the design that best seems to match the demands of the application. The fact that everyone can see the emerging application and track its progress is particularly important because software specifications are not normally complete enough to guide the development. In effect, rapid prototyping enables stepwise development of the application. Problems can be detected earlier and solved before they become too serious.

New Tools

What makes rapid prototyping possible is the availability of a set of new tools that combines the use of highly interactive development systems and new means for representing and reasoning about knowledge.

Highly interactive development systems consist of interactive development hardware in the form of AI or engineering workstations coupled with interactive knowledge-based system application development software. Typically, these systems use extensive graphics to display information contained in the knowledge base, whether that information is encoded as facts (data), relationships, rules, or procedures. Developers can use these graphics to trace the reasoning process of an application as it progresses through a test case. Users can employ them to monitor the progress of the reasoning process. In some cases, the user can interact with the application by setting various dials, switches, and other such devices, as well as by referring to appropriate places in a drawing or other pictorial representation of the problem domain.

Whether graphic aids or simpler menu aids are employed, the result is essentially the same—rather complex knowledge can be created and tested in a surprisingly short time. Because these development systems are designed to be highly interactive, very little time is required to compile and link the application since the tools normally subsume this function.

The various techniques for representing knowledge and reasoning about it (e.g., rules, frames, blackboards, and multiple-environment techniques) can be used alone or in combination to improve significantly the solution of certain types of problems. Using these techniques, knowledge crafters can build and test some pieces of a prototype knowledge base in about as much time as it takes to sketch out the design. A development team can thus try many more design sketches than would otherwise be possible, evaluate multiple candidate designs, and discard designs that prove to be too unwieldy. Frequently, a development team can also consider alternative reasoning methods for the same knowledge structure and generally tune the reasoning process to match the demands of the application.

These tools thus offer knowledge crafters the ability to develop rapid prototypes of larger, more complex applications, which results in:

- Frequent, easily measured milestones
- A larger number of solutions to a problem being tested
- Developers, experts, and users collectively resolving errors, misunderstandings, and other problems in the design and development of the application.

Consequently, rather large prototype portions of a knowledge-based system application can be constructed in a fairly short period of time (often between four and eight weeks) permitting experts, users, and management to make frequent assessments of how well the application works.

Although this rapid prototyping capability in no way prevents errors, misconceptions, or other problems from arising, it provides for early detection and correction of these problems. It also offers everyone involved an opportunity to evaluate the step-by-step progress achieved in developing the system. If such evaluations are made carefully, the risk of producing an unacceptable application after a series of prototype versions has been built and tested can be much lower than that for producing ordinary software with conventional programming techniques.

Good Programming Practices

The availability of good prototyping tools to assist in building knowledge-based system applications is no reason to abandon many of the sound, well-proven techniques that have been used successfully in the past to help produce ordinary computer systems. Because knowledge-based system applications are also just pieces of software, traditional software development techniques are clearly useful for producing these applications, too. Surprisingly, some people building knowledge-based system applications today have ignored traditional application development practices; predictable problems have resulted. Although artificial intelligence technology has contributed greatly to the building of knowledge-based system applications, such technology is intended to augment—not replace—the many good programming practices that have evolved over the years for producing computer applications.

Good Communication

The first element of good programming practice is to keep the organization well-informed about the status of the application being developed. Initially, effective communication involves documenting the problem, risks, and business issues, a step that begins with the feasibility study. One of the most important documents to be produced is a written description of the application design that must be understood and endorsed by everyone concerned with the project, including management, members of the user community, and the experts, as well as the persons actually building the application. Because knowledge-based system technology is new, persons not directly involved in the project may have widely disparate or basically incorrect views of what the technology can accomplish. The written design serves as a document of understanding. Written documentation is particularly important for project staff; for them, it serves two very important functions:

1. It provides a platform for debating various design issues.
2. It provides a written standard to which everyone can work.

Project Control

Any successful software development project requires careful project control, including the use of:

*   Milestones, to measure progress

- Version control, to keep portions of the software (and documentation) synchronized
- Testing control, to help manage the testing and validation process.

All milestones must be clearly stated and defined as unambiguously as possible. In this way, no one should question whether a particular milestone has been met. Establishing frequent, easily ascertainable milestones enables most people to recognize and understand the development status of the application.

Project control should also address the similar issues of version and testing control. Although both issues seem superfluous at project initiation when nothing has been created, they become very important as the various portions of the application are integrated.

Embedding Knowledge-Based Systems in Existing Systems

The earliest knowledge-based system applications, including MYCIN, CADEUCES, R1, and many of the early adviser-type systems, were essentially "cream-skimming," that is, stand-alone applications that could easily be justified by the significant benefit they provided for their organizations. Many of these applications were built using special software support such as LISP and Prolog. Data were entered from the keyboard with outputs directed to a text display screen or to a printer.

The newer knowledge-based system applications are more closely tied to other systems; they frequently access one or more data bases and sometimes other applications in the course of working toward a solution. Typical of such applications is the seat optimization system that has been constructed for Northwest Airlines. This application resides on a LISP workstation, which in turn accesses several of the airline's data bases stored on other machines, which it then uses for reasoning about adding or deleting the number of seats in various fare categories to maximize the expected revenue for a particular flight on a particular date.

As similar applications penetrate the world of business and industry, they will be required to work even more closely with existing computer systems. Some applications will need to be embedded as a part of (and sometimes a small part of) large, existing systems. The design of the knowledge-based application will thus have many additional constraints placed on it, including:

- The knowledge-based system application must coexist with, if not run on, the mainline hardware used for computing within the organization.
- The knowledge-based system application must run under normal operating systems and coexist with, if not run as a part of, ordinary application programs.
- Regardless of the underlying language for the knowledge-based system application, that language must be supported (at least in

delivery fashion) on the computer system to run the delivery version of the knowledge-based software. Moreover, other portions of the overall application, which could be written in any language, must be able to communicate with this knowledge-based module.

- The knowledge-based system application must be able to communicate with a variety of data bases, on the same machine or others, from which it can draw information as needed.
- Access to the knowledge-based system application must be provided through existing terminals. Requiring more than one terminal or display on a user's desk or in the workplace is not acceptable.
- Knowledge-based system applications must be able to operate with existing computer networks to access remote data bases, to invoke other portions of the application resident elsewhere, or to be invoked from other nodes on the network.

General Human and Organizational Constraints

Having several people work closely together on a complex project imposes numerous constraints on knowledge-based system applications that do not exist for other types of computer applications. Some are caused by the newness of the technology, which requires that extra care be taken to smooth its introduction into the organization, while other constraints relate more to the technology itself, which requires working with one or more experts to capture knowledge, represent it, and reason about it in the application.

The New Kid on the Block

In most organizations, knowledge-based technology is new and not always welcome. Some persons view it with unreasonable skepticism, while others may espouse it with abandon. To encourage the doubters to support the technology, the "project champion," as described in Chapter 2, is particularly helpful. This person of stature in the organization paves the way for others to cooperate with the project, generates enthusiasm among supporters, and moderates unwarranted enthusiasm.

Getting Support from the Experts

Because many experts have never been involved in developing ordinary computer applications, they have little or no comprehension of computers, and certainly very few indeed understand anything about knowledge-based systems technology. Therefore, the knowledge-crafting team must ensure that the expert understands the goals of the application and is not intimidated by the technology.

Chapter 3 discusses the knowledge acquisition process at length, and much of that process deals with interactions between the knowledge-crafting team and the experts. Long before this process begins, however, each expert must be made an ally of the project. If the experts can be convinced that the application will beneft them directly (e.g., make their jobs easier), they will tend to bend over backward to be cooperative.

Knowledge-based applications can capture only a portion of the total expertise on a subject. That portion can often relieve experts of the day-to-day, routine work, however, leaving them free to concentrate on more difficult and challenging problems. The promise of such an outcome is often a key factor in obtaining the experts' support.

User-Related Problems

User-related problems normally occur with any type of computer application, although for knowledge-based applications these problems can be more acute. These applications deal less with numbers than with symbolic information, which can be misinterpreted. Furthermore, the delivered knowledge-based application may often in some way modify a process currently involving several people or jobs in the organization. Developers need to understand how the knowledge-based application can best serve the organization in a nonconfrontational way.

A common problem is the improper use of terms or nomenclature presented to the user. The experts, users, and developers normally communicate in the same native language, which includes many words with similar meanings but slightly different connotations. This situation occurs most frequently in application domains where jargon gives unusual meanings to ordinary words. Other user-related problems can involve the system interface and the user's environment. Such user-related issues are discussed throughout Parts I and II of this book.

Organization-Oriented Problems

The structure of the organization itself can also present a host of problems. Because knowledge-based system application projects tend to cross normal organizational lines of authority, reaching a consensus about the appropriate actions to take can be difficult.

Other organizational problems can arise when an application is disseminated widely within the organization, as might occur with a financial advisory system distributed among a large bank's many branches. Keeping the various versions current and determining who is permitted to use the application under what conditions are important problems to resolve.

Possible Legal and Competitive Problems

Potential legal issues and problems with competitors must also be considered. Suppose a knowledge-based system is built to diagnose failures in an organization's product, such as a piece of machinery. If certain parts are known to fail more often than others, and this knowledge is placed in a knowledge-based diagnostic system, this fact could lead to a lawsuit over known (but unfixed) problems.

The same type of application could also provide significant insight to a competitor. If the competitor could uncover the expertise used to diagnose problems in another organization's products, the firm could improve its own product as well as use the information to discredit its competitor.

In some industries using a knowledge-based application could be too new for the culture of that organization. Even though the application was tested and found to be safe and accurate, the novelty of the application may open up its use to lawsuits. Of course, in other cases, because knowledge-based system applications are arguably "standard practice," failing to use such a system may also be the basis for a lawsuit.

Organizations that understand knowledge-based system technology, however, will be able to anticipate the impact of these systems on their businesses and should be able to avoid serious legal and competitive problems.

Crafting a fine sailing yacht requires a team of individuals with many talents. In addition to naval architects, designers, and builders familiar with modern-day materials, there must be people to consider the sailors' needs, both while under sail and at anchor, to test the yacht's endurance and sea worthiness, and to validate that the yacht meets the sailors' requirements. Similarly, crafting a knowledge-based application requires a multitalented team. In addition to experts, designers, and builders, there must be people to consider the users' needs, to test the quality of the application's advice, and to validate that the application meets the users' requirements. Chapter 2 discusses the assembly of such a development team.

Forming the Development Team

Before turning to discussions of the feasiblity study and other activities that transpire in building a knowledge-based application, we first need to consider the composition and organization of the development team.

Often, a group of five to six persons is the best size for developing a knowledge-based system application. Forming such a small, cohesive group tends to result in a less formal, more flexible management style and structure that can deal more effectively with the cross-organizational issues that can arise in this type of project.

Thus, the project organization for a knowledge-based application should center around a team with the following members:

- A project champion to facilitate the project's successful completion
- A project leader to manage, coordinate, and run the project
- Two persons experienced in knowledge acquisition and knowledge crafting, to handle the technical aspects of the knowledge-based portion of the project and to provide on-the-job training for the apprentices (Additionally, one of the knowledge crafters may act as assistant project leader.)
- Two persons to act as apprentice knowledge crafters to take over the enhancement and maintenance of the system when it is finished.

The remainder of this chapter is devoted to discussing how this type of project team might be formed and how it might function. In reading this material, you should keep in mind that many knowledge-based application development projects tend to span more than one part of an organization and that consequently members of the project team may not all come from the same suborganization. Therefore, team members (especially the knowledge crafters, who are rather scarce) should be very sensitive to cooperating with other members of the team and the various suborganizations involved in the project.

Management

Unless an organization is experienced in developing knowledge-based system applications, it should try to obtain help from other sources in the parent organization, such as a centralized corporate knowledge-based application development group, or from consultants or vendors. Occasionally, an inexperienced organization has created an application entirely on its own, but this course of action can lead to serious difficulties.

If a centralized corporate knowledge-based application development group exists, the developing organization may contract with that group to spearhead the development of the application, and in so doing obtain help as necessary from that group, elsewhere in the organization, or other sources. In other cases, when no such group has been formed, the developing organization may choose to spearhead the development itself and obtain help from outside sources.

In either of these approaches some members of the development team are likely to come from outside the immediate organization. Such indirect reporting roles make managing the project a little more difficult than it might otherwise be, and whoever assumes the management role needs to understand how to work in such situations.

The Project Champion

In many successful projects, a person of rather broad stature in the organization decides to champion the cause of knowledge-based systems technology and smooth the way for the project to operate as efficiently as possible. Such "project champions" are certainly not blind devotees of the technology; rather, they are individuals who believe that the technology is likely to have a substantial payout for the organization, and who are willing to use their influence to assure the best conditions possible for the project.

The project champion serves several important functions. At times, this individual can cut through red tape single-handedly. At other times, by knowing the appropriate people in the organization, the project champion can quickly have a question resolved. Thus, the main role of this person is to assure that problems are dealt with properly and to keep the lines of communication open between various interested parties. Additionally, the project champion may be expected to coordinate project reviews and milestone checkpoints and report the progress of the project to upper management.

The Project Leader

Another critical team member is the project leader. The project champion and the project leader are not normally the same person; the project champion is usually a corporate generalist, whose position derives from the ability to view a wide range of corporate activities and who can cause things to happen. The project champion provides the authority and the resources for the project leader, who is the specialist dealing with the day-to-day problems of developing the application. The project leader is essentially biased toward the needs and schedule of the development effort, which in turn must be balanced against the capabilities of the technology and the skills of development team members.

The project leader must be familiar with the application and the department for which it is being built. Moreover, this person should clearly understand the needs of the prospective users; thus, if a choice must be made, the project leader should be oriented toward the users rather than toward the technology.

Naturally, the project leader should understand knowledge-based system technology, but finding such a person can be very difficult. Therefore, the person chosen for project leader should be eager to learn as much as possible about the technology. This person should also be able to work well with the skilled knowledge crafters, who must carry much of the technical responsibility for the knowledge-crafting portion of the project. If possible, the project leader should have five or more years experience in developing computer applications, with some of that time spent in a managerial role, as well as a masters degree or equivalent in computer science.

The Assistant Project Leader

When the project leader cannot assume the role of technical leader in the knowledge-crafting effort, a second person should be selected to take the role of "lead knowledge crafter" or assistant project leader. This person should be a highly qualified knowledge crafter with experience in developing two or more knowledge-based system applications. Although such persons are rare, the success of the knowledge-crafting effort may depend on their abilities.

The assistant project leader should have a background in artificial intelligence technology with a masters degree or equivalent in computer science. The person should be able to work well with the particular experts in this application, as well as with members of the user community and others. This individual should work especially well with the other knowledge crafters and be able to train the apprentices.

Staffing

Given a moderate-sized project, and an organization lacking knowledge-based application experience, we suggest using a knowledge-crafting team built around two full-time knowledge crafters assisted by two full-time apprentices.

Roles of the Interviewers

The main task of the two knowledge crafters is to interview prospective users and experts to determine the required capabilities of the system and obtain the expertise to be placed in it. Additionally, the knowledge crafters must weigh ideas of how to structure the knowledge into a design for the application. Finally, they must turn the design into a tested, running application.

The role of the two apprentices is first to learn knowledge-based system technology and then to assist in applying that technology to craft the application.

Why Two?

Having two knowledge crafters on the team is important. In knowledge crafting, communicating ideas is vital to the success of the application. A single knowledge crafter would not have anyone with similar training with whom to discuss knowledge representation and reasoning issues. One person would, therefore, be responsible for synthesizing all of the knowledge obtained from the expert and representing it properly in the application.

Knowledge crafting is not an exact science (hence our aversion to the commonly used term, "engineering"). At least for the near future, a small number of persons will need to view a problem from different perspectives, so that together they can come to a much deeper understanding of the problem than any one of them might be able to do alone.

On the other hand, if many more than two persons are involved, the project tends to bog down, as many committee efforts do, and quality diminishes. A three- or possibly four-person team can work effectively (especially in larger, more compartmentalized projects), but certainly for first-time projects small groups of two persons are much more productive.

These same arguments can be applied to the apprentice team. Two apprentices can communicate with one another and help each other during the learning process. In their assignments they should learn to work in teams in the same way as the knowledge crafters. They will also work as a team after they assume responsibility for the application.

The Knowledge-Crafting Team

Today, knowledge-crafting teams are being formed from several sources:

- A central, corporate-wide knowledge-based application development resource center within the parent organization
- New persons recruited into the organization
- A consulting organization
- Personnel associated with a knowledge-based software tool vendor.

Resource Centers

In some instances, a centrally located, corporate-wide resource center can assist in developing knowledge-based system applications. These centers may have sufficient resources to handle entire knowledge-based application development projects, or they may contract with independent consultant groups or hardware or software vendors to provide specialized help.

One prime advantage of such a group over other sources is that its primary allegiance is to the parent organization. Although members of the group may still be learning about knowledge crafting and be less informed than outside specialists, they are likely to be more experienced in understanding the organization, its needs, and the corporate culture. In cases where the center cannot do the work itself, it can often locate appropriate outsiders based on its understanding of the problem and knowledge-based systems technology.

Certain organizations are more amenable than others to adapting to a new technology, and the means by which new technology is introduced in an organization depends partly on an organization's ability to handle new technology. Organizations that conduct research tend to be more adept in assimilating new technology than organizations that do not have a research focus.

New Hires

When an organization does not have the luxury of having a central resource center, it may decide to hire people from outside, although many recruiting efforts have not been very successful. Quite often, a qualified AI researcher is hired to develop applications and train a knowledge-crafting team. Although such persons surely understand knowledge-based system technology and AI techniques in general, they do not always fare well when removed from their research environment because they do not fully understand the needs of the organization. Often they are not interested in doing development work. An organization should therefore look for persons who can be expected to do well in application development. If an organization has decided to hire new people, it might consider retaining an independent consultant to help find and select suitable people.

Independent Consulting Organizations

Consulting firms can also assist an interested organization in selecting and developing a knowledge-based application and in transferring the technology. Several high-quality independent consulting firms, such as Arthur D. Little or SRI International, can handle all aspects of developing knowledge-based applications.

To assure independent and unbiased help in selecting these tools for use in the application, these consulting companies should not be involved in selling either hardware or software. As an organization becomes more proficient in the use of the technology, it can reduce its reliance on consultants and use them only to help in assessing new problems, in auditing existing development projects, or in installing new technologies.

Vendor Services

Software and hardware vendors usually can offer valuable consulting assistance. Such vendors can train people in the use of their products, as well as assist in developing an application. Their services, though, should not be confused with the services of an independent consultant; the help they offer is strongly biased in favor of solutions that their product can handle. Vendor consulting services are best employed to help determine how the vendor's software can be used for a given, specific type of knowledge representation and reasoning; consulting firms, on the other hand, are best employed to help determine what specific type of knowledge representation and reasoning is required for the application in the first place.

An Apprenticeship Program

Given the need for on-the-job training in all aspects of knowledge crafting, as well as for the continuing maintenance, enhancement, and extension to the application once it has been delivered and accepted, any organization planning a knowledge-based application should designate a number of potential apprentices. Department members or others from the parent organization should be named as apprentices, receive initial training in knowledge-based system technology, and go on to participate in the day-to-day development of the application under the guidance of the knowledge crafters. As the job progresses, the apprentices can begin to take over some of the actual project work; by the time the project is near completion, they should be capable of doing much, if not all, of the work. On completion of the project, they would continue to support that application as well as to develop new applications.

The apprenticeship technique helps guarantee that the resulting application is maintainable. Of course, it also provides an excellent way to train additional knowledge crafters, and many organizations today use apprenticeships to expand their group of trained knowledge crafters.

Several reasons have been cited for combining apprenticeship with the development of a knowledge-based application. However, the most compelling reason for having an apprenticeship program is that the number of trained knowledge crafters is very small, and obtaining trained persons to spearhead the design and development of the application is difficult. Requiring these people to provide follow-on support for the application after it has been developed is therefore apt to be unrealistic.

Today, a few academic institutions such as Stanford, MIT, Carnegie-Mellon, University of Michigan, University of Tokyo, and University of Sweden teach the theory behind knowledge-based systems, but only the University of Sweden at Linköping offers a degree in applied knowledge engineering (crafting). In the near future, however, the appropriate educational infrastructure will be put in place to train people.

When computers first became available, for example, there was a critical shortage of trained people. As the acceptance of computers increased, junior colleges, universities, and other programmer training centers rose to meet the demand.

Selecting Candidate Apprentices

Good candidate apprentices can be found among end-users, experts, and other computer-literate people in the organization. Certainly, apprentices chosen from the end-user community are apt to be more highly motivated than others, which would increase the likelihood of producing a useful, high-quality application.

Identifying a single guideline for selecting apprentices is not possible. In general, successful apprentices and knowledge crafters exhibit many of the following characteristics:

- They are highly inquisitive, imaginative, creative, and motivated.
- They interact comfortably with all kinds of people.
- They have a good understanding of computer system design and implementation techniques.
- They are oriented toward applications rather than research.
- They are interested in knowledge crafting.

A recent computer science graduate often makes a good apprentice. Because such persons are newly trained and highly motivated, they frequently do quite well. However, their background and lack of practical training may bring them into conflict with old-timers in the organization who have spent years learning a subject that is far removed from anything having to do with computers. While a good foundation in computer systems is a very important criterion, it does not guarantee success. Such a background is extremely helpful in building software systems, but knowledge crafting is not just a different type of programming. Knowledge crafting is an entirely different activity that needs to draw on more than just computer science principles.

In almost all cases, generalists are needed. Appropriate specialists can usually be found to cope with a particular problem, but most of the significant contributions to a knowledge-crafting project involve the synthesis of information obtained from experts, end-users, management, and others. By their very nature, generalists are good at this and must be preferred accordingly.

The candidate should also possess a strong outgoing personality and be challenged by and interested in new things. Knowledge crafters usually spend a great deal of time with experts in fields rather unfamiliar to them. Therefore, anyone with a quick analytical mind who gets along well with a wide variety of people from all walks of life should make an excellent candidate.

Finally, selecting apprentices with different backgrounds (e.g., one in computer science, the other in a domain area) is often the best solution. However, these persons should be trained in both areas, so that they do not become compartmentalized as computer or applications specialists. Such a rigidly organized group would be slow to act and unable to synthesize information well enough to craft a good application.

Apprentice Training

Once the apprentices have been selected, they should undergo a short period of formal, fundamental knowledge-crafting training. (The project leader may also take the same program.) Such training is available from a few sources, including:

- Computer manufacturers
- Knowledge-crafting consulting firms
- Knowledge-crafting software tool vendors
- Some academic institutions.

Computer manufacturers such as Digital Equipment Corporation and IBM offer training courses. IntelliCorp has a course series for KEE™ users, as does Inference Corporation for ART™ and The Carnegie Group for Knowledge Craft™. Universities such as Carnegie-Mellon, MIT, and Stanford offer courses in knowledge-based systems theory, and, as mentioned before, the University of Sweden in Linköping offers coursework leading to a degree in knowledge crafting. SRI International in California has developed a "Knowledge-Crafting Bootcamp," which is a very intensive, 11-day training program specifically tailored to helping a client's apprentices.

The training course should emphasize general technological skills rather than the use of particular hardware or software. Learning to use a particular tool is easy in comparison to learning the principles behind its effective application; facility with a tool can often be acquired on the job.

The subject material should be presented by combining theory with application exercises. Much of the initial training can be done without using a real computer. Many problems are better worked out with just pencil and paper. Obviously, though, more advanced problems require access to a computer, preferably one configured with the same hardware and software that is to be used for the development of the application.

A wide range of knowledge-crafting techniques should be presented to the apprentices, even though some of them might not be used in the application at hand. A broad understanding of knowledge-crafting techniques provides the necessary breadth for structuring the problem during the design phase of the project. In particular, the following list of topics should be covered:

- An introduction to knowledge-based systems
- Rule-based reasoning
  - simple rule-based systems using backward chaining
  - simple rule-based systems using forward chaining
  - simple rule-based systems using combinations of forward and backward chaining
  - pattern-matching techniques
  - rule-based systems using variables
- Frame-based reasoning
  - frame-based knowledge representation
  - inheritance
  - object-oriented programming, frames, and methods
- Other
  - multiple environment techniques
  - model-based reasoning
  - blackboarding techniques
  - LISP programming techniques (if applicable)
  - use of an AI (LISP) workstation (as applicable)
  - exercises using the particular software tool to be used in developing the application (e.g., ART™, Epitool™, KEE™, Knowledge-Craft™, OPS5, S.1™).

Once the formal training has been completed, the knowledge-crafting team can begin work on its first application, in particular, developing the application's requirements (Chapter 4), assessing its feasibility (Chapter 5), and developing a basic design or structure (Chapter 6). Key to the performance of these preliminary tasks, however, are the interviewing skills and procedures needed to elicit information from the various project participants. Interviews can be conducted in a variety of ways, but we have found the approach to knowledge acquisition described in the next chapter to be especially effective.

CHAPTER 3

Acquiring Knowledge

Although the yacht craftsman is an expert at constructing a high-quality vessel, a better sailing yacht can be constructed when the design team has access to and understands the subtleties of the naval architect's expertise. This requires the design team members to meet with experts in their own environment and to work together to capture and structure the knowledge necessary to design the vessel that will meet the sailors' requirements. Similarly, the knowledge crafter is an expert at constructing a high-quality knowledge-based application, but a better application can be constructed when the design team has access to and understands the subtleties of the expert's knowledge in that application domain. This requires the knowledge-crafting team to meet with experts and to work together to capture and structure the knowledge necessary to build an application that will meet the users" requirements. Chapter 3 discusses the process of acquiring and organizing knowledge from an expert.

This chapter discusses various interviewing techniques that developers can use to obtain knowledge from experts. Before starting these interviews, however, the knowledge crafters should review various publications, textbooks, or other written material to become as familiar with the subject as possible. Further, some experts may have written various documents on the subject that the knowledge crafters can understand and use to provide at least part of the knowledge they seek. Once this literature review is finished, however, the developers usually find that they still must hold a series of interviews with the experts to capture the remaining knowledge.

Because the knowledge obtained from the expert lies at the heart of a knowledge-based application, the process of obtaining that knowledge is key to building a successful knowledge-based application. Although obtaining system requirements from management and prospective users is not unique to knowledge-based applications, the process of acquiring heuristic knowledge from a small number of experts is unique to the development of such applications. The chance for error is great, and the acceptable means for capturing and testing such information are numerous. The "two-on-one" interviewing technique described in this chapter has been found to work effectively, while other less rigorous methods have often failed.

Interviewing

The principal means of obtaining knowledge from experts is interviewing them in person. Because the amount of accurate information required is significant, the knowledge-crafting team and the experts must plan on spending considerable time together. The expert can become impatient with what appears to be seemingly endless, trivial questions. In some cases, the expert can also become bored with the process and give only halfhearted attention to the line of questioning. Consequently, the knowledge crafters must be sensitive to the feelings of the expert and adjust the interviewing accordingly. The expert's time must be considered as precious, and the knowledge crafters need to use it efficiently.

Two-on-One Interviewing

Team interviewing, especially the two-on-one technique, is strongly recommended for knowledge-crafting projects. If the knowledge crafters conducted the feasibility study portion of the project alone, they would be joined by the apprentices in further interviews in later portions of the project. During the final stage of prototype development, the apprentices alone may constitute the interview team.

While team interviewing can intimidate an expert, the gain in accuracy and the amount of information obtained from using this technique usually outweighs any adverse side effects. Besides, as the project progresses, even a timid expert becomes accustomed to the members of the team, and any initial sense of intimidation diminishes. Thus, if the mem-

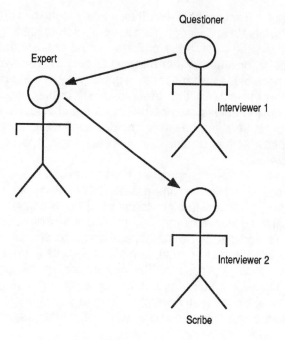

Figure 3-1 First Line of Questioning

bers of the team work sensitively with the experts, team interviewing may not cause as much discomfort as one might otherwise imagine.

The two-on-one interviewing technique involves a pair of knowledge crafters, one to act as the questioner while the other acts as a scribe. The roles of these two people reverse frequently—whenever the questioner ends a line of inquiry. This process of acquiring information is similar to a multiple-branch tree search. The interviewing team searches the breadth and depth of the tree to obtain and verify the maximum amount of information in as little time as possible.

The interview session starts with one person taking the role of the questioner, the other the role of the scribe, as shown in Figure 3-1. The questioner thoroughly explores one line of inquiry. As the questioning proceeds, the scribe notes the questions and answers. In time, as the concepts begin to crystallize, the scribe may begin to sketch a tree-like relationship between nodes of reasoning, especially those that may not have been fully explained. When the questioner has exhausted a particular line of inquiry, which usually takes no more than five to ten minutes, the questioner should defer to the scribe, and the roles of questioner and scribe interchange, as shown in Figure 3-2.

This process should continue throughout the interview session, with roles of questioner and scribe changing roughly every five to ten minutes, as the dynamics of the interview indicate. However, before the questioner relinquishes the questioning role, that person should verify that the answers to the questions have been understood and recorded correctly. When the roles are finally switched, the questioner signals this event by asking the scribe for any further questions on the specific issues. When the scribe is satisfied that all the points in the previous line of inquiry have been covered, that individual then begins a new line of questioning.

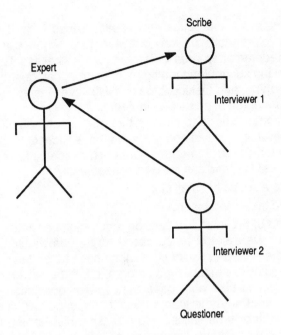

Figure 3-2 Second Line of Questioning

General Questions for the Expert

To focus the interview sessions, the questioner should iteratively pose three basic questions:

1. What do you do next?
2. What does that mean?
3. Why do you do that?

These questions or ones like them serve to delineate an information tree. The first question probes the next node in the question tree; the second question is aimed at defining the new question node; the third question strikes at the reasoning for the action. The information must be verified frequently, however, which requires the questioner to play back the answers to the expert and listen carefully for nuances that were not initially recorded. Such playbacks are also useful for verifying the scribe's notes.

The knowledge crafters must not lose sight of the larger picture while focusing on first one piece of knowledge and then another. They must also determine boundary conditions. Where are the limits in the problems to be considered? Where are the limits in the knowledge that is to be brought to bear on the problem? What constitutes a complete or full answer to the problem?

Making Little Steps Then Big Steps

Although the two-on-one interviewing method is efficient at completing an information tree, more than one such tree is likely to exist, and the process as described can fizzle after several iterations of questioning.

When this happens, the scribe can usually sense it; at the next questioner/scribe role switch, the new questioner can change the topic, perhaps to a predetermined area of interest or to other facets of the same problem. Making such a leap too soon, of course, can destroy the current line of questioning, and making it too late will have wasted some time and probably some of the expert's endurance.

Getting some experts to change their focus can sometimes be difficult. In general, the questioning should be switched to another area somewhat remote from the current area. This technique maximizes the information obtained and can be summarized as:

- Take a series of small steps.
- Then take a long step.

At the end of the interview session, each member of the interviewing team should have a set of notes based on the questioning of the other team members. The process of combining these notes need not be arduous if simple rules are established beforehand. If the two knowledge crafters use the same size note paper, start each questioning node on a separate line, and note the time a questioner/scribe switch occurs, then the notes can literally be spliced into a reasonable representation of the question tree. This method also works effectively when a question node is visited several times; the various strips of paper recording those visits can actually be placed adjacent to one another, exposing all of the questioning that occurred at that node.

Recording Aids

The benefits of recording interview sessions seldom warrant the trouble of making the recordings or the time required to review them. Only when the team is faced with a fast-talking, wide-ranging expert do such practices seem worthwhile.

Recorders, especially video recorders, can easily intimidate both the experts and interviewers. Moreover, nearly all recording devices require some attention during an interview session. Fussing with the equipment can be quite disruptive.

Once the interview is concluded, the knowledge crafters must then listen to each reel of the recording serially at the same speed it was recorded. The whole process can be more cumbersome and time-consuming than it is worth.

Some experts, however, talk so fast about so much that a recorder is necessary for sorting out what is said. In such cases, the recorder can monitor the overflow or overload points in the interview. At these times, the interviewing team should note the time of each overload point so it can be correlated with the recording.

Interviewing Multiple Experts

If several experts are to be interviewed, separate interview sessions should be conducted with each one. After the first round of separate interviews, the similarities and differences should be noted, and a second round of separate interviews can be used to determine how each expert's information meshes with that of the others. Interviewing a group of experts tends to result in a consensus of opinion, but it is the individual opinion of each expert that is really needed. Sorting through conflicting information is usually easier than extending expertise obtained by consensus, particularly since the process of obtaining consensus may suppress information. In a group situation, dominant individuals may bring their opinions to the fore. Other ideas may be dealt with summarily, causing some individuals to withhold contrary views.

What about interviewing several persons with overlapping, complementary expertise? Often, multiple experts provide different views of the problem; for example, a problem in VLSI design may require the expertise of an electrical engineer, a physicist, a materials scientist, and a specialist in optics. Each of the experts views the problem from a different, highly specialized viewpoint. To build a knowledge-based application containing appropriate contributions from each expert, the interview team needs to deal separately with each one in turn to understand the knowledge that each person has to contribute to the problem. Additionally, the interview team, having gathered at least some of this knowledge, must then work with the whole team to understand how the various elements of expertise interact.

A common failure of interview teams is the attempt to find the expert with the truth and to disregard the experts with the false information. This approach in effect forces the knowledge crafters to judge expertise of which they have only cursory appreciation. A better approach is to regard each expert as equivalently accurate and to blend what at first seems to be conflicting information.

Limitless Knowledge?

Each expert has developed extensive knowledge over a period of many years. The magnitude of that knowledge base can be awesome, causing novice knowledge crafters to wonder how all that knowledge can be captured and organized within an application. They may fear that they are about to embark on a never-ending crafting process. Fortunately, however, the knowledge crafter need not capture the entirety of the expert's knowledge, just that part that is relevant to the class of problems to be addressed by the knowledge-based application.

Problems with Experts

So far, the discussion has been limited to mechanisms and methods for interviewing. What can go wrong? Unfortunately, a great many problems can occur. For example:

- The expert may provide incorrect information.
- The knowledge crafters may misunderstand the information.
- The knowledge crafters' questions may introduce spurious expertise into the knowledge base.

- The expert's terminology may not be understood.
- The expert's explanations may wander aimlessly.
- There may be frequent interruptions.
- The experts and the knowledge crafters may not get along because of personality differences.

Truth

An expert may give false information either unintentionally or deliberately. In cases where the wrong information was unintentionally provided, that misinformation is usually detected in the verification process, through an independent source, if available. So that the application does not fail, a comprehensive set of test cases should be developed early in the project.

Unfortunately, a few experts deliberately lie to the knowledge crafters, possibly to thwart the building of the application, possibly to glamorize what is perceived to be the real, lackluster expertise. Such cases can generally be detected fairly easily because the deceptions are typically not consistent. When this general problem is detected, the knowledge crafters must very carefully seek its resolution. If the experts are tactfully confronted with the inconsistencies, they may cooperate more fully.

Misunderstanding

The other side of the coin is that the knowledge crafters misunderstand what the expert says. The knowledge crafters may not have taken the time to have the expert verify what they had been told, although even then the information can be misunderstood.

One way for the information not to be misconstrued is for more than one person to hear it, as occurs during the two-on-one interviews. In this case, two persons have to misunderstand instead of one. To minimize any confusion, however, the questioner should summarize the newly obtained information for confirmation after a line of questioning has been completed. The questioner would normally do this by asking the expert: "Did I understand you to say that ...?" or "Then, I understand that ...?." In other words, information is presented to several individuals from different perspectives to increase the likelihood that any inconsistency or misunderstanding, should it exist, will be detected. As with false information from the expert, the knowledge crafters' misunderstanding can usually be uncovered as the designing and building of the application unfolds. However, just as for traditional program development, the sooner the error is discovered, the easier it is to fix it.

Question Bias

The knowledge crafters must pay careful attention to the manner in which they ask questions. It is very easy to pose leading questions to the expert, questions that may bias the knowledge obtained during the interview session. Many experts, for example, have not taken the time to examine their own expertise or to organize or structure it. Further, most experts are flattered by the attention and recognition the project bestows on them, and they have a human tendency to try to please the questioner. When presented with questions about the logic of their approach, these individuals find they lack the knowledge to answer the queries as phrased. In an effort to please, however, they respond with their best guess on how one might proceed if approaching the problem in the manner indicated by the questioner.

A knowledge crafter's inattention to question phraseology can thus elicit spurious data rather than expert knowledge. The insights being recorded so carefully are not the heuristics used by the expert to solve problems but rather an off-the-cuff opinion on the actions that would likely be taken if the knowledge crafter's approach were followed. As a consequence, a set of guesses rather than studied expertise can be incorporated into a knowledge base, leaving the knowledge crafter puzzled about why the application does not produce the expected answers.

Accordingly, knowledge crafters must focus on what the expert actually *does* (as reported by the expert) rather than on what the expert *might do* with the knowledge as captured and structured by the knowledge crafter.

Terminology

Knowledge crafters must also be extremely sensitive to the expert's terminology. If both the knowledge crafters and the expert speak the same native language, then the knowledge crafters will likely assume that several words with approximately the same meaning are equivalent, that other words have their common or traditional meanings. Yet, many fields develop a special jargon, and common words take on very special meanings. Because the expertise is typically technical, although possibly not in a technical field, the knowledge crafters must be sure to understand the precise meanings of the terms used.

Surprisingly, misunderstanding is sometimes less of a problem when the native language of the interviewers is different from that of the expert. Here, although the two parties must share a common language for communication, more attention is often paid to identifying and defining terms. Knowledge acquisition that requires the use of an interpreter for the expert and the knowledge crafters is extremely difficult, however, and may not prove to be practical.

Wandering

Some experts tend to refrain from answering the immediate questions and instead cover a wider range of topical information that may not be germane to the particular line of reasoning being developed. When this happens, the knowledge crafters should try to focus attention back to the topic at hand. Such wanderings are not always harmful, however, for they can help the knowledge crafter develop a broad picture of the expertise.

Sometimes, of course, the expert wanders completely off track to a discussion about family, hobbies, or vacations, for example. Surprisingly, a little diversion may be good because it can relax the expert and the knowledge crafters alike. Of course, these side trips cannot become the rule of the day; the expert's attention must be refocused—gently, though.

A few experts find it difficult to focus their attention, perhaps because they are afraid of the process or are preoccupied with other things or want to sabotage the project. If this problem occurs only occasionally, and stronger prodding fails to focus the person on the problem at hand, then the session should probably be rescheduled. If the problem recurs, another expert may need to be found.

Interruptions

Interview sessions should not be interruptable. For the day-long sessions that often occur during the feasibility study and the development of the overall design, breaks should be scheduled at mid-morning, noontime, and mid-afternoon. Telephone calls and messages should be held for these breaks, if at all possible.

Sometimes the business conducted by telephone during the breaks gets out of hand, stretching out to an hour or more and seriously affecting the interviewing process. In such cases, partial-day schedules may be employed. By making the expert available for work-related problems for a quarter or a half of each day, the knowledge crafters may be able to enforce a ban on phone calls during the knowledge crafting part of the day. (The partial day schedule provides a fringe benefit, in that the knowledge crafters have time to review the material covered during the day and to prepare for the next day.)

Sessions are best held in quiet, comfortable settings away from the normal workplace of both the expert and knowledge crafters. In this way other people cannot easily contact the participants, and the participants do not sense the normal pressures of work. (However, some sessions should be held in the expert's workplace, since the knowledge crafters need to observe the expert at work.)

By far the worst type of interruption, though, occurs when the expert is called away for some days to handle a crisis. The real problem with this type of interruption is not the immediate break in the schedule, but the loss of the expert's reflections concerning the application at the time of the interruption. When the expert returns, a number of days can elapse before the momentum is restored. If such occurrences are frequent, the progress in obtaining expertise can be very slow.

This question of expert availability must be faced squarely during the feasibility study; management and the expert must be willing to commit meaningful blocks of the expert's time for knowledge acquisition interviewing, or the project will not likely succeed.

Preparing for Interviews

Both the knowledge crafters and the experts should be prepared for the interview sessions. Precious time can be wasted by poor planning.

Preparing the Expert

The experts should prepare for the knowledge acquisition interviews in the following ways:

- They should learn the primary goals of the application and understand the relationship of those objectives to the application.
- They should consider how they use their expertise to solve the application.
- They should get to know the knowledge crafters so that they are not intimidated by them.
- They should be convinced about the importance of the application.

Such preparation may take some time to accomplish, although one or two preliminary, relaxed meetings with the team may be adequate for this purpose. However, the introductory process cannot be hurried, and the actual knowledge acquisition interviewing process should not be started while the experts still appear to be reluctant to cooperate.

Preparing the Interviewers

The knowledge crafters also need to make some preparations:

- They need to review the general subject matter relating to both the expertise and the application.
- They need to establish the interview schedules and make the necessary day-to-day arrangements.

To help the knowledge crafters gain at least a superficial understanding of the expertise, the experts should be asked to recommend books, articles, and reports that give a layperson's description of the field. Such interest also helps to establish good rapport.

If possible, the knowledge crafters should also observe the experts at work, being careful not to distract them. The knowledge crafters should note the environment, the presence of other persons, the use of tools or other aids, and the interactions that take place.

Early Interview Sessions

The first interviewing sessions are concentrated sessions during the feasibility study and the overall design phases of the project. The feasibility study interviews typically take between two days and two weeks, while the overall design phase interviews may be broken into two or three sets of interviews, with each set taking between two days and two weeks, depending on the scope and magnitude of the application.

After the interview process has been established, but before the actual interviews begin, the knowledge crafters, apprentices, and experts should meet in a relaxed setting. The knowledge crafters should explain to the experts what knowledge-based systems are, how they are put together, and what is is to be accomplished in the interviews. They should attempt to interest the experts in the work, persuade them to be cooperative, and stress that every effort will be exerted to conserve their time. The informal discussions can be used to obtain the experts' full support for the interview schedule. Only after such agreement has been reached should the schedule be published.

Ongoing Interviews

Ongoing interview sessions occur periodically after the overall design has been completed while the series of prototype versions is being built and tested. The nature of these interviews depends on the complexity of the development tools and technology being used and on the means by which the knowledge is to be represented in the particular application. For example, rule-based reasoning requires that the expert examine individual rules in detail, while frame-based reasoning requires comparatively less examination of generic rules and closer examination of the knowledge stored in the various frame taxonomies.

As with initial interviews, ongoing interviews are best conducted in a concentrated, continuous series of sessions, typically lasting between one and five days. These interviews are needed to ascertain that information previously obtained from the expert is complete and that the knowledge crafters have faithfully represented this information in the knowledge base. Before beginning the interviews, the knowledge crafters must therefore have reviewed the knowledge obtained to date and implemented a first approximation of the prototype.

The problem of ascertaining that the knowledge has been faithfully represented in the knowledge base often requires that the expert understand at least a little of the way in which the knowledge is represented and how the reasoning process works on the representation. While it is fairly easy to explain rules and rule-based reasoning to an expert, it may be more difficult to explain frame-based reasoning, reasoning using multiple environments, or blackboarding techniques. On the other hand, it may be more difficult to explain and understand the interaction of many interacting rules than an equivalent representation of knowledge using frames.

Testing Interviews

Once the first prototype version has been produced, and the knowledge crafters believe it works properly, the application must be tested to ensure that the knowledge is represented accurately and that the reasoning process operates properly on that knowledge to solve the problem of the application. Testing interviews are intricately involved in that process.

Test interview sessions typically span several weeks, but the expert's time and involvement can be limited to about one hour per day over that period. Each test interview session should therefore be terminated at the earliest of:

- The satisfactory completion of the test case
- The encountering of a stumbling block that cannot be ignored for the rest of the test interview session or quickly fixed with time for more test interviewing
- One hour.

To maximize the information obtained in these sessions, the knowledge-crafting team should use the two-on-one technique with the questioner running the test at the computer while the scribe takes notes. Here, though, the roles of questioner and scribe would normally not change in the course of the hour, although they should change from day to day to take advantage of the different perspectives of the two knowledge crafters.

During the remainder of the workday and until the next test interview session, the knowledge crafters have the job of tuning the knowledge base to match the information uncovered in the interview session. With early prototype versions, one day is usually just enough; with the later prototype versions, having similar test interview sessions with other experts or prospective users during the same workday may also be feasible.

When the next day's interviews begin, the previous day's test case should be reviewed from the beginning so that the expert can see how the suggested changes have been incorporated into the application. This very rapid turnaround of changes keeps the expert's interest level high and makes knowledge-based reasoning systems workable.

Role of Apprentices in Interviewing

If possible, the apprentices should observe the initial interviews and begin to participate in the intermediate interview sessions, providing that the experts are not intimidated by the added number of people. If the apprentices can attend these interview sessions and the associated design sessions, they can observe the whole knowledge-crafting process, both its problems and its successes.

A particularly effective practice is to have the apprentices do much of the day-to-day test interviewing. In this way, the apprentices learn more about the detailed functioning of the application and begin to take over the project. However, the knowledge crafters must closely supervise all modifications of the knowledge base to reflect any problems raised by experts or prospective users.

Developing the Requirements

The sailor's requirements should dictate the design of a yacht, and many of those requirements center around the cockpit layout under sail. What may seem pleasant or inconsequential at the dock may prove to be annoying or essential when under sail. Thus, an extensive list of cockpit requirements dealing with the positioning and accessibility of winches, sheets, halyards, cleats, fairleads, travelers, and stays must be assembled. Additional requirements lists must be developed for areas below decks, especially the galley, navigation desk, and head areas. Similarly, the user's requirements should dictate the design of a knowledge-based application, and many of those requirements center around the man-machine interface. Not only should an extensive list of the user's requirements be assembled, but requirements must also be developed from managers and experts. Chapter 4 discusses the process of obtaining, ranking, and blending a set of requirements for a knowledge-based application.

Once the preliminaries (e.g., team formation, formal instruction) have been completed, the knowledge-crafting team can focus its attention on the real problem—namely, the crafting of a knowledge-based application. The foundation for that effort is a set of objectives and expectations, which are to be collected from the major groups associated with the project—management, the experts, the potential users, and the knowledge crafters themselves. Because these desires are often incomplete and conflicting, the team will need to integrate them into a complete and consistent set of requirements This process is further complicated by the shifting of the application's goals over time. As management, experts, and users learn more about the technology and its capabilities, their perception of the application's role will change.

The knowledge-crafting team will actually go through the requirement development process twice. The first time, in connection with the feasibility study (see Chapter 5), will produce a broad but fairly shallow set of requirements. The second time, in connection with the application design (see Chapter 6), will add much greater detail to the requirement set.

The Design Process

The initial steps in the process of crafting an application system design, whether rough for the feasibility study or more detailed to support implementation, involve the formulation of the application requirements. This task can be accomplished in two steps:

1.   Understanding the application environment
2.   Establishing the requirements.

The next steps in the design-crafting process involve the specification of:

- The knowledge structures and reasoning mechanisms to be used
- The development tools to be used
- The delivery vehicle to be used.

The remaining steps concern the evaluation of the design as established to meet the requirements, which involves considering the design:

- Technically—the degree to which the design can be used to represent and reason about the knowledge
- Physically—the degree to which it can satisfy restrictions on size, speed, or usage of specific facilities
- Economically—the degree to which it can provide an appropriate benefit-to-cost ratio, given the development risk
- Environmentally—the degree to which it can operate within the context of the users' job function and the organization's culture.

As illustrated in Figure 4-1, establishing the requirements is part of an iterative procedure, for the design and the evaluation processes can af-

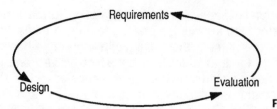

Figure 4-1   The Design Process

fect the requirements, leading to a respecification of one or more of the requirements, which in turn leads to some redesign and a further reevaluation.

For the feasibility study, the focus is on the requirements and evaluation steps, with the design steps being performed in a more cursory fashion. Once the feasibility study has been completed, however, the focus shifts from the requirements and evaluation steps to the design steps.

Understanding the Application Environment

Defining a set of application requirements is the initial entry into the design process cycle shown in Figure 4-1, and the first step in defining those requirements is for the development team members to understand the application domain and the use to which the application system is to be put. They don't have to become domain experts, but they do have to become informed about the environment for which the application is to be built. Additionally, the design team members must understand the use to be made of the application. These insights will derive from information about:

- Who will be using the application
- What type of physical environment is required
- What types of decisions the application is to make
- What the time frame for those decisions is
- What types of information are to be used
- What the sources of that information are.

This information will provide a basic framework that will facilitate the team's subsequent work in formulating requirements (e.g., ensuring that all the necessary issues and considerations surface), developing a design (e.g., selecting appropriate knowledge representations and reasoning structures), and then carrying through with the actual implementation, from prototype development to delivery system deployment.

Establishing the Requirements

Once they understand the application, the knowledge-crafting team can begin to formulate the application requirements. Depending on the stage of the project, establishing the requirements may proceed in one of two ways:

1. Broadly but rapidly for the feasibility study
2. More thoroughly, as a prelude to the design and prototype development tasks.

The knowledge-crafting team should document all of the proposed requirements, objectives, goals, and desired capabilities, along with a measure of the strength with which each is held or of the importance of each to the organization. Unlike conventional system development efforts, knowledge-based applications are more often guided by many broad but flexible objectives than by a narrow set of hard requirements. Only by understanding the complete set of requirements and their relative priorities can the knowledge crafters design and develop an application that will best serve the organization.

If the feasibility study has been completed, many developers are tempted just to "try something," to "see how it looks." After all, they now know a considerable amount about the application and believe that they can overlook the development of requirements, relying instead on a rapid prototyping capability to correct design errors.

This attitude of "let's get started" is understandable, particularly for those team members who have not previously been through the process of crafting a knowledge-based application system. With the feasibility study completed, they have already met with the experts, knowledge has been acquired about the domain, and some of the requirements are obvious. With sufficient information available to "get started," there may not be sufficient self-discipline to wait until all the necessary information is available.

Nevertheless, this process can (and does) work. We were associated with one project in which the project leader was insulted that we should expect a written statement of the application's requirements to be provided before implementation. "What an archaic idea!" The project leader proposed that the requirements be set forth only after the application was completed, for only then would the requirements be fully known.

The price paid for such a trial-and-error approach to requirements specification, however, is that initial prototypes turn out to be wrong in some way. As a consequence, more iterations, more development, and more redevelopment are required. The improved development process afforded by rapid prototyping only obscures the underlying problem. The capabilities of the technology must not be permitted to lure the developer into poor software development practices. Central to any software development (and a knowledge-based application is a piece of software) is the availability of a set of requirements against which the application can be designed, implemented, tested, and validated.

Requirements should be viewed as providing the basic guidelines for the knowledge crafter. Whenever design trade-offs are to be made, whenever structures or approaches are to be selected, the requirements and their relative importance provide criteria for comparing and selecting design alternatives. Thus, establishing and agreeing on the application's requirements is a prerequisite to the design and implementation process.

Whose Requirements?

Although four major groups of individuals will contribute to determining the requirements, the desires, interests, and needs of each group are by no means consistent. These conflicting pieces must be integrated into a set of requirements that is not only internally consistent but also acceptable to all parties.

The four groups that should contribute to defining the requirements are the following:

1. **Management**—This group is often more concerned with the operating environment of the deployed application (the so-called delivery system) and with the achievement of the projected costs and benefits estimated during the feasibility study than they are with the logical capabilities of the application. More than any other group, managers can offer a perspective on how the knowledge-based application could or should affect the organization's operating environment (e.g., the manner in which it serves its customers, the way in which it staffs its operations). However, members of this group are often fascinated with how they perceive the application (e.g., how they would like to work with the man-machine interface) rather than with how it might affect user personnel.

2. **Experts**—This group is typically concerned with the completeness of the knowledge base and the correctness of the reasoning procedures. Experts tend to focus on the quality of the decisions reached or the diagnosis made rather than on the effectiveness of the overall system in an operational context.

3. **Users**—This group is generally concerned with how its members will interact with the system (e.g., how they will input data to it, how easy it will be to use, how it will affect their job). They concentrate on the personal impact of the application on them rather than on the effect of the system on the overall organization.

4. **Developers**—This group is responsible for separating out the impossible or unrealistic ideas of the management, experts, and users—for bringing consistency to the inconsistent. Thus, this group might not be expected to contribute to the direct specification of requirements. The developers' biases (e.g., a desire to use the latest tools, to produce a "polished" system) need to be recognized, however, for they can affect the process of establishing the requirements.

Management's Requirements

Management's requirements generally relate to policy matters, which clearly affect the knowledge-crafting project. For example, management may require that certain aspects of the application be advisory and that the recommendations be reviewed or approved by a staff member before any action is taken. Another example might be management's requirement that the application operate on the organization's existing mainframe complex and deliver service through an existing telecommunications network to terminals that already exist on the users' desks. These types of requirements significantly limit the development and design choices available to the knowledge crafter and hence may affect many other aspects of the ultimate application system.

Some management requirements, such as the ones illustrated above, are legitimate exercises of managerial authority, but others just reflect personal preferences. For example, a manager who will not be a direct user of the system may "require" a certain capability (e.g., natural language input) that would not be necessary for the actual users (e.g., keyboard-proficient clerks making frequent use of the application). Permitting this type of requirement to persist could seriously affect development time, application performance, and cost-effectiveness.

Some requirements, however, are unstated. Management may never explicitly acknowledge that a particular type of delivery system is essential—or unacceptable—yet design after design will be rejected until one is presented that finally reflects the unstated requirement. The manager may not be trying to be deceptive, only unaware of the importance subconsciously being placed on the requirement. Thus, part of the knowledge-crafter's challenge is to capture all of management's requirements, stated and unstated, and then to sort out the priority or attention that should be attached to each.

Experts' Requirements

Most of the experts' requirements relate to the boundaries of the application domain, the nature of the knowledge that must be provided for decision making, and the frequency with which knowledge changes must be reflected, although experts will also have some requirements involving the characteristics of the interface (e.g., the application must appear to be "smart"). Again, the challenge facing the knowledge crafter is to sort out the necessary from the unnecessary. Because experts are primarily concerned with the reasoning capabilities of the system, they may get carried away in specifiying the boundaries of the application, making its domain of expertise too broad. For example, an application that can address 95% of the potential cases may well be acceptable from a business perspective, but the expert might insist that the system hande 99% of all possible cases.

Users' Requirements

Users' requirements can dramatically affect the time required to develop, test, and deliver an operational knowledge-based application. Underlying their requirements are considerations relating to their own capabilities and the environment in which the system might be used:

- **Physical abilities**—involving such considerations as user facility and comfort in using a keyboard
- **Educational level**—involving such considerations as user familiarity with domain language and terminology. (The interface

language for a financial planning knowledge-based application will be significantly different if the user is a member of the general public rather than a member of a bank trust department.)

- **Permissible training**—involving such considerations as the amount of training to be given to the user. (A customer can be given far less training than an employee.)
- **Environment**—involving such considerations as the conditions under which the system will be used. Will the user's hands be occupied, raising the importance of nonkeyboard input alternatives (e.g., voice input)? Will the user's eyes or attention likely be on other tasks, leading to a need for audible or other forms of outputs and alarms?

The user interface to the system becomes a particularly significant issue whenever the user community does not consist solely of persons who are used to dealing with computer systems on a regular basis. When the users are handicapped or culturally different from the knowledge crafters, the interface problem can become acute. In most cases, the knowledge-crafting team must devote a considerable amount of time and effort to planning and developing the user interface. To put this problem in perspective, we know of applications that were developed in which 40% of the project effort went into the user interface. Most projects do not require quite this degree of emphasis, but just a cursory once-over of the interface problem is clearly inadequate.

Developers' Requirements

The needs and capabilities of the knowledge-crafting team also affect the application's requirements. Some of the influence is appropriate, some inappropriate. For example, defining development facility capabilities is properly an area for knowledge-crafter input. Although a knowledge-based application could be built in assembly code without any access to higher level tools, the organization might find that no one would wish to be involved in such an arduous process.

On the other hand, members of the computing profession can overemphasize the importance of working with the latest tools in the most advanced facilities. Hence, the knowledge-crafting team members must take a hard look at their own requirements and separate what is needed from what is desired.

Formulating the Requirement Set

Once an initial set of requirements (or perhaps, more accurately, an initial "wish list") has been elicited from all participating parties, the real work begins. Wishes must be converted to valid requirements. The set of requirements may have to be extended to cover areas omitted from consideration. Finally, the requirements from the various participants have to be made consistent.

Issues to Be Addressed by Requirements

Although the specific requirements to be formulated depend on both the individual organization and the application, they should generally address the following issues:

- **Development resources**—hardware, software, knowledge-crafter labor, expert labor, calendar time, overall cost
- **Expert availability**—total time as well as contiguous time blocks
- **Functional capabilities**—logical functions that the system is to offer to the user, the breadth of the domain within which the system is to operate
- **Operational environment**—number of users, number of different locations, cost per delivery vehicle, operating cost, processing speed, integration with current user working environment and procedures, integration with current computing systems
- **User interface**—text, graphical, menu, natural language, audio
- **Information sources**—user input, central data base, real-time sensors
- **System outputs**—text output to user, graphical output to user, audio output, real-time output to other devices, updates to data bases
- **Maintenance**—frequency of maintenance, skill level of maintainers.

Requirement Priorities

The knowledge-crafting team must attach priorities to requirements at the time they are formulated. Not only will these assist in resolving any inconsistencies and conflicts that later arise, but they will also aid in developing a subset of requirements that can feasibly be met. Even though these requirements might be complete and internally consistent, all such requirements might not be able to be satisfied given the nature of the domain, organization, and current technology. The priorities enable the knowledge crafters to select those requirements to satisfy as well as those to set aside.

Are Those Requirements Real?

Many organizations are treating knowledge-based applications development as special projects. These efforts frequently involve special teams of individuals and are conducted outside of normal data processing software funding and development channels. This situation may set the stage for intelligent users to view a knowledge-based application project as a means to bypass their organization's lengthy queue of pending requests for traditional software development.

We were associated with one knowledge-based application development project in which users were requesting a capability to produce a variety of reports. Although these reports did not appear to require the reasoning capabilities of the proposed application, users nevertheless insisted that these reporting capabilities were necessary. On further inspection we found that a normal software development request for this capability would be backlogged in a three-year queue within the data processing department. With the knowlege-based application being funded off budget (i.e., from nondepartment sources), having access to the necessary files, and having a projected one-year development cycle, these users found the project to be a natural vehicle for obtaining the reporting capability they desired.

Are Those Requirements Realistic?

In one respect it is unfortunate that knowledge-based systems technology is so impressive because this quality can lead to unrealistic expectations within an organization. Requirements based on such expectations can preclude satisfying other, more important needs of the organization.

For example, consider a proposed requirement to add a high-resolution graphics interface to an application that might otherwise be served adequately by a textual display. Further assume that this application is to be used by many individuals having no computer science training. Accepting the graphics requirement could seriously affect the project's development, if not kill the project outright during the feasibility study. Possible complications include:

- **Specialized user training**—Completely isolating a LISP machine from a user is very difficult. An accidental error can easily place a user in a LISP error window. A novice user would have no clue as to the appropriate action to take. Consequently, much more training would have to be given to members of the application's user community.

- **New or duplicated terminals**—The graphics requirement would preclude use of the text-type terminals currently employed by the users for other processing tasks. The organization would thus need either to place a second terminal on each user's desk or to convert existing software systems to interface with the new knowledge-based application terminal.

- **Delivery system development**—The development system required to produce the desired graphical interface might not have a delivery capability on the existing mainframe or microprocessor equipment. In that case either new hardware would have to be acquired or the application would have to be "reprogrammed" so that it could execute on existing processors. In either case, considerable cost would be involved.

In such situations, the knowledge crafters must work carefully with all parties to ensure that the requirements being submitted are meaningful and are not the result of unrealistic expectations.

Just How Solid Are Those Requirements Anyway?

Once a complete, consistent set of requirements has been formulated, just how firm a foundation can it be expected to provide? Can it be counted on as a design base? Alternatively, must the set be regarded as immutable? The answer, of course, is that the requirements will (and should) change. They must not be considered inviolate, either in the sense of counting on permanency for application development or in the sense of fearing that once established they cannot be changed and must therefore be "perfect."

Ideas about the character and role of the application—and thus its requirements—will change as it evolves. This process is very natural, which is why the feasibility study for and subsequent design of a knowledge-based system are iterative processes. We have stressed the importance of developing requirements before crafting the application design because we believe that a better initial design can be crafted as a result. However, we are under no illusions that the knowledge crafter could ever specify a complete and perfect definition of the application.

Shifting Requirements

Further, as users and experts begin to learn about the technology's capabilities, they will change their ideas about what they desire from the application. Additionally, the knowledge crafters may make new suggestions as they learn more about the problem domain. The requirements will legitimately change, but not because the knowledge crafter had specified the wrong requirements. The requirements to be developed by the knowledge-crafting team should not be viewed in the same light as those developed for a traditional software development specification.

Because knowledge-based systems are a relatively new concept, most individuals in an organization are unfamiliar with what these systems can do and hence are unsure about their requirements. Accordingly, an ongoing educational process covering the capabilities and implications of the technology must be part of the requirements specification process.

Once some of the participants have seen a rough prototype of "their" system in operation, they will immediately begin to develop new notions of what the system should and should not be able to do, of how the system should be deployed within the organization, and so forth. Rapid-prototyping capabilities are particularly helpful for this task. They permit the design, in response to changing requirements, to be revised more quickly with a lesser expenditure of development resources.

Redesigning as Requirements Are Clarified

The need for redesign following initial prototyping should not be viewed as a condemnation of the initial requirements phase of the project. Although the current state of crafting knowledge-based systems is such that the requirements are unlikely to survive the development process without modification, the initial requirements can provide design guidance that can help the developers avoid major mistakes in direction.

The building of a knowledge-based application can be likened to some of the operations research techniques that search a mathematical space for an optimum point. The better the starting point (the initial solution) for the search, the more efficient the search process. Similarly, the better the starting set of requirements for a knowledge-based application, the more efficient will be the design and development process. Fewer iterations will be required, leading to a shorter, more effective process.

Summary

Requirements are the guideposts for an application. They are absolutely critical if an organization is to develop a meaningful application in an efficient manner. Further, the better the requirements specification, the more effective the design and implementation. Throwing together "something" so that an initial design can be prepared and prototyping can get under way is a losing cause. This fact seems so obvious, but it is often overlooked in practice. An inappropriate or erroneous set of requirements will lead to a system that is not suited to the organization's needs; thus, it will not be used or at best will be viewed unfavorably.

On the other hand, knowledge crafters should not become so concerned about the significance of each requirement that it becomes immutable. The project should not be delayed while requirements are pinned down in excrutiating detail. Because the requirements will (likely) change during the development of the knowledge-based system, the focus should be on establishing requirements that are good but not necessarily "perfect."

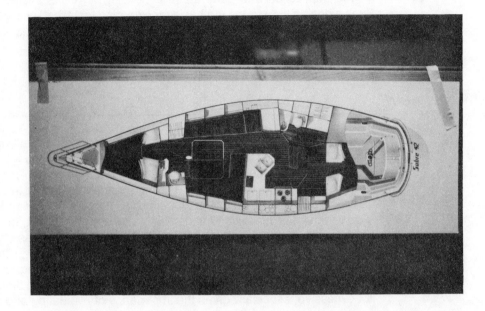

Conducting the Feasibility Study

The yacht designer sketches a below-deck layout in order to evaluate the characteristics of a potential design with respect to satisfying the requirements at a cost consistent with the benefits. By shifting the functions assigned to match the available space, the designer seeks to maximize the room for a salon, galley, head, and sleeping quarters within the constraints set by the requirements and the overall size and shape limitations of the yacht. Similarly, the knowledge crafter sketches a structure for a knowledge-based application in order to evaluate the characteristics of a potential design with respect to satisfying the requirements at a cost consistent with the benefits. By altering knowledge representations, control structures, and interface capabilities, the knowledge crafter seeks to maximize the functionality of the application within the constraints set by the requirements and operating environment of the application. Chapter 5 describes this preliminary design and evaluation process, termed a feasibility study.

Before launching into building a knowledge-based application, an organization should conduct a comprehensive feasibility study to understand better the scope of such an undertaking and the risks associated with doing it. A good feasibility study determines preliminary requirements for the application and uses them to develop an initial system design. Such a design then forms the basis for exploring technical, economic, and other issues associated with the application, thereby producing a fairly accurate estimate of what the development will entail.

Overview

For a feasibility study to achieve its intended goals, a team of professionals trained in knowledge-based systems technology must perform it while working together with the organization's management, prospective users, experts, and apprentices. The material presented in this chapter has evolved as the result of our conducting numerous studies across a wide variety of organizations and subject domains. No doubt, many ways can be used to complete such studies, but our experience has shown this approach to be effective where others have failed. Although the study encompasses most aspects of the intended application, it frequently does not take more than one to four weeks to complete. The cost, therefore, is not excessive, especially given the importance of evaluating and minimizing the risks of the proposed undertaking.

How Does a Study Work?

As described earlier in Chapter 4, the feasibility study cycle shown in Figure 5-1 usually proceeds cyclically from a partial determination of the requirements, to a tentative design to meet those requirements, to an evaluation of the system, and then back to the determination of additional or revised requirements, and so forth.

The various feasibility issues are assessed as the requirements are determined and the initial design is derived. As the process unfolds, technical, economic, and other findings indicate the feasibility of the application. However, the feasibility study only exposes comparatively preliminary and rather rough requirements and design components. The process of fully defining the requirements for the application was described in Chapter 4, while the process of developing the design from these requirements is explained in Chapter 6. This chapter addresses that part of the cycle that is most closely related to the feasibility study—the evaluation phase.

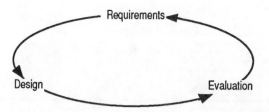

Figure 5-1 The Feasibility Cycle

(In Chapter 11 we describe two feasibility study schedules based on the methods described in this chapter—one for the study of a single application and one for a study to select a first application from a group of five candidate applications.)

The Study Team at Work

The study usually begins with a series of one or more introductory meetings in which company members explain the intended purpose of the proposed application to the knowledge crafters and other interested persons. These meetings are followed by a series of interview sessions with management, prospective users, and experts (usually in that order) to uncover preliminary details of the requirements and begin the feasibility (requirements-design-evaluation) cycle. Several tentative designs can then be prepared and evaluated. As the discovery process continues, contradictory requirements, expectations, or design weaknesses must be identified and resolved with the appropriate persons in the organization. Through several cycles, the requirements are refined, and some of the tentative designs are modified or discarded. By the end of the process, the knowledge-crafting team should have a fairly broad but shallow set of requirements, along with one or two possible designs, from which a reasonably accurate estimate of the required development effort can be determined. If no such design remains, the application as conceived may not be possible, and further effort may be required to design a system that is feasible if some requirements are relaxed.

Issues to Be Examined

A variety of issues are to be considered and evaluated as part of the feasibility study. Examining these issues in a logical progression is seldom possible. Information must be gathered from many sources, including people with other commitments and busy schedules. Thus, the knowledge-crafting team must arrange meetings with appropriate individuals to fit their schedules.

Regardless of the order, however, the feasibility study must examine three types of issues:

1. Technical issues
   - Suitability of the problem
   - Characteristics of the knowledge
   - Characteristics of the experts
   - Interfaces
   - Validation and testing

2. Economic issues
   - Benefits
   - Costs
   - Risks
   - Pioneering

3. Cultural issues
   - Corporate culture
   - User environment.

Technical Issues

A number of technical issues needs to be addressed during a feasibility study for a prospective knowledge-based application. Logically, the first issue that should be considered concerns the suitability of the problem for solution by knowledge-based technology.

Suitability of the Problem

A knowledge-based system is not a panacea; it cannot solve every problem. "Horror stories" abound of disasters resulting from attempts to address problems using inappropriate technology. The knowledge crafters, therefore, must assess whether the problem to be solved is one that should even be attempted using a knowledge-based approach. Such an assessment includes determining:

- The possibility of an algorithmic approach
- The boundaries of the problem
- The sources of the expertise
- The suitability of the expertise for the problem
- The type of expertise
    - data gathering versus data analysis
    - common sense reasoning
- The required development time.

Is There an Existing Algorithmic Solution?

One of the first issues that needs to be explored is the possibility of an algorithmic solution to the problem. By definition, an algorithm offers a guaranteed solution that is optimal under the assumed conditions, while a knowledge-based solution is heuristic and approximate. The risk that a successful knowledge-based application can be produced is thus higher than the risk associated with producing an application based on a known algorithm. In addition, the cost to capture and test the appropriate expertise is normally greater than the cost of implementing an algorithmic solution. Therefore, knowledge-based applications should only be attempted when other types of solutions are not possible.

Is the Problem Clearly Bounded?

Many applications, knowledge-based and otherwise, fail because the problem is not clearly defined and bounded. This lack of definition in turn leads to ambiguity in what constitutes an answer to or solution for the problem, thereby hindering knowledge crafters attempting to develop and evaluate solutions.

The major issue that the knowledge crafters must resolve during the feasibility study is not so much whether the problem is well defined as whether the problem, or some subset thereof, can be suitably bounded and defined. The existence of an ambiguously defined but boundable problem is not fatal; it merely requires the insertion of an additional definitional task at the beginning of the development project.

Does Any Expertise Exist?

Knowledge-based applications require a source of expertise. Quite simply, without the expertise, knowledge cannot be placed in an application. For instance, a knowledge-based application that could accurately predict stock prices or winners in a horse race would be extremely valuable; however, since no collection of humans has that type of expertise, a knowledge-based application built to solve these problems is not feasible. Surprisingly, many persons contemplating building knowledge-based applications overlook the fact that their desire for a knowledge-based application arises from their desire for the expertise.

Does the Expertise Fit the Problem?

Even if an organization has widely acclaimed experts available, the knowledge crafters must assess the amount of expertise that can actually be put in a form to benefit a nonexpert user. Determining whether the expertise alone can solve the problem or, conversely, whether the absence of the expertise materially affects the solution of the problem is one way to answer the question. Another way is to determine how successfully the problem is being solved today. If existing solutions devised by the expert are inadequate, then a knowledge-based application would not likely improve the situation.

Is the Character of the Expertise Representable Using Today's Technology?

Unfortunately, the current state of knowledge-based technology does not allow all types of expertise to be represented in a system. Therefore, the knowledge crafters must ascertain that the expertise associated with the problem domain is such that it can be successfully incorporated in the application. The following subsections describe two types of expertise that are difficult to embed within a knowledge-based application.

Is the Expertise Related to Acquiring Data?

A very good measure of whether an application is suited to knowledge-based techniques is to test whether an expert's skill derives from the analysis of information (that exists or that anyone could collect) or from the acquisition of information (that anyone could then analyze). If the expertise is related to the analysis of information, many of the tools available today may be relevant. However, these tools are ill-equipped to deal with expertise that is related to acquiring information.

Consider, for example, the expert who uses a highly developed sense of touch to identify minute flaws in a piece of metal. The expertise lies partially in the finger tips of the expert and the interpretation of personal sensory inputs. The knowledge-based system cannot perform such an analysis. Similarly, the analyst who derives data from a broad array of loosely connected, general sources (e.g., a collection of yesterday's news, a two-week-old magazine article, and a letter from a friend in Washington, D.C.) is drawing on a breadth of data that is beyond the scope of today's technology to scan and abstract.

Successful diagnostic-type, knowledge-based applications, for example, often rely on information that a less-experienced individual would be able to collect (e.g., the patient has a low blood-sugar reading, the loan applicant claims to own a fully-paid-for Rolls Royce). The skill of the expert, then, lies in analyzing the available information. Knowledge crafters should be concerned about application feasibility if they find, for example, that the expert's success is based on an ability to deduce that the loan applicant is lying from subtle body mannerisms or eye movements. Generally, knowledge-based applications are most applicable in situations where the expertise relates to the interpretation of data and not the acquisition of those data, where novices can obtain the data but not interpret it.

Does the Expertise Involve Common-Sense Reasoning?

From birth, human beings amass a huge amount of intuitive, implicit, so-called "common-sense" knowledge; codifying and entering such a body of knowledge into a computer is a research topic. Moreover, no one yet knows how to "teach" a computer to acquire this type of common-sense knowledge on its own. Yet, reasoning with this type of data is a hallmark of human problem solving.

Consider a three-year-old boy with a cup of milk on a table. We can safely assume that a child of this age is ignorant of hydrodynamics theory, partial differential equations, and other scientific knowledge. Yet that child knows that the milk will run out of the cup across the table if the cup should be tipped over. Further, he can reason from this knowledge to analogous situations that he might not have previously encountered. That is, presented with a glass of something he had never tasted (e.g., mango juice), he could reason that the juice would flow out of the glass if the glass were upset.

Therefore, the feasibility study must examine the nature of the expertise needed for the problem and determine the amount of common-sense reasoning inherent in the solution process. If the problem area should depend heavily on such common-sense reasoning, constructing a successful application may be virtually impossible.

The amount of common-sense reasoning present usually becomes evident during interviews with the expert, when many of the conclusions are supported by common-sense "nonexpert" reasoning. On the other hand, the same reasoning may also be second nature to the knowledge crafter. Unfortunately, this commonality may trick both the expert and knowledge crafter into believing that the explanation is adequate.

The knowledge crafter should also consider how different the expert's knowledge is from anyone else's. That is, would an average person have known what the expert purports is his special knowledge or expertise? When such differences are hard to distinguish, common-sense reasoning may be the cause. Again, it may be difficult for the knowledge crafter to make an objective estimate.

In certain cases where common-sense reasoning comprises some portion of the application, the knowledge crafters may be able to isolate the sections containing that reasoning and attack the remainder. For this separation to be successful, however, the experts will need to explain the common-sense portion of the reasoning (which may not be feasible) and prevent such reasoning from pervading the remaining portions of the application.

Is the Development Time Reasonable?

A final criterion for determining application suitability is the estimated calendar time required to develop the application. If the final prototype can be developed within a period of one year, then the size and scope of the application are probably within the capabilities of today's technology; otherwise, the requirements of the application are likely to exceed what is currently possible outside the laboratory.

Characteristics of the Knowledge

Assuming that the problem is suitable for a knowledge-based approach, the knowledge-crafting team must then examine the characteristics of the knowledge, including:

- The size of the knowledge base
- The complexity of the knowledge
- The time needed to obtain the knowledge
- The time needed to reason with the knowledge versus the time to react to the answers
- The form of the knowledge.

These characteristics may indicate that one or more representation techniques should be avoided, while others may appear to be especially suitable. Often, though, these characteristics tend to steer the knowledge representation selection process along a path leading toward the use of a set of techniques that includes several methods for representing the knowledge.

In considering the characteristics of the knowledge, the knowledge crafter should remember that each of the three categories of knowledge may need to be considered separately.

- **Permanent**—Knowledge that can be built as an integral part of the application since it will not change (e.g., the fact that an electrical current produces a magnetic field).
- **Static**—Knowledge that remains unchanged from one use of the application to the next but that is likely to change during the life of the application (e.g., the sales tax rate is 6.5%).
- **Dynamic**—Knowledge that will change from one use of the application to the next (e.g., the applicant's name is Smith) or knowledge that may change during the execution of the application (e.g., air pressure in the brake line is 85 pounds).

Size

The size of the application alone may dictate the particular knowledge representation techniques that might be used. Indeed, the size of some applications makes them impossible to develop using today's technology, both in terms of the amount of storage required to hold the knowledge and, more importantly, in terms of the time required to capture the knowledge, test the validity and accuracy of the application, or run it in a production mode. The size of the application thus should be measured in several ways.

First, the total overall size of the application needs to be estimated to determine whether the application can fit the constraints of the delivery computer system. Many applications that have been proposed cannot fit on computers of today.

Second, the separability of the knowledge into smaller units needs to be estimated. For instance, if the knowledge can be contained in the computer but only as a single monolithic mass, the knowledge would be considerably more difficult to capture and validate than an equivalent amount that could be compartmentalized into several smaller sections that could be manipulated independently. Substantially larger applications can be built when the knowledge can be segmented in this way. Such a division of the knowledge derives from a common engineering approach to problem solving—taking a large and/or complex problem and breaking it down into a number of smaller, more manageable parts or subproblems that can be solved separately.

Complexity

The complexity of the application must also be estimated. A knowledge base may not be very large, but if the knowledge is highly complicated or confusing, knowledge crafters may not be able to capture and test it in a reasonable amount of time. Usually, though, complex knowledge bases are also quite large so that both size and complexity tests fail simultaneously.

An automobile engine diagnostic problem, as shown in Figure 5-2, illustrates the knowledge complexity issue by subdividing a problem into segments capable of being treated separately.

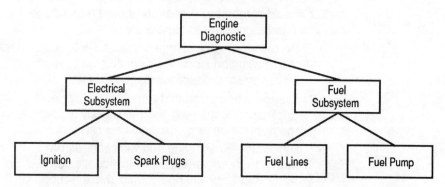

Figure 5-2 An Engine Diagnostic Layout

In this problem the electrical subsystem and the fuel subsystem are natural groupings, and each can readily be subdivided further. Thus, diagnosing individual problems is relatively easy. The major subsystem at fault is determined, and then those subsystems involved are methodically isolated. The total body of knowledge is not used to diagnose any one problem. The knowledge is segmented into sections that can be used as needed.

In some cases, however, interdependencies within the knowledge make such logical partitioning impossible, and the application must use all of the knowledge in each reasoning step. Clearly, such a reasoning process is much slower. In addition, the acquisition and testing of the knowledge are more difficult because all the knowledge must be tested in light of all possible data that might be provided to the application.

Stability of the Knowledge

The knowledge must remain stable long enough for the knowledge crafters to capture it, place it in an application, test it, and get some use out of it. If the knowledge changes faster than the time necessary to build it into an application, a meaningful knowledge-based application cannot be built. Fortunately, most knowledge is sufficiently stable to be used effectively. Because the time required to build and test a complex application can easily extend over a year, however, the life of a completed application may not be long enough to recoup the investment spent in building it. The time required to build an application to handle complex tax questions, for instance, may only be slightly less than the expected life of the tax laws behind the knowledge.

What about the person who has taken years to build up his expertise? Does it take an equivalent number of years to build such knowledge into an application? Generally, capturing the knowledge for an application does not take as long as developing the expertise. The expert's learning process is not methodical, but includes a lot of time-consuming trial and error.

Some expertise, though, is not easily transferred. In one case knowledge crafters wanted to collect the expertise of a master tool and die maker who had nearly 40 years of experience, including a 20-year apprenticeship. When asked to examine faulty parts made by a poorly designed die, the knowledge crafters could not see, feel, or comprehend the problems the master was describing. Surely, knowledge-based applications are not a substitute for the years of training some people need to become qualified experts.

Stability of the Input

One way to evaluate the stability of the input is to consider the amount of time available to reflect on the data and react to it before the answer is no longer valid. Invalidity may occur because the computer takes too long to derive the answer, because the inputs change too fast, or because the time to analyze the answer is too long with respect to the stability of the input. While this problem is frequently referred to as the "real-time" problem, that term may be misleading because real time normally refers only to short (e.g., subsecond) time spans with rapid responses.

Form of the Knowledge

Humans often think of knowledge as numbers (e.g., 72), facts (e.g., it is raining), symbols (e.g., good), and relations (e.g., she is my sister), especially when dealing with computer systems which have been designed to process numeric and symbolic data. Yet, many types of problems are not addressed by humans in these terms.

Consider pattern knowledge, for example. To determine the next move, the chess master frequently compares the pattern observed on the playing board with patterns he has seen before. The pattern signifies a situation, and his response is to that situation. Despite superior skill, the master cannot reason about the implications of literally millions of possible moves. Thus, any attempt to duplicate his playing ability by calculating the implications of alternative moves using the rules of chess will be doomed to failure. (A researcher may or may not be able to develop a chess playing program that can beat the master using such an approach, but that individual will not be able to duplicate the performance of the master since a different approach is being used.)

Similarly, the crew scheduler for a bus company frequently reacts to pattern information rather than to readily available numerical information. Computers do such a nice job of performing arithmetic operations rapidly and reliably that the knowledge crafter is often tempted to look for knowledge related to arithmetic computations. Thus, explanations of scheduling decisions are couched in terms of "driver with the least hours left to drive" or "driver located farthest from home terminal." Yet, the human scheduler is not very good at calculating and updating such an array of statistics on every driver as the schedule is assembled. Again, the scheduler observes patterns, and the expertise that the knowledge crafters must capture relates to the identification of such patterns and the associated responses that tend to produce good schedules.

Characteristics of the Experts

Quite apart from the character of the expertise or knowledge, the knowledge crafters must be concerned with the experts' suitability for the application development, including their:

- Availability to the project
- Interest in the application
- Ability to articulate their expertise
- Personal motivation.

In addition, the knowledge crafters must consider the commitment of management and the number of experts whose special knowledge must be reflected in the application.

Are the Experts Available?

Because the knowledge-acquisition process can be long and difficult, the experts should agree ahead of time to devote the necessary effort to this process. When the expert is rarely available, this process becomes even more time-consuming, possibly preventing the application from being built.

The knowledge crafters should be duty-bound to conserve as much of the experts' time as possible, by studying the subject area before the interviewing begins and by recognizing that the experts have numerous demands on them. Therefore, as described in Chapter 3, the knowledge crafters must plan to use the experts' time sparingly, obtaining a maximum of information in a minimum of time.

We know of one system that was taken to the first-prototype stage and then abandoned. The prototype demonstrated that the application would meet its design requirements and that it would provide more than the projected level of benefits. Yet, because the organization did not believe that it could spare the expert from his ongoing duties for a sufficient period of time to complete the application and put it into operational use, the project had to be cancelled for lack of available expertise.

Are the Experts Interested in the Application?

If the experts are actively interested in the success of the application, they will be extremely useful in helping the knowledge crafters capture, evaluate, and validate their expertise. On the other hand, if the experts are not especially concerned about the project, the knowledge crafters will have to work much harder to elicit the knowledge, and the chance that key information will not be volunteered (and hence overlooked) is considerably greater.

In many ways, the knowledge crafters should not expect the experts to be interested in the project at the outset of the feasibility study. The expert may not have been informed about the possibility of the project or even about knowledge-based applications. On the other hand, the expert's lack of interest may be caused by other factors. In one case, we spent a lot of time just trying to schedule the first meeting with the expert. He was clearly not interested in helping with the application—as evidenced by the fact that he soon left the company to join a competitor.

One way to convince experts about the importance of the project is to show them how the application will benefit them directly. A typical gain might be a lighter workload involved in dealing with day-to-day problems and thus more opportunity to handle more challenging problems.

Are the Experts Articulate?

The experts' fluency and articulateness are usually evident in the first interview. The experts must be sufficiently articulate to explain their expertise; the knowledge crafters need to understand it. The experts must therefore be able to explain why they do something, under what circumstances they do it, and the purpose they have in doing it—an often difficult task. In doing this, the experts will often remark that they have learned more about their expertise than they had learned in some time.

Being articulate should not be confused with being able to speak the same language. A knowledge-crafting team may work with experts who do not speak a common language, or the two groups may use different terminology in their respective professions. When these significant language differences are present, the apprentices may need to act as interpreters.

We were once involved in the feasibility study of a knowledge-based system to determine the proper feed mix for individual cattle. After spending some time listening to a cattleman explain the nutrients in various feedstuffs, we realized that the real unanswered question was whether the cow would find the mixture sufficiently appetizing to eat it. Unfortunately, the only expert on this issue was the cow. We had to abandon further consideration of the application because the cow was not sufficiently articulate to explain her food preferences to the knowledge crafters. Although this episode may seem absurd, it is typical of the kinds of unexpected situations that can occur in a feasibility study. People take it for granted that other humans are reasonably articulate and that they can understand one another, but the issue of being articulate is a real one not to be overlooked.

Are the Experts Motivated?

Any desire for the application not to succeed may be related to the perceived threat of the knowledge-based application to the experts' position in the organization. Since these fears may be valid, they need to be carefully considered; when they are unfounded, the knowledge crafters should work to dispel them as quickly as possible.

Sometimes the experts will exhibit outright hostility toward the idea of the application and refuse to talk with the knowledge crafters. Other times the experts may be willing to talk with the knowledge crafters but strongly voice their objections. These cases are sometimes the easiest to handle because the experts are being forthright and may be receptive to discussing the problem. The difficult cases involve those experts who seem to be receptive to the project but who provide no concrete, useful information at all.

One way to overcome the expert's lack of motivation is to try to find real benefits of the application for the expert. When the reasons for the unwillingness to participate are not apparent, a blunt, straightforward approach may get the expert to explain himself or herself. If attempts to motivate the expert fail, the only alternative may be to try to find another source of expertise.

We encountered one expert who strongly believed that his knowledge was his source of power and respect, that without it he would be like Samson with a haircut. Therefore, his "cooperation" with the knowledge-crafting team was only superficial, just enough to make it appear to his management that he was providing wholehearted support. His lack of motivation to communicate his expertise significantly reduced the quality of the application.

Management Commitment

A recent SRI survey(1) of major United States corporations revealed that successful knowledge-based applications were nearly always associated with situations in which management was interested in and committed to the project. The availability of experts can be used by knowledge crafters as a good measure of expert interest and management dedication to a project. The expert can use the availability issue as a smokescreen for lack of interest in the project; if management is not fully supportive of the project, expert availability will likely become a problem.

One good sign of management commitment is the presence of a project champion (see Chapter 2) and the direct management support of that person. The absence of a project champion might very well signal that management is not seriously interested in the undertaking.

How Dispersed Is the Expertise?

If the knowledge needed for an application can be found in a single expert (even though several of those experts might be available), the dispersal of the expertise is not an issue; there is a single voice of authority. The same tends to hold true if more than one expert works on the application, but they represent complementary views of the problem, as might occur when a physicist, chemist, and engineer collaborate on a manufacturing design problem.

The complexity of development increases, however, when multiple experts with overlapping expertise will be involved in the application development. Often these experts will give conflicting opinions based on the same information or, should they agree on the solution, will differ on the approach to be used in obtaining it. In some cases the use of even two experts can cause a problem. Building a single application that relies on a collection of conflicting experts would be very difficult at best, and building an application where the expertise is even more diffuse is probably not possible at all.

Interfaces

Knowledge-based applications are increasingly being built in an integrated mode. Rather than being stand-alone systems supporting analysts, these systems are tied to other elements of an organization's normal data processing operations. Thus, consideration of a knowledge-based application's feasibility must involve an examination of the application's interfaces, including:

- Access to (from) the knowledge-based application from (to) other portions of an encompassing application
- Access to external data bases
- Access to or from other computing equipment
- Security issues, such as:
  - permitting the use of a knowledge-based application but prohibiting the user from reading or copying the knowledge base.

permitting the reading and modification of certain portions of a knowledge base while prohibiting the modification of other portions of the same knowledge base.

Access to or from a Knowledge-Based Application

During the feasibility study, all access requirements to or from a knowledge-based application need to be studied carefully. Calls into a knowledge-based application can occur at poorly timed intervals, and the purpose of the call needs to be weighed against the priorities of other activities.

Not all knowledge-based application tools permit calls from outside the tool, and some tools that permit such calls leave various internal tables in an unpredictable state. To avoid this type of effect, some toolmakers have restricted the call path, permitting only a proscribed set of parameters to be passed in any one call to a single entry point in the tool. This safeguard can also frustrate developers in those cases where external application elements need to access various data structures in the knowledge-based application (e.g., information stored in the frames of a frame-based reasoning application).

Calling external code from the knowledge-based application may not be any more difficult than calling such code from other ordinary routines, provided that a simple subroutine calling mechanism is used, that is, the called routine returns to the calling routine in the knowledge-based application. However, more elaborate coroutine linkages are normally not supported.

Access to External Data Bases

Because many knowledge-based applications operate in conjunction with other computer-based applications, they must interact with one or more data bases, some of which may reside on external computers. Therefore, the feasibility study must consider the extent, if any, that both internal and external data bases will be used as part of the application. For instance, if the volume of data to be transferred is high, or the frequency of data transfers is high, additional burdens are placed on the application in terms of the hardware that must be used and its physical location with respect to the data bases. Performance criteria for handling certain external data bases may not be met with currently available hardware, or the cost of the necessary hardware may be prohibitively high for the application. Other applications using the data base may create additional constraints. Chapters 6, 7, and 9 discuss external data bases in greater detail.

Access to or from Other Computing Equipment

Interfaces with other computing equipment may impose demands on both the development facilities and the delivery environment. These demands typically center around the ability of the system to access appropriate amounts of data in a timely fashion or to obtain or provide information from other computing resources within an allotted time slot.

If the demand for these services is small, a loosely coupled system may make more sense. The integration of loosely coupled system elements tends to be less complicated in cases where performance and volume are not important. When tighter coupling is required, the development of the application may take more time and effort.

Security

Every external interface has associated security concerns. In addition to the normal security issues (e.g., determining that the user is authorized), knowledge-based applications present two issues that are frequently of prime concern:

1. While the knowledge base must necessarily be used in the course of running an application, management may want to preclude the user from examining the contents of the knowledge base.

2. While portions of the knowledge base may be made accessible to the user for the purposes of customization, management may want to preclude the user from changing any other parts of the application knowledge base.

The first type of security is often relatively easy to achieve. All knowledge base display mechanisms can be removed from the delivery software package.

The second type of security is more difficult to provide since the user is permitted to examine and modify portions of the knowledge base. Special-purpose knowledge base "shells" are developed for special application areas; the user then customizes the shell for a specific application, but is not allowed to customize the underlying portions of the shell to prevent damage to the whole shell. Presently, most knowledge-based application development and delivery tools do not permit selective modification of the knowledge base, but the need for this facility is likely to increase as the popularity of such special-purpose shells increases. We have received several requests to tailor and enhance general-purpose shells and thereby form special-purpose shells that will aid domain specialists in creating knowledge-based systems in a particular domain.

Validation and Testing

Issues related to validating the application and testing the expertise in it must be addressed at least as early as the feasibility study because they are central to the development of a useful application. Useful expertise must not only be acquired, but must also be thoroughly validated and tested to be worthwhile. These issues are addressed further in Chapters 6, 7, and 8.

Normally, the expert must plan to devote some time to helping test that the knowledge obtained is represented sufficiently well in the application to solve the intended problems. This process is different, however, from validating that the application actually meets the design objectives as well as the needs of the organization and the users.

Economic Issues

A knowledge-based application must be an economical undertaking; the cost of producing such applications is just too great in terms of time and effort for it to be otherwise. Nevertheless, in selecting an initial effort, an organization should opt for a straightforward application with a smaller payout instead of a complex one with a greater return. In this case, a "sure winner" is better than the riskier big payoff.

Conducting a reasonable economic analysis for a knowledge-based system is not substantially different from analyzing the benefits, costs, and risks of an ordinary software project. There may be a few additional twists to consider, however.

Estimating the Benefits

First, the benefits to be derived from the application need to be described. The knowledge crafter can begin this process by pretending that the application has been completed and is fully operational. What significant impacts are seen?

- Lower processing costs?
- Less scrap or fewer losses?
- Increased equipment utilization?
- Reduced processing, throughput, or delivery time?
- Improved product quality?
- Reduced risk or financial exposure?
- Improved product design?

This list can be refined or extended by investigating the possible impact of replacing the current analysis process with the knowledge-based system:

- Faster decisions?
- Lower cost of advice?
- More consistent decisions?
- Availability 24 hours per day?
- Availability in remote locations?
- Lower training costs?
- Improvement in user attitudes?

Proceeding through these types of considerations should provide the knowledge crafter with a basic list of benefits. Next, the associated value (in monetary terms) should be estimated for each benefit. In those cases where the benefit is primarily qualitative and thus difficult to quantify, a value of zero should be assigned. Such benefits fall into the category of "frosting on the cake"; they provide an extra benefit, but they should not be the basis for justifying the project's desirability. This process of identifying and quantifying benefits should be thorough, but unlikely benefits should not be included.

When a first pass of the benefit evaluation has been completed, the benefits with unknown values should be reexamined in light of all the benefits that have been described. If a certain benefit whose value has not been quantified appears to be insignificant in comparison to a benefit of known value, the value of the unknown benefit should continue to be recorded as zero. On the other hand, when a given benefit of unknown value appears to be far more significant than benefits with known values, a range of values should be estimated with the value nearer the lower edge of the range recorded.

Several iterations of the benefit list may be required for everyone to feel confident about the accuracy of each estimated value. However, by the end of the process, the sum of the benefit values should provide a conservative and valid benefit picture.

Estimating the Costs

As the feasibility study progresses, the design of the application will become more apparent. From one or two preliminary designs, the cost of developing the application can be estimated. Elements to consider when determining the cost are:

- The hardware and software tools needed for development and delivery of the application
- The demands of the delivery version and how the application can evolve from prototype to production
- The number of prototype versions of the application that will be required and the time and manpower necessary for building them
- The expert time required for obtaining the knowledge and validating it
- The time and manpower needed for testing and validating both the prototype versions and the pilot versions of the application
- The time and manpower required to train apprentices
- The time needed to move the prototype version to a pilot environment
- The time required to distribute the pilot version to the final environment(s)
- The resources needed to provide user support (manuals, training, consulting)
- The time and manpower required to provide ongoing maintenance for the application.

Although manpower costs are easily determined on an hourly, weekly, or monthly basis, the number of required prototype (and possibly pilot) versions of the application can significantly affect the time required and hence the overall project costs. The prototype version count therefore needs to be estimated very carefully, as does the testing and validating time and the time to move the prototype to pilot stage.

Note that both direct and derivative costs must be considered. Thus, for example, the direct costs of the hardware and software facilities needed for both development and delivery can readily be calculated. The derived costs are much more difficult to estimate, however. The capabilities of the development hardware and software will affect the time (and hence the labor cost) required for the development effort. Similarly, reducing development costs can increase delivery costs, and vice versa.

Unfortunately, the technical approach and the cost of the application are not independent. Thus, after estimating the costs based on the technical approach, the knowledge crafters may want to revise the technical approach, which will alter the costs. This interrelationship is one of the reasons that the feasibility study is considered to be an iterative process, as shown in Figure 5-1.

After all the cost items have been carefully estimated and totaled, they can be compared with the expected benefits. If the benefits outweigh the costs, the application would appear to be feasible. However, a reasonable return on investment must occur in a relatively short time (within a year) to justify the expense of building the application. If the spread between the benefits and the cost is small, for example, the money may be better invested elsewhere. Additionally, since these figures are only estimates with a chance of error, the benefit-cost ratio should probably be two or larger (depending also on the actual monetary values involved).

Examining the Risks

Up to this point, the discussion has focused on technical feasibility and on the relative benefits and costs of producing the application. A third element, however, must also be considered in determining the economic feasibility of an application, namely, the risk factors associated with developing it. Risks are primarily technical (e.g., the risk that a certain means for representing the knowledge will prove inadequate for the application) or economic (e.g., the risk that the costs will exceed those forecast or that the benefits will fall short of those forecast). Other risks include the risk that the expert will become unavailable, the risk that management will lose interest in the application, or the risk that the application will not satisfy the user's needs.

An important part of the feasibility study is therefore an evaluation of the severity of the various risks and the likelihood that the undesirable events might actually occur. This analysis can be very difficult when several risk factors are present. If the risks cannot be directly combined, the knowledge crafter may have to categorize each risk as low, medium, or high and take extra precautions (assuming the project proceeds) in each area where a medium or high risk assessment was made.

Pioneering Considerations

Occasionally, in its benefit-cost analysis, an organization needs to consider whether it should be the first or the second to employ a particular type of knowledge-based application. If it is the first, obviously it will be responsible for developing the application on its own ("blazing the trail" so to speak); if it is second, lessons can be learned from the trailblazer, and the application may even become available from a third party at some savings.

In deciding whether to be a pioneer, an organization must first determine whether the application could be used by other organizations and hence whether a third party would likely offer such an application in the near future. Many times, an application is peculiar to one organization. Other times, a third party would not be interested in producing such an application, perhaps because of its high cost.

If a third party can reasonably be expected to produce a similar application in the near future, defining the payout period for the application is the best way to evaluate the pros and cons of waiting. If the payout period is short (e.g., a year), then proceeding with the application is probably advantageous. A third party would not likely have the application ready during the payout period because of the extra time required to produce a broader, more general-purpose application for a broader market. In cases where the payout period is much longer, it may indeed be better to wait and be second.

Cultural Issues

Some knowledge-based applications have no human interface; they accept input from one program (or data base) and provide output to another program (or data base). Thus, issues related to the human interface are really a part of the evaluation of other programs. Many knowledge-based applications, however, do interact with the user. Therefore, in conducting the feasibility study, the knowledge crafters must consider the impact of the prospective application on the user community. That impact will be influenced by the corporate culture and the user's environment.

The Corporate Culture

The corporate culture in which the application will operate is influenced by many factors, including:

- National culture
- Type of business or industry
- Management style or philosophy.

Consider an application designed to assist a senior manager. Such an application might be readily accepted in the United States but would encounter resistance in Japan, since in the Japanese culture the use of a keyboard by a senior manager would be considered degrading.

Similarly, users in an organization that has a history of adopting advanced technology may be more willing to accept a knowledge-based application than users in an organization that requires little use of technology. Users in an organization in the computer industry may be more willing to accept advice from a computer than users in a different industry. Users in an organization making heavy use of computer terminals will have both keyboard skills and familiarity with computers and thus may be less intimidated by the knowledge-based application than would other users.

The User Environment

The users' wants and needs must determine the nature of the application interface. Typically, the training and experience of the users and the expert are significantly different. Therefore, if the users are going to obtain any benefit from an application, they must be able to understand the terms being used. For instance, the users of a knowledge-based legal advisory application are likely to be persons from all walks of life, while the expert might be a highly trained attorney. This application should not bandy legal terms such as *habeas corpus* and *quid pro quo,* which have no meaning to the typical layperson using the application.

Additionally, the abilities of the users must be considered. The user-application interface is vital, and its design includes such issues as how the users interact with the application (is the user keyboard-literate?), whether the users are handicapped by the environment in which they are to use the application (workers in a factory, for instance, may have to wear gloves), and whether the cultural understanding of the user matches the representation of the knowledge as well as the purpose of the application.

Another consideration is the amount of user training that will be necessary for the completed application, the number of likely users, and their expected frequency of use. The fewer the users and the more frequent their use of the application, the wider the range of abilities the application can accommodate, and the greater economic feasibility of providing special training for the application. Typical of such (nonknowledge-based) applications today is an airlines reservation system. However, if a very large number of people will use the application infrequently, the cost of providing specialized training will be prohibitively high. With infrequent use, the user easily forgets how to use the application. Automatic teller machines (ATMs) are typical of this type of user interface.

Finally, the knowledge crafters must consider the impact of the application on the working environment. Consider the situation, for example, where employees work together in teams to solve problems. Such an environment provides a considerable opportunity for socialization. A knowledge-based application that enabled each person to solve problems individually without assistance might generate considerable hostility. Even though the quality of the solutions developed by each user might be improved, the greater isolation and lack of socializing would be seen as a severe handicap.

Constraints

Every project operates under a set of constraints, be it related to budgets, personnel, time, or facilities. The knowledge crafters must obviously factor these constraints into their investigation of application feasibility. Usually such constraints only cause minor perturbations in a design approach and hence in the feasibility assessment.

Sometimes, however, these constraints can become severe, as illustrated by the following:

- The application must be developed on a personal computer in Basic.
- Only one person is available to work on the application, half time.
- The application must be delivered on each secretary's word processor.
- The developers are expected to be on call to fix bugs in other programs.
- Personnel in Department X, who will be users of the application, must not know about the project.
- The application must be completed by year-end (which happens to be two months away).
- The application must not cost more than $10,000.

Such restrictions indicate both an organization's (lack of) commitment to the application and the hostile environment in which the application would be developed. Although only extreme constraints (such as those illustrated above) would render a project totally infeasible, various constraints, stated and unstated, often affect the time, cost, and risk of a project. Some obvious examples are constraints on the development and/or delivery environments in terms of hardware or software tools and restrictions on the availability of personnel. Some less obvious examples are the nature of the development facilities, the amount of travel required by all concerned, and pressures in the workplace. Some constraints may be negotiable (e.g., the availability of personnel or facilities), but others may not be (e.g., delivery system requirements).

Pulling It All Together

So far, this chapter has discussed the many issues that need to be examined in a feasibility study, as well as the iterative process for determining the requirements, developing a rough design, and then evaluating the ability of that design approach to satisfy the requirements cost-effectively. Toward the end of the study, the knowledge crafters need to integrate all the findings, so that a definitive conclusion on the application's feasibility can be reached.

The investigation can be summarized into five categories: requirements, design, costs, benefits, and risks. Combining them graphically, as shown in Figure 5-3, leads to the conclusion that, for the identified requirements, a preliminary design can be defined, which has certain cost estimates and related benefit estimates that may or may not make the development of the application attractive.

Quite often a feasibility study ends nicely with a clear determination of the feasibility of the application, but some studies do not conclude so neatly. First, an absolute requirement may not be met (e.g., there is no expertise), and the application cannot be built. In such cases, the feasibil-

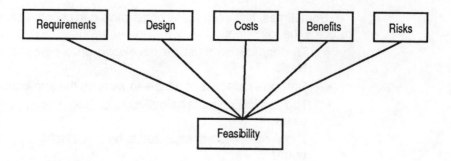

Figure 5-3   Deriving the Feasibility

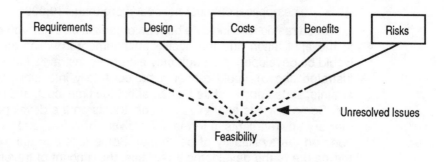

Figure 5-4   A Partial Derivation of the Application's Feasibility

ity study simply terminates with the understanding that the application is just not feasible. Second, and more likely, is the case depicted in Figure 5-4, where existing snags prohibit all factors from being tied together.

When this happens, the knowledge crafters are faced with three alternatives:

1.   Determine whether trade-offs might be possible (e.g., relax some restrictions, narrow the design to a subset problem) so that a worthwhile application can be developed

2.   If several alternatives exist, each one leading to a feasible application, continue with the development effort, selecting the winner when more is known

3.   Abandon the effort.

References

1)   Fried, L., *Commercial Use of Expert Systems: A Survey of U.S. Corporations,* Report # BIP 86-1068, SRI International, Menlo Park, Calif., 1986.

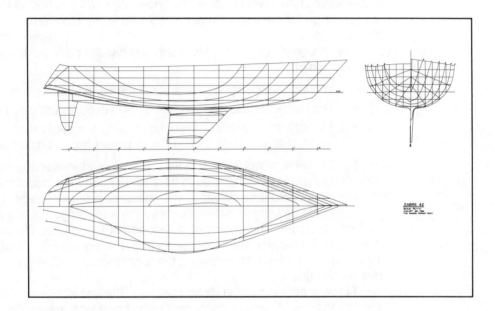

Crafting a System Design

The hull lines shown here form the overall envelope of the hull, within which the keel, rudder, ballast, auxiliary propulsion, cabin, exterior deck, mast, and sailplan must fit. Although these lines appear simple in the drawing, they are the result of integrating a great many factors into the yacht's overall design. Similarly, the knowledge-based application forms an envelope, within which the inference engine, knowledge structures, control structures, man-machine interfaces, and external interfaces must fit. Although a completed application may appear quite straightforward and logical, it is the result of integrating a great many factors into the design. Chapter 6 discusses the factors that must be considered and the process of developing a single, consistent design.

As discussed in Chapters 4 and 5, once the requirements have been specified for an application, work can begin on developing a specific design for it. The design may be constructed at a high level for a feasibility study or in much greater detail in preparation for prototype development. Regardless of the level of detail, the knowledge crafter's task is to formulate a design for the application that will satisfy the requirements as best as possible.

The design process consists of several parallel activities leading to a specification of:

- The knowledge structures and reasoning mechanisms to be used
- The hardware and software tools to be used for development
- The delivery vehicle to be used to bring the application to those who will actually use it once development has been completed.

Note that these activities cannot be conducted independently, even though they are to be conducted in parallel. For example, decisions about the knowledge structure influence the choice of a development tool. The selection of a delivery vehicle influences the knowledge representations that can be used. The choice of development tool affects the available options for knowledge representations and delivery vehicles, and so on. Thus, good communication among the team members during the design process is critical.

At the conclusion of the design process, the knowledge crafters must confirm that the design is consistent with the design assumptions originally developed during the feasibility study. Should the design contradict any of those assumptions, the knowledge crafters may need to repeat part of the feasibility study to ensure that these changes have not affected the feasibility of the application.

Crafting the Design

As a practical matter, a knowledge crafter cannot proceed serially through the development of a design without backtracking or iteration. Many of the factors influencing the design need to be considered together in parallel—a difficult task for most people. The best approximation to such a parallel process is to cycle through the design steps a number of times. We refer to this iterative process as *crafting a system design;* it is a vital step occurring early in the overall process of developing a successful knowledge-based application.

Much has been written about the *rapid prototyping* capabilities provided by many of the knowledge-based system development tools available on the market today. Many developers believe that this new technology has finally freed them from having to follow some of the traditional software development practices, practices that are often perceived to constrain individual programmer freedoms. Thus, they dispense with many elements of a top-down design and begin from the bottom up by developing a very rough prototype, experimenting with it, showing it to the users, finding weaknesses in the design, and then iterating through another prototype development phase.

Need for Traditional Design

Certainly this approach to developing an application system is much more feasible today using the new knowledge-based technologies than was previously possible using traditional languages such as COBOL and FORTRAN. Nevertheless, the ability to do rapid prototyping should not be confused with the desirability of relying on this technique as a design tool. Even if the knowledge crafter intends to take a rapid-prototyping approach to the first implementation of an application, the team can save time and effort by doing some top-down designing first, before a line of code or a single rule is written.

Despite the care taken in preparing the initial design, the design will likely change over the course of the implementation. The expectation of design change, however, is not an argument for skipping the design step; it is only an argument for not overemphasizing the first design. The knowledge crafters should not attempt to craft the "perfect" design initially. On the other hand, the better the initial design, the better the initial prototype and hence the fewer changes that will be required. Thus, the duration of the overall development process can be reduced.

Avoid Overdesign

Although having a design against which to implement an application is critical, the knowledge crafter must not forget that a design is a two-edged sword. Every design decision eliminates an additional element of flexibility. Each specification eliminates all alternatives to the specified element. Therefore, decisions about some aspects of the design should be deferred.

Deferring a decision for the sake of flexibility does not, however, give the knowledge crafter license to ignore the area in question. The design must set forth what has been decided about the area and what alternatives remain available. In particular, the following information should be set forth:

- **Requirements**—all known requirements that pertain to the affected area
- **Constraints**—any constraints that bear on the area or any problems that have arisen to affect the area
- **Feasible alternatives**—the options that remain open, that have not been foreclosed by other decisions or considerations. (Presumably, the postponed decision will select one of these alternatives.)
- **Eliminated alternatives**—options that once appeared feasible but that have since then been eliminated. The reasons for elimination should be set forth; not only may they be helpful in narrowing the remaining choices at a later date, but they may also prevent needless reexamination of old, previously resolved issues.

The Representation of Knowledge

The first major area involved in the design process concerns the selection of the various forms of knowledge representation to be used, the choice of the inferencing mechanisms to be applied to those representations, and the assignment of various categories of knowledge to those representations. Part III describes several techniques for representing knowledge in a knowledge-based application, together with certain pitfalls associated with each technique and an indication of application areas in which that technique might be useful for representing particular kinds of information.

Knowledge Structures

Knowledge can be represented and structured in a knowledge-based reasoning system in a variety of ways. The form of representation can significantly affect both the efficiency with which knowledge can be stored and updated as well as the efficiency with which the necessary inferencing can take place using knowledge in that form of representation.

Chapters 13 through 17 describe five types of knowledge representations. Most application systems can best be served by multiple representations, with different portions of the knowledge base being represented in different ways.

Inferencing Mechanisms

Just as knowledge can be structured and represented in a variety of ways, so an application can reason about that knowledge in many ways. The inferencing mechanism does not necessarily parallel the representational form. For example, both procedural knowledge sources (e.g., blackboard) and nonprocedural sources (e.g., rules) can reason about frame-based knowledge. The inferencing mechanism must suit the type of data analysis that is to be performed.

As with the representational form, many application systems are best served by multiple reasoning mechanisms, with different mechanisms being employed at different stages in the analysis to process different portions of the knowledge base.

Resolving Representation Issues

Because the feasibility study is usually too brief to determine the exact techniques required at various points in the application, this issue must be resolved during the design phase. Some determinations can be made rather quickly, such as whether the application will require model-based, blackboard, or multiple-environment representations. Each of these techniques addresses a distinctly different form of knowledge-based reasoning that the knowledge crafters should readily recognize.

If, during the feasibility study, the knowledge-crafting team finds that any one or more of these techniques might be necessary to handle the application, they should conduct a considerably more detailed study to ensure that the initial determination was valid. This confirmation, in turn, will tend to solidify requirements for both the delivery and the development facilities, the latter of which might conceivably affect user requirements.

Limitations on Choice

Under certain conditions the desired application might not be feasible with today's technology and tools. For instance, a model-based reasoning system might not be compatible with the demands of an untrained user group, or a multiple-environment system might not fit in a small delivery environment. The size and decomposability of the knowledge base can also preclude use of certain forms of knowledge representation. For example, if the knowledge base is very large and cannot be segmented, rule-based reasoning may not be possible.

At present, the adequacy of delivery environments for knowledge-based application development tools is of great concern to many parties. The various organizations involved in producing, marketing, or using knowledge-based development tools are trying to develop solutions to the delivery problem. The current situation of a rather limited number of delivery options will improve, but the problem of moving a tool to an *arbitrary* delivery environment can be expected to continue for some time. Moreover, this problem is likely to remain acute for exotic delivery environments, such as the processor in a camera or in specialized shop-floor computing equipment.

Selecting Appropriate Knowledge Representations

Previous subsections have highlighted the need to break the problem into pieces and to select appropriate knowledge representations and inferencing mechanisms for each piece. But what representation(s) should be used for each part? The general issue is addressed at considerable length in Part III. This section only provides some guidelines about appropriate use of various representations for the knowledge crafter seeking to construct an application design.

The first step is to decompose the problem into relatively self-contained pieces. Because this task can be difficult, the knowledge crafter may wish to experiment with different decompositions to find one that does a fairly good job of minimizing connections between sections but maximizes the homogeneity of the knowledge in each section.

A cue can be taken from the character of the problem. What are the things that will be reasoned about? What are the different types of knowledge to be applied? What are the control functions to be applied during the reasoning process? What are the different levels of abstraction? These and similar problem-oriented cues can be used to develop an appropriate decomposition.

The next step is to examine the characteristics of the knowledge contained in each decomposed piece. For the purpose of discussion, these characteristics can be summarized in four categories:

1. Knowledge about the domain
2. Knowledge about control of the reasoning process
3. Knowledge about the application interface
4. Knowledge about the condition of the knowledge.

Knowledge about the Domain

Some domain knowledge can be clustered about "objects" or "items." Such knowledge relates to the characteristics, properties, or behaviors of these objects. This knowledge can often be divided or stratified by conceptual levels of detail or abstraction. A frame-based representation with inheritance can appropriately be used in many of these situations. Such a representation is particularly helpful when behavioral knowledge is also to be represented because rule-based or procedural-based information can be reflected within the frame structure.

In other cases, domain knowledge cannot be clustered into groups. Each piece of knowledge is in some sense unrelated to any other piece. In such instances, n-tuples or unordered lists may be used for representing the knowledge.

Knowledge about existing relationships (i.e., a relationship that is essentially a property of an object) can often be encoded within a basic frame structure. However, knowledge about dynamically changing relationships is often best represented implicitly in rules or in a procedure rather than explicitly in a frame. Depending on how the knowledge will be used (see the following subsection on control), rules or procedures may be stored in slots in a frame, or they may be represented as knowledge sources in a blackboard system.

If the domain knowledge is truly procedural, it should not be forced into a nonprocedural representation. Before resorting to conventional programming for a portion of the knowledge, however, the knowledge crafter should ascertain that the knowledge is indeed truly procedural and that it does not just appear to be procedural because that is the form in which it had been previously represented. It may turn out, for example, that the procedural part of the knowledge is actually control knowledge, while the remainder of the knowledge is nonprocedural domain knowledge.

Knowledge about Control

Most knowledge-based applications maintain control over the reasoning or problem-solution process. The application accepts basic data from the user and then requests additional data from the user or from a data base as needed. At the completion of the analysis, a recommended solution is output. Although the user may have influenced the solution process by means of the data initially provided, the course of the analysis was controlled throughout by the application. Accordingly, the knowledge-crafting team should consider how knowledge about control of the application should be structured and represented.

For certain types of problems a single type of control is applied to the entire solution process. In selection, categorization, or diagnostic types of applications, for example, backward chaining may be the only mechanism needed. Similarly, if the application is oriented toward the determination of the implications of new data items as they are either derived or input, then a basic forward chaining reasoning mechanism may suffice.

In other cases a straightforward procedural approach may be all that is needed. Thus, for example, if the solution process involves deriving as much information as possible about the current situation from the given data and then trying to determine the state of the situation, a procedure initiating a forward reasoning pass followed by a backward reasoning pass would probably be the only control mechanism required for the reasoning process.

If the solution process can be viewed as a "generate and test" procedure, additional options are available. If the possible solutions to be tested can be enumerated, then a multiple-environment representation could very appropriately be used. On the other hand, if the solution to be tested has to be "designed" from an infinity of possibilities, then the design team may need to test each alternative before proceeding to the next. In this case, a multiple-environment representation would not be very effective.

A blackboard representation can be very effective in those situations where the reasoning process is very complex and is to be controlled in a dynamic manner depending on partial results.

The "style" of the solution process can also influence the form of representation to be used. For example, if a number of partial solutions are to be available for use by the inferencing mechanism during the solution process, a multiple-environment representation would be helpful. On the other hand, if the problem is to be solved and then resolved using different levels of abstraction, a blackboard approach may be more productive. Knowledge sources on the blackboard could be either rule-based or procedural.

If the solution process relies on predictions about the consequences of events (e.g., temperature will increase at sensors 5 and 12 if valve 3 fails in the closed position), then a model-based representation may be appropriate. The design team will find it relatively easy to test hypothetical situations and determine expected behaviors when working with knowledge represented in this form.

In some cases, the solution process can be viewed as a cooperative one. No individual knowledge source can solve the entire problem, but each can contribute to the solution. In addition, knowledge sources indicate to each other what information would be most helpful to permit them to contribute further. In essence, then, the knowledge sources contribute to the development of goals to guide the solution process. This type of cooperative solution methodology also fits into a blackboard system very nicely.

An extreme example of the cooperative approach is one involving the expert in the solution process. In such situations the knowledge crafters do not have sufficient knowledge about the problem area to construct an application that can solve a problem independently. The expert must work in tandem with the knowledge-based application, with the latter aiding the expert in conceptualizing and understanding the problem. Accordingly, the expert maintains control of the reasoning process; the knowledge-based application serves as an intelligent assistant rather than an advisor, responding to the requests of the expert, developing the implications of solution approaches that the expert might like to pursue, and implementing actions that the expert might like to take.

Finally, regardless of the locus of control, the user may need to exercise certain procedural controls during an analysis. For example, the effect of a data input may need to be reversed or a checkpoint may need to be taken.

Thus, in summary, the knowledge crafters must carefully consider the control structure and the implications of that structure on knowledge representation. No longer can they assume that a one-pass, consultation type of control will suffice.

Knowledge about the Application Interface

Knowledge crafters must also consider the application's interfaces in selecting the forms of knowledge representation. Most often, such a consideration focuses on the man-machine interface. The following issues can influence the choice of representation:

- **Explanation**—If the user is to be able to request explanations of terms and concepts from the application during execution, can that knowledge be represented and retrieved from the knowledge base using the planned representations?

- **Justification**—If the user is to be able to request justifications for conclusions and recommendations, can that information be derived from the knowledge base using the planned representations?

- **Checkpoint and restart**—Checkpointing an analysis is often desirable, either to break up a long session or to save a particular state that can be reinvoked if errors are made or if a different solution approach is to be tested. Can the planned representations support checkpointing and a restart from a previously taken checkpoint?

- **Knowledge sharing**—If a number of different analyses are to be performed on the same case or state, can that knowledge be shared using the planned representations?

- **Security**—It is often desirable to preclude user access to certain parts of the knowlege base. Will the planned representations support access limitations on part of the knowledge? Or is the entire structure either accessible or nonaccessible?

The man-machine interface is not the only interface that needs to be considered, however. Increasingly, applications must interface with other computer systems. Thus, for example, if data are to be abstracted from a data base on another computer system, will the selected knowledge representation facilitate the identification of the data needed, the subsequent conversion of those data to the appropriate representational form, and the placement of such data in the knowledge base?

Knowledge about the Condition of the Knowledge

The condition of the knowledge can often guide the selection of knowledge representations. For example, if the knowledge crafters have no knowledge about an appropriate solution strategy, then they have no knowledge about how to search for the best solution. They must thus "try everything"; a multiple-environment representation might assist in reducing the number of possible alternatives to be explored.

In some cases the solution process is ill defined and cannot be precisely specified. Part of the application development process may involve experimentation with some of the knowledge about the solution process. A blackboard approach can be very helpful when the control strategy is not well established. In such a situation a rule-based representation has advantages over a procedural one. Procedures need to be almost completely specified to be effective, while rule-sets can often be set up as skeletons, permitting test runs to be made and development to continue until such time as the appropriate relationships between parts of the application have been established.

Similarly, if some of the domain knowledge is ill defined, part of the application development process may involve experimentation with different sets of knowledge. Again, a blackboard approach may be helpful, since knowledge sources can easily be removed and replaced. (Of course, the blackboard requirements, such as independence of knowledge sources, must still be met.)

Another factor in selecting the representational form involves the degree to which behavior is understood. If some portion of the application's behavior is fully understood, that behavior can be captured fairly specifically, for example, as a model, a procedure, or a table. On the other hand, if the behavior is not fully understood, then the knowledge crafters must resort to heuristics. In such a situation, a rule-based representation might be more appropriate than a model-based one.

The expected condition of the data to be provided for a specific problem is also a consideration. If many data items are expected to be missing, a rule-based representation may be most appropriate. The condition portions of the rules ensure that what can be applied will be applied and that the rest will be ignored. That is, the rules can operate on whatever is available. It is generally much more difficult to organize procedural knowledge so that it can still be applied in the face of unspecified amounts of missing data.

Selecting Development Tools

The second of the three general areas to be addressed by the application design concerns the tools and facilities that the knowledge crafters use in building the application. The selection of appropriate development tools and facilities, hardware and software, derives from the application requirements, but these requirements can often point toward conflicting selections.

For example, the application requirements provide the basis for the system design. Thus, the design might call for the use of a blackboard system. On the other hand, those same application requirements might also imply the use of certain types of facilities, such as those currently available to or already in use within the organization. Thus, the requirements might also call for the use of IBM mainframe hardware and terminals. Existing facilities such as an IBM mainframe may not, however, have such capabilities as a blackboard system. As a consequence, the requirements, and perhaps the design itself, might need to be modified. The need for such changes reinforces the importance of an iterative development approach.

The existence of such conflicts implies that some difficult trade-offs must be made. The use of existing facilities may unduly restrict the features or capabilities that can be provided in the application system or may make application development a more lengthy, resource-consuming process. Yet, providing all the desired features and capabilities may prove sufficiently expensive to nullify the expected benefits to be derived from the system. The priorities established when the requirements were developed will be particularly helpful in balancing such opposing considerations and in reaching an appropriate compromise.

Hardware

The hardware facilities that can support a knowledge-based development effort can, for system development purposes, be divided into three major classes:

1. Mainframes
2. Workstations
3. Microprocessors.

Mainframes

If the organization already has a central mainframe installed with ample capacity, there may be significant out-of-pocket cost advantages to using that hardware to support the development process. However, this advantage must be counterbalanced with the fact that LISP-based software tends to run inefficiently on mainframes and to interfere with the efficiency with which other work can be processed on the mainframe at the same time. Thus, a mainframe solution is relatively more attractive when non-LISP software tools will be used. The range of knowledge-based development tools available on mainframes today is also somewhat restricted.

Another weakness of mainframe development environments is the present dearth of high-resolution graphics support for system development or deployment. Thus, a mainframe solution would look more attractive when a character-based dialog with the developer or end-user is sufficient and a windowing environment with icons and images is not needed.

On the other hand, a very significant advantage of a mainframe approach lies in accessing data bases. Many applications require access to organizational data bases, which are commonly located on central main-frame-based systems. Although computers containing these data bases frequently permit remote access, making the connection from a program running on the same computer system is frequently easier.

Workstations

Workstations currently provide the greatest capability for the developer, but they also entail significant capital investment. The workstation market can be divided into two subgroups: those based on LISP machines and those constructed from conventional processors.

1. LISP machines provide the best development environments for LISP-based software, but they are special-purpose systems. They are much more difficult to connect to the conventional systems that may form a part of the overall knowledge-based system. Major LISP-based workstation vendors are Symbolics, Texas Instruments, and Xerox.

2. Workstations built on conventional processors tend to interface more easily to conventional systems and to be more powerful for non-LISP-based application systems. Such workstations in many cases do offer a LISP language capability, but the development environment using LISP is not as capable or comprehensive on these workstations, and the memory requirements to run a LISP-based application can be significant. On the other hand, the LISP environments offered on many of these systems are being improved, and many more development tools are being offered in non-LISP versions. Major engineering workstation vendors offering systems suitable for knowledge-based system development include Apollo, Digital Equipment Corporation (DEC), Hewlett-Packard (HP), Sun Microsystems, and Tektronix.

Microprocessors

Microprocessor systems offer the least capital-intensive way to develop a knowledge-based system. Given the existing state of the art, however, most development tools require large memories and a fair amount of processor horsepower. Thus, systems developed on microprocessor systems today tend to be restricted in terms of the software they can use, the size of the system that can be developed, or the capabilities that can be utilized in the system. Most microprocessor-based application developments have used either IBM PC or IBM PC-AT (or compatible) computers.

On the other hand, the power and memory available on microprocessor systems are increasing rapidly, and prices are falling. Consequently, capability restrictions should soon be relaxed. The future should see these systems pushing into the lower part of today's workstation market. The blurring of the distinction between workstations and microprocessors should be hastened as systems built around the Intel 80386 microprocessor chip become more widely available.

Software

A variety of software is now available to assist the developer in the crafting of a knowledge-based system. Software development tools can be divided into four categories:

1.   Large-scale tools
2.   Small-scale tools
3.   Specialized tools
4.   General-purpose tools.

Large-Scale Tools

Large-scale tools offer a broad range of capabilities, but they can be fairly expensive, often costing tens of thousands of dollars. On the other hand, these tools provide quite comprehensive development environments for knowledge-based systems. They generally offer a range of forms of knowledge representation and several reasoning mechanisms. Many offer truth maintenance systems. All offer some type of general-purpose programming language as an underlying default to enable the user to provide specific functions, control, or capabilities not included in the basic package. ART™ from the Inference Corporation, Epitool™ from Epitec AB, KEE™ from IntelliCorp, and Knowledge Craft™ from the Carnegie Group, Inc. are representative products in this category.

Small-Scale Tools

Like the large-scale tools, small-scale tools provide a high-level "language" for knowledge-based application development. Their capabilities are restricted, however; the types of knowledge representation, knowledge-base size, or reasoning afforded are more limited than their larger cousins. Such tools are less costly to acquire and can be executed on computer systems having less processor power and/or smaller memory sizes. In fact, these tools are frequently designed to run on microprocessor-based systems. They may or may not offer an underlying general-purpose programming capability; one of the ways that these tools gain their ability to operate with lower resource requirements is to restrict the users' flexibility and capability. M.1™ from Teknowledge and EXSYS™ from EXSYS are representative products in this category.

Specialized Tools

Specialized tools are organized so as to assist the user in building a particular type of system. Knowledge representation is predetermined, as is the reasoning mechanism. Most of these systems are of the induction type, wherein the developer provides a series of examples. The tool then uses those examples to develop a rule-set by induction and produces a finished system. Expert-Ease™ from Jeffrey Perrone & Associates and RuleMaster™ from Radian Systems are representative products in this category.

Other types of tools are specialized for particular types of applications and offer only a single type of reasoning capability. OPS5 and its various derivatives (forward chaining), Prolog (backward chaining), and S.1™ from Teknowledge (backward chaining) are representative of this type of product. Specialized tools can be very effective development aids—but only if the particular system structure offered is appropriate for the problem at hand. All too often, a specialized tool is selected because of its availability, but its unsuitability for the particular problem leads to later development problems and subsequent disappointment with functional capabilities.

Several organizations are currently working on specialized versions of broadly capable development tools. Thus, for example, a tool might be developed to assist knowledge crafters in constructing chemical analysis or hardware diagnostic application systems.

General-Purpose Tools

General-purpose tools are those that might underlie or be used to construct a high-level tool. Despite all the excitement surrounding knowledge-based systems, such systems are nothing more than computer programs operating on a set of data bases. As such, *any* computer programming tool (e.g., assembly language) could *in principle* be used to develop knowledge-based applications, although as a practical matter, developer resource constraints dictate that some type of higher level language capability be used. For some types of systems, particularly real-time and military systems, an intermediate language can satisfy certain constraints on the system's operational environment. In such cases, knowledge crafters often resort to one of the tools that underlie the more general knowledge-based system development tools described above. Thus, systems have been developed in such languages as Pascal, LISP, and Prolog. In some cases these developments have been facilitated with object-oriented programming tools such as Flavors (from a number of vendors) or Loops™ (from Xerox).

Delivery Considerations

The third of the three general areas to be addressed concerns the mechanism by which the application will be delivered or made available to the user. The hardware and software to be used for this purpose is commonly called the delivery system.

The computer system used for developing a prototype knowledge-based system and for supporting experimentation with that prototype need not be the same as (and will likely be different from) the system that is used for delivering the application to the user (who will employ it in an operational context). The application requirements, originally developed for the feasibility study and subsequently refined, can be divided into two categories, depending on whether they relate to the development process or to the operational use of the application.

The development system is oriented toward the needs of the developer. Special, sophisticated software facilities are often desired, which may in turn require considerable hardware power. Thus, the hardware and software solutions to support the developer are often quite capable and complex but also relatively expensive.

On the other hand, the requirements for the system used to deliver service to the end-user in an operational environment will likely be considerably different. The knowledge-based application may be used by many individuals (in one or more locations) or may be used in several geographically distributed locations. In either case, a number of terminals or workstations will be required, making the cost of each unit a significant consideration. At the same time, the user does not have the expertise (nor in many cases the interest) to work with system internals. Hence, the features and capabilities that must be provided by the delivery system are usually not as substantial as those of the development system.

Approaches

A variety of delivery vehicles can be envisioned, the choice depending on the requirements of the application and the organizational environment in which the system will be used. The following four approaches represent major categories of delivery vehicles that developers might consider when crafting an application design:

1. Terminal-based delivery systems
2. Workstation-based delivery systems
3. Microprocessor-based delivery systems
4. Combination approaches.

Terminal-Based Delivery Systems

A terminal-based approach uses terminals connected to a larger host computer, possibly a mainframe, as the interface to the end-users. Thus, all processing for the knowledge-based system takes place remotely from the user on a shared system.

Advantages

This approach has several advantages:

- Terminals can be provided in quantity at relatively low cost.
- Terminals are particularly advantageous if the ones already on users' desks can be used to access the application.
- Terminals are advantageous if they can be connected to the host system through the regular communication network.
- A single copy of the application can be used to support all the users, minimizing the problems that can occur when multiple copies exist (e.g., a user loads an obsolete version on a local workstation).

- If the host computer is (or is connected to) the organization's central computing facility, access to data in organizational data bases may be simplified considerably.

Disadvantages

On the other hand, this approach has several disadvantages:

- Generally, the bandwidth between terminal and host is such that many types of graphic interfaces cannot be provided, restricting the delivery system to a text-type interface.
- Other computing activities taking place on the host may interfere with the application's responsiveness as perceived by the user.
- Knowledge-based processing systems tend to be large users of memory space and processor cycles, which would cause such a system to disturb the processing of other work on (or the serving of other users connected to) the host.
- The relative cost-effectiveness of this approach is generally poor for applications involving few users or for mainframes without sufficient excess capacity available.

Workstation-Based Delivery Systems

Workstation-based delivery systems are similar to workstation-based development systems in that they dedicate a processor with considerable power and memory to the service of the user. However, both the hardware and software aspects of this approach are considerably different for delivery purposes.

The workstation hardware is generally a smaller, less powerful, but considerably cheaper version of the development system. For example, less disk storage and main memory are generally required. On the other hand, connections to external data bases or other data input sources may be necessary.

The development tool used to construct the application may come in two versions, one for development and one for delivery. If the application is delivered in object form, then the delivery version need not even have a compiler.

Similarly, many features of the software that support debugging and browsing of internal data structures can be omitted from the delivery version. Not only does this reduce the capacity requirements placed on the delivery hardware, but in many cases software vendors offer reduced-capability delivery versions of their development tools at a significantly lower cost.

Advantages

The workstation delivery approach offers both advantages and disadvantages that the application designer will have to weigh in reaching a recommendation.

Among the potential advantages are:

- Workstations can operate independently of a host, eliminating interference between knowledge-based system processing and other host-based computing activities.
- Workstations can provide more responsive service to the user.
- The best graphics facilities are generally offered by workstations.
- Converting a development version of the application to execute in a delivery environment requires only minimal effort, a particularly important consideration when the application is likely to have frequent updates or modifications.

Disadvantages

Among the potential disadvantages are:

- Some workstations are difficult to connect to external data bases.
- This approach can be costly if the hardware/software needs of the application cannot be sufficiently reduced from the development version.
- This approach can also be costly if there are many users of the application or even many sites at which users are located.
- Users may find it awkward to switch between two separate systems at their desks (e.g., a personal computer and the workstation), to say nothing of the desk space that would have to be given up to accommodate two displays.
- Many workstations operate independently, making application version control more difficult than a centralized approach because of the larger number of copies in existence and the role of each user in maintaining version currency.

Microprocessor-Based Delivery Systems

This approach uses a microprocessor-based hardware system (e.g., a personal computer) to deliver the application. An application developed on a microprocessor system can usually be converted to a delivery version with little difficulty. However, the application may still need to be modified to fit on systems having smaller memories than the development system. Converting an application from a workstation-based development system is likely to be much more difficult, although the products of some development tool vendors may facilitate this process.

Advantages

Reliance on microprocessor-based systems for delivery offers a number of advantages for deployment of the application:

The microprocessor can operate independently of a host, eliminating interference between knowledge-based system processing and other host-based computing activities.

- Microprocessors can provide more responsive service to the user than can systems relying on a host connection.
- Microprocessors provide a relatively inexpensive delivery vehicle, particularly in comparison with workstation-based approaches. Even in situations where many application units are to be deployed, the cost of this approach may be minimal since most users may already be employing personal computers in the course of their existing duties.
- Currently, microprocessor-based systems tend to be easier to connect to external data bases or other data input sources than many workstations.
- Users would not need to switch back and forth between two separate systems at their desks (nor would space be required for two different displays); they might be able to use a single microprocessing system for their current work and for the knowledge-based application.

Disadvantages

Among the potential disadvantages are:

- The microprocessor may not be sufficiently powerful to support the types of graphics found on workstation-type delivery vehicles. It also may not offer a large, high-resolution display.
- This approach can be costly if the hardware/software needs of the application cannot be sufficiently reduced from the development version; larger memories or coprocessors would have to be added to each unit in the field.
- This approach can also be costly if many of the users (or even many of the sites at which users are located) are not already equipped with personal computers.
- Most microprocessor systems are operated independently, with each user bearing the responsibility to load the most recent version of the application. Consequently, version control is more difficult than for a centralized approach.

Combination Approaches

Various delivery vehicles can be constructed using a combination of the above three approaches. The following three combinations illustrate the possibilities:

1. Microprocessor-host
2. Cross-compilation
3. Application rewrite.

Combination Approaches: Microprocessor-Host

A microprocessor can be established as a powerful and smart terminal connected to a host processor. The host processor would contain the complete knowledge base and would perform all the reasoning or inferencing on that knowledge. A portion of the knowledge base would be stored redundantly in the microprocessor to enable it to respond rapidly to user requests. The microprocessor would also be responsible for providing the graphical interface.

This approach, then, aims to eliminate some of the terminal-host disadvantages (e.g., minimal graphical capabilities) and microprocessor disadvantages (e.g., inadequate capability to perform the necessary inferencing) while capitalizing on some of the advantages of each approach (e.g., access to host-based information and availability of compatible microprocessors in the users' workplaces). On the other hand, the application system will still need to be converted from a development version to a delivery version operating in the microprocessor-host mode.

Combination Approaches: Cross-Compilation

This approach simply uses two different hardware systems for development and delivery; however, the development system has the capability of cross-compiling a version of the application system that will execute in the delivery environment. This approach also means that the delivery system can be distributed as object (rather than source) code, reducing problems associated with a broad user population attempting to modify the application system.

A knowledge crafter using this approach could develop an application on a workstation and then deliver it either on a mainframe or on a microprocessor. With appropriate tools, the "conversion" from development system to delivery system should be minimal. However, the knowledge crafter pursuing this approach should proceed cautiously. Cross-compilation is frequently fraught with such problems as only a "core" set of features able to be cross-compiled or certain capabilities able to be ported only if modified manually. Thus, an early cross-compilation test should be made with a broad range of capabilities.

Combination Approaches: Application Rewrite

Like the cross-compilation approach, this approach permits the application developer to use two different systems for development and for delivery purposes. Basically, development would be conducted on a development system in traditional fashion. The design-develop-redesign-redevelop iteration would proceed until the developer had an operational software specification for the application. Work would then proceed to rewriting (or writing from scratch) a delivery system.

Because of the availability of very good specifications, the cost of producing the delivery system using a rewrite is much less than the initial system development costs. On the other hand, the preparation of the development system is still an expensive process, so the application rewrite, though cheaper in relative terms, could still be quite costly in absolute terms.

A major advantage of this approach is that the application can be delivered on a totally different type of hardware (using potentially different software tools) from the development system. The constraints and restrictions of tool-based approaches can be avoided. Any unique characteristics of the application can be used to reduce processing requirements.

The major disadvantage of the rewrite process, of course, is the time and labor required to produce the delivery version. As a consequence, the overall application development process is a more time- and resource-consuming one. Furthermore, such a rewrite, from development to delivery, is not just a one-time commitment. The application (if it is not gathering dust on a shelf somewhere) will be updated, modified, and extended. Those responsible for the maintenance of the application will need either to use the development version for development, debugging, and testing (and hence have to again apply all the changes to a different system) or to work directly with a delivery system that lacks development features and that will be much more difficult to maintain.

Environment

The preceding subsections have compared several delivery options, but a delivery option cannot be selected without the knowledge crafters considering the environment in which the system will operate. Such issues should be reflected in the application requirements. For the purposes of illustration, however, consider the following six delivery environments and the effect that each might have on the application design and the selection of a delivery system:

1. An environment in which a very small number of professionals share a single system

2. An environment in which a number of trained individuals use a number of copies of the system in an office setting

3. An environment in which a number of untrained individuals use a number of copies of the system in an office setting (e.g., an application for customers to use in a bank lobby)

4. An environment in which a number of trained individuals use a number of copies of the system in an industrial shop floor setting

5. An environment in which the application is embedded in a larger computer system complex and the "users" are other system elements

6. An environment in which the application is embedded in a product to be used by masses of people (e.g., a camera).

One Delivery System

In the case of a small number of professionals sharing a single system, the development environment itself is probably the best candidate for the delivery environment. Thus, moving from the development to the delivery environment should not require any effort. Even today, an organization can select a moderately capable development facility, such that its extra cost relative to a less expensive delivery facility would be less than the cost to move the application from the development environment to another environment for delivery.

Many Delivery Systems

In the case of a number of trained individuals (e.g., employees) using the application at the same time, a number of delivery systems will be required. The expense of moving the application from a development to a delivery environment is probably economically justifiable.

Untrained Users

In the case of a number of untrained individuals (e.g., customers) using the application at the same time, two costs are incurred: moving the application to another system, and making a very simple, easy-to-understand user interface for the wide range of capabilities and levels of computer sophistication typically found in a community of untrained individuals. The cost of this user interface can be significant and can approach or exceed the cost of building the rest of the application. Hence, the ability to provide it on the delivery system will be a dominant consideration in the selection of that system.

Environmental and Cultural Issues

In the case of the application being used on the factory floor, the dominant concern is to provide hardware and software that can survive the rather hostile environment of a shop floor. Here again, the user interface requires painstaking care to design and test, both with respect to environmental issues (the users may be wearing gloves) and also with respect to the language and understanding of shop-floor personnel. Although the users may be trained to use the system, they are not likely to be familiar with computer systems or possibly even with the language of the expertise contained in the application.

Interfacing as a Component in a Larger Application

In the case of an embedded application, the "user" is another computer program. Thus, the actual interface to and from the knowledge-based portion of the application is quite straightforward. However, the information transmitted between this portion of the system and other portions of the system must be exact; no human is there to fill in any details that might be implied or missing. Consequently, to develop an application for use in this type of delivery environment, the fully developed prototype must be moved to the delivery environment and then undergo rigorous system testing in the context of that environment. For large and complex systems, this testing will require very careful planning. These problems are in addition to the normal problems of placing a knowledge-based system on a mainframe.

Embedding the Application in a Device

In the last case, where the application is to be embedded in some sort of everyday equipment, the moving of the application to the delivery environment probably implies a total rewrite to the exacting demands of the target hardware—a situation made even more difficult because the delivery hardware often has extremely limited capabilities. Such a move with small applications is technically possible using today's technology, but the process of moving from the development environment to the delivery environment and of testing the application in that environment is likely to dwarf the other portions of the project in time, effort, and cost.

A Summary of Delivery Environment Issues

Each of the various environments cited here (or others similar to them) presents special problems in the development of a knowledge-based application. The demands of the delivery environment cannot be ignored in the feasibility study, in the overall design of the application, or in the prototyping effort.

Knowledge crafters often want to design a prototype of the application without regard for the problems that will be presented by the delivery environment. If they ignore delivery, the prototype version can at best be used to capture, represent, and test the knowledge for the application. In such situations moving the application to the delivery environment will frequently require a total redesign and rewriting of the application.

Interfaces

The preceding subsections have focused on the delivery mechanism (e.g., hardware and software), but a number of considerations relating to interfaces are also critical to the design of the delivery version, as well as to other aspects of the application's design, such as the form of knowledge representation or the development tool to be used. The four types of interfaces that must be considered are:

1. Man-machine interfaces
   - text and image interfaces
   - graphical interfaces
2. Data base interfaces
3. Real-time interfaces
4. System interfaces.

Man-Machine Interfaces

The man-machine interface is particularly important; it is a critical factor in determining the end-user's acceptance of and willingness to work with the application. Other areas of a knowledge-based system development project are more intellectually challenging and interesting, but they are unlikely to have as significant an impact on the user's acceptance of the completed system.

The man-machine interface must be designed especially for the intended users, which can be a significant undertaking. The interface should be appropriate for the users' keyboarding capability, computer system skills, operational domain knowledge, and expected usage pattern.

Man-Machine Interfaces: Text and Image

When the user might need to input a very wide array of data, a keyboard interface may offer the greatest flexibility. However, when the system can reasonably predict a small set of possible choices, then a menu selection interface might be more effective. When dealing with concepts rather than numbers in a menuing mode, the user may find it easier to interact with icons rather than text names or commands.

Dealing with textual output is generally not as difficult, since the application is not restricted by human typing speed. However, care must be taken with respect to overall volume of text, highlighting, scrolling, and window placement for best comprehension.

Often the delivery interface requires that development interfaces be hidden from the user or eliminated, leaving a customized interface that is "user proof." Not only must there be no traces of the underlying system during normal usage, but also an error or other user action should not place the user under system control or produce an error message from the underlying system. The only interface the user should see, under any circumstances, is the specially constructed application interface.

Man-Machine Interfaces: Graphical Interfaces

Sometimes the information to be communicated to the user is geographical in nature, depicting positional relationships. This type of information can be communicated to the user much more effectively in graphical than textual form. The old proverb about a picture being worth a thousand words is very apropos. Thus, applications involving analysis of complex electrical or mechanical circuits, molecular structures, or battle management situations may require sophisticated graphical representations.

There are a number of techniques that may be used to enable a greater amount of information to be communicated from a given display. For example, modifications to the size, shape, or texture of a symbol or icon may be used to communicate additional information about that symbol. Color can similarly be used to communicate information in an added dimension, such as speed, capacity, height, or state.

Graphics can be particularly important in applications in which the user will be part of the solution process. In such cases, graphical output can greatly facilitate the user's understanding of the evolving solution and making a decision as to the next action to be taken. Consider the Strate-Gene™ system from IntelliGenetics™ which has been constructed to assist molelecular biologists plan cloning experiments.

As shown in Figure 6-1, the application maintains a display of a portion of an evolving DNA chain. In response to user commands, the application can indicate the sites at which a particular enzyme would cut the DNA molecule, insert a molecule or fragment into the DNA chain, display a preferred source or destination location from which to obtain or place a particular type of gene, and so forth. Imagine the difficulty of communicating this type of information to the user without the aid of graphics!

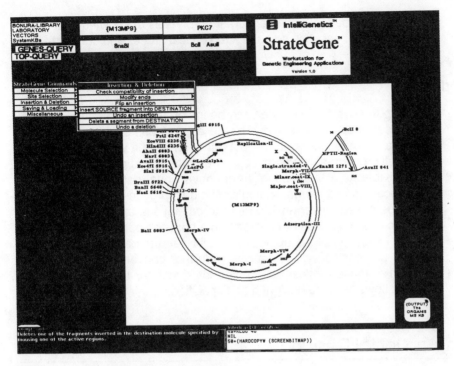

Figure 6-1 A Complex Graphics Interface

Data Base Interfaces

The data base interface is also critical to the users' acceptance of the system. Often, part of an application knowledge base is extracted from a data base maintained and used by the organization's traditional data processing programs. Clearly, the knowledge-based system should be able to access such data bases routinely. Not only does this capability ensure that reasoning takes place on the most recent values for data items of interest, but it also eliminates the need for users to key in data that are known to be in existing data bases. Many prospective users will believe that an application lacking the minimal intelligence to access existing data could not possibly have the greater intelligence needed to reason with those data.

Real-Time Interfaces

If an application is to use real-time data from transactions or from a controlled process, the knowledge crafter will need to evaluate carefully the mechanisms available to acquire and process these data in a timely fashion. Because most existing development tools have not been particularly oriented toward real-time operation, the knowledge crafter might have to consider the addition of special hardware (e.g., a coprocessor for data handling), software (e.g., a priority-driven control structure to interrupt lower priority processing to handle the arrival of a new real-time data input), or a combination of these. In any event, a specialized control mechanism will be required to ensure that rule-sets or knowledge sources are selected for execution so as to keep critical processing current in real time.

System Interfaces

Computer system interfaces can be important for some applications. To be most effective, knowledge-based applications should not be constructed as stand-alone systems, but rather should be viewed as a part of the overall problem-solving process. Therefore, the application may need to be callable as a "subroutine" from conventional data processing routines executing on the organization's main data processing facility. Or the knowledge-based system might need to call for the execution of certain data processing routines or functions on a host computer. Or the outputs from the execution of the application might need to be communicated to the data processing system for use in further conventional processing. For each of these modes, appropriate interfaces for the desired control and data flows must be designed and specified.

Developing an Initial Design

Having considered the relevant design topics, the knowledge crafter can now formulate an initial system design. This design will be comparatively rough to serve the needs of the feasibility study, with only minimal documentation. Following the conclusion of the feasibility study, the design must then be refined and described in greater detail as a prelude to implementation of the application.

The design process can be viewed as a matching process, fitting the needed capabilities and facilities for the development and delivery systems with the capabilities and facilities available in the respective environments. There will rarely be a perfect match. In some cases the design will have to be modified to fit the facilities that are available, while in other cases the available facilities will have to be modified to suit better the needs of the evolving design.

The designer proceeds to consider the constraints on the facilities, both external (e.g., availability and cost) and internal (e.g., design needs), then the constraints on the design, both external (e.g., user requirements) and internal (e.g., facilities available), and then the constraints on facilities again. This iteration proceeds until sufficient modifications have been made in the available resources or in the capabilities and facilities needed to satisfy the application.

The development of the initial design is important for it will be the basis on which the knowledge crafters develop the initial prototype. The more appropriate this design turns out to be for the application, the less backtracking and redesign required, the fewer prototype development cycles needed, and the sooner the implementation will be completed. Nevertheless, a considerable amount of (often) critical information is not known at the time the initial design is prepared. As a consequence, the initial design may be erroneous; it may contain inefficiencies; it may reflect misconceptions; there may be omissions. The novice knowledge crafter, seeking to craft the "perfect" design, should not be distressed at this turn of events.

Design Content

The assembled design must address two basic areas: the structure and content of the application, and the environment in which that application will be developed and used.

Application Structure

The design of the application structure must specify four aspects of the application's internal characteristics:

1. **Structure of the knowledge**—a description of the identity and organization of the knowledge, including:
   - the identity of the knowledge items or components that are to be contained in the knowledge base
   - the organization of the various types of knowledge
   - the representational form to be used for each item of knowledge.

2. **Inference mechanisms**—the manner in which the system is to reason with the knowledge

3. **Control mechanisms**—the procedure(s) by which various inferencing mechanisms are applied to particular portions of the knowledge base

4. **Data interfaces**—the manner and connections by which data and information are passed in and out of the application, from the following sources and to the following destinations:
   - human users
   - data bases
   - sensors (or real-time data collection systems)
   - computer systems (for further processing or for control).

Some aspects of this design will be dictated by the requirements, while other portions will be derived from (or implied by) the consequences of those requirements.

Application Environment

The design of the application environment must specify both of the environments in which the application will be used:

- **Development environment**—the context in which the developer will work with the system
- **Delivery environment**—the context in which the user will work with the system in an operational or production mode.

Application Environment: Development

The development environment specification outlines the facilities that must be provided to the developer. These include the necessary hardware as well as the software tools to develop and execute the control logic; acquire, store, and examine the knowledge; and test and verify the entire application.

These facilities also include the mechanisms for interfacing with sources and destinations for information. Data may be provided to the development environment in the same way as they will be provided to the delivery environment via:

- An actual data base
- Sensors connected to actual processes
- Human users.

Alternatively, the data may be provided via simulated interfaces:

- Local or internal files that model the actual data bases
- A simulator to generate and supply data inputs
- Scripts reflecting interactions, either tailor-made for testing or reproduced from logs of actual user sessions.

The use of an embedded simulator, for example, might be specified to drive real-time inputs to and receive real-time outputs from the application system while it is under development.

Application Environment: Delivery

The delivery environment specification outlines the facilities that must be provided to the ultimate system user, which may be a computer program, a human being, or a combination of these. The facilities to be specified include the delivery hardware as well as run-time software support that will execute the application. The various types of interfaces to be specified include the man-machine interface as well as connections to external data sources such as data bases and sensors.

Design Completion

Once the feasibility study has been completed and the implementation project approved, the design must be completed, confirmed, and documented. Completing the design involves a repetition of the same steps taken for developing the initial design. And despite the fact that an initial design has already been prepared, the process will likely still be an iterative one. However, this time the focus will be on formulating the design details and extending the depth of the rough design prepared for the feasibility study.

Design Confirmation

Once the knowledge crafters decide the design is fully specified, they must verify that it is consistent with the assumptions made about the design during the feasibility study. To the extent that these assumptions are incorrect, that the actual design is considerably different from the one outlined in the feasibility study, the knowledge-crafting team will need to reexamine the feasibility of undertaking the application. Because several elements of the original feasibility study will not change (e.g., the benefit analysis), only a portion of the work will have to be repeated. Failure to reexamine those portions, however, could lead to considerable disappointment when the completed application is delivered.

Design Documentation

After being confirmed, the design must be documented. The contents of this documentation must be such as to:

- Clarify the design that has been formulated
- Provide an official description for approval and evaluation purposes
- Guide the development team during the knowledge acquisition and system implementation process.

The same document may not serve all three purposes. A description of the design appropriate for management is likely to be strikingly different from what needs to be communicated about that design to a developer. Not surprisingly, more than one document may need to be prepared.

The design being documented will have resulted from an iterative process, during which one or more aspects of the design will have been revised or modified. The documentation therefore permits all aspects of the design to be viewed together, which helps to ensure that the overall design is complete and consistent, that all derivative changes implied by a given change have indeed been made.

The design documentation also serves as the formal description of the application, thereby permitting management, experts, users, and developers to agree on the acceptability of the design, to judge that, despite all the compromises that might have been made, the resulting design will still adequately serve their particular needs, the needs of their peers, and the needs of the organization. Although user representatives will use this documentation in judging the application design, this documentation should not be confused with the user's manual that will ultimately be required.

Finally, the design documentation serves as a guide to each team member, communicating the design philosophy, so that appropriate trade-offs can be made as work proceeds at more detailed levels and so that a consistent implementation approach can be used across the entire application. The design document must therefore be updated as the design changes. Knowledge crafters often resent this need to take time out to update the documentation, particularly when they are working in a rapid prototyping mode. However, failure to maintain the documentation will only lead to later problems, as anyone who has constructed a complex software system using a development team can appreciate.

Next Steps

After the design has been approved by all participants, the knowledge-crafting team can shift its attention to the knowledge acquisition and application implementation process, which is described in Part II.

PART II

Crafting a Knowledge-Based Application

The craftsman must be patient and exercise care to ensure that the lines of the hull are perfect and that the hull surface is as smooth as possible to reduce drag as the yacht moves through the water at various heel angles. Similarly, the knowledge crafter must be patient and exercise care to ensure that the knowledge placed in the application is complete and consistent and that the implementation produces a smooth man-machine interface. Chapter 7 describes the prototyping process that leads to a fully functional application operating in a laboratory or development environment.

Crafting the Prototype Application

Once an overall design for an application has been accepted, the development process moves to the prototyping phase, during which a series of prototypes is built. The primary purpose of the prototyping phase is to build a complete version of the application to test whether sufficient and appropriate expert knowledge has been obtained and represented properly for solving the class of problems associated with the given application. A secondary, but often very significant, purpose of the prototype is to provide a realistic test of the application's man-machine interface. The suitability of this interface is central to the acceptance of the system.

The prototyping process can be thought to be divided into three stages:

1.   An initial stage, in which a first prototype is created from design information

2.   An interim stage, in which a series of increasingly more capable prototypes is derived from the initial stage prototype by testing and review with experts and prospective users

3.   A final stage, in which a completed prototype is produced from the interim stage efforts.

General Prototyping Considerations

No matter what prototyping strategy it might choose to use, the knowledge-crafting team must consider the following issues.

Breadth of Prototype Development

Throughout the prototyping process, the design must be kept as broad and as deep as possible to avoid producing a system that is too restricted for later expansion. To present information in its clearest light, humans try to synthesize and then simplify it. However, premature or over-simplification during the prototyping can prevent important details from being included. Although some prototypes may have to be scrapped as the designers learn more about the application, a prototype should be dropped only after unforeseen problems make it impossible to develop it further.

Initial End-User Information

The end-user community must be consulted early in the prototyping process; these people—and not the experts—will ultimately use the system. Frequently, the end-users have had very different training from the experts and use different terminology. If the developers do not take these differences into account, the system can easily appear so foreign that no end-user will understand or be able to use it.

In assessing the user's comments, however, the developers should remember that the development environment (e.g., a LISP workstation) may be very different from the ultimate delivery environment (e.g., a shop floor terminal), and prospective users may have difficulty in relating one system to the other. Moreover, in examining an incomplete system, the user may not be able to visualize how the final system will appear. Programmers normally can understand and appreciate incomplete systems undergoing development, but knowledge crafters should not expect users who are unfamiliar with computers to have a similar ability.

Despite the difficulties in obtaining end-user evaluations, it is imperative that this information be obtained. An approach we have found effective is for one knowledge crafter to work directly with the user at the workstation, demonstrating the application's capabilities while the other knowledge crafter notes all comments, questions, and criticisms. This process avoids information loss while permitting the demonstration to proceed smoothly. Before completing the session, however, the end-user should be given an opportunity to exercise the man-machine interface and work directly with the application.

Designing the Application

While developing the prototypes, each team member should become familiar with all of the components, even though specific persons may be responsible for designing certain sections of the application. The knowledge-crafting team should plan numerous meetings to review the overall development, as well as to examine the details of each section. When all the sections appear to be compatible, the team should hold one or more work sessions to explore alternatives to the overall development and to the various major sections contained within it. Although the overall design may at first seem valid, this design has not been made with complete information; some assumptions may later prove to be invalid.

Evaluation

The rationale for prototyping, and the motivating factors for moving from one prototype version to the next, stem from the developers', users', and experts' evaluation of the prototype. Although prototyping is addressed in this chapter and testing in the next, the process is not one of "develop, then test." The evaluation process depends partly on the components of the application; that is, a testing capability has to be designed and built into the prototype.

Working Remotely

If the knowledge crafters are based outside the immediate organization but work with a team of local apprentices, then the next major version of the prototype can be under construction at a remote site while the apprentices conduct the daily expert interviews and handle the less complex errors found in the previous prototype version. Of course, these two groups must carefully coordinate their activities, often by working together for periods of a week or more during the reviews. Certain knowledge-based technologies (e.g., plain rule-based reasoning systems), however, may not provide adequate facilities, and other technologies may result in knowledge representations that are too complex to permit development to proceed in parallel at multiple sites.

Strategies for Prototyping

At least three strategies can be used successfully to build the prototypes:

1. Build an initial prototype for the whole application, test it, and refine it in successive prototype versions.

2. Build an overall skeletal prototype, perhaps with one or more complete sections, test it, and enhance it in subsequent prototype versions by completing and testing other sections in the context of the whole application.

3. Build separate prototype pieces of the application, testing each piece in turn, and merge the pieces into a final prototype for the complete application.

First Strategy

The first development strategy is generally preferred, particularly for relatively small applications. Because the entire application is contained in the first prototype, testing, evaluation, and refinement can proceed on the basis of having a complete application at hand.

Second Strategy

The second development strategy works well for larger applications that cannot easily be completed in a short time. By first building an overall skeleton along with the major knowledge representation structures to be used in the application, developers can then flesh out the skeleton with more and more detailed sections, permitting each section to be integrated into the framework of the whole application as it is built. This strategy tends to produce well-integrated applications that might be too large to develop using the first strategy.

Third Strategy

The third development strategy works well when the application involves two or more independent disciplines that overlap only minimally. One prototype can be built, tested, and refined to reflect the knowledge of one discipline, while another prototype can be created for a second discipline, and so forth, with the whole system being integrated in a final prototype. With this strategy the knowledge-crafting team can be divided into two or more groups, each building different sections of the application in parallel. The problem with this strategy is that the final integration of the application can be difficult, a problem that is especially severe when the man-machine interface is an important part of the application. This strategy also reduces the opportunity to develop common knowledge representations across sections. Therefore, this strategy should be avoided for building all but those applications that have multiple disciplines with minimal overlap.

Documentation

While producing these various prototype versions, regardless of which development strategy is used, the team must update the project documentation to reflect the revised state of the application design. When good knowledge-based system development tools are used to build these interim prototypes, the documentation, and not the prototype itself, usually requires the most work for updating.

Many knowledge-based system development tools have considerable on-line/in-line documentation capabilities that can be used by the knowledge crafters to document the detailed design of the application (e.g., the purpose and structure of rule-sets, rules, frames, and slots). If the knowledge-crafting team uses these capabilities in a disciplined manner, simple programs can be used to extract application design documentation. This approach has two advantages. Not only will the team's documentation effort be reduced, but the documentation will be assembled from representations in the application, information that is more likely to be kept current than information described independently in a separate design document. Note, though, that capturing such design documentation automatically does not obviate the need for a higher level document that describes the overall structure of the application and the manner in which the various components work together.

Prototyping Using the First Development Strategy

The first development strategy entails building a complete prototype in the initial stage, refining it in the interim stages, and completing the prototype in the final stage of development.

Building the First-Level Prototype

The first-level prototype of the application should follow closely from the overall system design, but focus on the building and testing of the general overall knowledge structures and rule-sets for the application. In an application implemented using rule-based techniques, this task entails establishing the various rule-sets and the control logic, often outside the scope of the rule-based system itself, that selects the particular rule-set and how it is to be interpreted (i.e., forward-chained or backward-chained). In an application implemented using frame-based techniques, this task usually first entails establishing the appropriate information taxonomies and the information contained in them before creating any rules or methods. In an application implemented with multiple environments, the various types of environments must be determined first. Although these determinations should have been made during the overall design effort, the actual implementation of these mechanisms must be done early in this prototyping effort to ensure that the earlier design efforts were indeed correct.

Because not everything in the first prototype version will likely work as planned, the knowledge crafters should expect that the prototype will have to be revised, tested, and reevaluated before it works properly. Therefore, constructing a broad but shallow version of the system at first is advisable. Such a design can be analyzed, modified, developed, and tested until the underlying structure provides adequate support, at which point the lower level details can be added. This approach concentrates the early prototype development activity on developing a sound overall framework for the system, flushing out the major structural problems first. It means that the effort to complete the lower level details is not likely to have to be redone because of overall design changes. This emphasis on breadth is particularly important for the initial prototype, for it is this prototype that will support the first testing of the man-machine interface.

An Iterative Series of First Prototypes

The task of producing the complete first-level prototype is therefore one of producing a series of first prototypes, testing and evaluating them, refining the design, and rebuilding again. As the underlying prototype design begins to become more supportive of the application, more details can be added to the application, again with further testing, evaluation, refining, and rebuilding, until all of the application structure works properly within the prototype framework.

The core knowledge-crafting team can often perform the first-level prototyping task without the apprentices, although their daily participation in the development of the prototype affords them an excellent opportunity to study and learn many knowledge representation and knowledge-crafting techniques. If such participation is not feasible, however, the core team should devote several days during the review of the completed prototype application to explain every detail of the design to the apprentices. Not only should the knowledge crafters explain the details of the application, but they should also explain the rationale underlying the design choices that led to those details.

The typical time required to produce a first-level prototype is between four and eight weeks. This prototype should meet certain preset, easily determinable milestones and, at completion, be shown to everyone connected with the project, especially the end-users, the experts, and project management, to ascertain that the general structure of the prototype meets the requirements established for the overall design. The purpose of this review is really threefold:

1.   To demonstrate that the prototype has been developed according to the predetermined specifications

2.   To collect information about errors or other problems in the system (especially user interface problems) that need to be addressed in the intermediate prototype stage

3.   To give management, experts, and users their first glimpse of what the technology can provide and of the "look" and "feel" of the planned application. (This may be the first direct observation of a knowledge-based system for many individuals.)

The evaluation can be performed much more quickly and easily if the necessary supporting data are readily available. Testing considerations (as set forth in Chapter 8) must therefore be factored into the design and included as a part of the prototype implementation.

Building Intermediate-Level Prototypes

Because the information gathered during the first interviews before a prototype has been developed is by necessity theoretical, without an actual system to test the knowledge, the expertise that goes into the first-level prototype can sometimes be too shallow. With the availability of a demonstrable application prototype, however, the knowledge-crafting team has a vehicle to communicate with the experts, a vehicle that can use the knowledge acquired thus far to make correct or (more likely at this point) incorrect decisions.

The prototype application therefore gives concrete evidence as to whether the expertise contained in it is adequate for solving the problem. Although the goal of the initial prototyping effort was to produce a cohesive, coherent prototype version of the application, the goal of the intermediate prototyping effort is to refine the knowledge contained in the system so that it is adequate for solving the class of problems associated with the application.

Reviewing Each Intermediate Prototype

After the initial prototype has been completed and reviewed with the knowledge crafters and apprentices, several meetings should be held among management, prospective end-users, and experts to examine issues relating to:

- The overall appearance of the prototype system
- The user interfaces
- Missing or inadequate areas of knowledge or functionality
- Errors in the knowledge or its representation.

Any inconsistencies, errors, or omissions uncovered during the reviews should be evaluated and resolved. The knowledge crafters should anticipate that some of these discrepancies will affect the overall design; such hands-on reviews tend to highlight problems that were not obvious in the paper design.

Although a strategic set of milestones can be established for the final intermediate prototype application, the development team may need to create and track each intermediate milestone tactically as various conditions arise.

Prioritizing the Contents of the Next Version

Following this review process, the developers should list in order of importance the design changes, omissions, and errors as well as any knowledge modifications to be considered in a series of interim versions of the application. All of the suggestions and comments that come out of the review process should be preserved, even if finally assigned a low priority or declared to be outside the scope of the application. Without such a record of proposals and dispositions, old issues may continue to surface in future review sessions.

Although the modification list may not initially identify every serious problem with the knowledge, such problems will gradually surface as the application moves from prototype to prototype. Each new prototype both subtracts from and adds to the list of modifications to be made.

To address some of these problems and evaluate the modifications, the knowledge crafters should begin a series of frequent, detailed interviews with the experts and the testing authority, preferably conducted during one-hour sessions, such as those described in Chapter 3, and held regularly (e.g., at the same time each working day). In the time between the end of one interview session and the beginning of the next, the knowledge crafters can usually correct most relatively minor errors that have been identified.

Batch Serious Errors or Attack Them Serially?

For more serious problems, the development team may need to schedule additional time to evaluate the impact of the errors on the application and to redesign certain portions of the prototype. These problems can be handled serially one by one or temporarily put aside to address other problems of that prototype version. When only a minimum of exhaustive testing has transpired, the latter method is better. If several intermediate prototype versions have already been tested when a serious problem is encountered, it may be more advantageous to attack that problem immediately.

The intermediate prototyping task is therefore used to correct the problems detected in the logic of the knowledge base and in the overall application by testing and refining a succession of prototype versions. A major improved version can be expected every four to six weeks, followed by a general round of reviews. Overall progress on the project can be tracked from these reviews; as new problems arise, they can be evaluated and merged with previously identified problems to be handled in subsequent prototype versions.

This process should converge rather rapidly. Depending on the size and complexity of the application, an acceptable prototype application should result in four to eight such prototype cycles, for a total of between 16 and 48 weeks. Note that everyone associated with the project has the opportunity (and duty) to evaluate progress at each review period and that frequent milestones are the key to success in this type of work.

Building the Final Prototype

According to the first development strategy, the final prototype is typically the latest prototype version built following completion of all milestones and review sessions. This final version, together with final documentation, must be prepared for a final, comprehensively exhaustive review with management, members of the intended user community, the experts, the testing authority, and other interested persons. Although this version may differ considerably from the ultimate system that is to be delivered to the users, it must serve as the basis for a go/no-go decision on whether to enter the pilot delivery phase.

Therefore, a detailed plan and schedule for the pilot phase effort must be drawn up. While such a plan clearly should have been available at the time the project was initially considered, six months, a year, or possibly more may have passed since project inception. Given the rapid advances in hardware and software development occurring these days, the pilot strategy should be reexamined in light of these advances.

Prototyping Using the Second Development Strategy

When the application is too large to be built in a single initial prototype effort, knowledge crafters may wish to use the second development strategy, creating and testing an initial prototype of an overall application skeleton to which various detailed sections can be added and tested in subsequent intermediate prototype versions until a final completed prototype is obtained. The application skeleton consists of a framework embodying the structure for the complete application but with very little detail or substance attached to that framework; hence the term *skeleton.* Although only one or two areas of the application are detailed initially, the development team can demonstrate the operation of the application on selected cases. Then, as the team moves from prototype version to prototype version, the various skeleton sections can be filled in one by one.

Building the Skeleton

The danger in this method is that the skeleton will not adequately support the detailed sections of the application when they are added later. Therefore, the knowledge-crafting team must carefully review the design of each detailed section to identify its skeletal requirements.

For applications involving rule-based reasoning, the skeleton may involve control code used to select among various sets of rules, a set of variables to hold information, as well as various rule-sets that reason about the problem as a whole before invoking more detailed rule-sets to focus on narrower sections of the problem. For this development strategy to work well with a rule-based reasoning tool, the rules must be grouped into rule-sets; otherwise, the subsequent addition of rules to a single rule-set may result in rules being fired or not being fired as originally intended. Testing and fault isolation become much more difficult tasks as well.

Another less devastating problem (and one that is not constrained solely to rule-based reasoning tools) is that some tools require different formats for forward-chained rules and backward-chained rules; therefore, if a rule-set is to be forward chained and backward chained at different times in the application, two copies must be maintained for this purpose. Moreover, as the development of an application unfolds, the knowledge crafters sometimes change the chaining direction of a given rule-set. Finally, in developing the skeleton for an application using rule-based reasoning, the knowledge crafters should determine the need for variable information and how that information is to be created and referenced by the various portions of the system.

For applications involving frame-based reasoning, the knowledge crafters first need to lay out the general knowledge taxonomies for the application and then create the skeletal control and rule-sets that go with the taxonomies. In some respects the task of creating the underlying skeletal taxonomies may be more difficult than creating the skeletal structure for a rule-based application, primarily because the underlying taxonomies in a frame-based application typically contain much of the knowledge represented in the application. This knowledge must be structured properly for the subsequent detailed sections to operate correctly. Once these taxonomies are in place, the remainder of the application development should be less difficult.

Testing must be regarded as an integral part of the skeletal prototyping effort. Regardless of the reasoning techniques used, the skeletal portion of the application needs to be tested thoroughly to ensure that the appropriate structure and reasoning capabilities are included.

Milestones

Knowledge crafters can identify the appropriate milestones for both the skeletal section and the ensuing detailed sections by determining the expected behavior of the system for various tests and then testing to ascertain that the actual behavior matches those expectations. Thus, the testing for the skeleton and the detailed sections can be used to determine a set of rather easily verified development milestones (see Chapter 8). Here again, milestone reviews should be open to management, prospective end-users, and experts alike, although these people may have a more difficult time understanding the status of the application at any given point in its stepwise development than understanding the development status of a complete system.

Building the Subsequent Sections

Once the general skeleton has been built and tested, detailed sections can be added to the skeletal framework and tested either serially or in parallel until a final prototype is obtained. After a detailed section has been built, it should be tested and reviewed with management, prospective users, and experts to ensure that the knowledge is adequate for solving the appropriate portions of the problems to be addressed by the application.

In developing and testing the detailed sections of the application piecewise, however, the knowledge crafters must be especially cautious in identifying which sections solve which portions of the problems and in building and testing the prototypes accordingly. Certain problems that are not part of the detailed sections or the overall skeleton can be overlooked. The information taxonomies found in a frame-based reasoning tool help prevent this situation, but they are not guaranteed to solve it. (In fact, knowledge crafters should expect to modify the framework to accommodate certain of the new cases considered.)

Again, because they are shown an incomplete application, management, prospective users, and experts may have difficulty understanding which portions of the problems are handled by the different sections and which sections are present or absent in the system at a given time. The knowledge crafters should thus expect the testing and refinement to take a little longer than for a complete prototype.

After a full prototype has been developed, several additional prototype iterations are typically required to test the entire application and to resolve errors in the knowledge or in its use in the application. These intermediate versions are essentially the same as the intermediate prototype iterations described earlier in the context of the first prototyping strategy.

Building the Final Prototype

The second development strategy is similar to the first in that the final prototype follows from the last complete intermediate prototype and reflects any required changes. The final prototype should serve as the focal point of an exhaustive review to determine: (1) that the prototype version of the application indeed meets the criteria established for the application at the time the overall design was completed; (2) that the knowledge is correct, sufficiently complete to meet the needs of the application (in terms of case coverage), and used properly; and (3) that the interfaces to the users and other computer systems operate as intended.

Prototyping Using the Third Development Strategy

The third development strategy may apply for large applications that have two or more independent disciplines with little overlap. When the boundaries between the disciplines are well marked and understood, the development team may be able to develop separate sections for each discipline in parallel and join them at the end of the prototyping phase. Since the sections are integrated after development (rather than before as for the second strategy), the knowledge cannot be shared between the sections (i.e., the logic contained in these sections cannot refer to a common knowledge or fact base). Figure 7-1 shows a typical application containing three sections, each to be developed in parallel and joined later by a controlling section.

In determining whether to use this approach, knowledge crafters should also consider the application requirements for a man-machine interface. For applications that rely significantly on human interaction, one of the first two development strategies may be more appropriate; they bring the man-machine interface to the testing stage much more quickly. Only if the human interface is a relatively minor consideration (or well specified in advance) should the third development strategy be used. In that case the man-machine interface cannot be tested until the last stage of development.

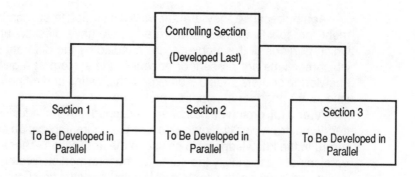

Figure 7-1   An Example of Parallel Development

Developing and Integrating the Independent Sections

Because the independent sections can be developed in parallel, each section can be developed and tested as a complete application using the first development strategy. This approach, however, results in the development of a set of rather independent sections that must then be integrated to form a single application.

If each section represents an independent set of expertise, then the preferred way to integrate the sections is with an additional set of expertise that chooses among the results of the others. For instance, an advisory system for helping to design highly complex mechanical equipment could have sets of expertise for engineering, manufacturing, procurement, and marketing. A set of design expertise could then be added to the other sets, thereby synthesizing the expertise from the various disciplines. Obtaining and testing that synthesizing expertise can often be quite difficult.

Perspective

Knowledge crafters must understand the prototyping process, recognizing that it is a supplement to, rather than a substitute for, the design. Knowledge-based applications today are crafted, not engineered; they evolve over a period of time. Fortunately, reasonably good software tools are available to facilitate this development/redevelopment process.

Evaluation is critical to the prototyping process, regardless of the particular development strategy used. An effective evaluation process is required if the benefits of the prototyping process are to be realized. In the next chapter, the testing and validation mechanisms that underlie the evaluations discussed in this chapter are considered.

Evaluating the Prototypes

Once a new yacht is constructed, the yacht builder must evaluate it under stress. Here the yacht is undergoing sea trials to establish its general seaworthiness. Its performance under various points of sail will also be evaluated against comparable data from other yachts. Similarly, once the prototype application has been constructed, the knowledge crafters must evaluate that prototype's performance characteristics. A knowledge-based application's performance as measured by various test cases must be recorded, evaluated, and validated against the operational needs of the users. Chapter 8 describes the process of evaluating the prototype knowledge-based application.

The crafting of a knowledge-based system involves two basic activities: system construction (the prototyping process described in Chapter 7) and system evaluation (the subject of this chapter). Although these topics are addressed serially in two chapters, the activities themselves are intertwined. A prototype is constructed, evaluated, and then another prototype developed. Moreover, although the actual evaluation comes *after* the development of the prototype, the planning for that evaluation must come *before* its development.

The evaluation process must consider a number of issues, although these relate primarily to the following three categories:

1. **Testing**—Does the prototype do what it is supposed to do (e.g., does it meet specifications)?
2. **Debugging**—If the application doesn't do what it is supposed to do, why doesn't it?
3. **Validation**—Does the application actually solve the problem that it was intended to address?

The Evaluation Process

After completing the acquisition of a section of knowledge from the expert, organizing that knowledge into the appropriate representational forms, and embedding the knowledge into the evolving knowledge-based system, the knowledge crafter can savor a rather satisfying moment. Yet, the crafter's accomplishment is not really complete until the system has been evaluated. The knowledge crafter must resist the temptation to "assume it works" or "guess that it's OK" and proceed with further development.

Planned Evaluation

Furthermore, the knowledge crafter must plan that evaluation before the prototype is constructed. Test cases must have been identified and collected; "hooks" or special testing facilities must have been designed and implemented in the application. Otherwise, the evaluation process becomes far more difficult. With sufficient lead time, the knowledge crafter may be able to collect currently unavailable data or build certain facilities (e.g., reporting the level at which each aspect of a decision was made) into the prototype. Such facilities are invariably easier to provide if incorporated during prototype construction rather than being retrofitted afterwards.

Multilevel Evaluation

The evaluations should take place at different levels, with the activities planned to fit the level of development. The data requirements and test cases needed to support the examinations at different levels are similarly different. Testing, for example, should include daily tests of the additional knowledge obtained from the expert, periodic tests of the knowledge relating to a particular area, and then broad tests of knowledge relating to sets of areas.

Validation should be treated in the same way. Commonly, validation is viewed as a process performed at the end of the development to determine whether the completed application satisfactorily addresses the problem it was intended to solve. However, some validation issues should be addressed before the application is complete.

For example, consider the issue of the man-machine interface. Knowledge crafters could certainly wait until the application is fully developed before determining whether the members of the user community could work with the interface as effectively as planned. As a practical matter, however, this issue should be resolved as quickly as possible during development. Because few experts and prospective users have had experience with knowledge-based systems, the design specification only approximates what people expect (or hope) might be the appropriate man-machine interface, and testing will only confirm that the specification is being met. It will not address the question of whether the specification is appropriate. Hence, the validation issue must be addressed long before the application is completed.

Case Data

Case data or sample problems are critical to the evaluation of a knowledge-based system. Before developing any prototype, the knowledge crafter should identify the types of case data that are available (or that can be made available) for several reasons. First, this exercise will assist in the identification of critical areas that will be untestable if additional data cannot be collected. Second, the listing of the data that will be available permits the evaluation program to be designed around them. Finally, testing procedures using these data can be built into the application so that the available data can be used most effectively.

Case data must serve a number of functions. Very specific cases are required to test that certain situations are handled properly. (These data might be viewed as "manufactured" because they are tailor-made to test certain aspects of the application's reasoning.) Other cases are required to permit evaluation of the application's handling of typical or common situations. (Such data might, for example, be collected via some mechanism that recorded key data on problems currently being presented to experts for solution.) Still other cases might be generated somewhat randomly to represent the breadth of situations that might at some future time be presented to the application for solution. Taken together, the case data must exercise or test the characteristics of the most critical parts of the application's behavior.

Case data can also be important to the administrative process. As was discussed in Chapter 7, control of the development process requires establishment of schedules and milestones. Developing a knowledge-based application is no different in this regard than developing any other type of software. Passing certain tests represents an easily defined milestone to mark project progress, and case data can be used to establish such tests.

Case Solutions

Unfortunately, generating case data is much easier than generating the solutions that go with those data. After all, a random number generator with a range filter can be used to generate data for a large number of cases very quickly. However, determining the desired response of the application for each such case can be a nontrivial task. Because the knowledge-based system is itself the subject of evaluation, it cannot be used to generate solutions. Thus, the expert must often analyze and develop solutions for each case. Clearly, then, the volume of data that can be effectively used by the knowledge crafters is very severely limited. Even actual cases taken from organizational files of problems previously solved must be reviewed, since the historical solution may have been improper (e.g., developed by a novice rather than an expert). Typically, therefore, the case-data problem should be viewed as a case-solution problem; the ability to generate solutions and not data is what tends to limit the case data that can be developed for an application.

Testing

Testing is the process of examining a system as it is developed to ensure that it is meeting all specifications. Thus, the prototype development process outlined in Chapter 3 called for each day's knowledge obtained from the expert to be tested before development proceeded further. Such testing serves two purposes: it verifies that the previous knowledge was indeed captured and reflected properly in the application, and it indicates where additional development and knowledge crafting are needed.

Testing takes place at several levels, depending on the stage of prototype development. For example, some testing must be very detailed, verifying that under certain conditions a particular rule or knowledge source (procedure) was activated. Other tests are performed at the system level, verifying that a given set of results is obtained from a given set of inputs.

Ideally, testing should be a continuous process. As pieces of the application are assembled, they should be tested. Just as a mechanic might test a generator being rebuilt for an automobile (by testing each component as it is placed in the generator, then testing that the generator operates mechanically, then testing that it works electrically, then testing that it functions properly when installed in the automobile), so should the testing of a knowledge-based application be conducted in many stages. Tests must cover more than just the correctness of the system's rules, structure, and logic. Because characteristics of the application itself must be considered, tests of such parameters as memory requirements and execution time must also be performed.

Finally, the knowledge crafter must remember that testing consists of two activities, not one. The test must be performed, and then the result must be evaluated. Thus, test-case generation must include not only the preparation of the input data to be provided to the application for testing but also the preparation of the output data that are expected to result when the test is performed.

Testing Objectives

Developers commonly think of testing as relating only to whether the system is performing as intended, as measured by performance against a set of tests. Determining that the application is functioning properly at all levels over the benchmark tests is obviously necessary and important. However, the more critical (and more difficult) aspect of testing is to determine the degree to which the application might produce the desired results for an untested or unexpected case. Many knowledge-based systems are sufficiently complex that they cannot be tested for all possible combinations of input data. Therefore, the testing must be oriented toward assuring the knowledge crafter (as well as users and management) not only that the application performs correctly on the available test cases, but also that it will likely perform correctly on cases that have never been processed previously.

No known procedure exists for meeting this goal, but the following four issues, if addressed satisfactorily, should give knowledge crafters greater confidence that their application will perform as expected when presented with new or untried situations:

1. **Completeness**—Is anything missing?

2. **Consistency**—Does each part interface properly with every other part of the application?

3. **Robustness**—Will the application depart gradually from correct results as the number of missing and/or incorrect data items increases?

4. **Sequence Independence**—Is the application's nonprocedural knowledge completely free of sequence dependencies?

Testing Objectives: Completeness

Testing for completeness presents the problem that rarely can "everything" be defined. The developer can certainly test that the application has a mechanism to treat all possible values for each item of input data, but should there be additional mechanisms? The knowledge crafter's position is the uncomfortable one of trying to determine whether something unknown is missing. The situation is analogous to that of the programmer who is asked to estimate the number of undetected errors remaining in his code. An application might have, for example, three rules for dealing with a data item: one for when the item has a negative value, one for a value of zero, and one for a positive value. This set of rules seems to cover all possible values (excluding UNKNOWN) for the item, but does it? Perhaps to operate properly, the third rule might need to be represented as two rules: one covering positive values less than or equal to 100 and the other covering values greater than 100.

The search for completeness can proceed in two directions. One is the direct course, organized according to the structure of the problem. Working with the expert, the knowledge crafter questions each aspect of the system. In the case of the rule that should have been split, the knowledge crafter would ask the expert whether any situations had arisen where knowing the specific value of the item would have made a difference (as opposed to knowing only that the value was positive). This approach can be fairly effective at finding a number of missing items, but it fails, of course, when the expert forgets the case that requires making an additional distinction.

The other course is an indirect one that may detect problems less efficiently than the direct approach. This procedure requires knowledge crafters to generate additional test cases that relate to the design or structure of the knowledge-based system rather than to the knowledge domain of the application, since the expert will likely have helped establish test cases that relate to user problems or commonly encountered situations. By focusing on a different set of areas where cases might not be processed properly, knowledge crafters can catch situations that might otherwise go undetected.

Testing Objectives: Consistency

Consistency testing addresses the problems that can arise if each system component does not provide the data needed by every other component in the expected fashion. Assumptions about knowledge structures, reasoning mechanisms, and data formats must be identical for both the creator and the user of data.

Some consistency problems relate more to form than to function. Thus, a bit of knowledge may be generated in one format (e.g., name of paint color) but expected in a different format (e.g., inventory number assigned to that paint color) by another part of the system. Similarly, the units may be different. Thus, the height of a wall may be recorded in feet by one part of the system but used as if measured in meters by another part of the system.

Other inconsistencies arise in terms of functions that are performed. Two portions of the system may assume that range checking of a value is performed by the other part, with the result that range checking is never performed and an out-of-range data value may be used. Consistency problems frequently are introduced if the application has many sections and proper version control is not maintained.

Although the use of knowledge-based techniques does increase the opportunity for consistency problems to arise, these same techniques can be harnessed by the knowledge crafter to reduce inconsistencies. In addition to the usual approaches to inconsistency reduction (e.g., specifications, definitions, dictionaries, change controls, regression tests), the reasoning capabilities within a knowledge-based application can be focused on the problem of improving internal consistency within that application. An approach for doing this is described in the consistency checking subsection.

Testing Objectives: Robustness

Robustness is a measure of an application's ability to continue to produce correct judgments or outputs in the face of deteriorating input. The input may be reduced in quantity (i.e., more data items have the value UNKNOWN) or quality (i.e., more data values are incorrect). The better an application can maintain its performance in the face of such input degradation, the more robust it is said to be.

An application may also be termed robust when deteriorating input data produce proportionally deteriorating responses. That is, a slow decay in input quality should be met with a slow decay in output quality.

Testing robustness is much easier than building robustness into an application. Test cases from the standard set being used can be modified by substituting UNKNOWN for selected values or by substituting random numbers or characteristics for them. Usually, the knowledge crafter would not actually generate random values. Instead, data would be modified in ways that were representative of the ways in which actual data presented to the knowledge-based system might be corrupted (e.g., a dropped negative sign for a value, the symbol for a different but related color).

A fringe benefit of robustness testing is that solutions for these modified cases do not have to be developed. Because the characteristic being tested is the ability to produce the original results, the original solutions can be used for these test cases.

The most difficult part of robustness testing can be the development of an appropriate measure for determining the quality of the solution or the "closeness" to the desired result. This measure must reflect the degree of change in the solution considered in its entirety, not just the amount of change taking place in individual data items. Generally, the closeness of the solution to the desired one will depend more on certain data items than others. Consider, for example, a commuter transportation problem. An input error specifying "driving to work" rather than "riding the train to work" might have little effect on travel time or commute cost but might lead to a significantly poorer solution since the rider would not be able to read while in transit.

Robustness: A Further Definition

Another way to view robustness is from the standpoint of the application's likely ability to handle new cases satisfactorily. The degree to which future performance will reflect past performance depends on the robustness of the application design. If the application has been tuned to maximize correct performance on a set of test cases, the knowledge crafter should be suspicious of the application's ability to handle future cases equally well.

Consider the problem of picking securities whose price on the stock exchange will go up in the next four weeks. Even experts are not correct in their evaluations 100% of the time, so that good performance is measured by x% of the judgments being correct. However, by examining the cases where the application's judgment was wrong, an analyst (or even an algorithm) can modify parameters within the application so as to increase the percentage of cases properly evaluated. Such optimization is analogous to the classic curve fitting problem in which a mathematician can always find a polynomial that will pass perfectly through any given set of points; it is just that the "perfect" polynomial so constructed will not necessarily pass through an additional, but previously undisclosed, point.

Similarly, tuning an application based on test cases can be misleading. Even if the test cases used are representative of actual problems, knowledge related to the particular problems in the sample (rather than the real world) will be embedded in the application. Not surprisingly, the application will not perform as well on actual problems as it can on those test cases.

Knowledge can be created and refined from new data; existing knowledge can be added to the application to handle a problem with a test case. However, knowledge must not be created on the basis of the test cases, for it might well be spurious. Knowledge-based systems are a mechanism to share existing expertise, not one to generate new or additional knowledge.

Testing Objectives: Sequence Independence

A particular problem for the novice knowledge crafter is maintaining the sequence independence of nonprocedural knowledge. Many forms of knowledge representations are not procedural, such as the rule-based reasoning described in Chapter 13. Nonprocedural knowledge does not contain information for controlling the execution sequence. Rather, it contains logic related to the solution of the problem, and that logic (coupled with the factual data for the problem) dictates the execution order.

Consider a set of production rules. Each rule is based on the assumption that it is executable (can be fired) whenever its predicates are true. No procedural information is implied by the order in which the rules are listed in the rule-set. The inference engine will determine the order in which executable rules will be fired, based on the particular data being reasoned about. Thus, execution order can vary from case to case.

Because most conventional programmers have worked extensively, if not exclusively, with procedural programs, they tend to think of problems in procedural terms and hence frequently include implicit procedural information in the rules they prepare. Such rules are no longer independent, and their execution order becomes critical to performing the reasoning correctly. Therefore, whenever a rule-set has been working without difficulty but suddenly provides strange results on a test case having similar but different values, the knowledge crafter should suspect that the test case might have violated some implicit sequencing logic that had been implicitly assumed for the nonprocedural rule-based representation.

A fringe benefit of testing rule-based knowledge bases for sequence independence is that the development of new test cases (and solutions) can sometimes be avoided. The order of rule firing is often partially determined by the order in which data are made available or hypotheses are presented for testing. Hence, varying the order in which data are presented to the system can produce different execution orders that might uncover sequencing dependencies. Permutations of data order in test cases are easy to generate and should not affect the solutions for those cases. Thus, new solutions for the permuted cases need not be developed.

In other situations, the data provided in a test case are such that underlying sequence dependencies will be avoided, regardless of input data order. The knowledge crafter must then rely on a broader range of test cases to detect these problems. Such cases should be as structurally different as possible, embodying considerably different ranges of input values and producing widely varying output results. In this way, the knowledge crafter can test different rule firings as well as different sequences of firings.

Identifying implicit procedural knowledge or sequence dependence in a knowledge base is important for two reasons. Obviously, removing a source of error is important. More subtly, however, identifying such a problem can help the knowledge crafter to understand better the knowledge that is to be represented, which frequently leads to a simpler, less error-prone, easier to maintain representation.

Testing Techniques

Testing is a very straightforward process. The particular set of test data (the test case) is fed into the application and processed, often with the aid of special testing facilities provided by the application development tool. The difficulties associated with testing lie instead with the development of appropriate test cases and with evaluating the results of a test. Test case development has already been addressed, but test case evaluation deserves some explanation.

Some errors are so damaging that their effects cannot be missed. Other errors can be detected by comparing the results with specifications in a design document (e.g., as would be the case for execution-speed tests). Still others can be detected by comparing the results with precalculated values, historical data, or judgments made by the domain expert. Other types of errors are much more difficult to detect, because the results are correct but the underlying process is in error (e.g., offsetting errors yield a correct result).

The major problem is finding all the errors that might exist in a knowledge-based application, and this problem is far from solved. A variety of techniques, however, can facilitate the testing process:

- Test cases
- Tracing
- Consistency checking functions
- Rule firing-order variation
- Regression testing.

Test cases may be further subdivided by the role they are intended to play. Thus, cases may be directed toward testing reasoning logic, human interfaces, or application functionality, as well as toward demonstrating capability to users and management. Case data may also be categorized by the source of the data. Thus, cases may be collected from historical files, sampled and recorded from ongoing transactions, or specifically generated to test certain aspects of the application.

Some of these testing techniques (e.g., regression testing) are traditional ones and will be treated only briefly. Others (e.g., consistency checking functions) are an outgrowth of some knowledge-based representation capabilities and represent a new technique. Some (e.g., tracing) are traditional but take on new meaning when applied to knowledge-based representations.

Test Cases

Test cases provide the major vehicle for testing and demonstrating the capabilities of a knowledge-based system. Unlike tracing, which is directed toward determining *how* the system arrived at its conclusions, test cases are directed toward determining whether the system can reach the *proper* conclusions. (If the proper conclusions are not reached, then the knowledge crafter will have to employ one or more debugging techniques to identify the reason that improper conclusions were drawn.)

Accordingly, the knowledge-crafting team must place considerable emphasis on developing case data before even the first prototype is crafted. A testing program must be defined, identifying the types of cases required to serve the various testing requirements for the application. The sources of the necessary data must be identified, and preparations made to capture, record, generate, or abstract the necessary data. Desired or acceptable outputs for each set of inputs must also be identified.

Test Cases: Facilities

The knowledge crafters must also prepare for the testing process itself, not just for the test data. If sequences of tests are to be run automatically, the development tool may need modification so that inputs for these cases can be batched. That is, a control mechanism should be established (if not already present in the development tool) that will permit the knowledge crafter to identify a set of cases, with the system then setting up and processing each one in sequence without further human intervention.

Of course, each test case involves a series of inputs and a set of expected answers. Thus, the knowledge crafter also needs a mechanism to compare application outputs from a test case with the expected results.

Automating the input as well as the output comparison process is particularly important for those test cases that will be exercised repeatedly. A testing bottleneck will occur if the developer has to conduct man-machine dialogs for each test and then pour over a set of output data. Hence, it is critical that the actual dialog be replaceable by scripts, references to case input files, or the like, and that the conclusions or output from processing the test cases can be compared automatically against expected values.

Although automating the testing process is advantageous, not all test cases should eliminate the man-machine interface. To the contrary, testing the user interface is very important, and some test cases should be specifically oriented toward testing it. Further, the developer can often obtain insights into potential problems by browsing through output resulting from such a test.

Test Cases: Types

In developing data for application testing, the knowledge crafter must determine the types of test cases that will be required. This task requires investigating the purposes to be served by each test. Thus, for example, test cases might be required to demonstrate that:

- Particular types of reasoning or particular sections of the logic are functioning
- Particular functional capabilities are working properly (e.g., menu generation, ability to reverse the effects of a user input)
- Typical or representative problems can be addressed satisfactorily
- Difficult problems can be handled
- The application has substance, that it can provide more than intuitive results, that it can handle tricky problems.

One of the knowledge crafter's main concerns is the reasoning capability of the application. The knowledge crafter would therefore select cases that would test particular aspects of the reasoning. If a knowledge base for a menu planning application contained a section on the nutritional requirements of diabetics, for example, test cases involving menus for diabetic individuals would be of interest.

On the other hand, management is less concerned with the detailed characteristics of an application's capabilities. Instead, these individuals often focus on the general behavior of the application. Test cases should demonstrate the power, depth of reasoning, or problem difficulty that can be handled. A case demonstrating the application's ability to handle common or high volume types of problems quickly and effectively would be desirable. However, test cases for this purpose would not need to provide a forum for demonstrating the full range of the application's functionality.

Test Cases: Testing Plan

Having identified the purposes to be served by the test data, the knowledge crafter must next identify the specific data to collect. For example, if data to test the reasoning leading to the generation of a diabetic menu are to be developed, the knowledge crafter will need to decide what aspects of the menu generation process to test. Will two or two thousand cases be required to exercise the logic adequately? Do these cases need to be tailor-made, each testing one specific aspect of the internal logic, or should the law of large numbers be relied on? (The latter approach argues that if a sufficiently large number of cases are selected randomly, they should provide a reasonable test of all the underlying capabilities of the application.) Even if a specific number of cases were determined to provide an adequate test of application logic, resource availability and time constraints may dictate that a lesser number of cases be used. Thus, case selection must be focused on meeting particular testing targets.

Further, in developing a testing plan, the knowledge crafter must remember that the generation of the expected results for a test case does not prove that the application is properly designed and satisfactorily operating. Errors may compensate for each other, leading to correct results for the test case but erroneous results when applied to actual problems. Again, cases that will detect certain types of problems or errors must be identified.

The testing program must be developed *before* the prototype application is constructed. Not only is time required to prepare data (or to arrange for the collection of data not currently being recorded), but the test plan may reveal certain aspects of the application that might not be testable using data that could be made available. The knowledge crafter would then have the opportunity to modify the design prior to implementation so as to facilitate testing with some other mechanism.

Test Cases: Sources

Having established the testing plan, the knowledge crafter must then determine how the various sets of case data are to be collected or developed. Three major sources of data should be considered: historical, collected, and generated. The costs and data quality associated with each of these approaches must be compared with the data requirements set forth in the test plan.

Sources: Historical Data

Because most organizations have considerable historical data on the problems that the knowledge-based system is to address, these records can be a fruitful source of test data. The knowledge crafter can either collect a sample of typical or representative problems or search for problems exhibiting specific characteristics or properties. The historical source of data ensures that the cases are realistic, that they are representative of actual problems that the organization needs to solve, and that they are not contrived.

Using historical data often has three significant disadvantages, however. First, the data are rarely complete. The historical record is a synopsis, yet the testing of the knowledge-based application requires a full set of data. Second, the historical solution may not be the desired solution. (After all, one reason for developing the knowledge-based application in the first place may have been due to dissatisfaction with the chosen solutions.) Thus, each case must still be analyzed (solved) by an expert to develop the proper solution for comparison with the application's output. Third, the historical data are frequently on paper rather than in electronic form. Hence, the data must still be captured, checked, and organized for entry into the knowledge-based system.

Sources: Collected Data

Another approach involves the collection of case data from the current operation of the organization. This technique has the advantage of permitting the knowledge crafter to design whatever type of data collection procedures might be appropriate. Thus, complete data can be captured, often in a machine-processable form.

On the other hand, these data collection procedures have several disadvantages. They can be disruptive to normal operating procedures. Moreover, because the data are not summarized, categorizing the cases is more difficult. As for data taken from historical records, the solution for each case must be developed by an expert.

Perhaps the most serious drawback of this approach, however, is the lack of control over the types of cases being presented. The normal course of business dictates what types of cases are presented. A case that will test a particular aspect of the application is often very difficult to find.

Sources: Generated Data

The other major approach is the generated case. This case is completely artificial, being created solely to test a particular aspect of the application's knowledge base, reasoning capability, or functionality. This approach has the advantage that data can be created fairly inexpensively and can be tailored to test particular components of the application.

This approach has two serious drawbacks, however. First and foremost is that solutions need to be created for each test case generated. The expert must develop these solutions; they cannot be "generated" as can the input data of the case. Further, since these cases are "unrealistic," the expert may not be eager to invest the time and personal effort to develop the solutions.

The other drawback is that the cases are artificial, which may be an issue for certain applications. In some domains, the artificiality of the case significantly affects the behavior of the knowledge-based application. Hence, these cases would not test some of the system capabilities that will be exercised by actual problems.

Tracing

A common testing technique used with knowledge-based systems is tracing. Tracing can be used in two ways: as a testing mechanism (discussed here) and as a debugging tool (discussed in the subsection on debugging). Tracing has two major advantages for a testing program. First, it can be focused very specifically on parts of the knowledge base. Thus, it can provide the developer with a more specific test of a particular aspect of the application (e.g., is RULE 46, which deals with preparation of fish for a diabetic, being fired?) than can an examination of the output or conclusions from the application's execution.

On the other hand, the developer still needs some data to cause the application to take a meaningful path to trace. This requirement leads to the second advantage of this approach. To focus on particular aspects of the application, the knowledge crafter will likely use the generated approach for data. However, unlike that approach, tracing does not require that expert solutions be developed. Because the trace is undertaken to track whether the proper decisions are being made in a particular area, the problem need not be run to completion. Tracing, by eliminating the need to generate solutions, permits an expert to support a larger amount of other testing activities without an increased time commitment.

The tracing approach is not without its liabilities. In many situations, it is not at all obvious what combinations of input data will produce an execution pass through a particular portion of the knowledge base logic. Thus, generating the required input data may be a much more difficult task than it might at first appear to be. Second, the approach is frequently misused.

Ideally, the knowledge crafter would generate a set of expected responses to go along with the input data for a trace test. That is, the "solution" for these input data would be to see RULE 25 fired, then an instance of the object SPECIAL-MENU created, and then RULE 51 fired. In actuality, however, many knowledge crafters develop the solution dynamically. That is, when the trace shows that RULE 25 fired, the knowledge crafter makes an on-the-spot decision on whether RULE 25 should reasonably have fired at that point. Usually these individuals believe themselves to have become sufficiently competent in the domain to make this type of decision.

Although the dynamic development of solutions may appear to be an effective use of resources (particularly if the test will not be repeated once the particular area or module is checked out), this technique has two associated risks (analogous to type I and type II risks in statistics). First, the result may be nonintuitive. That is, RULE 25 fires, the knowledge crafter believes that it should have fired, but the situation is not straightforward and the expert would judge that the rule should not have fired. The second risk is more subtle. RULE 25 does not fire, but this fact is hardly noticed as the knowledge crafter did not expect it to fire. Yet, the rule should have fired.

Many techniques have been developed for tracing the execution of conventional programs. These can be applied to knowledge bases as well. In addition, many knowledge-based system development tools offer tracing capabilities that are oriented toward some of the special characteristics of the knowledge base. Thus, facilities may be provided to monitor rule firings, enabled-but-unfired rules, modifications in the knowledge taxonomy, and so forth. Several techniques based on an *active values* capability (see Chapter 14) can be used to trace and display (in several forms of presentation) various characteristics of the knowledge base that might be of interest. Thus, the knowledge crafter could trace changes in the value of a slot in a frame, changes in the number of instances created from a frame (or the number of subclasses from a class), and so forth.

Consistency Checking Functions

Some knowledge-based techniques also provide a means for testing a knowledge-based application. An application being built with an *object-oriented programming* structure (see Chapter 14) is illustrative. This structure enables consistency checking functions to be placed in the knowledge base. Thus, each unit or object in the knowledge base can be given a method (function) that will perform such consistency checks as it requires. That is, the method can verify the presence of all other objects whose presence its own object requires as well as the absence of states or conditions with which its object is incompatible. When a new version of the application is developed, the consistency of that system can be quickly checked by sending a message to every object requesting it to verify that the new system is consistent from its point of view.

Even more sophisticated capabilities can be embedded within the object structure. A method can be added to each unit that, when invoked, will respond with the capabilities of that unit. Thus, the consistency checking method associated with an object can determine whether functions or capabilities required by that object are available in any of the other objects present in the system.

Determining the consistency of a rule-based system (see Chapter 13) is a very difficult logical problem that is beyond the scope of this book. However, individual rule-sets may have characteristics that can be exploited for the purposes of consistency or completeness checking. Such tests would not be complete in and of themselves, but they might be able to screen out a good percentage of the inconsistencies that might arise. If the rules are incorporated into a frame-based taxonomy, then such tests could be performed automatically on the rule-sets as well as on the frame-structured knowledge.

These types of capabilities enable the knowledge crafter to arrange for a variety of tests to be performed automatically. A consistency checking subroutine could, of course, be established in a traditional programming language, performing the same types of consistency checks. The unique feature of the approach described above is the decentralization of the testing function. Functions can be associated with each unit in the knowledge base. As the unit is developed (or modified), relevant tests can be constructed. The knowledge crafter can specify such tests much more reliably in the course of working with the affected unit than when subsequently working on a system-wide testing routine.

Rule Firing-Order Variation

As mentioned previously, one of the common problems found in knowledge-based systems is the incursion of sequence-dependent or procedural information into nonprocedural representations. Such pernicious errors can cause symptoms that are very difficult to debug. The order in which rules currently fire or procedures are currently invoked may be appropriate given the way in which the application happened to be developed and the test cases are being processed. Because the implicit procedural requirements are not violated, the system performs as intended. Later, however, when some simple, innocent-appearing changes are made, the system begins to behave erratically. The changes, although logically correct in themselves, alter the implicitly required rule firing sequence, resulting in the unexpected behaviors. (Knowing that the problem is a procedural sequencing problem makes it easier [though not easy] to isolate than if the knowledge crafter is simply confronted with a strange behavioral symptom.)

A good way to detect a sequence-dependent problem (but unfortunately, not the best way to isolate it) is to change the sequence in which the nonprocedural activities are performed. This action may cause the system to "trip" over the underlying but hidden sequence dependency, bringing it to light. Altered execution sequences can be enforced in a variety of ways.

Many systems have positional dependencies. For example, if three rules are eligible for firing, the one first listed in the rule-set of such a system will actually be fired. Thus, reordering the rules (which should have no logical effect) may alter behavior. Similarly, if frames and slots in a knowledge taxonomy are organized alphabetically, the order in which relationships are created or destroyed might be affected by name changes. A text editor can be used to perturb spellings for testing purposes.

Every rule-based inference engine has some form of tie-breaking mechanism to select the next rule to be fired from among those in the set of rules eligible to be fired. The mechanism may be an unsophisticated one (e.g., the "pick the first rule" approach described in the preceding paragraph) or it may be quite complex (e.g., an algorithm involving a search strategy). Some inference engines provide knowledge crafters with a set of mechanisms that can be selected by changing a parameter value, while others provide a place for knowledge crafters to insert their own methods. Regardless of the adjustment procedure, however, knowledge crafters are provided with a means to alter the firing order of rules without changing rule positions or naming conventions. (Altering the rule firing order may affect the execution efficiency of the application, but this is not a serious consideration during the testing for sequencing dependencies.)

In a forward-chaining application, modifying the order in which data are presented to the application can also affect the firing order of rules. Because such a change should not affect the results, permutations of data input order might suffice to detect the existence of a sequence dependency.

The knowledge crafter can also test for implicit sequencing dependencies by changing the values of the data provided to the system. This approach, however, tests different rule firings as well as different sequences of firings, so any sequence dependencies may be partially obscured. Further, because the adjustment of input data values can cause the output values to change, solutions will need to be developed for these modified cases. Nevertheless, this approach can be effective.

Regression Testing

Because an iterative or evolutionary procedure is implicit in the development method, regression testing is particularly important for knowledge-based systems. Whenever the application is significantly modified or whenever one prototype is replaced by another, a standard set of test cases should be run to verify that the new version can at least duplicate the results obtained by the old version for that set of cases. In other words, the regression test verifies that whatever changes and additions were made in creating the new prototype did not destroy the level of functionality that existed previously.

These tests are not intended to aid the developer in understanding system behavior but rather to confirm that "everything is still OK." Accordingly, human involvement in these tests is not needed; automated procedures for running tests and comparing test results are thus particularly desirable for these tests.

The regression test set must not remain static, however. New capabilities will be added to the application as it evolves from prototype to prototype. Correspondingly, new cases will have to be added to the regression set to test the newly added features or facilities; otherwise, the regression testing will have less and less relevance over time.

Debugging

The testing process just described is oriented toward the detection of errors, not their identification. Once an error condition has been detected (e.g., by execution of a test case producing an erroneous result), the knowledge crafter enters a debugging mode in an effort to identify the underlying cause of the detected problem.

The knowledge crafter can use a variety of tools to track down the offending bug. The best ones to use will depend on the hardware and software supporting the development effort, the analytical capabilities of the knowledge crafters, and the characteristics of the application itself. The following six categories of tools can be enlisted for debugging a knowledge-based system:

- Standard tools
- Rules
- Methods
- Daemons
- Justification or support
- Problem-dependent monitoring.

Each of these classes of tools is briefly described in the following subsections.

Standard Tools

The numerous tools developed over the years to assist software developers in debugging their systems are applicable to debugging knowledge-based systems. Although the structures of a knowledge-based system and a conventional program are different, both systems are nevertheless computer programs. Thus, all of the traditional debugging tools and mechanisms can be used to debug a knowledge-based application.

Many so-called AI practitioners like to propound that "AI programs" are inherently different and thus that traditional approaches and considerations do not apply. However, such statements are frequently motivated more by a desire to avoid some of the undesirable activities (e.g., documentation) associated with conventional program development methodologies than by a perception of true inapplicability. The knowledge crafter should take advantage of those debugging tools that are available on the development system being used.

Tracing techniques are a case in point. Although tracing is an effective testing technique, it is probably used more frequently for debugging. Tracing the logic step by step can often show the knowledge crafter where the reasoning took a wrong turn. Some of the facilities found in knowledge-based systems can be used to facilitate tracing. For example, the reasoning of a rule base can be traced backward in some systems. Instead of having to reexecute the test case with tracing enabled, the knowledge crafter can begin with the reported results and then trace backwards through the reasoning process to detect where it might have gone astray.

Rules

Software developers sometimes use special debugging codes that they create. Following a trap or the arrival of the application at a particular state, the system gives control to a routine to check variable values and relationships, to report values, and to make modifications if need be. The knowledge crafter has the same alternative available, but with no restriction on using a procedural routine. Either a procedural or nonprocedural approach could be used as most appropriate.

When encountering a certain state or condition, the application could begin processing a debugging rule-set. This set of rules can check values and relationships, display or record values, and so forth. The advantage offered by the rule-set is the nonprocedural specification of the task to be performed. That is, the knowledge crafter may find it easier to specify the logic associated with the debugging task to be performed than to specify the procedure to be used in performing that task.

Methods

The knowledge crafter can use the *methods* mechanism of a knowledge base, relying in part on object-oriented programming for debugging purposes. For example, each time a message is received by an object or unit in the knowledge base, a debugging method, tailored to that unit, could be executed. This method could take such actions or report such data as might be appropriate for that unit.

This mechanism conveniently investigates a number of aspects of a knowledge-based system. For example, information on the creation and destruction of units can easily be obtained. If knowledge sources or rule-sets are stored in a knowledge taxonomy within a frame structure, this same mechanism can be used to follow the chain of control from rule-set to rule-set or knowledge source to knowledge source.

This mechanism is particularly advantageous in that it can be easily tailored to the application. Further, by using the inheritance mechanism of the frame structure, the debugging methods can be quickly tailored to operate in different ways at different logical levels in the knowledge taxonomy.

Daemons

Many systems that offer a frame-based reasoning capability provide for some type of monitoring capability on the values contained in frame slots. Typically, such *daemons* (e.g., active values) are employed in the normal course of the application's execution; however, the knowledge crafter can use this monitoring capability as a very handy dynamic debugger.

An active value or daemon, for example, could be attached to a slot in a particular unit. Whenever the value in that slot was accessed (as part of a fetch from or a store to that slot) a specified procedure would be called—hence the term *active value*, for the slot value can be viewed as being activated. Any action involving it will be trapped.

The knowledge crafter can use this ability to gain control at the time of access to a slot for a number of purposes. The action being performed (fetch or store) and the value of the slot (both pre- and post-access) can be recorded or displayed. The value itself can be filtered, screening out unwanted or erroneous values so that execution can continue. Various calculations can be performed, rule-sets can be triggered, values in other slots and frames can be checked, and tracing can be enabled or disabled.

As in a conventional program, the knowledge crafter will find this capability particularly helpful when a value is being changed unexpectedly by an unknown source. The active value provides a convenient trap for the unwanted store. Many knowledge-based system development tools offer a set of default active value routines. Thus, the knowledge crafter can obtain such facilities as an always-current display of a slot value merely by creating an instance of one of the standard active value routines and attaching it to the slot of interest.

Justification or Support

When the execution of a test case produces an unexpected result, the knowledge crafter is faced with the problem of determining just why the system produced that conclusion. As mentioned previously, a tracing procedure can be activated, the test case can be reprocessed, and the knowledge crafter can watch each step that the application system performs. Unfortunately, for many applications and test cases, this process can be very long and tedious.

Once again, however, some of the capabilities of knowledge-based systems can be harnessed to assist the debugging process. In this case, the knowledge crafter can take advantage of the support or justification facilities that are generally associated with system conclusions. (Although such support is often application dependent, the mechanism is usually provided by the development tool.) Thus, the knowledge crafter can use the WHY or HOW commands to determine in application terms the reasoning or support underlying particular conclusions.

At best, such questioning can lead the knowledge crafter directly to the problem. At worst, it will probably only narrow the focus of the search for the system bug. However, localizing the search is a significant benefit, for it enables tracing techniques to be used more effectively.

Knowledge crafters are often frustrated during the development of a knowledge-based application by the volume of support text that needs to be crafted into the system. Performing a competent job can become tedious and boring. Yet, if the insights available at the time of development can be captured in the support framework, the benefits will flow to both the application user *and* the developer.

Problem-Dependent Monitoring

The preceding subsections have addressed debugging techniques that can be applied in general. However, specific problems often have particular characteristics that, if monitored, will reveal how the solution is progressing and can provide the expert or the knowledgeable developer with some insight about the behavior of the solution process. Thus, for example, if the solution of a problem should cause the system to pass through a particular series of states, the knowledge crafter would find it helpful to monitor the sequence of states entered by the application. Further, the point at which the application departed from the expected state sequence, and the identity of the unexpected state entered, will likely assist the knowledge crafter in developing some hypotheses about the character of the bug being sought.

As another example, consider an application dealing with a piece of machinery. Monitoring the differential between the temperatures reported by two different sensors might reveal a considerable amount of information about the underlying process and hence about the reasoning path that the application should be following. In some cases numerical values may not even be required, since it is the *pattern* of change that is a critical indicator of the equipment's condition or of the underlying process' status. Thus, knowing the pattern of variation in the temperature difference (e.g., monotonic, oscillatory, random) might provide the knowledge crafter with a sufficient clue to guide the debugging search.

The knowledge crafter should thus select appropriate problem-dependent items or relationships to monitor, items that will provide insight into the underlying process and thus guidance in locating where in the reasoning process an error might be occurring. Often, problem-dependent information can be very helpful in pinpointing the location of problems. Armed with more refined location or cause information, the knowledge crafter can frequently identify or isolate the bug fairly easily using other tools.

Validation

Validation refers to the process of determining that the application, as constructed, actually solves the problem of interest. The testing and debugging activities previously described focus on the mechanics of the reasoning process. Does the application operate in accord with the specification? Has each section of the expert's knowledge been recorded and implemented properly?

Validation focuses on whether the specified result is the right result. The application may be producing the right result for the wrong reason, but that is a testing concern, not a validation concern. Validation is concerned with whether the application is solving the user's problem. Will its use enable the user to make better or faster decisions, reduce cost or loss, reduce risk, or increase revenue? Validation is clearly required at the completion of the development process, but not all such testing need be delayed until then. Some validation effort can (and should) be performed as the application prototypes are being developed.

Because suitable results should have been obtained for all test cases at each stage of development, a knowledge crafter might argue that a fully tested application had already been validated. This misconception is particularly prevalent if the test cases were chosen to be representative as well as difficult. With the application providing the proper advice under a variety of circumstances, the knowledge crafters may feel that little or nothing remains to be done for validation.

Validation Coverage

The topics to be covered by the validation effort are oriented toward demonstrating that the application behaves appropriately in context. That is, when exercised by the user in the customary environment within the organization, will the application provide appropriate results? Obviously, the advice or solution developed by the application must be logically correct, but a number of other factors must be considered.

Basically, these factors relate back to the feasibility study, verifying that the application can deliver what was originally intended. With development nearly completed, are the deployment and expected operational costs for the application in line with original estimates? These cost figures encompass many concerns that were originally separate. For example, the impact of a knowledge base's size would be reflected in the application roll-out cost. Thus, the consideration of the cost side of the equation provides a convenient summary measure for many factors.

While the cost-related evaluation represents a narrowing or a summarization, the benefit-related evaluation is frequently much broader and more difficult to perform. Although the focus is on the realization of the expected benefits of the application, the potential benefits are more difficult to encompass in a summary measure and are often treated on several axes. These axes include:

- **Scope**—Can the application satisfactorily address the full range of problems originally targeted?

- **Productivity**—Can the user process problems at the expected rate (e.g., the proscribed number of cases per hour)?

- **Effectiveness**—Independent of the quality of the application's solution, can the user work with the application to produce solutions of the desired quality?

- **Skill level**—Can users, having only the projected levels of training and experience, use the full capabilities of the application to advantage?

- **Training**—Do users actually develop greater insight into problem solving as a byproduct of using the application? (For example, does working with the application provide the equivalent of some period of training by an expert or of on-the-job experience?)

- **Compatibility**—Is the operational mode of the application compatible with the customary working mode of the users? This concern encompasses not only the extent to which the application is compatible with work flows but also the degree to which the application is sociologically compatible with user work habits. (For example, if users previously worked in two-person teams, does the application preserve the team approach?)

Although validation is concerned with the issue of user and application performance, many aspects of performance are not included in the validation effort. Consider, for example, the application's man-machine interface. An interface that causes frequent user errors through poor positioning of items on the screen or poor naming conventions may detract from user problem-solving speed and contribute to user frustration but probably will not affect the problem's solution. Accordingly, many of the issues surrounding use of the system (e.g., man-machine interface, processor response, training materials, support) are not addressed as part of validation, but these are significant concerns; they are addressed in Chapter 10 as part of the pilot testing activity.

Validation Authority

Although the knowledge-crafting team will generally be responsible for running the validation tests, a variety of individuals will be involved in evaluating the test results and thus contributing to the conclusion that the application is valid. Many of the cost issues can be addressed by the knowledge crafters since they have the most detailed knowledge of application requirements. Issues of scope should be handled by management and the experts, while users and experts are primarily responsible for the assessment of productivity, effectiveness, skill level, and training. The compatibility issues are best addressed by the users. The individual assessments must then be integrated, and all parties must agree that overall the application has been validated.

Validation Tests

The various evaluations that go into the validation are not made in the abstract; they are performed with respect to some specific situations that are set up, conducted, and monitored by the knowledge crafters. In other words, validation is performed in the context of tests, and like any testing situation, advance plans must be made for the testing conditions to be established, variables to be measured, and so forth.

Two general types of tests are required for validation—more test cases and live tests. The first type of testing is needed to correct for the curve-fitting problem, while the second type ensures that the application actually addresses the problem rather than a surrogate for the problem.

More Test Cases

The evolutionary process of developing an application results in an extensive amount of testing. New knowledge that is added has to be tested, as does each successive prototype. Given the typical difficulty of obtaining solutions to test cases, the knowledge crafter tends to use a given set of cases over and over again. Such reuse causes the knowledge crafter to run the risk of "curve fitting," even if it does not occur consciously.

Each time the application failed to produce the desired result for a test case, some fix was applied. Ignoring the fix of obvious errors (e.g., name typos), the issue becomes one of how (i.e., the mechanism by which) the application was modified to produce the desired results. If some new factor was introduced that had not been previously considered, does that factor represent new insight into the problem or does it merely represent a convenient correlation that will assist the application in producing proper test case results? If the weighting of a particular type of evidence was adjusted, does that represent a better understanding of the underlying knowledge about the domain, or does it represent a change that will produce a correct result for the present test case without changing the results for other test cases?

To ensure that the application is suited to addressing the problems of interest and not just the particular set of test cases used, the knowledge crafters need to run an additional set of test cases through the application, cases that were not used during its development. These additional test cases should be fairly broad and cover the full range of functionality expected from the application. Note, however, that the tests focus on the logic of the application. They seek to demonstrate that the application has not been made overly specific, that it can address a broad spectrum of situations satisfactorily and not just a set of case problems. Although successfully addressing these additional cases indicates that the application is logically equipped to process problems of the specified type, this success is only a necessary, but not sufficient, condition for deployment of the application.

Live Testing

Each application is designed and constructed to solve an operational problem. Solving that problem logically does not necessarily mean it can be solved in an operational context. The user community must be able to use the application effectively in a production mode.

Therefore, real users with real problems must use the application to solve those problems in an appropriate time frame. At this point in development, the users will be working with a development prototype instead of a production version of the application, but this situation should not be viewed in a negative way. Using the application in an operational context with the man-machine interface is the important test.

In addition to addressing the operational characteristics of the application, however, these tests must also address the application's logic. The advice provided, given the way the user employed the application, must be correct. Thus, an expert, either concurrently or later, must examine each of the problems and rate the solution developed by the user.

Next Evolutionary Step

With the completion of the various prototypes, as well as the various testing and validation activities, the application development cycle has been completed. The application now has all the requisite logical and functional capabilities, and the man-machine interface has been judged suitable for the intended user population. At this stage, however, the application runs on a so-called development system, which may not be an appropriate delivery vehicle.

The development hardware may have a number of drawbacks. It may be costly; it may be incompatible with the equipment currently employed by the users to handle other parts of their jobs (that the knowledge-based application is not intended to address). Similarly, the development software supporting the application is designed to support knowledge-crafting rather than operational usage. It may be larger than necessary, having features for developers, and development commands may be accessible to users.

The next step in the evolution of the knowledge-based system is therefore the conversion of the application from a development version to a delivery version and the deployment of that system in daily operations within the organization. The development of the delivery version (the operational pilot) is discussed in the next chapter, while the deployment of the pilot application system is discussed in Chapter 10.

With sea trials successfully passed, the yacht enters pilot production. A key checkpoint is shown here as the first pilot hull and deck structures come together to form an integral unit. The results of fine craftsmanship can be observed in the perfect mating of these large assemblies. Similarly, with the successful completion of the prototype evaluations, the application must be converted to a pilot version for testing in an operational mode. The results of fine craftsmanship will be observed as the pilot performs as well under operational conditions as the prototype did in a development environment. Chapter 9 covers some of the considerations involved in converting an application prototype to a pilot version.

Crafting the Pilot Application

The development of most knowledge-based applications follows the same general course from beginning through completion of the final prototype. Because the size and complexity of these applications can differ substantially, individual development schedules are quite varied. When the project moves into the pilot phase, however, the course of development becomes heavily dependent on the application.

The main purpose of the pilot system is to subject the application to the ultimate delivery environment and test it under controlled circumstances very similar to those expected to be faced by the final system. In this case, the scope of testing is not limited to testing just the expertise and the man-machine interface; rather, the testing program seeks to examine the effectiveness of the complete man-machine system in an operational context. The goal of pilot testing is to ensure that the expertise solves the problems presented by the application, that real users can interact properly with the system, and that the application is able to perform as intended.

The first task of the pilot phase—moving the application from the prototype development environment to the delivery environment—is addressed in this chapter. The testing of the pilot application is addressed in the next chapter. Because delivery environments can be quite different, the process of moving the application from the prototype development environment to the pilot delivery environment will vary from application to application. For instance, in some cases the hardware and software used in the prototype and delivery environments may be identical, while in other cases they may be drastically different. Thus, the effort to move an application from one environment to another can range from negligible to substantial.

To cover a wide variety of pilot development situations, this chapter introduces four rather different applications to show how each might be treated during the pilot development phase. While other applications may not match the characterization of any one of these examples, the reader should begin to see how various delivery considerations can affect the pilot phase of application development.

Illustrative Applications

Each application described is assumed to have been developed on an AI workstation with the aid of a knowledge-based development software tool. The four applications have been contrived to expose the variety of problems that can occur today in moving from the completed prototype to a pilot version of the system. Small variations in some of the applications can add even further complications. The delivery environments for the four applications are respectively:

1.   Delivery on an AI workstation

2.   Delivery on a number of cheaper, personal computers

3.   Delivery of the application as an element of a larger system in a complex mainframe environment

4.   Delivery on special-purpose hardware.

Today, knowledge-based software development tools tend to emphasize prototype development over operation in various delivery environments. Many tool developers, however, are working to support delivery versions of their systems for newer and larger personal computers or engineering workstations built using Intel-80386 or Motorola-68020 microprocessors. Much less support is available for the delivery of knowledge-based applications on mainframe computers, especially for applications requiring frame-based reasoning or multiple-environment tool support. Essentially no support is available for custom hardware.

Application 1

The first application is a knowledge-based design assistant for a small team of five architects. These individuals are to share a single copy of the system whose purpose is to help them design houses by working interactively with them to advise on such issues as building codes, use of certain materials, and good design principles. The knowledge base contains information about general architectural shapes, properties of building materials, and design rules as they relate to building codes for various rooms and systems in a private house (e.g., the kitchen, bathroom, furnace room, electrical system, plumbing system).

Application 2

The second application is a knowledge-based advisor to assist loan officers of a large bank in consistently evaluating commercial loan applications. The knowledge is to be derived from three loan experts who together have an enviable loan analysis record. One copy of the system is to be placed in each of the bank's many branch offices, where one or two loan officers are to use it for approving local commercial loan applications. To keep hardware costs low, the delivery hardware for the pilot system cannot cost as much as the workstation that was used for development. A large personal computer was selected, primarily because personnel throughout the bank are familiar with this class of machines, such machines already exist in the bank, and the machines can be used with other applications as well.

Application 3

The third application is a transaction validator for a real-time transaction processing system. Because the application is to be embedded as part of a larger transaction processing system running on a large mainframe complex, users will not interact directly with the application; rather, they will interact with the parent transaction processing system, parts of which will interact with the knowledge-based portion by means of subroutine calls. A single copy of the application is to be integrated into the existing system.

Application 4

The fourth application is a diagnostic system to be incorporated in a major manufacturer's line of kitchen appliances. The system is to be driven by sensor inputs within the appliance to provide display and audio output for the consumer using the appliance. The application is to be integrated into the appliance product line, and 50,000 units are expected to be sold in the first year.

Application 1: The Architectural Advisor

This application is the simplest of the four. Only a single copy is required, and the constraints of the delivery system are ideal for a moderate-sized AI development workstation, thereby permitting the development and delivery hardware and software to be the same. Because the cost of moving the application between the development and delivery environments usually far outweighs the added cost of using development hardware and software for the application, organizations recognize that using the development system for delivering the application makes a great deal of sense when only a single copy of the delivery system is needed. In this case, the superior graphical display capabilities of either an AI workstation or an engineering workstation are especially desirable for the architectural advisor.

The pilot development effort for this application is not entirely straightforward, however. Although the prototype should have been developed and tested previously, the knowledge-crafting team must still do a great deal of work to ensure that the expertise correctly solves the problem and that the users understand the application before it can be released for day-to-day use.

One problem is likely to be that the application is incomplete. Certain data may be missing and need to be entered into the application. For instance, not all of the building code data may have been entered in the prototype version if the application did not need that information in the knowledge base and just listed it in a report. Moreover, in many applications the planned user interface may include a very elaborate help mechanism, which the user can invoke for assistance at any point in the operation of the system. Although the mechanism would have had to have been developed and tested during prototype development, the actual contents of the messages and help panels (possibly including intricate graphics) may sometimes be left to be completed during the pilot development effort.

Another problem that will need to be addressed is system protection. The development software provides the full set of capabilities that were used to examine and modify the knowledge base during development. Some mechanism will need to be introduced to ensure that the users do not use these capabilities to modify, accidentally or otherwise, critical parts of the knowledge base. Many protection mechanisms are oriented toward safeguarding against intentional modifications. However, safeguards against accidental changes are critical in an environment in which users will be unfamiliar with many of the system's capabilities. Otherwise, users may get into trouble, inducing unintended (and likely unknown) side effects.

Application 2: The Mortgage Loan Advisor

The prototype version of this application will have to be translated to a delivery environment because of the expense of duplicating the prototype hardware for each of the bank's many branches. While the bank has selected personal computers for the application, two delivery system strategies could be used for this application:

1.   Move the application to the personal computer system and install (or use) one of those personal computers in each bank branch.

2.   Move the application to a central time-shared computer system and provide access to it via terminals and telephone line connections from each bank branch.

Both of these strategies assume that the full, high-speed graphics power of a typical AI workstation would not be required for the application. The computational power and graphics capabilities of present-day personal computers are still limited. Moreover, the transmission line bandwidths constrain the amount of graphics information a time-shared system can send to a terminal.

Using a Delivery Version of the Software Tool

If the development tool is available (possibly in a delivery configuration) on the pilot hardware, the easiest way to move this application to either one of the hardware alternatives is to run a copy of the prototype version of the application in the pilot delivery environment. Although this choice is theoretically possible, only a small number of development tools offer such a capability today, primarily because of problems inherent in the tool technology or in a tool company's supporting a myriad of development and delivery hardware environments. Software tools that do span different hardware often contain subtle differences that complicate the transition. In addition, the storage capacity and speed limitations of personal computers may severely restrict the efficacy of the combined tool and application.

When using a delivery version of the software development tool is impractical, the knowledge crafter will need to rewrite the application to use a different knowledge-based technology or a conventional programming language. In either case, the rewrite task is substantial, even though the prototype version of the application should have been written with such rewriting in mind. Thus, for example, features in the development tool that are known to be unavailable in the intended delivery environment should have been avoided to make the prototype resemble the pilot as much as possible.

As in the case of the first application, completeness and protection are concerns. However, if a delivery version of the software system is used, the absence of some of the more powerful development capabilities from that software will provide a measure of protection.

Is the Development Tool Worthwhile?

At this point, the knowledge crafters may wonder whether using an elegant knowledge-based tool for developing the prototype was the right choice. Without such tools, however, many prototype applications could not have been built. For example, the rapid prototyping capabilities of the knowledge-based development tool might have been used to formulate an understanding of the problem, a complete specification for the application, and a tested knowledge base, thereby permitting the application to be written using a conventional programming language. Similarly, the constraints imposed on an application by the delivery hardware might be addressed far more easily with the use of a powerful development tool, more than compensating for the subsequent conversion required.

The Promise of New Systems

We expect that a group of larger, more capable personal computers (e.g., those based on the Intel-80386 microprocessor) will be available in the near future. These machines are said to be much faster than previous personal computers with a good deal more storage capacity and better graphics capabilities. Because these machines are seen as a means for integrating the worlds of MS-DOS™, UNIX™, and knowledge-based systems, they are likely to be supported by the various companies making knowledge-based development software tools. Therefore, a substantial increase in the availability of delivery support for various tools on these new hardware systems can be expected.

Logical Testing of the Pilot

Because the pilot version is produced by translation from the prototype, the results of that translation effort must be carefully tested to ensure that the two versions are logically equivalent. Only then can the pilot testing regimen described in Chapter 10 be initiated.

Entering pilot system testing, however, does not signal the end of the prototype's utility, since the prototype can and should be used to correct or enhance the basic expertise contained in the application. If the expertise is found to be incorrect or incomplete, the changes to that expertise (as well as the subsequent testing of those changes) should be performed in the prototype environment, where better debugging and development tools might be available for this purpose. After being adjusted, the knowledge base can then be moved to the pilot environment for further user testing. Because this process should be expected to continue throughout the pilot testing and final development cycle, the interface between the knowledge base and the rest of the system (e.g., the user interface) should be carefully controlled to facilitate such upgrading of the knowledge base.

Application 3: The Transaction Validator

Although the translation, completeness, testing, and protection requirements for this application involve many of the same issues described with respect to Application 2, additional considerations may arise. First, the knowledge-based development tool for this application is less likely to run on a large mainframe than the previous application. Second, even if the tool runs on the mainframe, the large computer may not be able to meet the virtual storage demands of the application, either because its capacity is inadequate or because the active working-set size may be too large.

An alternative to running the application on a mainframe may be attaching one or more high-performance artificial intelligence workstations to that mainframe in a loosely coupled configuration. Such a configuration can function well when the demands of the overall system require a minimum of traffic across the coupling between the two machines. As faster workstations and data links become available, this configuration might become the preferred means for handling knowledge-based systems in transaction processing (or similar) environments.

Configuration Planning and Modeling

In planning Application 3, the knowledge crafters should focus on determining the ultimate delivery hardware configuration even before building the knowledge base. Large or complex knowledge-based applications may not be easily handled in a transaction processing system; for these applications, creating the pilot version is surely the most difficult step. To predict whether a certain configuration will be adequate, the developers should consider modeling the overall system before building it. Among the critical items to be considered are the demands on the mainframe computer in terms of instructions to be executed and accesses to main (virtual) storage.

Garbage Collection Issues

Although rule-based applications can be mapped onto mainframe equipment rather successfully (although not necessarily easily), frame-based or multiple-environment applications may be extremely difficult, if not impossible, to handle on a mainframe. Such applications tend to exhaust the available dynamic address space fairly rapidly, ultimately requiring garbage collection. The inability of mainframe virtual address systems to perform efficient garbage collecting has thwarted the development of fast and efficient LISP systems for such machines, particularly when real-time response constraints are involved. Although a real-time application may not actually be written in LISP, the developer will likely need to implement the same underlying storage management capabilities as LISP systems employ.

Application 4: A Built-In Diagnostic System

This application poses the most complex conversion issues of all the applications described here, and only simple, well-behaved applications can be considered for such extensive, unsupported delivery. Not only must the application be hand translated to the delivery environment, but it must also be very thoroughly tested in that environment to flush out as many problems as possible. The knowledge crafter should expect such a project to take many months to complete. As microprocessors become faster, smaller, and cheaper, much of the translation requirement will disappear, but the requirements that the application be absolutely error-free and protected from the user will not disappear, and those requirements overshadow everything else.

Summary

Knowledge-based applications systems have existed in a world dominated by the AI workstation. Today, that world is changing, at least with respect to delivery systems. Because the manufacturing volume of AI workstations will remain low in comparison to general microprocessor-based systems, such workstations will continue to command a higher price and probably will never be very suitable economically as delivery vehicles for applications where more than a few delivery systems are required. Unless manufacturers elect to stop making them, AI workstations will continue to be better for developing knowledge-based systems than more general-purpose, microprocessor-based workstations. Because knowledge-based development tool manufacturers appear to be striving to make their software applicable to delivery environments as well as development environments, the need to translate the application into a completely different form in the delivery environment will diminish. However, in time-sensitive cases, or cases such as Application 4, this need will diminish much more slowly.

The pilot production model of the yacht must be taken to sea for a further set of trials to detect any production flaws and identify any last-minute adjustments that are needed in sail plan, rigging, fittings, and so forth. Similarly, the pilot knowledge-based application must be tested in an operational environment, with actual problems being presented in realistic time frames, to detect any flaws and to identify any last-minute adjustments that are needed in the man-machine interface, response characteristics, or functionality. Chapter 10 discusses the conduct and characteristics of these operational tests.

Conducting the Operational Phases

With the completion of the pilot or delivery prototype of the application, the developers shift their attention from implementation considerations to operational testing and evaluation. These latter activities can be grouped into two categories or phases: a pilot operation phase, in which the pilot application is tested in an operational environment, and an operational phase, in which the application is placed in production use. However, this operational phase is just a name for a period of production operation that is subject to considerable monitoring and evaluation. It must not be viewed as an opportunity to turn the application over to operational personnel and wrap up the project. The operational phase, as defined herein, is an important part of the overall development effort.

Pilot Operation Phase

The pilot operation phase is basically an experiment, although the practical constraints imposed by the operational context restrict what can be tested. The pilot operation is similar to a period of actual operational use of the application, in that a delivery version of the application is being:

- Run on delivery hardware with delivery support software
- Used to address real problems of the organization in a timely manner
- Used by regular staff members.

Despite the similarities, however, the operational phase differs from a normal operating environment in that:

- The number of users (i.e., number of terminals connected to a shared system or number of workstations) is relatively small.
- The operating environment may be modified occasionally for experimental purposes (e.g., to determine experimentally the impact of different levels of operator training).
- The entire operation is heavily instrumented, so that a variety of information about the characteristics of the system and its usage will be available for evaluation purposes.

Essentially, the pilot operational period is an opportunity to learn as much as possible about the operating characteristics of the application. It is intended to identify any potential operating problems prior to full-scale deployment. For example, do users encounter any unforeseen difficulty in working with the application interface? Does the application have unanticipated interactions with other job activities (e.g., does the availability of the application at the user's workstation cause other systems to execute much more slowly)? At the completion of the pilot operation, the application should roll out into full production use without any surprises. The pilot should scale up to full operation without difficulty.

Plans for the pilot operation must be drawn up carefully in advance so that:

- Maximum information can be obtained from the period of instrumented usage

- Maximum advantage can be taken of the available opportunity for experimentation
- Experiments address the information most critically desired
- Data collection and summarization mechanisms to support the information needs can be developed and placed into the application and the surrounding operational environment as appropriate.

In other words, advance planning and preparation for the pilot operation are critical. Without such planning, valuable time will be lost while experiments are designed and prepared, and information later desired to support the evaluation will not have been collected and will not be derivable from the information that has been collected.

Much of the needed information can be obtained from the application itself with proper instrumentation and recording. Because part of the information relates to the user's behavior, however, mechanisms for monitoring or observing user behavior have to be prepared. Even though the human is not a literal part of the computerized application that has been developed, the user is an effective part of the overall knowledge-based system that is addressing the organization's problems. Accordingly, all aspects of the system's performance must be measured, not just the computer portion of the application.

In preparing for the pilot operation phase, the developers should be concerned about the following six categories of information:

1. The effectiveness of the man-machine interface

2. Productivity measures

3. The extent to which expected solution quality is actually realized

4. The degree to which expected benefits are actually being received

5. The adequacy of user support

6. The impact of the application on staff attitudes.

The degree of emphasis to be placed on each of these areas will depend on factors relating to the particular organization and the application, but all six areas should be accorded some degree of consideration in the evaluation.

Man-Machine Interface

The pilot operation provides a dual opportunity to evaluate the man-machine interface. It is both the first opportunity to study this interface outside of laboratory conditions and the last opportunity to study the effectiveness of this interface before the application goes into full operational use. For the first time, actual users will attempt to use the system in an operational environment to solve current organizational problems. The developer must therefore learn as much as possible about the effectiveness of the user interface from this preliminary experience prior to roll-out to full operational use, specifically focusing on the following six aspects of the man-machine interface:

1. **Understanding**—Some early knowledge-based systems involved little human participation (other than as the supplier of

the information). The system reasoned with the input data and provided advice at the end of the analysis—all without any logical interaction with the user. However, more and more knowledge-based applications being built today are designed with the user as a partner. Current knowledge-based systems are intended to work with the user to facilitate solution of the problem. The system is an advisor *throughout* the process, not just at the end of the process. If the pilot application is intended to operate in this mode, the knowledge-crafting team should determine the degree to which the interface can facilitate the desired type of interaction.

- Does the interface assist the user in conceptualizing the problem?
- Does the graphical representation of the knowledge and the solution process contribute to the user's understanding of the problem and its solution?
- Does the interface facilitate the user's own reasoning about the problem?
- Does the interface facilitate communication using terms of the domain or problem (e.g., does the user have to translate system inputs and outputs into and out of some more general, nonproblem-specific, terminology)?

2. **Usage pattern**—Users tend to develop personalized usage patterns once they become familiar with the operation of the application. A user will begin to employ the system in certain ways, to tackle each problem with a personalized approach. The developer should consider the degree to which the interface is compatible with that usage.

    - Does the application provide commands or functions that are not used?
    - Are there common sequences of commands or activities that should have some type of single command available to trigger them?
    - Does the user search for or try to use any capabilities that are not present?

3. **Efficiency**—The more the user works with the application (as opposed to merely receiving output), the more important it becomes for the developer to study the efficiency with which the interface can be used. That is, how rapidly can the user do something once a decision has been made to perform that action? These efficiency questions relate to the structure or organization of the interface, not to the particular information that is contained in that structure. (The latter point is the subject of the next item on usability of the interface.)

    - Does the interface have elements that are awkward to use? For instance, in a graphics environment, does the user frequently have to move the cursor long distances across the screen? Does the user have to switch back and forth from one screen to another?

- Could the interface be changed so as to reduce the time a user spends performing certain activities? For example, are menus available for selecting from standard entries (rather than having to keyboard the entry)? Is the cursor located at the probable choice on a menu rather than on the first item or off the menu?
- Is the system sufficiently responsive to the user's actions so that the delay in displaying responses does not decrease user productivity and increase user frustration?

4. **Usability**—Most knowledge-based systems involve some dialog with the user, ranging from requesting key input data to providing a continuing stream of advice, guidance, and commands throughout an analysis. The developer must ascertain that the terms in which this dialog is conducted are clear, concise, and unambiguous.

- Do the users understand the messages given by the system?
- Can users react quickly to responses from the system?
- Are interactions with the system confusing or subject to misinterpretation? For example, do users respond to data input requests with values that are measured in different units than the system expects?

5. **Mistakes**—The user interface should have been designed to facilitate the user's interaction with the system. The only difficulty is that "facilitated interaction" is a very difficult concept to measure. Accordingly, the developers may wish to consider some surrogate measures such as whether the interface contributes to user error. Data should thus be collected on the number and type of mistakes users make in attempting to work with the system.

- How frequently are errors made?
- Are errors primarily conceptual errors (e.g., wrong command) or mechanical errors (e.g., wrong spelling)?
- Are there similar or related commands that confuse the user?
- How rapidly can a user recover from an error? For example, is recovery simply a matter of providing a correct input or will some time elapse while the screen is redrawn for the user to regain control?

6. **Training**—Two elements of training are associated with a knowledge-based system. One element deals with the training the user receives from the system in terms of domain knowledge, of the analysis process for solving domain problems, and so forth. This element was addressed previously in the discussion of understanding. The other aspect of training is the education and practice required by a user to employ the knowledge-based system effectively to solve problems.

- How much training is necessary before a user can employ the system productively?

- How long does it take for a new user to become proficient in working with the system?
- Can the user take advantage of the full range of capabilities provided in the user interface?
- Is frequently needed information available in readily available summaries or through on-line help facilities?
- When the needed information is available, can the user find and access it easily?

Productivity

A variety of data about the resources consumed in using the system should be collected. Obviously, some of these measures are application-dependent, but the developer should collect certain general types of data to evaluate the pilot operation. These data will be particularly helpful in planning for the forthcoming roll-out of the system into operational use. The productivity data can be divided into two categories, those data that measure human productivity and those that measure computer productivity.

- **People**—The primary focus of this metric is on the quantity of work that the user can perform with the assistance of the knowledge-based system. (Quality is also a very important criterion, but it is addressed separately later.) Measures of speed should be of two types. The first type is for planning purposes and reports summary performance (e.g., problems solved by an average user per hour). The second type is for analysis purposes, so that overall performance can be improved (e.g., time required to set up problem, time required for data input, time required to think about system responses).
  - What is the elapsed time to solve an average problem (and how does this compare with current problem-solving methods)?
  - How many interactions with the system are required for the user to solve the average problem?
  - How much time does the user spend in the various stages of the problem-solution process? (The definition of these stages is obviously application-dependent.)
  - How much time does the user spend in performing various functional activities (e.g., data input, output analysis, thinking about the problem, waiting for a response from the computer system)?
- **Processing**—The primary focus of this metric is the effectiveness with which the hardware resources are used and the effectiveness with which the system delivers those resources to the user. Despite arguments that a terminal or workstation is like a telephone (and thus its utilization is irrelevant), figures about hardware utilization are very important for planning purposes, for they indicate the cushion or expansion capability that exists to address future system enhancements. Thus, regardless of whether

the application is running on a personal computer, an engineering workstation, or a mainframe via a terminal, the developer should be concerned about hardware performance.

- What processor utilization results when the application is processed?
- If the knowledge-based system runs on a shared processor dedicated to the application, how many people can use the system at the same time?
- If the application runs on a shared processor performing general tasks, to what degree does the execution of the application interfere with other processing (and vice versa)?
- How much memory is required to run the application effectively; for example, would a little more memory provide significant gains in processing speed and responsiveness?
- If the application deals with real-time input data, can the system meet the timing requirements for accepting input data items and for providing responses based on those inputs?
- What is the distribution of system response times to user inputs or requests? How does response time vary with the configuration and other activities taking place on the system?
- If the application is running on a workstation connected to a host computer, what volume of data is transmitted (in each direction) between the host and the local processor (e.g., for data base access and update)?

Solution Quality

One of a developer's primary concerns should be the quality of the advice given by the knowledge-based system. After all, it was no doubt the desire for improved solution quality that led to the development of the application in the first place. Measurement of solution quality implies that problem data will have to be captured as they are presented to the system so that experts can subsequently evaluate the quality of the system's advice. Issues to be addressed include:

- What percentage of the problems is resolved with an excellent (best, optimal, ideal) solution?
- What percentage of the system solutions is acceptable?
- Are there characteristics of the problem or of the answer that might aid the user in identifying bad or erroneous solutions generated by the system?

Benefits Received

When the knowledge-based system development project was undertaken, everyone associated with it (e.g., management, development team, users) had certain expectations (made explicit during the feasibility study) about the benefits that might derive from the knowledge-based application. No evaluation of the pilot operation would therefore be complete unless the issue of benefits was addressed. Accordingly, the developer must try to measure the benefits being derived from the system during pilot operation.

- Is each of the various types of projected benefits being realized?
- Are those benefits being received in greater or lesser amounts than predicted?
- Does the pilot operation experience provide any basis for believing that the magnitude of the benefits received will grow with time?
- What is the net effect of the greater amount of some benefits being received and the lesser amount of others?

These types of questions are generally very difficult to answer, which is why the feasibility study included defining good measures of benefits to be derived from the development and why the pilot operation period must be planned carefully in advance.

Adequacy of Support

A number of additional questions need to be raised about the general topics of training, user support, and documentation.

- **Training**—The developer needs to ascertain the adequacy of the anticipated training procedures used, considering duration or quantity, content, and style.
  - Did the instruction program cover the right topics? Was the user adequately prepared for the situations that arose when using the application?
  - Was the training period too long? Too short?
  - Were sessions too concentrated?
  - Was the method of training appropriate? Or should more emphasis be placed on written materials, on-the-job training, classroom instruction, machine-based training?
- **User support**—The developer must consider what types of user support functions are needed for the application. Again, requirements in this area will be very application dependent.
  - Could users surmount difficulties when they arose or did they have to contact support personnel (if available) or the developers?
  - How frequently did such difficulties arise?
  - Would better training, on-line help facilities, or other aids have prevented any of the observed difficulties?
  - How much time did support personnel spend in resolving a problem when it arose?
  - Does the resolution of problems require a physical presence with the user and access to the application or can assistance be provided over a telephone link?
- **Documentation**—The amount of user-level documentation needed will depend on the background of the expected user

population and the characteristics of the application. However, some level of documentation will likely be required, and the developers must assess the adequacy of that documentation. Unfortunately, such assessments will largely be subjective, but this fact cannot be an excuse for failing to make them.

- Are sufficient reference materials provided (e.g., user's manuals, command summary sheets, quick indexes)?
- Do these materials provide all of the information that users needed to operate the pilot?
- Is the information written in a clear, concise, and easy-to-understand manner? For example, is the user observed reading and rereading sections of the manual, trying something, finding it doesn't work and going back to the manual again?
- Is the user able to find the information that does exist in the support materials?
- Can the user find the needed information quickly and directly? Or is considerable searching necessary?
- Can a user reasonably be expected to handle all difficulties encountered if supported only by the available documentation? Or will a hot line or other access to a support person be required?
- What was the user's general frustration level in addressing system difficulties?

Attitudes

Because user attitudes toward a system can significantly affect the use made of that system, the developer should collect a variety of information about user attitudes during the pilot operation of the application. These data should of course be collected from the users of the system, but they should also be collected from the experts and management personnel as well. Information on attitudes can be divided into two categories: that pertaining to the situation as it is perceived and that pertaining to expectations about what is perceived.

- **Perceptions**—Perceptions are very important to measure because the user reacts to the perceived situation (not the actual situation). For example, if a user perceives the system response time to be too slow, he will judge the system on that basis. Reams of statistics to the contrary will be of no avail. It is surprising how effective attitude changes can be in "improving" system performance in comparison with actual system modifications.
  - Is the system easy to use?
  - Is the system's advice helpful?
  - Do users tend to accept the system's recommendations or do they override them?
  - Does the system improve user performance?
  - To what degree does the application provide the benefits originally projected?

- Is it worthwhile to invest the time and effort to run a problem through the knowledge-based system?

- Overall, does the availability of the knowledge-based system contribute to or detract from the user's job performance?

- **Expectations**—The companion concern involves expectations. A system might have a good level of performance, both perceived and actual, but if that level is less than the expected level, the system will still be viewed unfavorably. Hence, the developers should also obtain data about the user's expectations.

  - In general, does the system meet expectations?

  - Is it as easy to use as expected?

  - Is the quality of the decisions as high as expected?

  - Does the system improve the user's job performance to the anticipated degree?

  - Are the drawbacks of the system as serious as expected?

  - Is the organization receiving as much benefit from the system as anticipated?

Roll-Out Evaluation

The pilot operation phase is the last step before the application will be placed into regular operation. Accordingly, once data are available from the various tests and experiments performed during pilot operation, a number of evaluations must be made before the project can proceed to the operational phase. These evaluations relate to issues of modification, feasibility, and schedule.

- **Modification**—The types of modifications at this point in the development derive mostly from the observations and data taken from the pilot tests and experiments.

  - What hardware changes are necessary for the application to meet its design goals? A different computer system? More memory? A more powerful processor? A better link to a host processor? A different graphics display?

  - What changes must be made in the application's logic or knowledge base as a result of the operational trials? Must reasoning in certain domain areas be made more precise? Must certain functions be made more efficient? Are needed functions missing?

  - What modifications must be made in the user interface? Are wording changes needed in text messages? Is a different type of interface required for part of the reasoning process?

  - What changes must be made in the planned training program? Will greater support, involving either humans or on-line facilities, be required to assist the user community?

  - What changes in user community attitudes are necessary for the roll-out and production use of the system to be a success?

- **Feasibility**—Although the feasibility of the application will have already been assessed at several points during the development, the developers should verify that the project remains operationally feasible before full roll-out begins, particularly because the various changes identified immediately above might significantly affect the character of the project.
  - Based on the available data about hardware effectiveness and the proposed changes to support the application in an operational environment, are costs still in line with projections? Can compatibility requirements still be met?
  - Do the apparent costs of the desired training and support mechanisms fall within the planned limits?
  - Do solution quality and system usability appear to offer the same magnitude of benefits as originally projected?
  - Given the various changes in costs and benefits associated with the operational use of the application, is the benefit/cost ratio of the production version of the system still acceptable?
- **Schedule**—If the proposed modifications are minor, the original roll-out schedule may not have to be changed. However, if major changes in hardware or software or in personnel attitudes are required, the roll-out schedule may need to be revised.
  - Will roll-out have to proceed more gradually because of changes in training requirements?
  - Will roll-out have to be delayed because of required changes in application logic or interfaces?
  - Will required changes to hardware involve changes in equipment delivery dates or system interface completion?

With the completion of the evaluation and the formulation of the necessary plans for modifications and then roll-out, the project moves into its final phase, with the application being put into regular production use.

Operational Phase

Although the deployment and regular use of the application system mark the end of the formal development process, the project has not been completed. Management and knowledge crafters alike commonly make the mistake of assuming that the project has been completed when the application goes into regular production use and that the attention of the developers can be directed elsewhere. To the contrary, many of the considerations discussed during the development phases carry over into the operational phase. For example, periodic maintenance will be required as the domain knowledge or the environment changes. New versions of the system will be required from time to time, and regression testing (as well as other quality control tests) will have to be performed on these versions.

Evolution from Pilot to Operations

The application can shift from pilot operation to regular operational use in a variety of ways. The pilot may have proven to be so satisfactory that it is scaled up (e.g., terminals are added) and deployed directly. Alternatively, the data accumulated from the pilot tests may indicate that the system must undergo a number of revisions, with deployment taking place at a later date. Or, deployment may be delayed until more extensive training can be provided to a large number of users in geographically widespread locations.

Regardless of the manner in which the change to regular production use occurs, however, the operational phase can be characterized by five special areas of concern:

1. Documentation
2. Training
3. Maintenance
4. User support
5. Migration

Documentation

Two types of documentation are required for operational use—user documentation and system documentation.

- User documentation must cover not only the essential procedures for using the system, but also helpful hints on using the system to advantage, using it more efficiently, and getting out of trouble.
- System documentation is required to assist those who will be maintaining and enhancing the system. This documentation must cover the internal structure of the system as well as explain some of the reasoning underlying that structure.

Many of the representations used in knowledge-based systems are much more readable (or can be made much more readable) than conventional program code. Accordingly, novice knowledge crafters tend to rely on the self-documenting nature of the system. This is a serious error. Although these systems can be made easier to understand, they are certainly not self-documenting. System-level documentation is needed, particularly to describe the developers' purpose and intent. Information about alternatives not selected can greatly facilitate maintenance and avoid personnel spending time attempting to move the application down paths already found to be fruitless. Thus, all the requirements for documentation of a traditional program apply to knowledge-based applications as well.

Training

Two types of individuals need to be trained in one or more aspects of the application system—users and support personnel.

- Users need to be trained in the proper use of the system—a minor or major undertaking depending on the application. Some applications are sufficiently straightforward that only 15 minutes of on-the-job instruction would suffice. Others may be sufficiently complex that one or more days of classroom explanation, complete with training material, visual aids, and so forth, would be required.

- Support personnel need a variety of training. If the user population for the deployed application is sufficiently large, support personnel will be needed to provide user training as well as consulting support and problem resolution during operational use. In addition, other personnel will be needed to perform routine maintenance and to extend the functionality of the system. All of these personnel, whether playing single or multiple roles, must be given proper training.

Training is an ongoing activity. The personnel involved in a project change. They are promoted; they transfer within the organization; they change jobs and leave the organization. Hence, the organization must be able to replace both support personnel as well as users. Effective training provides a solution.

Maintenance

Maintenance support involves two different types of maintenance activities—update and extension.

- Update maintenance involves modifying the representations in the application's knowledge base in response to changes taking place in the external world. New domain knowledge may have been developed that needs to be represented in the system; one of the experts may have developed new heuristics that are particularly effective. New procedures may have been found to perform certain functions. Laws or regulations may have changed, necessitating a corresponding change in either the factual data or the expertise contained in the knowledge base (or both).

- Extension maintenance basically addresses system enhancement; it involves modifying the application to provide additional capabilities or new functions or to broaden the areas that the application can address. Adding a menu selection capability to the user interface would be an example of such a new capability. Broadening the coverage of the system might occur by modifying it to handle more types of situations (fewer exceptions) or additional specializations. Thus, for example, a credit authorization advisor (or loan officer assistant) that was constructed to address credit applications of manufacturing companies might be extended to cover retail and service companies as well. Alternatively, the application might be extended along a different axis so that it could support specialized types of loans such as secured loans collateralized by receivables and documentary letters of credit.

User Support

Someone must be available to assist users who are having difficulty or who have encountered a problem with the application that they cannot resolve. Depending on the size of the organization and the complexity of the application, a person may be assigned to this task on a part-time basis, or the individual may be just one member of a large support team.

For a system having a small set of users working together in one central location, a senior user may informally play this role. In other cases, all users together may perform this function. For large, distributed systems with many users in several geographical locations, at least one individual should be assigned to this task. Making such an individual available by telephone during operating hours to answer questions would provide the traditional "hot-line" support.

The type of support required also varies with the sophistication of the system and the capabilities of the user community. If the users are technically sophisticated, they may be able to handle most of the commonly occurring problems themselves. Only the technically difficult problems would be referred to a support person. On the other hand, a knowledge-based system built to be used by the public or by untrained personnel in a customer organization would have to be supported by an individual with quite different capabilities. The questions posed would be easier to answer, but more repetitive. Support personnel would have to exhibit both competence and patience in dealing with frustrated users.

Migration

Knowledge-based systems are generally viewed as advisory systems. That is, they are intended to aid a human in making better decisions; they are not intended to make the final decisions. The knowledge-based system is generally constructed because an algorithm to solve the problem was not available; consequently, the system is based on the heuristics and experiential knowledge that experts have accumulated over a period of time. This knowledge represents the closest approximation available to an algorithmic solution to the problem.

As experience is gained with the application over time, however, users may find that certain aspects of the advice are invariably correct. These aspects would then be logical candidates for migration to a more conventional system. Thus, the knowledge-based system could be viewed as an experimental test bed, trying ideas until appropriate solution mechanisms are found.

In some situations the knowledge-based system will be an adjunct to a larger host application. In such cases it may be fairly easy to migrate functions from the knowledge-based system to the host data processing system. In other cases a companion system might have to be constructed. In still other cases, the nature of the knowledge and the structure of the application might prevent removal of portions of the application from the knowledge-based system.

Because developing a knowledge-based application is always a learning experience, knowledge crafters must plan for the greater understanding of the domain that will accumulate over time. If functional migration appears feasible, plans should be prepared to identify candidate functions periodically and to evaluate their migratability.

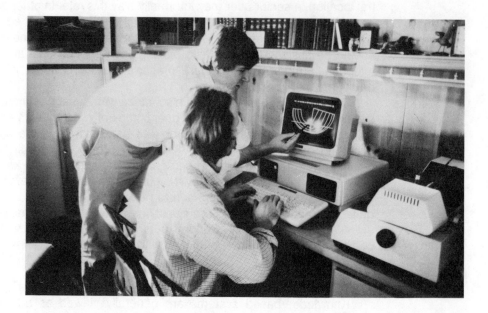

Preparing a Project Schedule

The design and construction of a quality sailing yacht involves a great many activities that must be scheduled and coordinated if the various components and assemblies are to be completed on time. Two members of the design team are shown here at a computer terminal developing such a schedule. Similarly, the design and construction of a quality knowledge-based application involves a great many activities that must be scheduled and coordinated if the various components are to be assembled, integrated, and tested on time. Chapter 11 discusses certain scheduling considerations and describes several sample schedules.

The sample schedules described in this chapter are intended to reinforce the knowledge-crafting concepts presented in previous chapters. They are not intended to be used as definitive schedules for developing a specific application, but they do illustrate issues that need to be reflected in a development schedule. The development phases considered in this chapter are the selection of an application, the feasibility study, the overall application design, the development and testing of the prototype versions, and the development and testing of the pilot versions.

Scheduling a Study to Select Among Candidate Applications

Frequently, an organization new to knowledge-based system technology does not have a single candidate application in mind, but would like to select an initial application from a set of about five possibilities. The application selected should meet the following criteria:

- Positive, identifiable, and measurable benefits
- No more than moderately difficult to implement
- Completable in less than a year
- A very low development risk.

To minimize the time and cost involved in conducting five rigorous feasibility studies for five potential applications, we recommend a two-week, intensive preliminary feasibility study to select one of the five candidate applications. This preliminary study is designed for an experienced, two-person knowledge-crafting study team working on-site with key personnel in the organization. Prospective apprentices are encouraged to work with the knowledge crafters. Figure 11-1 illustrates a two-week time frame for conducting such a study.

During the first Monday morning sessions, the knowledge-crafting team is introduced to persons representing the various candidate application areas. For each application area, appropriate persons discuss the overall goals and nature of the application, how it is currently handled, and who the users and experts are expected to be.

On Monday afternoon, the study team begins a series of half-day studies of each candidate application area. This series covers the nature and extent of the knowledge to be represented in each application, as well as any special issues relating to its final deployment (e.g., user interfaces or interfaces to other computing systems).

While the study of each application may differ slightly, approximately a quarter of the effort should be spent in understanding issues relating to the users and other computer interfaces while the remaining three-quarters should be spent in interviewing the experts to understand the size, depth, and breadth of the knowledge required for the application and the way such knowledge should be represented. Several evenings should be spent discussing design issues for each of the applications and, where possible, sketching one or more designs.

After all the candidate applications have been studied once, the knowledge-crafting team must make a second pass over the applications to concentrate on evaluating the expertise and how it might be represented. If possible, an initial design sketch is completed for each application. This process should be finished by noon of the second Monday.

Following the two rounds of study, each candidate is evaluated, and those candidates that clearly do not meet the criteria, those that are very risky, for example, are removed from the list. Of course, all candidates could be removed, in which case the study is terminated or extended to locate other candidates. (In our example, two candidates are removed.)

The remaining candidates are then evaluated further, especially to delineate the expertise and determine more accurately how it might be represented. This discovery process typically centers around detailed interview sessions with the experts. During this time, additional evening sessions may be required to refine the original design concepts for these remaining candidate applications.

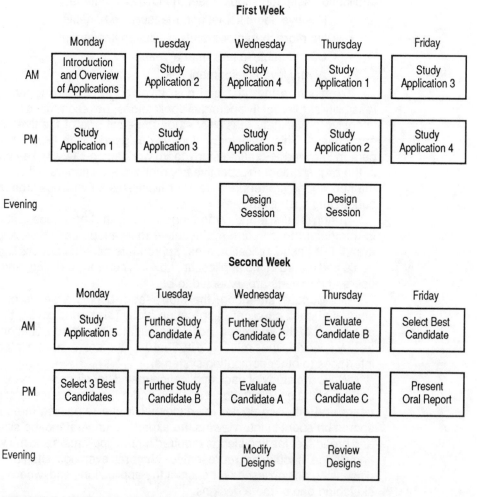

Figure 11-1 Preliminary Feasibility Study Schedule

The final step consists of selecting the best application among those reviewed, preparing a tentative plan to conduct a detailed feasibility study, and presenting the findings in an oral report to the appropriate persons in the organization.

Scheduling the Feasibility Study for a Preselected Application

Figure 11-2 depicts a schedule for the feasibility study of a small to moderate-sized application in which one to three experts are used to provide expertise in a single area. This schedule assumes that the development team includes knowledge crafters and apprentices, although the actual roles of knowledge crafters and apprentices are not distinguished here.

This schedule, which can last from two to eight weeks for this size application, includes the following 14 steps:

1. In this first step the knowledge-crafting team familiarizes itself with the problem area and the expertise involved by studying general descriptive material obtained from the organization, prospective users, and experts.

2. To launch the project, the knowledge-crafting team meets with representatives of management and the prospective end-users, as well as with the experts. The main purpose of the meeting is to focus on and review each person's motivations for the study and the application.

3. To give them a firsthand view of the dynamics of the application along with an overall impression of how the expert works to solve a problem, the knowledge-crafting team should observe the experts at work.

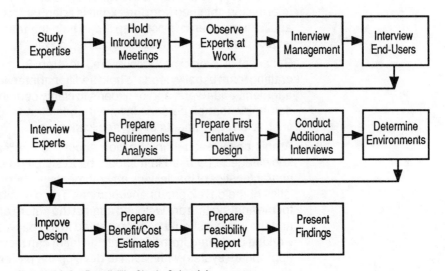

Figure 11-2 Feasibility Study Schedule

4. The team next interviews various persons in management to determine their view of the application and the expertise used to solve it. A key goal for this set of interviews should be the development of a management estimate of the potential benefits of the prospective application.

5. The knowledge crafters then interview members of the end-user community to determine their capabilities and requirements. These requirements should be compared to management's and any major conflicts resolved.

6. The team next conducts a series of in-depth interviews with each expert to determine the type of expertise used, how that expertise might be used to solve problems arising from the application domain, and the suitability of including that expertise into a knowledge-based system. These interviews are likely to require a substantial portion of the time taken for the feasibility study. The information obtained in these interviews needs to be correlated with that obtained during management and user interviews.

7. At this time, the team should have obtained sufficient information from management, the end-users, and the experts to produce a written requirements document that should be reviewed with the various parties. When approved, the requirements document should serve as a guideline for the development of the tentative design.

8. After reviewing the requirements document produced in the previous step as well as other information collected so far, the development team begins to sketch out a first, tentative design for applying the expertise to the problems that are to be addressed by the application and for interfacing the application to the users and possibly to various data bases and other computers. To some extent, this step can run in parallel with steps 6 and 7, although some design work cannot be begun until those steps are completed. In this step, the knowledge crafters determine whether the information obtained from the expert is adequate for designing the application; when it is not, step 9 can help the team focus on the weak spots in the information obtained so far.

9. Because of problems encountered in step 8, the knowledge-crafting team usually needs to hold additional interviews with management, end-users, and/or experts to clarify certain points and to determine that all persons involved understand the capabilities, cost, and requirements of the application.

10. At this point, enough information about the application and the knowledge to be used in it should be available to determine the characteristics of the delivery environment and then the characteristics of the development environment. The overall requirements for the final system are weighed against the nature of the expertise and the ways it should be represented in the delivery system. By working backward from this point, the team can thereby select the appropriate system with which to develop the prototype versions.

11.   Once the characteristics of the development and delivery environments have been determined, the team reviews the initial tentative design and continues refining it with these environments in mind. Additionally, the experts (and possibly representative end-users) are interviewed again to ensure that the major functions of the proposed application are understood and that the range of possible knowledge representation techniques available in the software development tool are adequate for the job. If several experts are being used to form a single corpus of expertise, this step should be used to verify that the respective pieces of expertise do indeed form a consistent whole.

12.   In this step the knowledge-crafting team determines the cost of developing the application as well as the benefits obtained from having it. Starting with step 4, the team should have been gathering information for determining the various benefits to be derived from the application. In this step those components are synthesized and contrasted with the expected cost for producing the application.

13.   In this step the team produces a written feasibility report describing the findings of the study. If the results of the study are positive, this document will serve as the basis for deciding whether to continue with the development of the system. The tentative design contained in this report will then serve as the starting point for the overall design effort.

14.   In this final step, the findings of the feasiblity study are presented to interested parties in the organization.

Of course, at any time in the study the development team may discover that the application is infeasible and should be abandoned. Alternatively, some of the steps may have to be repeated when certain details do not mesh properly.

Scheduling the Design Effort

The feasibility study should culminate in an initial overall design based on the information obtained during the study. The design effort must then refine this initial design and test it against the requirements of the application. Finally, once the design is complete, it must be documented and organized as a working plan for the development of the various prototype versions. Figure 11-3 depicts this overall process, which can take from 2 to 12 weeks, depending on the complexity of the application.

The process entails the following eight steps:

1.   First, the development team reviews the initial feasibility study design and conducts additional interviews with both experts and end-users to learn more about how the expertise is used to solve the problem and how the end-users might use the system. With this additional information, the knowledge-crafting team is likely to

uncover inconsistencies or incomplete areas in the expertise and have to refine their understanding of how the end-users relate to the expertise in the framework of the application. In addition, the knowledge-crafting team should formulate the detailed design of the man-machine interface and of all necessary support features, such as a help system (if required).

2. The knowledge crafters next review the refined design to evaluate its quality, both with respect to solving the problem at hand and to meeting the overall requirements for the application. Management, representative end-users, and experts alike are expected to participate in the review.

3. The development team then reviews the findings of the step 2 evaluation and further refines the design. By this time, the development and delivery environments for the application should have been determined.

4. The knowledge crafters, with help from management, representative end-users, and experts, evaluate the results of step 3 for completeness and for compliance with the requirements established for the application. After this review, the development team determines whether the design is complete and ready for prototyping. If it is not, steps 3 and 4 must be repeated until the design is fully developed.

5. The knowledge crafters now complete the documentation in preparation for a major design review and subsequent prototype development. Because design documentation should have been developed in parallel with the development of the design, starting with the initial feasibility study design, this step should be quite brief.

6. This step serves as the major review of the design. The knowledge-crafting team determines whether the design matches the requirements of the application sufficiently well to proceed with prototype development. Problems encountered in the review should be resolved by further design work (e.g., by cycling through steps 3 and 4) before prototype development can begin.

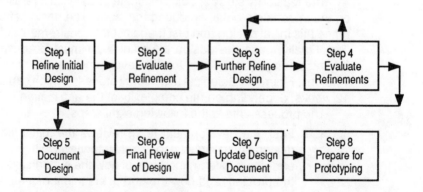

Figure 11-3 Design Schedule

7. In this step the team updates the design document to reflect any changes resulting from the design review.

8. Finally, the knowledge crafters prepare for prototype development by estimating the expected number of prototype versions, identifying how the prototyping is to proceed, and defining other milestones that will occur during prototyping.

Scheduling Prototype Development

The key to the successful development of a prototype application is the scheduling of a series of intermediate prototype versions with increasing coverage or functionality specified for each successive version. Just how many such versions are required depends on the number of areas of expertise involved, the total number of experts, and the overall size and complexity of the application. For a small to intermediate-sized application with a single expert, approximately four intermediate prototype versions may suffice, but for more complex applications involving two or three areas of expertise, eight to ten intermediate prototype versions may be required. Figure 11-4 shows a typical schedule for a small to intermediate-sized application requiring a single expert; a detailed description of these steps follows.

1. The knowledge-crafting team develops the first prototype of the application using the overall design specification developed previously. This version should contain the overall structures for representing the knowledge and the mechanisms to begin to reason with information stored in these structures. Typically, the knowledge crafters will encounter inconsistencies, which will necessitate additional interviews with the expert.

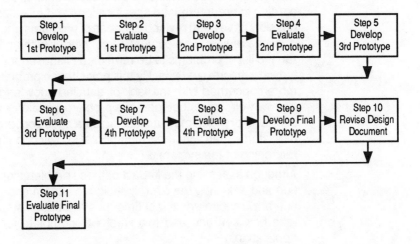

Figure 11-4 Prototype Development Schedule

The degree of completeness of this first prototype version cannot easily be predicted. Many details may have to be omitted at this stage. A minimal amount of detail is required, however, to test the ability of the overall structure to solve at least a piece of the problem.

This first prototype version should not take very long to build. Assuming that a workable development environment is used and that the development team includes two knowledge crafters and two apprentices, this version should take between four and eight weeks to develop and test.

2.   Next, the knowledge-crafting team, together with representatives of management, end-users, and experts, rigorously evaluates the first prototype with respect to the preestablished milestones. Problems detected in the version must be reviewed and priorities set for solution.

This step normally requires between one and two weeks. Additional time may be required for the development team to determine, document, and schedule any design changes that the evaluation may have mandated.

3.   The development team next develops the second prototype version based on the overall system design, as well as on any design changes required by the previous analysis. After the changes in the overall structure of the knowledge and the reasoning associated with it are made and tested, the appropriate detail can be added as originally planned. The emphasis in this and succeeding versions should begin to shift from representing and using the knowledge to developing and refining the prototype user interface and interfaces to data bases and/or other computers or systems.

The time to complete and test this version should be between four and eight weeks.

4.   The new prototype is subjected to a comprehensive evaluation according to predetermined specifications and milestones that may possibly have been revised because of problems uncovered in the previous review. This evaluation concludes with an itemized and ranked list of problems to be remedied in subsequent prototypes, typically the next version. By this point, these problems should be more concerned with the lack of detailed knowledge to solve a narrowly circumscribed part of a problem, problems with the user interface, or problems in accessing data bases or other computers or systems than with the fundamental knowledge structures and reasoning of the system.

Although assessing the impact of these problems on the application and adjusting the overall design to accommodate their solution may require additional time, this evaluation step should only take between one and two weeks to complete for this type of application.

5–8. Steps 5 through 8 provide for the production of two additional prototype versions and are similar to steps 3 and 4, except in the level of detail. In each case, the evaluation step should be rigorous and include additional detailed testing by end-users and experts.

   The time to complete these steps should be approximately the same as the time for steps 3 and 4, although more time may be required for additional testing and detailed analysis of problem areas.

9. After the fourth prototype version has been developed, the application should be complete, and step 8 should have uncovered any lingering problems. Therefore, the purpose of step 9 is to correct any problems and test a final prototype. This step should take between two and four weeks.

10. In step 10 the team makes any revisions to the design documentation that may be required as a result of changes effected in the prototypes. This step can operate in parallel with step 9 and may be considered as part of that step.

11. In step 11 the final prototype is reviewed in preparation for the pilot development effort. While most of the problems dealing with the mechanics of the application should have been solved during the construction of the intermediate prototype versions, the purpose of this final evaluation is to determine whether the problems of the application are actually solved satisfactorily by the expertise now contained in the system and whether the application in prototype form meets its design goals well enough to continue with pilot development. During this examination, certain problems may occur in the prototype and require fixing before the analysis can be completed. This step should take between two and four weeks.

   If the application involves more than one area of expertise, the prototype development schedule would be different from the one shown in Figure 11-4. For instance, with two areas of expertise, the schedule shown in Figure 11-5 might apply.

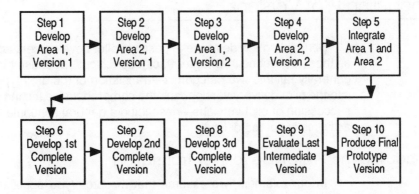

Figure 11-5 A Schedule for Developing Prototypes with Multiple Areas of Expertise

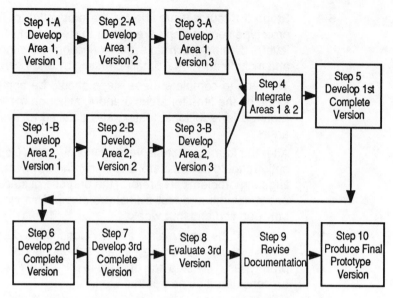

Figure 11-6 A Schedule for Parallel Protoype Development

Each step in this schedule includes both build and evaluate steps similar to those shown in Figure 11-4. In this schedule, however, each area is separately built, tested, evaluated, and changed. Several prototype versions are then used to integrate both areas of expertise as they relate to the whole problem area. This schedule also assumes a development team of two knowledge crafters working with two apprentices.

Greater parallelism can be obtained with two development teams, as shown in Figure 11-6. In this type of schedule each team works independently for three steps to develop one area of expertise separately from the other. After both areas have been developed to a predetermined point, the two teams work together to integrate the areas and complete the development of the application.

Scheduling Pilot Versions

Scheduling a wide range of possible pilot development activities, such as those described in Chapter 9, can be difficult. Because these activities generally fall into two categories—translation of the prototype application into the pilot delivery version, and the comprehensive testing of a possible succession of pilot versions—describing a general schedule for these two activities is not too difficult.

Scheduling the Prototype to Pilot Translation

In our example, we assume that the prototype application must be manually translated to the pilot system. Typically, this translation entails some restructuring of the knowledge base used in the prototype system. If the restructuring is unnecessary, the schedule for translating the knowledge

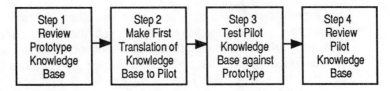

Figure 11-7 A Schedule for Pilot Development of the Knowledge Base

base may be substantially less complex. In fact, when both the prototype and pilot delivery environments offer some tool support, such a translation step may not be necessary at all. Figure 11-7 shows an illustrative schedule for a major translation effort.

The following description of the four steps does not include the time to complete them because of the widely differing prototype and pilot environments possible and the diverse characteristics of potential applications.

1. From the feasibility study through prototype development, the knowledge crafters should have planned for the pilot (and final) delivery environment. In this step the development team reviews the prototype design to ensure that the prototype environment has remained compatible with the requirements for translation to the delivery environment. If inconsistencies are discovered, the team must resolve these problems, amending the prototype or pilot environment as necessary. Finally, the development team should plan and schedule the actual translation effort, selecting milestones as appropriate.

2. In this step the development team translates the prototype to the pilot delivery environment. Wherever possible, this translation should parallel the functions and facilities contained in the prototype version, so that the testing facilities in the prototype tool can be used to compare intermediate pilot results with similar results in the prototype delivery version.

3. The knowledge crafters next conduct a rigorous test of the translated pilot knowledge base to flush out any inconsistent behavior between the knowledge bases of the prototype and pilot systems and to tune the knowledge base in the pilot delivery version to match that of the prototype version.

4. Finally, the knowledge-crafting team, as well as managers, experts, and representative end-users, conducts a general review of the pilot delivery system to determine that the knowledge base has been translated successfully. This step includes making any necessary revisions to the design documentation.

This schedule only describes the means for translating the knowledge base from the prototype environment to the pilot delivery environment. It deliberately does not describe how the remainder of the system is taken from prototype to pilot because that process depends almost entirely on the nature of the specific application.

In many cases the knowledge base cannot be decoupled from the rest of the application because the operation of the inferencing mechanism in conjunction with the knowledge base influences or drives the user interface and other interfaces to data bases and/or other systems or computers. Therefore, as the knowledge base is moved, the remainder of the system, including various interfaces, must also be moved or translated into the pilot delivery environment; the process of moving these portions of the application may be substantially more complex than the process of moving the knowledge base.

Scheduling Pilot Testing

Once the entire pilot delivery version of the application has been created, pilot testing can begin. Although the wide range of possible applications prevents describing a detailed schedule for this activity, the general schedule shown in Figure 11-8 is typical for such testing.

1.   Management, experts, and representative end-users should work with the development team to test and evaluate the first pilot delivery version of the application. The pilot version should match or exceed the capabilities of the prototype.

2.   The knowledge-crafting team then refines the first pilot version based on the items uncovered in the previous step. Most refinements will affect the user and various other interfaces, not the functioning of the knowledge base.

3.   In this step the development team, with help from managers and end-users, tests the system to ensure that the refinements have been applied properly. If problems are uncovered in this step, the team may need to cycle through steps 2 and 3 one or more times.

4.   In this step the team must prepare various support materials and documentation, including user documentation and system maintenance documentation. Additionally, training and support plans for the remainder of the effort should be prepared at this point. Finally, any changes or corrections to the design documentation should be made at this time.

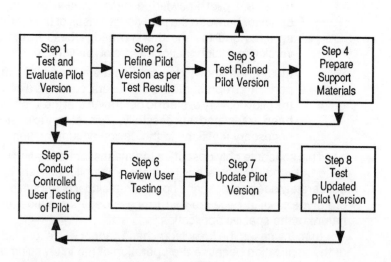

Figure 11-8   A Schedule for Pilot Testing

5.   At this point, the pilot system should be ready for controlled user testing. User reactions as well as problems with the operation of the system should be recorded for careful analysis by the development team and possibly by the experts.

6.   The knowledge-crafting team then reviews the results of the user testing and, if necessary, defines adjustments to the pilot version to correct these problems.

7.   The pilot version is changed to include the adjustments or refinements deemed necessary in the previous step.

8.   The development team, management, experts, and end-users test the updated pilot system. If additional refinements were found necessary, steps 5, 6, 7, and 8 would be repeated. One or more additional user testing cycles may also be necessary, so that steps 5 through 8 would be repeated several more times.

The crafting of a yacht involves a number of skilled activities, some of which are quite critical to the successful launching of a high-quality yacht. Similarly, a number of critical factors are involved in the construction of a knowledge-based application. Chapter 12 sets forth a selection of key principles to guide the knowledge crafter.

Crafting Successful Knowledge-Based Systems

In working with organizations to develop a number of knowledge-based applications, we have observed firsthand many factors that are especially critical to the successful development of such applications. This chapter presents our selection of the key principles that a knowledge crafter should remember in building a system. The absence of a factor from our list implies only that it is not as critical as others for keeping a project out of trouble or for facilitating progress; it does not imply that the factor is unimportant and can be ignored.

Our recommendations have been grouped into three categories for reference purposes:

1. **Design**—This category covers the determination of the general structure of the application system, the selection of the development tool, the selection of the delivery vehicle, and so forth.

2. **Knowledge crafting**—This category covers the knowledge acquisition activities coupled with system development and testing.

3. **Operations**—This category covers the pilot operation of the system, as well as the long-term operation and support of the application system.

Knowledge-based system technology offers a powerful capability; when it is properly used, organizations can obtain significant benefits. As with the use of any new technology, though, a knowledge-based application will not automatically provide wonderous benefits to every user. The technology has its pitfalls, and knowledge crafters must try to avoid these difficulties when building an application.

Design

Our first recommendations relate to the design phase because the design established for an application provides the framework for the rest of the development effort. A good crafting of the knowledge cannot compensate for a poor design.

Devote Adequate Resources to the Design

The knowledge-crafting team should carefully plan and develop the application's design. Properly performed, the design activity can make the rest of the development effort much easier. Rushed or skipped, it can make future activities much more difficult. When a project is initiated, the high interest and excitement pressures the team to "get going." This sentiment, coupled with the well-known capabilities of many knowledge-based systems for rapid prototyping, can tempt the knowledge crafters to short-change the design effort and start building the application too soon. Yes, rapid prototyping can overcome some of the problems resulting from a poor initial design. And yes, even the best prepared design will require subsequent revision. However, neither of these facts is an argument to omit the design phase.

We are aware of one project in which the development team jumped immediately into prototype development. Team members fanned out in parallel to interview experts, excitedly entering a rule into the prototype system whenever a piece of information was gleaned from one of the experts. When we asked whether the team needed to include rules covering a particular aspect of the domain, we were informed that the requirements would be defined by the completed prototype so that it was premature to exclude anything from the evolving prototype. Needless to say, the performance of the application became a significant issue, particularly during pilot testing.

Faith in the power of rapid prototyping is deep-seated. A critic of our methodology takes exception to our concept of a feasibility study (Chapter 5), arguing that rapid prototyping makes the concept of a feasibility study obsolete, that a developer should simply build a prototype to learn whether it can be done. But this action is a misuse of the technology. Rapid prototyping is ideal for exploring possible knowledge-base organizations; little information is generally available about this area of the application, and any insights must be developed experimentally. However, rapid prototyping contributes little to other aspects of the feasibility study.

The knowledge-based application, despite the different technology employed, is a computer program. The better the initial design for the system, the smoother the development effort will proceed. The facilities of the inference engine and development tools will still be more effective than conventional techniques; they will just be applied to a better base and hence contribute to an even better project. The capabilities of the technology should not be wasted on rescuing an ill-conceived, poorly designed project.

Decompose the Problem

When confronted with a problem that appears too large or too complex, the knowledge crafter should attempt to decompose it into smaller pieces that can be tackled individually. The best decomposition technique to use will depend on the characteristics of the particular problem.

Many types of problems are suited to a layered approach, with each layer representing the problem at a different level of abstraction. At the highest level of abstraction, the entire problem is covered. Because of that abstraction, however, the problem is a much simpler one to solve. The next lower levels of abstraction then consider pieces of the problem, as laid out by the top level solution. Here the complexity is greater, but the problem is smaller, with the net result being a simpler problem. This layering can be carried down as many levels as appropriate for the particular application.

Alternatively, the problem may be decomposable into a number of relatively independent pieces. Each subproblem can then be solved separately, and the results combined and assembled. Usually, because the pieces are not completely independent, the entire procedure will have to be repeated a few times before an acceptable solution is reached. However, because a smaller problem is addressed at each step, the solution process should still be faster than for the undecomposed problem.

All too often, decomposition is not considered during the design stage. A 50-rule demonstration version of an application may work beautifully, but the developers may fail to realize that the knowledge structure they have chosen will not scale up satisfactorily. We know of one rule-based application that encountered such difficulties. By the time the application had grown to 1,000 rules it was very difficult for any person on the project to understand the entire rule-set. By the time the rule count reached 2,000, the application was "out of control." Simple changes and additions produced unexpected side effects. Only by decomposing and restructuring the knowledge base was the project team able to deliver a successful application.

Decomposition is not a panacea since some problems cannot be decomposed meaningfully. The approach, however, is very helpful whenever it can be applied. Decomposition brings with it simplicity, and simplicity provides a multitude of benefits, including better problem conceptualization, cleaner design, and easier maintenance.

Fit the Structure to the Problem

The various forms of knowledge representation selected for an application must fit the characteristics of the problem. One of the worst mistakes that a knowledge crafter can make is to attempt to "force" an application into an unnatural form or structure. Such force fitting is usually done for the "best of reasons" (e.g., "we already have this tool so using it will be much cheaper"). The result, however, is a recipe for disaster.

We know of one project at a major corporation that selected a development tool for reasons that were unrelated to the characteristics of the application. After one year and one million dollars, a working prototype had been constructed. Some colleagues of ours were involved in a different but related application for another division of that corporation. The prototype for that application reached an equivalent performance level in one third the time at a fraction of the cost. Much as we would like to conclude that our colleagues were much more highly skilled, that was not the case. Both project teams were made up of equivalently talented individuals. The difference in results stemmed from the development tool used. One tool fit the problem while the other was a poor match; one team focused on development while the other was distracted by difficulties arising from the attempt to map the problem into the structure supported by the tool.

Generally, the complexity of an application grows exponentially with the degree of representational misfit. A common way to deal with an escalating level of complexity is to modify the scope of the application to better fit the tool being used, but then the application will not likely satisfy its original objectives. In addition, because of the compromises made to "get it working," user satisfaction with the resulting application generally declines as the degree of misfit increases.

Devote Adequate Resources to the User Interface

The knowledge crafters should recognize that the user interface is an extremely important part of the application, particularly for those applications that involve the user in the reasoning process. Such deep reasoning systems are intended to guide the user in the solution process rather than to provide the solution directly. Consequently, the quality and character of the interface directly affect the quality of the analysis.

Regardless of the role that the interface plays in the reasoning process, the interface is critical to the acceptance of the system. A knowledge-based system with little knowledge will not be viewed favorably, regardless of the man-machine interface, but even a superbly "intelligent" system will receive poor marks if the user interface is awkward or difficult to use.

Some user interface issues are obvious (e.g., a nontypist should not have to do much typing). Still others are a function of the problem. Other more subtle ones will only be discovered after a human user tests a prototype. A good knowledge-crafting project can devote from 25 to 45% of its resources to the development, implementation, and testing of the user interface and to the preparation of good user documentation.

Knowledge Crafting

Many of our recommendations apply to the knowledge-crafting process, including the acquisition of the knowledge from the expert(s), the development of the application system, and the testing of the various prototypes.

Generate Expert Interest

An *active* expert is one who actively seeks to develop and perfect the system. A *passive* expert is one who merely cooperates with the knowledge crafters, responding as needed to help them build the system. An active expert is much more effective than a passive one. Not only will more nuances in the expertise be detected and incorporated in the application, but an appropriate structure for the domain knowledge will likely be developed sooner and the expert will likely contribute expertise to some of the testing and debugging functions as well. The result is a better system developed in a shorter time.

Accordingly, the knowledge-crafting team should enlist the active aid of the expert. One way to appeal to experts is to show them how the application will assist in:

- Off-loading some of the current workload to more junior personnel, freeing time to permit the pursuit of more interesting tasks or the further enhancement of expertise
- Reducing the number of "emergency calls" that have to be responded to immediately
- Analyzing a problem more rapidly and more consistently.

One of the best mechanisms to generate an expert's interest, however, is to bring that person into the project at a very early stage. Working with the developing system as it evolves serves not only to build enthusiasm but also to instill a feeling of ownership. A working prototype should be built as quickly as possible. Once completed, the expert's ideas can be incorporated and demonstrated the next day. This ability to provide real, and nearly immediate, feedback to the expert is an important mechanism to generate excitement.

Use an Experienced Knowledge-Crafting Team

Few people would disagree with the advice to use experienced personnel on a project. However, many organizations are faced with situations in which experienced personnel are simply not available. The company seeking to develop its first knowledge-based application, for example, will rarely have an experienced knowledge-crafting team on its staff. Nevertheless, attempting an application development effort with a team lacking broad experience is a recipe for disaster. We have found that novices, no matter how well meaning, lack the perspective to avoid some of the technology's pitfalls.

All too often a novice gains experience for a development project by experimenting with a small rule-based tool on a microprocessor. This individual then brings a rule-based bias to the project, being unaware of the other types of representations that might be used more appropriately for some types of knowledge representation. The situation is like that of the African Bushman in the movie, "The Gods Must Be Crazy." Had that man's tribe been given a number of bicycles instead of the Coke bottle (and trained in their use and maintenance), those people would have believed that they had the most wonderful transportation mechanism imaginable. Furthermore, they could have put the bicycles to good use. Yet, these individuals would have had no knowledge or appreciation of other means of transportation that might be even more appropriate for serving certain travel needs, such as a boat for traveling along a river.

A bicycle may indeed be appropriate for a particular transportation requirement (e.g., delivery of financial documents in a congested downtown area), but it is far better to select knowledgeably a bicycle than to use one because it is the only known vehicle. Similarly, knowledge crafters should choose appropriate knowledge representations based on information about the alternatives rather than defaulting to the only representation with which they are familiar.

Advances in the technology pose further problems for the inexperienced knowledge crafter. Interfaces that permit many aspects of the technology to be hidden from the developer can now be built. This feature is often promoted because it permits knowledge crafters to develop applications without having to understand the technology. Reducing the skill and training needed is a desirable goal, but it can be achieved only if the technology has actually been simplified. Many aspects of knowledge-based technology today cannot be simplified to the degree sometimes advertised. The consequences of having developers use a technology they do not understand to build an application should be obvious. If a product sounds too good to be true, it probably is.

Consider the problem of reasoning under uncertainty. As discussed in Chapter 13, some reasoning methods are quite complex. Further, the conclusions drawn from a given situation will vary significantly depending on the type of reasoning employed. Yet, some tools hide details of the reasoning mechanism in the interest of simplicity, a successful move when the tool's behavior matches the developer's intuitive expectation. In other cases, however, the developer believes that the reasoning is being performed in a different manner, and thus the application appears to behave in unexpected or mysterious ways. Development becomes a frustrating and difficult process. Selecting a simplified tool because it permits inexperienced personnel to develop applications is a very risky course of action.

What, then, should an organization do if it wants to apply the technology but has not developed a team of experienced knowledge crafters? Basically, it must either acquire or develop such a team. Hiring experienced individuals will, of course, satisfy the hiring organization's immediate needs, but from a broader perspective this action does not address the overall needs of society for such individuals.

Developing an experienced team, on the other hand, requires a training program. The apprenticeship methodology described in earlier chapters is one approach. Qualified personnel (e.g., consultants) can be acquired to provide the experience, and existing personnel from within the organization can serve as the apprentices.

Formal education is another approach. Unfortunately, only a few existing courses are directed toward the process of knowledge crafting. Many vendors provide classes, sometimes with impressive titles, but most of them only provide instruction in tool usage. That is, these courses teach students *how* to use the commands of a particular tool but not *when* to use them.

What students need is experience in developing real applications rather than practice on toy problems. Only in this way can they understand the development issues as opposed to the programming issues. We know of one organization that provided a simple tool (along with some training in using that tool) to a number of its employees from a broad range of departments. As might be expected, this approach produced many people able to work with the selected tool but no one who understood its underlying principles well enough to develop a system.

This situation is analogous to the "blank paper" problem. Without training and experience in analyzing problems and structuring knowledge relative to those problems, an individual finds it very difficult to lay out an appropriate knowledge structure on a blank sheet of paper. Once a good structure has been developed (i.e., the paper has been written on), the logic is easily understood. Even the novice can then work with that structure, attach knowledge to it, and so forth. The problem lies in knowing what to put on the sheet of paper in the first place.

Do It Right the First Time

Not only should the development team carefully conduct the design phase, but it should also avoid shortcutting any knowledge-crafting activities. The savings that might be obtained by using a one-person knowledge-crafting team are illusory, for the insights of the second person (as well as the synergy between the two) make an important contribution to the project.

Because so little is known about building knowledge-based systems, knowledge crafters must experiment, testing different ideas as an application evolves. They should not be in such a hurry to construct the system as to eliminate this type of experimentation. Even though existing development tools enable small experiments to be quickly assembled and conducted, critics will nevertheless complain that such activities are wasteful. The knowledge gained from an experiment, however, will likely pay for the development cost of that experiment several times over, particularly for design concepts relating to the application's man-machine interface.

Plan Ahead for Testing/Debugging

Knowledge-based system development tools provide an array of facilities to assist the developer in testing and debugging the application system. Consequently, knowledge crafters can be lulled into a false sense of security, leaving testing and debugging issues to be considered "later." Unfortunately, those individuals will eventually discover that needed interfaces are missing, interfaces that should have been put into the system during implementation to facilitate subsequent testing and debugging.

Similarly, knowledge crafters should not build a system without specifying how it will be tested. What types of test cases will be needed and how will such data be obtained? How will test cases be introduced into the system? Must a driver be built so that the data for each case will not have to be entered manually each time a test is run? Can the testing be focused easily so that various sections of the application system can be tested as they are implemented? Planning ahead for testing and debugging may seem like drudgery, but the effort spent in advance will be paid back many times over in savings as the application is developed.

Watch Out for Spurious Knowledge

Test cases serve as a vehicle for examining whether the application (or some part of the application) is functioning as expected. The role of testing is to determine whether sufficient expertise has been accumulated and properly represented to enable the knowledge-based system to produce an appropriate solution for each test case. Failure to produce the desired responses for a test case is indicative of a problem, either a representational error or a lack of proper knowledge. If the problem is a knowledge problem rather than a bug, the knowledge crafter must remember that new knowledge must come from the experts, from research, from experiments—not from the test cases.

Using test cases to develop new knowledge is very dangerous. Although the application will be able to process the test data with much greater accuracy, the application's ability to process other problems properly will not have been improved. The temptation to draw the "obvious" conclusion from the test data in order to make the application perform better is one that must be resisted.

Consider as an analogy the knowledge crafter attempting to build an application that will predict prices in the stock market. In looking over a variety of data associated with the test cases (the last 20 years of stock market price history), this individual notices a direct correlation between the league represented by the winner of the January Super Bowl and whether the stock market rose or fell that year. Clearly, including this rule in the application will permit the knowledge-based system to predict correctly the direction of stock market prices for all test cases. However, our hapless knowledge crafter has only illustrated that a time series of finite duration can always be matched by some other time series—if one only looks hard enough. The "knowledge" that the identity of the Super Bowl winner influences stock prices is strictly spurious.

Deriving "relationships" from test data is not the only way to introduce spurious knowledge into a knowledge base. The knowledge crafters can introduce it unsuspectingly by focusing on the technology rather than on the expert. Consider, for example, the development of a scheduling system. The computer can provide a myriad of numerical data about the activities to be scheduled, and the knowledge crafters may attempt to obtain relevant expertise from experts about how they manipulate these data to produce a good schedule. Often such biasing questions as "What do you do with the job that has the greatest amount of processing left?" or "What do you do with the pilot that has had the greatest variance in flying time per segment?" are asked.

Because human beings are quite poor at carrying out large quantities of numerical computations, however, good schedulers tend to find approaches that involve tasks they do well (e.g., parallel processing to detect patterns) and avoid approaches that involve tasks they do poorly (e.g., numerical computations). Attempts to determine how an expert handles quantitative measures will therefore only elicit guesses on how those data might be used. Because most experts want to be helpful, they will try to provide answers to the knowledge crafter's questions, even if they have to invent them. Thus, many of the "insights" into the use of quantitative measures by the expert would likely be spurious. Knowledge crafters must focus on what an expert actually does without introducing any bias about what they think that expert is or should be doing.

Decompose the Testing Process

The decomposition of the testing process should parallel the decomposition of the problem; the test structure should match the problem or system structure. Test cases will be needed for the subsystem or component level, as will mechanisms to drive those tests. Trying to test a component of the application with a full-system test case is not only inefficient but frustrating as well.

Similarly, the knowledge crafter must recognize that some form of driver may be needed to conduct such a subsystem test, compensating for the missing portions of the system. Although savings realized in the testing process will more than cover the development cost, the construction of such drivers must be performed in parallel with the development of the application system (and the interface for attaching such test drivers should be part of the application design).

Stage the Receipt of Benefits

One of the more important reasons for developing an application in stages is to be able to derive an increasing level of benefits over the course of the development project. Not only is staged completion desirable from an economic standpoint (some payback occurs early in the project), but it reduces development risk as well (an early assessment of the system can be made before too many resources have been committed).

Another very important reason is that a staged completion retains the interest of all those involved in the project—experts, prospective users, and management alike. Seeing benefits begin to flow from the system keeps interest alive and builds enthusiasm. Such showcasing also provides early feedback from these constituencies, enabling design changes to be made or enhancements planned before too much effort has been invested in the development.

Some knowledge crafters are reluctant to show their system "before its time," arguing that people will be turned off by the lack of function. Their system should not be shown, but only because they have made inappropriate development decisions, such as leaving the man-machine interface to last, focusing instead on the development of the knowledge base and inferencing procedures. The concept of staged completion, however, is still valid. If the knowledge crafters had made adequate plans, the user interface could have been brought along the development path at the same rate as other portions of the system. Staged growth occurs in terms of system depth or breadth, not in terms of function. With a development plan oriented toward a staged delivery of system capabilities, the knowledge crafters can show a meaningful application to interested people at various stages of development.

Operations

Our final recommendations relate to the operational phases of the project.

Plan for Evaluation

The major focus during the pilot operation of the application should be on evaluation, which often requires that extensive data be collected. Some types of data may be collected manually, particularly when activities on the human side of the interface are measured, such as attitudes and time spent searching for information in manuals. A human observer equipped with a stopwatch is often sufficient. In other cases, data must be collected within the system about the desired aspects of system performance. In the best of circumstances, the data can be generated as a byproduct of normal operation so that the knowledge crafter will only have to record the data for later summarization. In other circumstances, however, the data desired for evaluation purposes may not even be calculated so that mechanisms must be implanted within the application to derive as well as record those data.

Retrofitting some of the data gathering and recording functions can be difficult and tedious if not properly planned. Thus, the necessary data gathering should be designed into the system. The experimental design (e.g., combinations of users, problems, and test environments) is only part of the process. The knowledge crafter must determine what is to be learned from the pilot operation and hence what data must be obtained from each experiment. Only then can the proper data collection facilities be prepared.

Ensure Availability of Adequate Support Services

To be applied effectively, the application system must be surrounded by a complement of support services. User-level documentation is required; user support (e.g., consulting) is needed. Personnel will be required to modify and enhance the system, keeping up with the domain as it evolves and extending the application's functionality over time. Without this type of support during the operational phase, the application system will quickly slide into disuse.

The issue, then, is one of quantity of the various services to be supplied (and of the means by which that quantity should be delivered). The quantity of (and delivery mechanism for) support services needed depends in large part on the environment surrounding a particular application. For example, a system being used by many individuals scattered in branch offices all over the country may require a 24-hour hot line to assist a user in trouble. While a system used by a few individuals in a single location might rely on those individuals for support, a large, complex system in a rapidly changing domain might require a large staff devoted to maintenance. On the other hand, a small, relatively stable application system might be maintained directly by the expert.

Obtain Support of Opinion Leaders

New technology does not introduce itself into an organization. A project champion is needed. Such a person is generally an opinion leader, a person who can motivate others to want to see new technology introduced into the organization.

With the backing of such an individual, the project team will find that experts become available, that resources for pilot testing are found, that maintenance and support teams are located, and that system roll-out to the operations group is accomplished. All too often, without the support of such a project champion, the knowledge-based application system will languish in the hands of the developers. The system falls into disuse at one or another stage of the development process and never proceeds to productive operational use. Large organizations are filled with inertia; a powerful individual is needed to help develop and maintain momentum within such an organization.

Accordingly, knowledge crafters should seek to identify such an individual early in the project (e.g., during the feasibility study) and take steps to enlist that person's support and active cooperation.

Summary

If our collection of recommendations could reflect but one concept, it would be *planning*. A knowledge-crafting team must:

- Plan for the man-machine interface
- Plan for the experimentation necessary to refine the design
- Plan for the best approach to generate enthusiasm on the part of the domain expert
- Plan for a rapid prototyping capability to permit contributions from the experts to be demonstrated quickly
- Plan for the staging of benefits
- Plan for needed debugging capabilities
- Plan for developing appropriate test data and validation data
- Plan for the necessary testing facilities
- Plan for testing tools that match the problem structure
- Plan for the data collection capabilities required to support the evaluation of system performance and capability during the period of pilot operation
- Plan for user training and support.

Clearly, plans alone do not make an application, and implementation is never a trivial undertaking. However, advance planning to ease the implementation problem has no substitute.

Many of our recommendations in this chapter relate to the proper use of knowledge-based systems technology. Viewed another way, this advice should help knowledge crafters avoid some of the difficulties that can arise in applying that technology. In particular, knowledge crafters must beware of:

- Relying on inexperienced personnel
- Confusing tool usage skills with knowledge about how to apply that tool to a problem
- Acquiring products that overly simplify the technology
- Scaling demonstration models up to full size
- Using tools whose structure does not match the problem
- Relying too much on rapid prototyping to atone for inadequate preparation
- Cutting corners to reduce costs
- Letting the technology rather than the expert drive the development activity
- Introducing spurious knowledge into the application

- Focusing on the reasoning aspects of the application to the exclusion of the man-machine interface
- Attempting the development of the application without adequate management and expert support
- Evolving a prototype into an operational application without adequate preparation for testing, conversion, and operational support.

PART III

Knowledge Representation

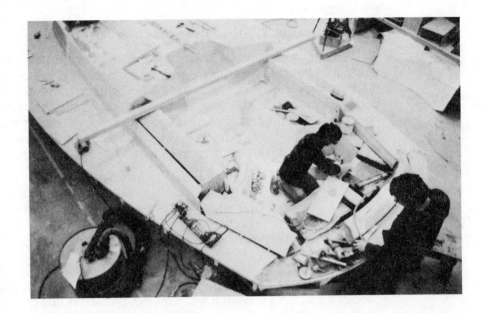

CHAPTER 13

Knowledge Crafting with Rule-Based Representations

The layout of the cockpit is guided by a collection of knowledge that has accumulated over the years. For example, the halyards must lead aft and be readily winched and cleated for ease of operation by anyone in the cockpit. The cleats must be placed aft of the winches at an angle consistent with the position of the crew and the seatback. The mainsheet traveler must be out of the way of the crew and yet available for easy operation by the crew and skipper. Consequently, the arrangement of the cockpit can be thought of as the result of the designers reasoning with a large collection of design rules. Similarly, part of the knowledge represented in an application knowledge base can be structured as a set of rules. These rules establish relationships between facts in the knowledge base and permit new facts or relationships to be derived. Consequently, part of the problem solution developed by an application can result from reasoning with a collection of rules. Chapter 13 discusses the ways in which knowledge can be structured and reasoned about by using rule-based representations.

Many knowledge-based software development tools focus on rule-based knowledge representation technology, among the more comprehensive of which are EMYCIN, OPS5, and S.1™. In each of these tool systems, rules are conceptually represented as IF/THEN statements with the logical form:

IF <predicate> THEN <consequent>

Using such statements, knowledge crafters formulate the knowledge they obtain from the experts into sets of such rules. The inference engine then analyzes and processes these IF/THEN rules in one of two ways: backward or forward. In backward-chaining, the inference engine works backward from hypothesized consequents to locate known predicates that would provide support. In forward-chaining, the inference engine works forward from known predicates to derive as many consequents as possible.

Backward-Chaining

In backward-chaining, the inference engine identifies a set of one or more hypotheses by finding those consequents that do not appear as predicate elements in other rules. Similarly, predicates that do not appear as the consequents of any other rule are marked as terminal predicates. The analysis process begins with the user specifying one or more hypotheses (either selected from the inference engine's generated list or selected from the set of rule consequents).

The reasoning process begins with the inference engine taking the first hypothesis and locating all rules having the hypothesis as a consequent. It then moves backward from the consequent to the predicate in each of those rules and tests the truth of the predicate. If any predicate tests TRUE, the consequent is established. It is added to (inserted into) the knowledge base, and the process either terminates or proceeds to examine the next user-specified hypothesis.

If the truth of no predicate can be determined, then each such unknown predicate is established as a new hypothesis and the process continues. The inference engine selects one of the new hypotheses, examines each rule having that hypothesis as a consequent, tests the predicate of each such rule, and so forth. This process forms a chain, linking rule predicates backward to the consequents of other rules—hence the term *backward-chaining*.

When one of the predicates being tested evaluates to TRUE, not only is the consequent of that rule inserted into the knowledge base, but the consequent of every other rule in the chain linking the predicate to the user-specified hypothesis is similarly inserted into the knowledge base and the user notified of the truth of the hypothesis. Again, the reasoning process either terminates or proceeds to examine the next user-specified hypothesis.

Should the backward-chaining process reach a terminal predicate and should the value of that predicate be unknown, either the user (or a data base) will be asked to supply the value, or the chaining along that path will be abandoned. Should the terminal consequents of all chains from the hypothesis test negatively, the testing of that hypothesis will be abandoned, and another one selected. This process continues until the appropriate number of user-supplied hypotheses has been proven true or until all hypotheses have been considered.

The system keeps track of the values of the predicates and only asks that a value be supplied when the predicate applies to a hypothesis being investigated and when the value of that predicate cannot otherwise be determined. These two properties permit the inference engine to behave similarly to a person questioning the user.

Backward-chaining is often used as the cornerstone of selection applications, in which one item is to be selected from a fixed set of items, for example, in diagnosing a particular failure to be one from a fixed set of known failure types.

Forward-Chaining

Forward-chaining also operates with sets of rules that look syntactically similar to backward-chaining rules. Each rule is examined, and each predicate is evaluated to determine its truth. The consequents of those rules with predicates evaluating to TRUE are then added to (inserted into) the knowledge base and the entire process repeated. The process continues until the truth of no additional consequents can be determined. Note that failure to derive the truth of a consequent does not necessarily mean that the consequent is FALSE; it only means that truth has not yet been established.

This process of reasoning from the consequent of one rule to the predicate of another forms a chain in the forward direction—hence the term *forward-chaining*. Conceptually, the reasoning process must evaluate the predicate of each rule whenever a new fact is inserted into the knowledge base. This, however, is very inefficient. Many inference engines maintain an elaborate set of pointers, enabling only those rules containing the new fact as a predicate clause to be reevaluated.

Forward-chaining essentially permits the knowledge crafter to use rules to develop as much information as possible from a limited set of initial data or to judge changes efficiently when a new data item is added. This type of reasoning would be appropriate in a monitoring situation, for example, in which it was desirable to learn as much as possible about the state of the monitored system based upon the available data.

A Simple Example

To illustrate the manner in which an inference engine might process a set of rules, consider a simple example of a set of rules that relates the type of day and my location to what I eat for lunch. These rules will be used first in a backward and then in a forward direction.

The Rules

The following seven rules constitute the knowledge base for the example. Assume that no other information is available at the time processing of the rules is initiated.

Rule 1:	IF	IT IS A WORKDAY
	AND	I AM IN THE OFFICE
	THEN	I EAT IN THE CAFETERIA
Rule 2:	IF	I EAT IN THE CAFETERIA
	THEN	I EAT SOUP AND A SANDWICH
Rule 3:	IF	IT IS A WORKDAY
	AND	I AM OUT OF THE OFFICE
	THEN	I EAT OUT
Rule 4:	IF	I EAT OUT
	THEN	I EAT CHINESE FOOD
Rule 5:	IF	IT IS A WEEKEND DAY
	AND	I AM AT HOME
	THEN	I EAT AT HOME
Rule 6:	IF	I EAT AT HOME
	THEN	I EAT SWEDISH PANCAKES
Rule 7:	IF	IT IS A WEEKEND DAY
	AND	I AM OUT SHOPPING
	THEN	I EAT OUT

The Hypotheses

The set of all basic hypotheses derived from this rule-set (i.e., the consequents that do not appear as predicates in any other rule in this rule-set) are:

1. I EAT SOUP AND A SANDWICH
2. I EAT CHINESE FOOD
3. I EAT SWEDISH PANCAKES.

The Terminal Predicates

Similarly, the terminal predicates (i.e., the predicates that do not appear as consequents in any other rule in this rule-set) are:

1. IT IS A WORKDAY
2. IT IS A WEEKEND DAY
3. I AM IN THE OFFICE
4. I AM OUT OF THE OFFICE
5. I AM AT HOME
6. I AM OUT SHOPPING.

How a Backward-Chaining Inference Engine Might Operate

The typical use of a backward-chaining rule-set is to prove a hypothesis. If you treat the above rule-set as the knowledge base for a backward-chaining inference engine, you would then select one or more hypotheses for testing from the list previously given. If you select all hypotheses for testing, the inference engine might operate as follows:

1. Select a possible hypothesis—

    1. I EAT SOUP AND A SANDWICH

2. Locate the hypothesis in the rule-set—

    <u>Rule 2</u>:   IF   I EAT IN THE CAFETERIA

                 THEN   I EAT SOUP AND A SANDWICH

3. Examine the predicates of the rule and determine whether they have been evaluated and, if not, evaluate them (In this case there is only a single predicate clause to evaluate.)—

    They evaluate to UNKNOWN

    (If the predicate had evaluated to TRUE, the hypothesis would be true and the process would terminate; if the predicate had evaluated to FALSE, then the inference engine would search for another rule having the same consequent as the hypothesis, i.e., the same consequent as the consequent of this rule.)

4. Locate a rule whose consequent contains one of the predicate clauses—

    <u>Rule 1</u>:   IF   IT IS A WORKDAY

                 AND   I AM IN THE OFFICE

                 THEN   I EAT IN THE CAFETERIA

5. Evaluate the predicates of this rule if they have not already been evaluated—

    They evaluate to UNKNOWN

6. Determine whether these are terminal predicates—

    They are:

    1. IT IS A WORKDAY

    3. I AM IN THE OFFICE

7. Ask the user for the value of each unknown predicate; if the value disproves the rule, select another path to the hypothesis, and, if no other path exists, try another hypothesis.

How a Simple Forward-Chaining Inference Engine Might Operate

The same rule-set can be used as the knowledge base for a forward-chaining inference engine. In this case, however, no hypotheses are provided because the rules are not used to try to derive the truth of any particular consequent. Rather, they are used to derive all possible consequents that can be derived from a set of predicates (actually from a set of values that cause one or more predicates to evaluate to TRUE).

If you provided the knowledge base with values such that the predicates

2.   IT IS A WEEKEND DAY

5.   I AM AT HOME

would evaluate to TRUE, a forward-chaining inference engine might operate as follows:

1.   The rules containing either of the provided predicates are located

Rule 5:	IF	IT IS A WEEKEND DAY
	AND	I AM AT HOME
	THEN	I EAT AT HOME
Rule 7:	IF	IT IS A WEEKEND DAY
	AND	I AM OUT SHOPPING
	THEN	I EAT OUT

and one is selected—

Rule 5 is selected.

2.   This rule is interpreted (*fired*)—

Rule 5:	IF	IT IS A WEEKEND DAY
	AND	I AM AT HOME
	THEN	I EAT AT HOME

and the consequent I EAT AT HOME is given the value TRUE.

3.   A search is made for a rule containing I EAT AT HOME as a predicate—

| Rule 6: | IF | I EAT AT HOME |
| | THEN | I EAT SWEDISH PANCAKES |

4.   The rule is interpreted (*fired*)—

I EAT SWEDISH CAKES is given the value TRUE.

5.   A search is made for a rule containing I EAT SWEDISH PAN-CAKES as a predicate—

No such rule exists.

6.   The process terminates.

Attributes of Rule-Based Applications Development Tools

Inference engines with rule-oriented processing capabilities have several attributes, as described below.

Rule-Sets

As indicated, each of the rule-based reasoning techniques simultaneously works on a group of related rules—the rule-set—to obtain information by a parallel matching of predicates or consequents. The order in which the rules are listed in the knowledge base should be unrelated to the order in which they will be considered or fired.

In some tools, only a single rule-set is permtted. In other tools, the rule population can be divided into proper subsets. Thus, only the relevant rules at a particular point in the inferencing process need be considered at any one time. For systems with a large number of rules, this subsetting capability can significantly improve execution efficiency and enable the knowledge crafters to decompose the problem.

Rule Format

Some rule-based tools provide both a backward- and a forward-chaining inference engine that operates on rules written in the same format. That is, the same rule (or the same rule-set) can be exercised in either a forward or a backward direction. Other tools require that forward-chained and backward-chained rules be written in different formats.

This latter type of tool is undesirable in situations where a rule-set is to be used in different directions at different times during the inferencing process. Two essentially identical rule-sets are not only esthetically displeasing, but also inefficient in the use of memory (duplicate storage) and error prone (the usual problem of maintaining two identical versions as modifications are made).

Controlling Rule-Set Execution

Those rule-based tools that permit multiple rule-sets to be defined generally provide some mechanism to control which rule-set is to be executed in which direction during the inferencing process. The knowledge crafter can thus select both the rule-set and the type of chaining to be used. In some rule-based tools, the mechanism used is the *meta rule,* which may have the form of regular rules or a special format. In other such tools, knowledge crafters may be provided with a special control language, or they may be required to use the underlying language of the tool (e.g., LISP), which is outside of the rule system. The use of meta rules results in a more cleanly defined system, while the special control language may provide for a somewhat simpler control specification. While utilizing the underlying language may require greater knowledge on the part of the developer, it also provides greater flexibility and fewer restrictions.

Pattern Matching

Inference engines, such as the one used in the previous forward-chaining example, use a *pattern-matching* algorithm that enables them to match a new data value with only those rules that reference that data value. Thus, predicates need be tested only for those rules that might be affected by the new value. The effectiveness of the pattern matcher in an inference engine can significantly affect the tool's execution efficiency. Not surprisingly, the matching scheme incorporated in the inference engine is one of the truly distinguishing characteristics of individual software tools.

Another characteristic of some pattern-matching algorithms is the ability to evaluate a given predicate only once, even though it might appear in more than one rule. Thus, in the previous example, if IT IS A WORKDAY is evaluated in connection with Rule 1, the resulting value will be used in Rule 3. The predicate clause will not have to be reevaluated to determine if IT IS A WORKDAY is true. (In this example, the evaluation of each predicate clause is trivial; however, in many cases predicates can become quite complex and require considerable computation to evaluate.) Not only do such pattern-matching algorithms contribute to the efficiency of the inference engine's operation, but they also prevent some of the side-effect problems that can occur from multiple evaluations of a predicate (see the subsection on multiple evaluation of predicates below).

Some inference engines are much less sophisticated and much more brute force in approach. Rather than working only with those rules whose predicates include new facts or newly provided data items, some forward-chaining inference engines arbitrarily test every rule in the knowledge base to see if it can be fired. If any rules are actually fired, then every rule in the knowledge base (that has not already been fired) will again be tested, and so on until no further rules can be fired. Were such an inference engine to be used in the forward-chaining example above, at least one predicate in each of the seven rules would be tested in Step 1, in each of six rules in Step 3, and in each of five rules in Step 5. Obviously, the inference engines of such tools are inefficient. When such a tool is used, the rule base must be segmented as much as possible to minimize the number of rules that must be considered at each step.

Closed-World Mode

Backward-chaining inference engines sometimes offer a *closed-world mode* assumption, under which a predicate evaluating to UNKNOWN will be given the value FALSE if no other information can be derived or obtained. In other words, anything that cannot be proven TRUE is assumed to be FALSE.

Some forward-chaining inference engines offer an analogous capability in which the negation of a consequent will be recognized as true if the consequent is not contained in the knowledge base.

Theoretical Equivalence of Backward- and Forward-Chaining

The forward- and backward-chaining techniques can be viewed to be equivalent. Knowledge crafters can reformulate the rules in one rule-set to form a new rule-set such that the information that was derived from one rule-set using forward-chaining can be derived from the other using backward-chaining (and vice versa). Thus, both forward-and backward-chainers need not necessarily be provided by the inference engine, although having both is certainly much more convenient for the knowledge crafter.

Variables

Some rule-based inference engines enable variables to be used in rules. This capability permits a single rule to be used in place of many rules. A variable contained in a rule's predicate may take on several different values, causing the rule to be *instantiated* several times, once with each different value of the variable. Thus, a single rule can be fired multiple times. This economy of representation is valuable for two reasons: not only do many fewer individual rules have to be written, stored, and processed, but, more importantly, the higher level form of representation enables the knowledge crafter to have a better grasp of the application's knowledge structure. The latter provides economy in rule development and structuring.

To illustrate, assume that we have the following set of rules:

Rule 1:   IF   THE HOUSE IS PAINTED RED
           THEN BUY RED GLOSS TRIM PAINT

Rule 2:   IF   THE HOUSE IS PAINTED GREEN
           THEN BUY GREEN GLOSS TRIM PAINT

Rule 3:   IF   THE HOUSE IS PAINTED BROWN
           THEN BUY BROWN GLOSS TRIM PAINT

Rule 4:   IF   THE HOUSE IS PAINTED WHITE
           THEN BUY WHITE GLOSS TRIM PAINT

Using the common convention of beginning a variable name with the question-mark symbol (?), these rules can be replaced by the following single rule:

Rule 1:   IF   THE HOUSE IS PAINTED ?COLOR
           THEN BUY ?COLOR GLOSS TRIM PAINT

If the knowledge base contains white and green houses, then the rule will be instantiated twice (once with the value white and once with the value green), so that both white and green gloss paint would be purchased.

Certainty Factors

Some inference engines also permit a weighting or *certainty factor* to be associated with each rule, as well as with each data item in the knowledge base. Thus, in the preceding rule-set pertaining to what I eat for lunch, the sixth rule might be written as:

RULE 6:   IF   I EAT AT HOME
          THEN I EAT SWEDISH PANCAKES (.6)

This rule can be interpreted to mean that if I am eating at home I will eat Swedish pancakes only 60% of the time.

A major characteristic of a rule-based tool is the manner in which it handles the logical processing of certainty factors. The combination of certainty factors in the predicates of rules involves an entirely different form of logic. Unfortunately, no one approach has universal applicability. Certain methods are appropriate for certain types of situations but not for others.

The following example illustrates the difficulty:

RULE 1:   IF   I EAT SOUP
                AND   (I EAT A SALAD
                OR   I EAT A SANDWICH)
          THEN I AM NO LONGER HUNGRY

Now, if I EAT SOUP has a certainty of .6, I EAT A SALAD a certainty of .3, and I EAT A SANDWICH a certainty of .5, then what certainty should be attached to I AM NO LONGER HUNGRY—.5, .3, .18 or some other value? One approach, based upon so-called fuzzy logic, was employed in the early MYCIN(1) system, in its various derivatives (e.g., EMYCIN, S.1), and in many PC-based development shells. Another approach involved the use of Bayesian logic, and was utilized in the Prospector(2) system.

The situation becomes even more complex when systems that use a three-valued logic are examined. The certainty range of 1.0 is divided into three intervals: the interval for which there is supporting evidence (i.e., TRUE), the interval for which no information is available (i.e., UNKNOWN), and the interval for which there is contradictory evidence (i.e., FALSE). The methods for examining the evidence are commonly categorized as evidential reasoning. They derive from the work of Dempster(3) and Shafer(4), and have been embodied in the Gister(5,6) system.

The logical handling of uncertainty by the inference engine being used must be understood. Without such an understanding, the knowledge crafter is likely to find that the inferencing mechanism performs differently than expected.

Problems with Rule-Based Systems

Most commercially available development tools provide some type of rule-based inferencing capability; a few provide only a rule-based inference engine. Several problems can arise when a rule-based knowledge representation is used within a system.

Multiple Evaluations of Predicates

A knowledge crafter can easily fall into a trap caused by multiple evaluations of a predicate. Although a predicate is assumed to be evaluated once successfully (and then the rule fires) or once unsuccessfully (and the rule then lies dormant), the inference engine will often reevaluate that predicate more than one time. Because an unsophisticated inference engine, for example, cannot determine if a change to a knowledge base will affect a given predicate or not, it reevaluates the predicate.

A rule predicate whose evaluation merely causes reference to be made to some data in the knowledge base poses no risk. The reference does not change the state of the knowledge base; if the inference engine were to evaluate the predicate more than once, the only side effect would be some extra computation. Rules often become more complex, however, incorporating representations that, when evaluated, will change the state of the knowledge base. For example, a predicate might contain reference to functions whose evaluation would not be free of side effects. Such functions often arise in the context of meta rules that attempt to control the selection and application of rule-sets. A counting function that adds one to a value each time it is called would be a simple example. It modifies a counter each time it is called so that another rule can determine the desirability of causing a state change. A less subtle example would be a predicate containing a function that requests input from (or provides output to) a user. Redundant predicate evaluations will produce redundant I/O for the user.

If the inference engine being used is one that permits multiple evaluations of a predicate or predicate clause in a rule, then the knowledge crafter must be very careful not to include any term within a predicate whose evaluation would have a side effect. Finding bugs caused by this behavior can sometimes be tedious.

Large Rule-Set Overloads

The development of large rule-sets can pose two types of problems for the knowledge crafter: inefficient execution and unmaintainable rule-sets.

If the inference engine does not have an efficient pattern-matching capability, a large rule-set will necessitate significant levels of computation (searching repeatedly through rules that do not apply or are irrelevant to the current state of the reasoning process). Moreover, the size of the rule-set may exceed the available physical memory, leading to considerable swapping activity as the system moves from one rule to another. (This latter effect will occur even if the inference engine uses a pattern-matching algorithm, unless the rules can be grouped logically.)

The second and more critical problem relates to the capabilities and training of the person attempting to work with the rule-set. Different people are more or less able to follow a number of logical relations and thus understand the knowledge base. If the rule structure or knowledge base is particularly complex, the knowledge crafter may not be able to define the optimum number of rules that should be contained in the rule-set.

As a general target, however, 50 rules in a rule-set seems manageable. The knowledge crafter should thus organize the knowledge representation for the problem so that the complete collection of rules can be broken down into proper subsets containing fewer than 50 rules each. The capabilities of some individuals and the problem type will increase or decrease that number, but only minimally.

If the problem does not appear to decompose nicely into small, independent rule-sets, the knowledge crafter should consider different representations of the problem or different organizations of the knowledge base. To avoid extra developmental difficulty (to say nothing of longer-term problems in maintaining the rule base), the knowledge crafter should be willing to spend considerable effort to find an appropriately decomposable structure for the knowledge base.

Uncertainty about Certainty

Regardless of the mechanism used to combine certainty factors within a rule, all of the techniques involving numeric certainty factors assume complex logical relationships between the rules and the various states which the reasoning process can enter. Further, it is very difficult for the knowledge crafter to ensure that the desired relationships hold over a large rule-set. Some development tools have special facilities to aid in the preparation and verification of appropriate weighting factors for rules, e.g., KAS(7) contains several tools to assist the knowledge crafter in establishing certainties for the Prospector system and in testing the effects of those assignments. Although such facilities are a considerable help, establishing the proper operation of a numeric certainty system across a large rule-set still remains a significant problem.

A Misfit to the Problem's Structure

Perhaps the most difficult problem to be faced by the knowledge crafter, particularly one not having had wide experience in developing knowledge-based systems for a variety of problems, occurs when the knowledge structure of the problem does not naturally fit the chosen form of representation. Such a difficulty might arise, for example, if the natural form of the problem would require one or more nonrule types of knowledge representations while the knowledge crafter wanted to use (or was required to use) a development tool that only offered a rule-based form of representation. Such a misfit can significantly affect the odds of completing a successful knowledge-based system.

Procedural Fever

The rule structures used in a rule-based system are not well suited for representing procedural information. With procedural information, the knowledge crafter must be concerned with the *order* in which rules fire, yet the entire focus of rule-based representations is to take ordering considerations out of the developer's hands. Representing procedural knowledge in a rule-based system thus entails considerable debugging. Because many developers (particularly those with limited [nonAI] computer experience) tend to think in procedural terms, they tend to build procedural representations—even when representing nonprocedural knowledge and even when using rule-based structures. Note, however, that some knowledge is best represented in procedural terms (e.g., algorithms to calculate numeric quantities), and no attempt should be made to represent that knowledge in nonprocedural terms.

Selecting an Appropriate Representation

Having identified that portion of the knowledge base that is best suited to a rule-based form of representation, the knowledge crafter then must select the type of reasoning (i.e., forward, backward, or both) to be performed on each rule-set.

In some organizations, a particular development tool has already been selected, perhaps for other applications. If that tool offers only one type of rule-based reasoning, then the developer's choice is clear (even though unsatisfying). Situations that force the problem representation to fit the tool (rather than selecting the tool to fit the problem) often create insurmountable problems.

The logic of the problem will favor one type of inferencing over the other. Many knowledge-based applications lend themselves to writing rules one way versus another. Convoluted or complex rules can easily make the knowledge base much more difficult to create, understand, and maintain.

Application Context

The context of the application may significantly affect the choice of the rule-based reasoning mechanism to use. Consider the following situations as an illustration:

- A system being designed to monitor a real-time process or a transaction-processing system will be receiving new data items from time to time. The purpose of the system is to determine the implications (if any) of each new data point. This situation is a natural fit for a forward-chaining type of inferencing.

- A system being designed to diagnose a problem will generally start its analysis with "all" the available facts. The purpose of the system is to determine the type of failure that has occurred. Additional tests are to be performed or additional data provided only if necessary to determine the existence of a particular problem state of interest. This situation is a natural fit for a backward-chaining type of inferencing.

- A different system, similarly intended to diagnose a situation, has many potential problem states. Again this system would begin with "all" the available information, but, based on the available information, it would first seek to determine the subset of problem states in which the system might reside. It would then determine whether the system was actually residing in any of those states. This situation is a natural fit for a forward-chaining type of inferencing to determine the set of potential states and then a backward-chaining type of inferencing with each of the possible states as a hypothesis to be investigated.

Performance

The performance of one reasoning technique over another may be significantly different for a given rule-set or for a given inference engine. Backward-chaining techniques may reduce the search set rather quickly; the pattern-matching abilities of some forward-chaining inference engines are very efficient. Thus, it may be significantly more efficient for the knowledge crafter to employ reasoning in one direction rather than the other when dealing with a particular problem structure or when using a particular tool.

References

1)   Shortliffe, E. E., *Computer-Based Medical Consultations: MYCIN,* Elsevier, New York, N.Y., 1976.

2)   Duda, R. O., P. E. Hart, and N. J. Nilsson, "Subjective Bayesian Methods for Rule-Based Inference Systems," in *Readings in Artificial Intelligence,* B. L. Webber and N. J. Nilsson editors, Tioga Publishing Company, Palo Alto, Calif., 1981.

3)   Dempster, A. P., "A Generalization of Bayesian Inference," *Journal of the Royal Statistical Society,* Volume 30, 1968.

4)   Shafer, G., *A Mathematical Theory of Evidence,* Princeton University Press, Princeton, N.J., 1976.

5)   Lowrance, J. D., T. D. Garvey, and T. M. Strat, "A Framework for Evidential-Reasoning Systems," *Proceedings of the Fifth National Conference on Artificial Intelligence,* AAAI, Menlo Park, Calif., 1986.

6)   Lowrance, J. D., *Evidential Reasoning with Gister: A Manual,* SRI International, Menlo Park, Calif., April 1987.

7)   Reboh, R., *Knowledge Engineering Techniques and Tools in the Prospector Environment,* Technical Note 243, Artificial Intelligence Center, SRI International, Menlo Park, Calif., June 1981.

CHAPTER 14

Knowledge Crafting
with Frame-Based Reasoning

The first prototype hull will be cast from a model, the framing for which is shown here. By organizing the hull as a series of frames, the design team is able to create an overall shape that meets the design requirements and to provide a structure on which the yacht can be built. Similarly, part of the knowledge in an application knowledge base can be organized as a set of frames. These frames will contain the essential structural information on which part of the application's reasoning can be based. Chapter 14 discusses the ways in which knowledge can be structured into frames and the ways in which frames can be related to each other and reasoned about.

Frame-based representations provide a mechanism for structuring certain types of knowledge in a knowledge base. The types of knowledge that can suitably be structured using a frame-based organization can range from collections of related facts, to relationships between such collections, to rule-based and even procedural representations of knowledge.

The knowledge-structuring capabilities provided by a frame-based form of representation facilitate the development of a knowledge-based application in two ways. First, they assist the knowledge crafter in understanding the relationships that exist among the data being assembled. Second, they enhance the ability of the inference engine to operate on those data as well as on those structural relationships.

A *frame* can be viewed as a collection of related information about a topic. This information may be factual or procedural (e.g., data or functions). A frame may be taken to represent a *class* of similar objects; other frames, representing *subclasses* or specific *instances* of those objects, can be formed from the initial class frame. The properties (e.g., knowledge) contained in a class frame can be inherited by its subclass and instance frames. Rule-based and procedural knowledge representations can operate efficiently on frame-based representations. A style of programming, termed *object-oriented programming*, has been developed on the frame foundation.

Frame-based representations offer an attractive way to structure a knowledge-based application and, together with frame-based reasoning, offer a powerful way to analyze problems. They also facilitate the rapid prototyping of knowledge-based applications and the modification of the knowledge base.

Frames

A *frame* can play a number of roles. Initially, however, the frame can be likened to a data record as used in such programming languages as COBOL, Pascal, or PL/1. In this sense, a frame consists of a named set of named fields containing data that are in some way related. Just what that relation is, of course, depends on the particular problem.

Frame

A frame is basically a structure for holding various types of knowledge. Frames are given names, with the presumption that the knowledge contained within a particular frame is in some way interrelated. Conceptually, a frame represents an item (i.e., a physical object) or a concept (i.e., an idea). The contents of the frame then describe that item in some way (e.g., its characteristics, its properties, its behaviors). Continuing the house painting example of Chapter 13, frames might be established for HOUSE, OUTSIDE-PAINT, and INSIDE-PAINT as shown in Figure 14-1.

Although the term "frame" is used in this book to represent such structures, this terminology is by no means standard. Thus, other authors and speakers may refer to frame-like structures as *units, objects, concepts, schema*, or *entities*.

Slot

The internal structure of a frame can be characterized as providing a set of *slots* in which the knowledge associated with a frame can be stored. Once again, standard terminology for this internal structure does not exist. Thus, others may refer to the slots of a unit or concept as the *parameters* or *behaviors* of an object or as the *attributes* of an entity or concept. As with frames, slots are individually named, again with the presumption that any knowledge that might be placed in a slot would relate to that slot's name.

For the house-painting example, the OUTSIDE-PAINT frame might have slots to contain information about the COLOR of the paint, the PRICE at which it can be purchased, the types of SURFACES on which it can be used, the application INSTRUCTIONS, the TYPE of base used for the paint, and whether the paint will dry with a GLOSS finish, as shown in Figure 14-2.

The slots shown in Figure 14-2 are only illustrative. If relevant, many more slots might be added to hold information about can size, trade discount, drying time, solvents that could be used for clean-up, manufacturer, chemical content, production lot number, and so forth. The development of a knowledge-based application is like the development of a traditional model, however. In both cases only those characteristics that are essential to the problem at hand need be abstracted from the actual system and represented in the model. Thus, only that knowledge about the paint that might be relevant to the reasoning to be performed should be captured and stored in the frame.

What Goes in a Slot?

Values or facts that are related to the frame are one of the major types of knowledge that can be stored in slots. (Other types of knowledge that can be stored in a slot, such as class relationships, are discussed

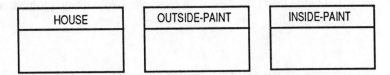

Figure 14-1 Three Empty Frames

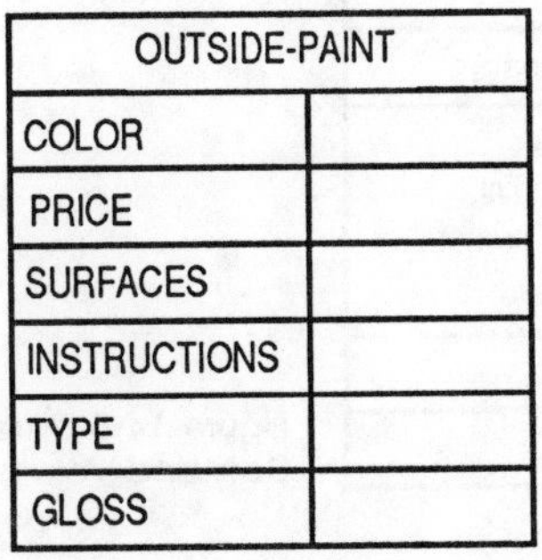

OUTSIDE-PAINT	
COLOR	
PRICE	
SURFACES	
INSTRUCTIONS	
TYPE	
GLOSS	

Figure 14-2 Frame with Slots

later in this chapter.) These data can be stored in a variety of formats, depending on their characteristics. Thus, some values might be stored as numbers, while others might be stored as symbols or character strings.

A slot might hold a single value or a set of values. Depending on the particular reasoning system being used, the order of the values contained in a slot can be made to be significant. Consider, for example, a planning application that passes through a number of states in reaching a solution. Each state might represent the use of a particular strategy in trying to develop a plan. A slot might be used to hold historical information about the system states that the application had entered (i.e., the strategies that had been applied) thus far in attempting to develop the plan. That is, each time a transition was made to a different state (i.e., a different strategy was to be applied), the state name would be included in the list of states contained in the slot.

The manner in which information is stored in a slot can be significant. For example, if the knowledge crafter is interested in the sequence of states visited by the application (i.e., the sequence in which the strategies were applied), then the symbol for each state visited should be appended to the list of states previously visited, thereby preserving the visiting order. On the other hand, if only the identity of previously visited states (e.g., which strategies had been used at least once) is of interest, the order of the values in the slot would not be significant. Thus, a state symbol would only be added to the list in the slot if it did not duplicate a symbol already contained in the slot.

An Example

In terms of the house-painting example, the COLOR slot might have a symbolic representation (e.g., "RED" rather than "fire-engine red" or "color 7329"), while the PRICE slot might have a decimal representation. The SURFACES slot might be a multivalued slot containing a number of terms for the surfaces on which the paint could be applied. The INSTRUCTIONS slot might contain English text describing the manner of application of the paint, while the GLOSS slot might have a logical representation (e.g., "TRUE"). See Figure 14-3.

OUTSIDE-PAINT	
COLOR	RED
PRICE	12.99
SURFACES	(Wood Stucco Concrete)
INSTRUCTIONS	Prepare surface by removing any loose paint, dirt, or grease. Apply primer . . .dry for 12 hrs.
TYPE	Latex
GLOSS	TRUE

Figure 14-3 Frame with Slots and Values

Value Forms

As the example illustrates, many different forms might appropriately be used to represent values. An application developer would typically employ some of the following types of representation in a system:

- Numerical
  - integer
  - decimal
  - floating point (engineering notation)
- Logical
- Symbolic
- Text
- Graphical or pictorial.

Restrictions

So far, no restrictions have been placed on the possible contents of a particular slot. Thus, while a decimal value might logically be expected in the price slot (e.g., 12.99), nothing would prevent an entry of TWELVE DOLLARS AND NINETY NINE CENTS from being made. Even worse, a nonprice value could be stored in the slot (e.g., LATEX). Since such values would not be very meaningful, certain restrictions on slot contents must often be applied. Although several types of restrictions might be applied, only three are discussed at this point:

1. Restrictions on the form of the representation (e.g., only decimal values permitted)
2. Restrictions on the values that can be stored (e.g., only prices between 9.99 and 19.99 permitted)
3. Restrictions that are independent of specific values (e.g., no more than three values in the slot).

Representation Restrictions

To be able to process knowledge contained in the slots of frames, the reasoning system must be able to interpret the values in a slot unambiguously; it must know (and be able to understand) the form of representation of the knowledge in the slot. Consider the COLOR slot, for example, containing the value RED. For the term to be meaningful, the inferencing mechanism must interpret RED as a symbol (from which the meaning "fire-engine red" might be inferred) rather than as text (i.e., the three letters R, E, and D).

To accomplish this, the knowledge crafter can attach a restriction to a slot, limiting the form of the value(s) that can be stored in it. In the case of the COLOR slot, for example, the following restriction could be applied:

RESTRICTION: (VALUE-TYPE: SYMBOL)

Similarly, the PRICE slot might be restricted to hold decimal values, the GLOSS slot logical values, and so forth.

Value Restrictions

Ensuring that a slot's value has the proper form of representation only solves part of the problem, for the value itself, when interpreted correctly, must also be meaningful. Assume for the moment that there continue to be only four colors of outside paint—fire-engine red (with symbol RED), chocolate brown (with symbol BROWN), creamy pearl (with symbol WHITE), and forest moss (with symbol GREEN)—as described in the previous chapter. Under these circumstances, the symbol MAGENTA in the COLOR slot would be in error, just as a value of $ or % would be in error. Yet, both MAGENTA and $ are valid symbols. Thus, a further restriction must be attached to the slot, limiting the specific symbols that can be stored in it to only those that represent valid paint colors. In the case of the COLOR slot, for example, the following restriction could be applied:

RESTRICTION: (CONTENT-ONE-OF: RED BROWN WHITE
                GREEN)

This restriction would exclude values that represented paint colors not offered (e.g., MAGENTA) as well as values that do not represent a paint color (e.g., $).

A variety of similar restrictions might be placed on other slots. For example, values in the PRICE slot might be constrained to fall within a range of numbers or to exclude certain numbers (e.g., even dollar amounts). Consider, for example, a slot containing the floor on which a particular office is located in a 50-story building. The restriction placed on such a slot might contain a mixture of ranges and specific values, such as:

RESTRICTION: (CONTENT-ONE-OF: G B LL M 2:12 14:48 P R)

On the other hand, because of the variety of floor names that might be possible (e.g., garage, basement, lower-level, mezzanine, penthouse, roof), the developer may need to specify only what may not be used as a floor name (e.g., the 13th floor).

RESTRICTION: (CONTENT-NOT-ONE-OF: 13)

Other Types of Restrictions

The developer might wish to apply several other types of restrictions in appropriate situations. For example, the maximum (or minimum) number of values that could be placed in a slot at any one time might be specified. Consider the house painting example again. If the mixing of paint colors is to be prevented, the COLOR slot could be constrained to holding a single color as follows:

RESTRICTION: (MAX-NUMBER-OF-VALUES: 1)

Similarly, the relation that the frame might bear to other frames can be constrained.

An Example

Taking restrictions into consideration, the OUTSIDE-PAINT frame might be set up as shown in Figure 14-4.

What Controls How a Slot Is Treated?

The previous subsections described some of the types of restrictions that a developer might wish to place on the contents of a slot, but such restrictions are not the only type of specification that might be used to control particular aspects of slot value processing. For example, the developer might like to specify the type font and point size with which a value should be displayed. Thus, some mechanism is needed by which such control information can be attached to slots in a frame.

Facets

This mechanism is the *facet*. Facets contain certain types of information that are related to a slot. A variety of different facets may be attached

OUTSIDE-PAINT	
COLOR	RED
	RESTRICTION: (VALUE-TYPE: SYMBOL)
	RESTRICTION: (CONTENT-ONE-OF RED BROWN WHITE GREEN)
	RESTRICTION: (MAX-NUMBER-OF-VALUES: 1)
PRICE	12.99
	RESTRICTION: (VALUE-TYPE: DECIMAL)
	RESTRICTION: (CONTENT-ONE-OF 9.99 12.99)
SURFACES	(Wood Stucco (Nonporous Concrete))
	RESTRICTION: (MAX-NUMBER-OF-VALUES 10)
INSTRUCTIONS	Prepare surface by removing any loose paint, dirt, or grease. Apply primer. . .dry for12 hrs.
TYPE	Latex
	RESTRICTION: (CONTENT-NOT-ONE-OF: Water-Based)
GLOSS	TRUE
	RESTRICTION: (VALUE-TYPE: LOGICAL)
	RESTRICTION: (CONTENT-ONE-OF TRUE FALSE UNKNOWN)
	RESTRICTION: (MAX-NUMBER-OF-VALUES: 1)

Figure 14-4   Frame with Slots, Values, and Restrictions

to the same slot, each providing a different type of control parameter or characteristic. The contents of the appropriate facet are checked whenever a particular type of action is to be performed (e.g., fetch, store, display, query) in connection with a slot value.

Standard Facets

A knowledge-based application development tool offering frame-based representations will likely provide a number of standard facets. That is, any application generated using the tool would contain the necessary program code or instructions to perform the required processing of any values contained in one of these standard facets. The application developer need only provide the appropriate contents of a facet in order for that facet to be effective in providing its intended function.

Adding a facet structure to a frame, then, provides a mechanism for representing the various types of slot value restrictions discussed previously as well as for representing other characteristics such as display format. Some of the standard facets that a knowledge-based application development tool might provide for each slot in a frame include:

- Permitted representational form(s) for the values in the slot
- Permitted values for the slot
- Maximum number of values permitted in the slot
- Minimum number of values permitted in the slot
- Display format for the slot's value
- Explanation about the purpose or meaning of the slot
- Text of question to be asked in the event that the user is requested to provide a value for the slot
- Text of response to be provided should the user question the purpose of the request for a slot value.

A variety of other facets that relate to inheritance and class structure relationships might also be made available.

Active Values

Facets can be used to support a number of special-purpose capabilities. Since access to a slot value in a frame takes place only after the system refers to the relevant facets controlling access, setting up a facet to indicate that a slot value is active is relatively easy. That is, any access to an active slot turns control over to an *active value* routine before access is made.

Frame-based systems commonly provide a number of standard active value routines that will plot, graph, or signal the value each time the slot's contents change. However, the knowledge crafter can also use active values as a monitoring capability by specifying a routine to be given control each time access is to be made to a slot. Access may be intercepted just prior to a data store or immediately after a data fetch. The routine receiving control may then modify or substitute values, log the access, or turn control over to the user to browse the knowledge base. This mechanism provides the knowledge crafter with an easily created filter, enabling values to be range- and type-checked either before they are stored or before they are returned to the requesting program or rule.

Active values can be used as a regular part of the knowledge representation. Thus, the storage of a particular value in a state slot can be used as the trigger to initiate the processing of a specified rule-set. However, active values also offer the knowledge crafter a handy debugging mechanism. An active value can readily be attached to a slot, with control being turned over to the knowledge crafter (or his debugging routine) when activated. Various system values can be examined and displayed before regular execution of the application is resumed. This capability is perhaps the most valuable testing and debugging tool provided by a frame-based system.

Developer-Specified Facets

Generally speaking, a knowledge-based application development tool cannot provide all of the facets that a developer might wish to attach to a particular slot. The ones described in the previous subsection could be viewed as generic facets, facets that are related to the reasoning process in general and that are unrelated to any particular application. Because additional problem-dependent facets are also needed, however, the development tool should offer a mechanism that will enable the developer to define and add facets that are related to the particular application. Of course, the developer will also have to provide the necessary programming to implement handling of the facet!

Consider the following example of a developer-specified or application-dependent facet, in which the developer wants to use the facet to record the source from which the current value of a slot was obtained (e.g., input by the user, initialized default value, derived using Rule 7 of Rule-Set 3). This facet would be analogous to the "why" facet. Instead of containing the text of an explanation, however, the facet would contain the source from which the current slot value was obtained. Specifying a new facet is generally quite easy with tools that permit developer-specified facets. In addition to creating the facet, however, the developer must also provide the mechanism to implement the facet's intent. In the case of the "how" facet, the developer would have to create a mechanism to trap any store into the slot, backtrack to determine the appropriate source designation for that value, store that designator in the facet, and complete the trapped store (i.e., putting the value in the slot as originally attempted).

Where Are Frames Useful?

Frames are useful in categorizing knowledge when that knowledge has some underlying structure. If the knowledge can be related to a set of objects or concepts, then at least a portion of the facts contained in the knowledge base can be clustered around those objects or concepts.

To illustrate, consider a knowledge base dealing with automobiles. By clustering the knowledge around each type of automobile, a user could obtain information on Chevrolets without having to search through all the knowledge about automobiles. This type of retrieval would take advantage of the frame structure, referring only to the slots in a particular frame.

Similarly, the user could obtain information on tire types without having to search through all the knowledge in the knowledge base, looking at a particular slot in a number of frames. This type of retrieval would take advantage of the slot structure. These two types of access to the knowledge are illustrated in Figure 14-5. The frame structure permits the knowledge crafter and the domain expert to view the contents and structure of the knowledge base in a way that facilitates greater understanding as well as a greater ability to detect inconsistent or incomplete data.

Thus, in the rough design portion of the feasibility study, the knowledge crafter should be looking at the characteristics of the knowledge that is expected to be placed in the knowledge base, identifying whether it will likely consist of a loose collection of unrelated facts or whether it will consist of a number of clusters of related facts. The knowledge crafter should search to identify not only what objects or concepts (around which knowledge can be clustered) but also how many such objects and concepts might exist. The larger the number, the greater the advantage a frame-based representation can provide.

Structure

Thus far, frames have not been related to each other in any way. The illustrations have just shown frames without any connection among them. In practical applications, however, the objects or concepts represented by frames often do bear some relationship to each other. Part of the power of a frame-based representation is its ability to capture such relationships and to represent this structure in the knowledge base.

One way to view such relationships is with the concept of refinement. That is, as attention shifts systematically from one frame to the next in a collection of related frames, the idea or object represented by each frame becomes progressively either more general or more specific. The description in the following subsections moves in what is commonly viewed as the downward direction, from general to specific. (Related frames are generally displayed as a two-dimensional hierarchy, with the more general frames at the top of the display and the more specific frames at the bottom. Hence, traversing frames from general to specific implies movement down the page.)

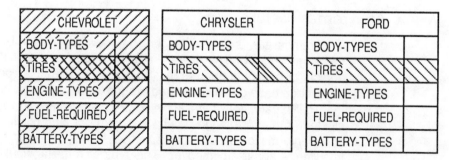

Figure 14-5 Knowledge Access by Frame and by Slot

Classes

The term *class* is used to denote a frame containing the knowledge about a set or class of objects of a given type. Thus, a frame might be established for the class AUTOMOBILES. All other clusters of knowledge about particular aspects of automobiles would be associated with subordinate frames. However, knowledge about unrelated concepts would be associated with frames in different classes. Thus, the knowledge base might contain the classes AUTOMOBILES, KITCHEN-UTENSILS, and SHOES, as shown in Figure 14-6.

Subclasses

The frames in a *subclass* represent a particularization or a specialization of the class to which they relate. Thus, the class AUTOMOBILES might have subclasses of DOMESTIC and IMPORTED, as shown in Figure 14-7. The frames representing these two subclasses would have more specialized information that pertains to one of the two types of automobiles (i.e., domestic cars or imported cars) but that does not pertain to the class of automobiles as a whole. The subclass provides additional knowledge beyond what is available at the class level. The subclass is thus different from a mathematical subclass; it represents a narrowing of the concept but also an expansion of the information about the concept.

Note that subclasses are themselves classes, for they in turn can have subclasses. To avoid confusion, we shall refer to classes and subclasses alike as classes. Since classes deriving from another class can give rise to further derivative classes, the concept specialization process can continue iteratively. Each lower class in the hierarchy represents a further specialization of the concept. (Or, looking at the hierarchy the other way, each class represents a generalization of a subordinate class.) Thus, the class DOMESTIC might have three subclasses representing automobiles manufactured by three companies: CHEVROLET, FORD, and CHRYSLER. The class FORD might in turn have two subclasses representing two different models manufactured: RANCHERO and LTD. This process could continue on to body type (e.g., sedan, station wagon) and other features. This class hierarchy is shown in Figure 14-8.

Although not shown in Figure 14-8, each of the other domestic automobile classes (e.g., CHEVROLET) could be broken down into model-based subclasses, and the IMPORTED class could have a similar class graph attached to it.

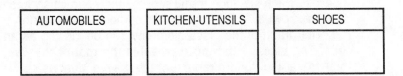

Figure 14-6 Three Class Frames

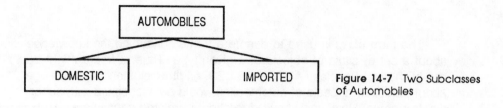

Figure 14-7 Two Subclasses of Automobiles

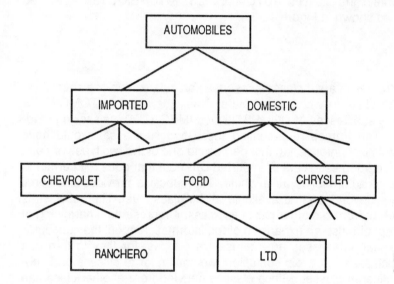

Figure 14-8 Class Structure of Automobiles

This class structure serves to structure the knowledge, and the resulting class hierarchy is often referred to as a *taxonomy*. Thus, the structure in Figure 14-8 would be referred to as the automobile taxonomy.

Instances

Sooner or later no further subdivisions are possible without losing the concept of a class that represents multiple objects. At this point, the next further specialization would be a particular *instance*. Each such instance would represent a specific case or instantiation of the general concept. Thus, as shown in Figure 14-9, the class RANCHERO might have three instances, with frames representing MY-FORD, JIM'S-FORD, and SUSAN'S-FORD. By convention, the dotted line represents a class-instance relationship while the solid line represents a class-subclass relationship. Each instance frame represents a particular automobile, having a specific owner, color, registration number, and so forth.

The graph of the class hierarchy can be viewed as an upside-down tree. The class at the top represents the root of the tree, while the instances at the bottom represent the leaves. Just as nothing grows from the leaves of a real tree, so does nothing grow from the leaves of the frame tree. There is no categorization more specialized than the instance.

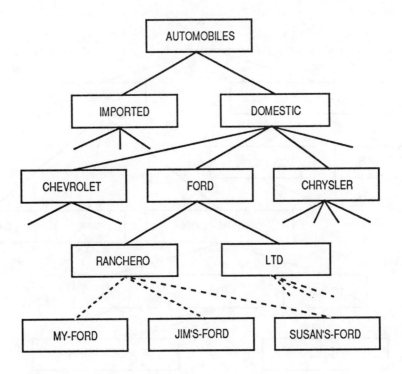

Figure 14-9   Automobile Taxonomy with Instances

Intersecting Hierarchies

The automobile taxonomy illustrated in Figure 14-9 was created as an isolated knowledge structure, but this need not be the case. Classes and instances can be related between taxonomies. Consider two other taxonomies, one representing the knowledge contained in the knowledge base about trucks and the other the knowledge about engines.

Figure 14-10a shows the class TRUCKS broken down into two subclasses, SPECIAL-PURPOSE and CARGO. The SPECIAL-PURPOSE class is further broken down into two subclasses, FIRE-TRUCK and TOW-TRUCK, while the CARGO class is broken down into GENERAL-GOODS, TANK, and CATTLE. The general goods class is broken down into 1/2-ton, 1-ton, and 2-ton subclasses, and the 1/2-ton class has two instances. A much broader taxonomy could be developed, but this brief one will serve to illustrate a point.

The Ranchero is an interesting vehicle in this context. Because it consists of the front half of a passenger car and the rear half of a truck, the RANCHERO class (or any instance of that class) relates to concepts in both hierarchies. This relationship is represented in Figure 14-10b by the dotted line connecting the instance MY-FORD to the class RANCHERO (making it a member of AUTOMOBILES) and to the class 1/2-TON (making it a member of TRUCKS), which means that MY-FORD is an instance of both classes and has all the properties of a Ranchero automobile and all the properties of a 1/2-ton truck. Such a passing of properties from

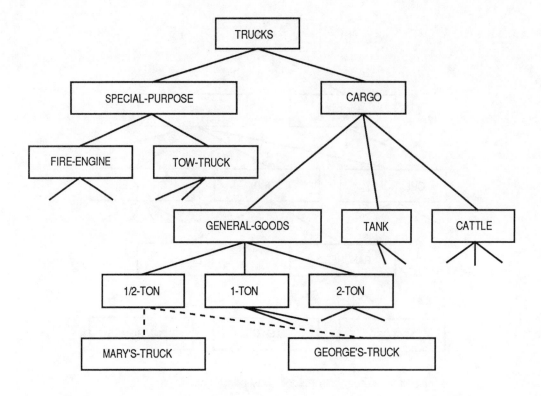

Figure 14-10a The Truck Taxonomy

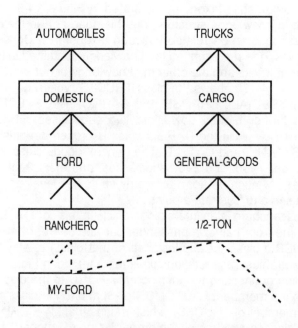

Figure 14-10b Skeleton of Two Taxonomies

class to class or instance and from multiple classes to another class or instance illustrates the inheritance of properties down through the knowledge taxonomy. The concept of inheritance is discussed later.

Connections can also be made higher up in the taxonomy (i.e., between classes). For example, the class RANCHERO could be related as a subclass of both the FORD and GENERAL-GOODS classes, as shown in Figure 14-10c. This relationship would imply that all Rancheros were domestic Ford automobiles and that they were all general-goods carrying trucks (no cattle trucks or fire engines), but it would not imply anything about the load-carrying capacity of the Ranchero. Thus, the connection between RANCHERO and GENERAL-GOODS implies that the RANCHERO automobiles are a particularization of the class FORD (and all classes above it) and of the class GENERAL-GOODS (and all classes above it). However, none of the knowledge in the tree extending below GENERAL-GOODS has any fixed relation to RANCHERO automobiles. Thus, RANCHERO vehicles are potentially eligible to have either 1/2-TON, 1-TON, or 2-TON capacities.

Now consider the engine taxonomy. As shown in Figure 14-11a, the class ENGINES is broken down into the subclasses DIESEL and GASOLINE. The GASOLINE class is further broken down into CARBURETED and FUEL-INJECTED subclasses. The FUEL-INJECTED class is further divided into cylinder-based subclasses. Although not shown in Figure 14-11a, similar subtrees would extend down from the CARBURETED and DIESEL classes.

Assume for the moment that MY-FORD has an 8-cylinder, fuel-injected, gasoline engine. The novice knowledge crafter might be tempted to establish a relation similar to the one shown in Figure 14-11b, making MY-FORD a subclass of both RANCHERO and 8-CYLINDER. After all, MY-FORD does have an 8-cylinder engine with all the properties indicated in the 8-CYLINDER, FUEL-INJECTED, GASOLINE, and ENGINES

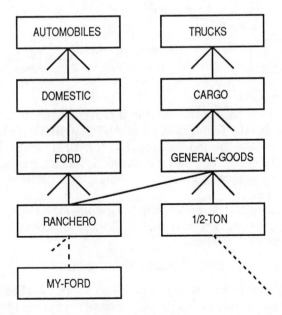

Figure 14-10c Skeleton Taxonomies with More Abstract Connection

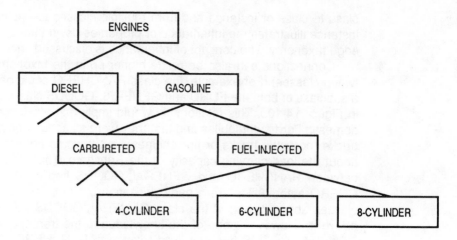

Figure 14-11a The Engine Taxonomy

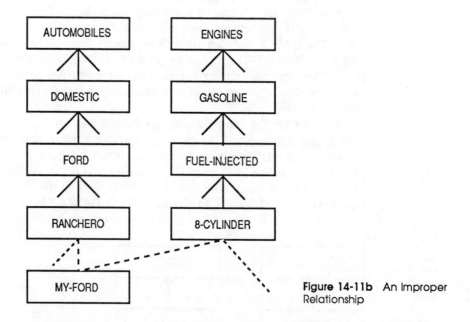

Figure 14-11b An Improper Relationship

classes. However, while MY-FORD is a particularization of the classes RANCHERO, FORD, DOMESTIC, and AUTOMOBILES, it is not a particularization of any of the classes 8-CYLINDER, FUEL-INJECTED, GASOLINE, or ENGINES. The car I am driving has an engine, but it is *not* an example or instance of an engine. Therefore, a different type of connection is needed.

The proper relationship is of the form *contains* or *has-a*. Thus, the knowledge crafter could specify that all Rancheros contain fuel-injected engines by using the relation:

RELATION: RANCHERO HAS-A FUEL-INJECTED

This relation is indicated by the solid line connecting the sides of the RANCHERO and FUEL-INJECTED class boxes in Figure 14-11c. Such a

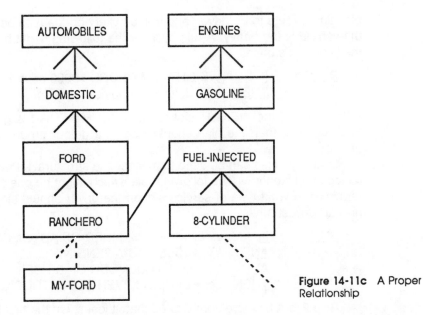

Figure 14-11c A Proper Relationship

relation indicates that every Ranchero vehicle has a fuel-injected, gasoline-powered engine. All of the characteristics of such an engine are available to the RANCHERO frame, but there is no implication that the RANCHERO is an instance of FUEL-INJECTED. Relations are discussed in greater detail in the section on relationship knowledge.

Where Are Structures Useful?

The arrangement of frames in a structural relationship offers several advantages. Most importantly, the visual representation of the relationships between frames aids the knowledge crafter in understanding the underlying structure of the knowledge, thereby facilitating the development of the application. Not only does it aid in determining where to place knowledge in the knowledge base, but it can guide the knowledge acquisition process. By viewing the structure and considering the areas in which knowledge has and has not been acquired, the knowledge crafter can determine where further acquisition efforts might appropriately be directed.

The structured relationship of the frames in a taxonomy is also a means of storing knowledge. The fact that MY-FORD is a RANCHERO provides additional knowledge about MY-FORD. Similarly, additional knowledge is provided by the linkages indicating that the car is manufactured by Ford, that it is a domestic vehicle, that it is a general-goods carrying truck, and so forth. This knowledge is available not only to the knowledge crafter but to inference mechanisms as well.

Frame-Based Reasoning

Because the knowledge contained in a frame's slots is available to inference mechanisms, a rule could reason about the characteristics of a frame by referring to its slot values. Assume that the application involves planning a route to be driven and that a rickety bridge is to be avoided if the vehicle is too heavy. A rule such as the following might be placed in the knowledge base:

RULE 1:   IF   WEIGHT of MY-FORD >3000 pounds
          THEN   take detour around rickety bridge

If the value of the WEIGHT slot of the frame MY-FORD is greater than 3000 pounds, then the plan should include a detour around the rickety bridge.

Similarly, rules can be used to process the structural knowledge contained in a taxonomy. The following rule, which might be one of a set determining at what type of service station the driver should stop to refuel his car, is illustrative.

RULE 2:   IF   ?VEHICLE is MEMBER-OF AUTOMOBILES
          AND   ?VEHICLE HAS-A ?ENGINE
          AND   ?ENGINE is MEMBER-OF DIESEL
          THEN   set REFUEL of ?VEHICLE to TRUCKSTOP

Rule 2 is a bit more complicated than it looks. On the first line the inference engine attempts to instantiate the variable ?VEHICLE with every frame, but only those instantiations that are members of the class AUTOMOBILES are kept. At this point, several vehicles might qualify, so several instances of the rule would be established (e.g., with vehicle-1, vehicle-2). The second line instantiates the variable ?ENGINE with any frame that ?VEHICLE points to with a HAS-A relation. Thus, if vehicle-1 had an engine and, say, a fuel-tank, the rule would be instantiated twice—once with ?VEHICLE = vehicle-1 and ?ENGINE = ENGINES and once with ?VEHICLE = vehicle-1 and ?ENGINE = FUEL-TANK.

The third line of the rule then throws out any instantiation of the rule for which ?ENGINE is not a member of the class DIESEL. Thus, only those rule instantiations for which the specified conditions are satisfied will be left at the end of line three. The fourth line then sets the slot RE-FUEL of the associated vehicle to the value TRUCKSTOP. If there were five automobiles with diesel engines, Rule 2 would be instantiated five times and would fire five times, once with each eligible automobile.

Similarly, rules can be developed that create structure in the taxonomy, associating one class with another. Reasoning with a knowledge taxonomy is not the exclusive province of rules, although many frame-based systems use rule-based knowledge extensively. However, procedural knowledge of the type found in blackboard systems (see Chapter 15) can process frame-based knowledge quite efficiently.

Hierarchical Reasoning

The arrangement of knowledge from general to specific within a knowledge taxonomy matches the type of reasoning that is used in many types of applications. For example, consider the problem of classifying a truck by its purpose or function. Usually the truck is categorized more by eliminating all of the functions that it cannot serve than by identifying its purpose. This elimination can take place at various levels in the hierarchy, depending on the type of knowledge known about the candidate truck.

Thus, at one level there might be a rule:

RULE: IF   MANUFACTURER of ?TRUCK is CHRYSLER
            THEN ?TRUCK is NOT MEMBER-OF FIRE-TRUCK

Assuming Chrysler does not manufacture any fire trucks, a single rule at this level can eliminate a number of class and subclass possibilities.

Another method of elimination can be illustrated at another level. For example, assume that the capacity of the truck could be identified as 1/2-TON. Then a rule such as the following would serve to put the identified function of any frame having a 1/2-ton capacity in the slot POSSIBLE-FUNCTIONS:

RULE: IF   CAPACITY of ?TRUCK is 1/2-TON
            AND   CAPACITY of ?POSSIBILITY is 1/2-TON
            AND   ?TRUCK NOT ?POSSIBILITY
            THEN ADD FUNCTION of ?POSSIBILITY to
                     POSSIBLE-FUNCTIONS of ?TRUCK

Because of the tree structure of the knowledge taxonomy, fewer frames need be considered at a higher level than at a lower level. Thus, the reasoning can take place more efficiently at a higher level if data availability and desired output permit. For example, consider the problem of identifying the type of truck to use to satisfy a particular requirement such as carrying a liquid. In this case, the inference engine might be able to select a tank truck as belonging to a class of trucks that would satisfy the requirement without ever considering the type or volume of liquid to be carried.

Planning can be carried out on multiple levels. For example, at the first level the reasoning goal would be to determine whether a type of truck equipped to transport a liquid cargo existed. Having determined this, the inference mechanism might then focus on a narrower problem, namely, checking the cost and availability of each qualifying tank truck.

Should no tank truck satisfying the cost and availability requirements exist, the inference mechanism might go back up a level to consider another type of truck that might be able to transport a liquid cargo (e.g., a general-cargo carrier with a portable tank placed in the cargo area).

The hierarchical structuring of frame-based representations is consistent with this type of reasoning. Even if the application does not involve a sequence of objects or concepts at progressively greater levels of detail, it may well involve multilevel reasoning, using completely different sets of objects at each level. Such reasoning can be greatly facilitated by having a compatibly structured knowledge representation.

At the time of the feasibility study and during the early design phases of the project, the knowledge crafter should therefore be looking at the characteristics of the expertise that is to be captured about the application domain. Questions such as the following should be asked:

- Do the objects and concepts of the domain bear a relationship to each other?
- Are there large numbers of related frames?
- Does the reasoning process involve multiple levels of detail about particular types of objects?

Affirmative answers tend to indicate an appropriate situation for the use of a frame-based representation.

Inheritance

The previous section indicated that frames at lower levels of a taxonomy could obtain properties from frames at higher levels in the taxonomy. Knowing that FORD is a subclass of DOMESTIC automobiles and of AUTOMOBILES permits certain additional information about Fords to be inferred, namely, that they had the general properties of automobiles (e.g., four wheels) as well as the additional properties of domestic cars (e.g., English rather than metric dimensions). The mechanism for passing such knowledge from frame to frame down through the taxonomy from general to specific is known as *inheritance*.

Passing Properties

Each subclass can be given certain properties of its parent class. Thus, the general knowledge about automobiles would be inherited (made available) in every frame at the DOMESTIC class level. This knowledge would further be inherited by each frame at the manufacturer class level (e.g., FORD), by the frames representing all the models of a manufacturer (e.g., the LTD class), as well as by each instance frame (e.g., MY-FORD). Similarly, the additional knowledge provided by the DOMESTIC class (i.e., the additional knowledge that is not contained in the class AUTOMOBILES that serves to distinguish the class DOMESTIC from the class AUTOMOBILES) would also be inherited downward to all frames at the manufacturer, model, and instance levels of the hierarchy.

The discussion thus far has focused on the inheritance of slot values from a parent frame to a child or offspring frame in an iterative manner throughout a structured hierarchy. However, a frame can inherit many types of properties from its parents. No individual development tool may provide the full range of inheritance capability, but the discussion in the next subsection is intended to show the types of inheritance that a knowledge crafter might find useful for a particular application.

Types of Inheritance

A slot in a frame might inherit a variety of properties, ranging from specific values to structural characteristics, as illustrated by the four types of inheritance described below.

Types of Inheritance: Slot

Slot inheritance takes place when the slot itself, but not its value, is inherited from a parent frame. Thus, in Figure 14-12a, the WHEELS slot would be inherited by every descendant subclass from the class AUTO-MOBILES, but the slot value would not be inherited. That is, the classes DOMESTIC and IMPORTED would have a property called WHEELS, but

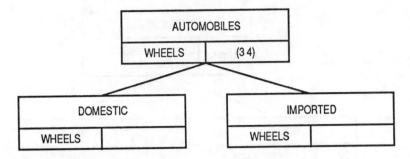

Figure 14-12a Slot Inheritance

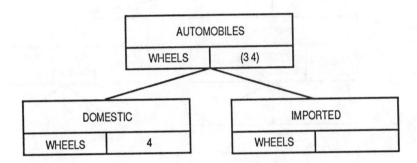

Figure 14-12b Noninheritance of Slot Values

there would be no implication about how many wheels a domestic or imported automobile might have. The (3 4) value of the WHEELS slot of AUTOMOBILES would not be inherited.

Further, the WHEELS slot of DOMESTIC might be given a value of 4, since no 3-wheeled automobiles are made domestically. As shown in Figure 14-12b, this assignment would not affect the value of the WHEELS slot of any other frame in the hierarchy.

Types of Inheritance: Value

Value inheritance takes place when the value of a slot in a frame is inherited from the corresponding slot of the parent. Thus, if the AUTOMOBILES frame had a slot called CARRIES with a value of (PASSENGERS, CARGO), the corresponding slots in the DOMESTIC and IMPORTED frames would be given the value (PASSENGERS, CARGO), indicating that those vehicles similarly can carry both passengers and cargo. Similarly, this value would automatically appear in the CARRIES slot of each descendant frame in the hierarchy as shown in Figure 14-13a.

If the CARRIES slot of CORVETTE were then to be set to passengers (since the sports car has no room for cargo), this value would appear in the CARRIES slot of all descendant frames. However, this change would not be inherited upward to any parent frame, nor would it affect the slot values in any other unrelated branch of the tree (e.g., the IMPORTED frame), as illustrated in Figure 14-13b.

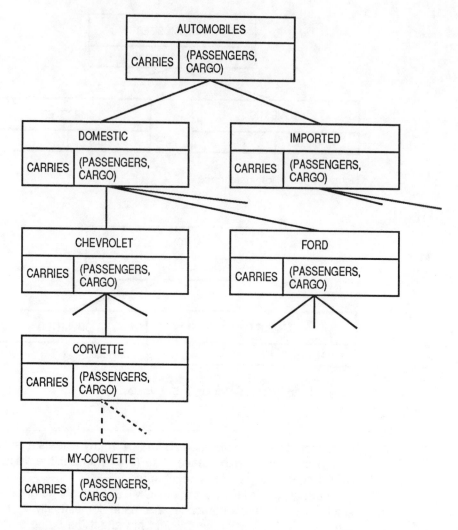

Figure 14-13a Value Inheritance

Types of Inheritance: Restriction

Restriction inheritance takes place when it is the restrictions on values, rather than the values themselves, that are inherited. Thus, a constraint on the WHEELS slot of AUTOMOBILES to permit only 3- and 4-wheeled vehicles would be binding on all subclasses and instances of AUTOMOBILES, but no specific value would be implied (see Figure 14-14).

Types of Inheritance: Null

In some cases inheritance is not desirable, and all of its forms should be inhibited. Thus, for example, the FORD frame shown in Figure 14-15 might have a slot named FLEET-MPG, containing the average miles-per-

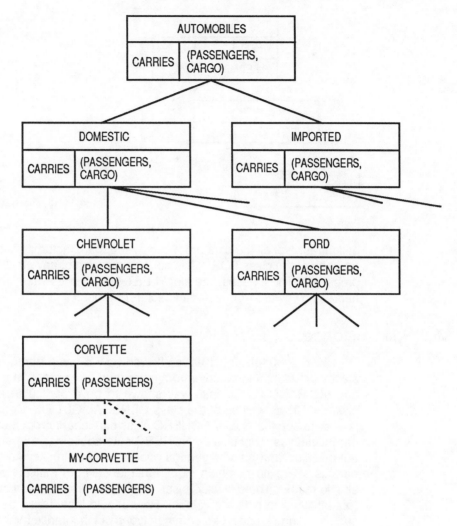

Figure 14-13b Downward Only Inheritance of Values

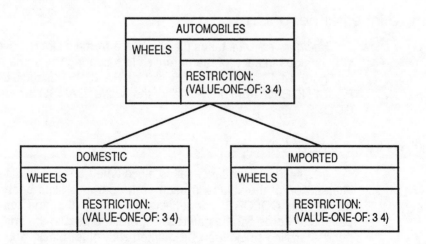

Figure 14-14 Restriction Inheritance

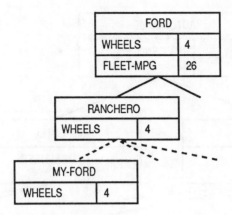

Figure 14-15 Noninheritance

gallon rating of all the cars produced by the manufacturer. This rating is a property of the class FORD; it is not a description of any class or instance properties. Thus, neither the slot FLEET-MPG nor its value should be inherited downward from the manufacturer frames.

Multiple Inheritance

Figures 14-10b and 14-10c showed how a given frame (whether instance or class) might derive from more than one parent. In the latter figure, the RANCHERO class was shown to be a particularization of the class FORD as well as of the class GENERAL-GOODS. Conceptually, it is easy to see that the RANCHERO class can inherit properties from both parent classes. That is, a RANCHERO automobile has properties of Ford automobiles and also of general-goods carrying trucks. As long as the parents share no common slots, inheritance from multiple parents is a simple matter. The difficulty arises when the parents have common slots (potentially with different values). How should inheritance be handled in such a circumstance? Two common types of inheritance might be used to deal with this situation: union and intersection.

Multiple Inheritance: Union

Union inheritance takes place when a frame's slot receives the union of the values in each of the parent's slots bearing the same name. Thus, in Figure 14-16, the CARRIES slot of RANCHERO receives the value PASSENGERS from FORD and the value CARGO from GENERAL-GOODS.

Multiple Inheritance: Intersection

Intersection inheritance takes place when a frame's slot receives the intersection of the values in each of the parent's slots bearing the same name. The COLORS slot reflects the colors that the vehicle can be painted. If Fords can be painted red, white, blue, brown, and green and if goods-carrying trucks can be painted red, blue, black, and brown, then intersection inheritance would provide red, blue, and brown as the pos-

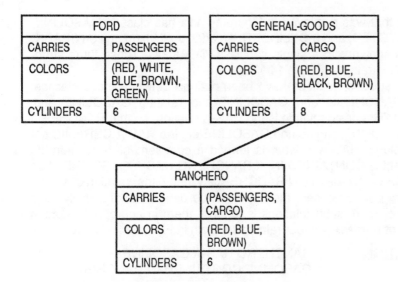

FORD	
CARRIES	PASSENGERS
COLORS	(RED, WHITE, BLUE, BROWN, GREEN)
CYLINDERS	6

GENERAL-GOODS	
CARRIES	CARGO
COLORS	(RED, BLUE, BLACK, BROWN)
CYLINDERS	8

RANCHERO	
CARRIES	(PASSENGERS, CARGO)
COLORS	(RED, BLUE, BROWN)
CYLINDERS	6

Figure 14-16 Union and Intersection Inheritance

sible colors for Rancheros. This intersection inheritance is illustrated in Figure 14-16.

A variety of other inheritance methods is also possible. For example, a slot value might be inherited from only the first (last) of the listed parents. Thus, Fords might have 6 cylinders and trucks might have 8. Rather than ending up with a combination (e.g., 7 cylinders), the Ranchero will end up with either 6 or 8 cylinders. (The CYLINDERS slot for RANCHERO in Figure 14-16 has a value of 6, reflecting inheritance from the FORD frame.)

When multiple values are involved, further inheritance possibilities arise. For example, a developer might like values to be inherited in the same order (reverse order) as they appear in the parents' slots or to be combined in the same (reverse) order in which the parents are listed. Depending on the facilities of the particular knowledge-based application development tool being used, these and other inheritance mechanisms may or may not be available. The knowledge crafter should investigate the inheritance needs of the form of knowledge representation being selected for the application and compare those needs with the capabilities of the available tools when selecting a tool.

Relationship Knowledge

The preceding subsections have focused on the storage of values in slots and the association of various types of restrictions with those slots. Knowledge about relationships can also be stored in slots. Consider, for example, a knowledge base with the classes AUTOMOBILES, ENGINES, and SPARK-PLUGS. A section of the AUTOMOBILES taxonomy that was displayed in Figure 14-9 consists of the classes DOMESTIC, FORD, and RANCHERO, and the instance MY-FORD. A section of the ENGINES taxonomy that was displayed in Figure 14-11a has classes GASOLINE, FUEL-INJECTED, and 8-CYLINDER. An additional taxonomy on SPARK-PLUGS is shown with a single subclass, CERAMIC. These three structures are illustrated in Figure 14-17a.

Some specific relations have been defined between these classes, relating RANCHERO and GASOLINE and relating GASOLINE and CERAMIC. The basic relation is the HAS-A relation, so that RANCHERO HAS-A GASOLINE engine and GASOLINE engine HAS-A CERAMIC set of spark-plugs. HAS-A is what is termed a complementary relation; its complement is CONTAINED-IN. If RANCHERO HAS-A GASOLINE, then GASOLINE CONTAINED-IN RANCHERO. When either relation of a complementary pair is defined, the other can be defined automatically. One way to implement such relations is to store them in appropriate slots in the relevant frames. The four relations shown in Figure 14-17a are:

RELATION: RANCHERO HAS-A GASOLINE
                 GASOLINE CONTAINED-IN RANCHERO
RELATION: GASOLINE HAS-A CERAMIC
                 CERAMIC CONTAINED-IN GASOLINE

Instances

The frame representation for part of a knowledge base will often remain static during an analysis. Thus, the knowledge crafter would create relationships such as those shown in Figure 14-17a during development of the application system, and these frames and relationships would not be changed. However, because other parts of the knowledge base will

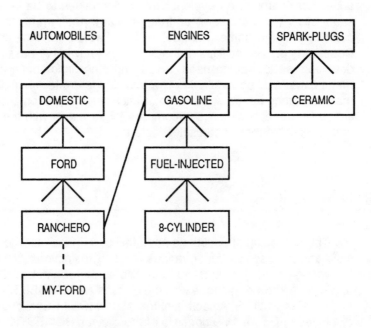

Figure 14-17a   Relations between Taxonomies

change dynamically during an analysis, the inference engine must be able to create (or destroy) frames and relationships programmatically during execution of the application.

Consider the case of Susan buying a new Ranchero. Her acquisition will necessitate creating a new instance of RANCHERO, SUSAN'S-FORD, as well as other relationships. Because RANCHERO HAS-A GASOLINE, an instance of GASOLINE will need to be created and SUSAN'S-FORD given a HAS-A relation to it. Similarly, because GASOLINE is linked to CERAMIC with a HAS-A relation, an instance of CERAMIC will need to be created and a HAS-A relation established from the GASOLINE instance to the CERAMIC instance. These relationships are depicted in Figure 14-17b, which is identical to Figure 14-17a except for the addition of all the frames and relations implied by the addition of the instance, SUSAN'S-FORD.

Rather than having to create each frame individually and to establish each relationship within the family, some knowledge-based system development tools will automatically create all referenced frames (that do not already exist) and all of the relationships between those frames whenever a new frame is created. Thus, the creation of SUSAN'S-FORD would trigger the following:

- Creation of an instance, SUSAN'S-GASOLINE, of GASOLINE
- Linking the instance to the parent (SUSAN'S-GASOLINE to GASOLINE)
- Establishing a HAS-A relation between SUSAN'S-FORD and SUSAN'S-GASOLINE

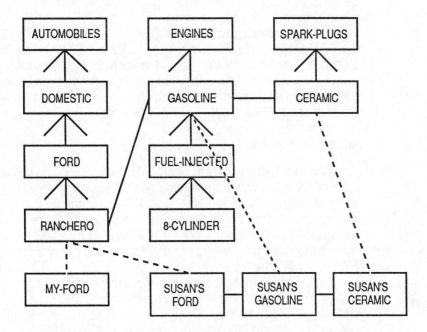

Figure 14-17b Relations between Taxonomies with a New Instances

- Establishing a CONTAINED-IN relation between SUSAN'S-GASOLINE and SUSAN'S-FORD
- Creation of an instance, SUSAN'S-CERAMIC, of CERAMIC
- Linking the instance to the parent (SUSAN'S-CERAMIC to CERAMIC)
- Establishing a HAS-A relation between SUSAN'S-GASOLINE and SUSAN'S-CERAMIC
- Establishing a CONTAINED-IN relation between SUSAN'S-CERAMIC and SUSAN'S-GASOLINE.

This ability to create a full subtree structure simply by creating an instance of a class is a very powerful capability.

Facets Revisited

In view of the class relationships that can exist between frames, additional facets can be created to constrain slot contents in terms of these relationships. Thus, the possible values that might be placed in a slot might be restricted to the name of a frame that is an instance of a particular class or the name of a class that is derived from another class. In terms of the automobile example, the following restriction would restrict the possible values for a slot to instances of DOMESTIC:

RESTRICTION: (INSTANCE-OF: DOMESTIC)

Thus, any instance of one of the domestic manufacturers (e.g., CHRYSLER) or of one of the domestic manufacturer's car models (e.g., LTD) would be permitted. However, one of the manufacturers (e.g., the class CHRYSLER) or one of the car model classes (e.g., LTD) would not be permitted. Likewise, no instances deriving from the IMPORTED side of the taxonomy would be permitted.

Similarly, restrictions such as DERIVES-FROM, NOT-MEMBER-OF, INHERITANCE-TYPE, INSTANCE, and EXCLUSIVE-MEMBERSHIP can be used to control the use of and reasoning with relations. Again, this area offers considerable additional power to a representational form, but different knowledge-based application development tools provide these types of capabilities in different ways, if at all.

Where Is Inheritance Useful?

Inheritance is particularly useful when the reasoning process involves creating new instances, modifying relationships, or adding new relationships. A change made to a slot in a subclass frame as a result of the reasoning process will be inherited down to all subordinate subclasses and instances. The knowledge crafter need not worry about, and the knowledge base need not make provision for, finding every instance and making the corresponding change.

Thus, if the application domain seems well-suited for frame-based representation, the knowledge crafter should examine the degree to which that structure may change or be filled out during the reasoning process. The more dynamic the knowledge base, the more important an inheritance mechanism may become. Even for static knowledge bases, inheritance can be valuable during the development process. (Although the ultimate knowledge base may be static, the knowledge base during the crafting process is likely to be anything but static.)

Order Out of Chaos

One system we have examined involved the checking of equipment configurations for completeness and consistency. This type of problem is a common one for a fairly broad range of manufacturing industries. This system was entirely rule-based and involved an extensive set of rules, each checking some aspect of the configuration. Understanding some of the relationships between the rules was difficult because of the number of rules to be examined.

A small version of this system was assembled using a frame-based representation (as well as a rule-based representation), which permitted the rules to be categorized and their number reduced. By taking advantage of the ability to reason about structures and relationships of equipment components, we were able to substitute a smaller number of rules operating at a more abstract level for a larger number of the original rules. Not only did this change provide an efficiency in representation, but it made the system less complex logically. This latter characteristic facilitated the developer's modification of the knowledge base.

Thus, the combination of a frame-based knowledge base structure with a rule-based reasoning mechanism can provide an application system structure that is far more powerful and efficient than the system that might be built using either representational form alone. In this case, the whole is definitely greater than the sum of the parts.

Other Types of Slot Contents

The preceding subsections have discussed two types of knowledge that can be stored in a slot—basic facts or values, and frame relationships. Additional types of knowledge can be placed in a slot, however. For example, rules or even entire rule-sets might be placed in a slot. Similarly, procedural or behavioral knowledge can be accommodated by placing a function in a slot. As a practical matter, however, rules are likely to be gathered in a rule taxonomy, with just a reference to the appropriate rule class contained in the slot. In this manner the categorizational power of a frame-based representation can be brought to bear on rule-based and procedural-based knowledge. The association of functions with a frame also provides the mechanism for implementing object-oriented programming, a concept that is discussed later in this chapter.

Rule-Sets

Chapter 13 discussed the development and use of multiple rule-sets in an application. In some knowledge-based development systems an entire rule-set may be stored in a slot, permitting rule-based knowledge as well as facts and relationship knowledge to be structured in the knowledge taxonomy. At the other extreme, each rule could be placed in a single frame, with a parent frame representing the entire rule-set. The inclusion of rules within a frame permits an application's rule-based knowledge to be structured in the same manner as the factual knowledge. Rules can thus be organized in a taxonomy and referenced from slots of other frames. Such rule references can be inherited downward in knowledge hierarchies from classes through subclasses to specific instances.

To illustrate, consider a frame-based taxonomy of rules relating to automobile failure diagnostics. The knowledge taxonomy has a root class called DIAGNOSTIC-RULES. This class contains no rules but represents the class of all diagnostic rules. It serves as the parent to three subclasses that respectively contain the individual rule-sets for each type of diagnostic: CARBURETOR-DIAGNOSTICS, ELECTRICAL-SYSTEM-DIAGNOSTICS, and BRAKE-SYSTEM-DIAGNOSTICS. As shown in Figure 14-18, the rules are distributed one rule per slot within those frames. Alternatively, each of these three frames could serve as classes representing the rule-set, with the rules contained individually in instances of those classes. Thus, not only does the frame representation provide a mechanism for decomposing the rule-sets and for referencing them, but it also provides a mechanism for structuring the relationship between the rule-sets.

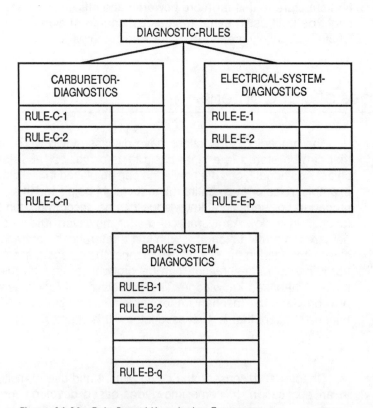

Figure 14-18 Rule-Based Knowledge Taxonomy

This structure permits not only a better understanding of the rule-based knowledge, but also a more efficient application of the rules, since only the rules in the relevant rule-set need be considered at any one time. Further, the frame-based structuring of rules permits relevant rules to be inherited from classes through subclasses to specific instances of rules.

Similarly, references to rules or rule classes can be inherited down through nonrule knowledge taxonomies. Consider the CARBURETOR-DIAGNOSTICS rule-set in Figure 14-18 to determine whether a carburetor is working properly. A reference to these rules might be contained in a slot within the AUTOMOBILES frame, representing the class of automobiles. These rules would then be inherited by all subclasses of AUTOMOBILES (e.g., CHEVROLET and CHRYSLER) as well as by specific instances of classes (e.g., MY-FORD). Thus, the carburetor diagnostic rule-set would be available to every class and instance for use as needed.

The inheritance of rule-sets (or references to rule-sets) offers a number of advantages. Assume that the carburetor diagnostic processes for Chevrolet and Chrysler automobiles are basically similar but differ slightly with respect to certain details. Thus, a basic set of diagnostic rules could be referenced at the level of AUTOMOBILES, and this set would automatically be made available to every subclass of AUTOMOBILES, as well as to any specific instance of AUTOMOBILES. The inherited rule-set could be slightly modified at a subclass level (e.g., CHEVROLET) by adding and deleting rules to reflect considerations unique to a particular brand of automobile.

Then each specific instance of an automobile (e.g., MY-FORD) would inherit references to an appropriate set of carburetor diagnostic rules. Given any instance of AUTOMOBILES, the inference mechanism could reference that frame's carburetor diagnostic rules without having to determine which rules might be applicable to that particular vehicle. Any general changes in diagnostic procedures could be reflected in the basic rules, and these changes would automatically be available to derivative classes and instances in the knowledge taxonomy.

Similarly, a change to the rules pertaining to Ford automobiles could be made to the FORD frame. These changes would be reflected not only in FORD, but also in all frames descendant from the class FORD (e.g., LTD, MY-FORD). However, these changes would not be reflected in the frames for any other type of car (e.g., CHRYSLER) or in frames representing more general subclasses of automobiles in the hierarchy (e.g., DOMESTIC). The benefits that can be gained from this representational form are enormous.

An alternative way of organizing the carburetor rules is reflected in Figure 14-19. The individual rules can be represented as instances, as shown in the right-hand side of the diagram. These are gathered together into classes (e.g., CHEVY-GENERAL, CHEVY-SPECIFIC). Because many of the general rules are common to several types of vehicles, they are related to more than one class.

The DIAGNOSTICS slot of the class AUTOMOBILES would then contain a reference to the GENERAL-RULES class, which in turn would provide access to the individual diagnostic rules. However, the reference to these rules would not be inherited; only the slot would pass down

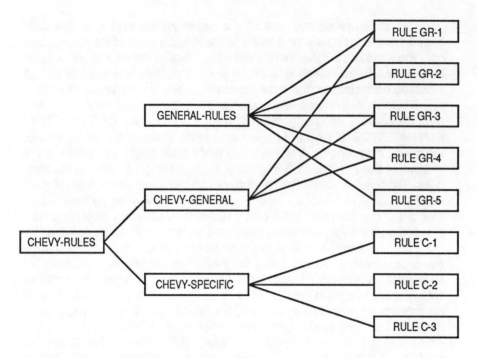

Figure 14-19 Alternative Rule Structure

through the hierarchy. At the level of the CHEVROLET class, a reference would be placed in the DIAGNOSTICS slot to the CHEVY-RULES. These in turn would provide access to the CHEVY-GENERAL rules (which are a subset of the general rules) and the CHEVY-SPECIFIC rules, which are unique to Chevrolets. CHEVY-GENERAL and CHEVY-SPECIFIC then provide access to the specific rules that are to be used for diagnosing a problem in a Chevrolet.

Procedures (Methods)

Slots may also contain functions, permitting procedural knowledge to be incorporated within the frame representation. (Such functions, when used to support object-oriented programming, are often referred to as *methods*.) Analogous to the inclusion of rules within a slot, the inclusion of a function or method provides a very powerful way to structure the distribution of procedural or behavioral knowledge within an application.

The automobile example of the previous subsection can easily be adapted to this case. Just substitute the term "function" for the term "rule-set" to create an appropriate example. All of the arguments made above with respect to rule-sets and inheritance apply equally well for functions and procedural knowledge representations.

In the case of functions, however, some specialized types of inheritance are provided by various knowledge-based system development tools. These inheritance mechanisms permit some procedural code at a subordinate level to be combined with a function inherited from a parent frame rather than being replaced by it. Thus, instead of making local

Prior to Inheritance

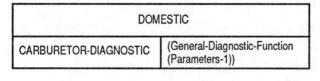

DOMESTIC	
CARBURETOR-DIAGNOSTIC	(General-Diagnostic-Function (Parameters-1))

CHRYSLER	
CARBURETOR-DIAGNOSTIC	(Special-Chrysler-Diagnostic-Function (Parameters-2))

Post-Inheritance Combination

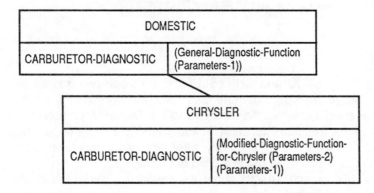

DOMESTIC	
CARBURETOR-DIAGNOSTIC	(General-Diagnostic-Function (Parameters-1))

CHRYSLER	
CARBURETOR-DIAGNOSTIC	(Modified-Diagnostic-Function-for-Chrysler (Parameters-2) (Parameters-1))

Figure 14-20 Before-Type Inheritance

changes to the inherited diagnostic function at the manufacturer class level (e.g., CHEVROLET) to reflect differences in procedures between different automobiles, those changes can be placed directly in the slots of the descendant frames. Then, instead of replacing the inherited function (as would customarily be the case), the modifications would be applied to that function. This technique permits local changes to be made to a function automatically at each level in the knowledge taxonomy. The knowledge crafter need not worry about whether all changes were made or whether they were made correctly in every frame.

Method Inheritance

Function or procedural knowledge can be inherited from parent to descendant frame in the usual ways. However, some special types of inheritance are desirable for procedural knowledge. The following two forms illustrate some of the possibilities.

Method Inheritance: Before

Before inheritance is so named because the function stored in the child's slot is applied *before* the inherited function from the parent has been applied. The top portion of Figure 14-20 shows a function in each of

```
General-Diagnostic-Function (Parameters-1);
General Function Code;
Return;
End;
```

Figure 14-21a   Skeleton of the General Diagnostic Function

```
Special-Chrysler-Diagnostic-Function (Parameters-2);
Special Function Code;
Return;
End;
```

Figure 14-21b   Skeleton of the Special Chrysler Diagnostic Function

two frames (DOMESTIC and CHRYSLER) when those two frames are unrelated. One references a general diagnostic function while the other references a special Chrysler diagnostic function. The lower portion of the figure shows the resultant function in the CHRYSLER frame, named "modified diagnostic function" for clarity, after inheritance has taken place (after CHRYSLER has been made a child of DOMESTIC).

Figures 14-21a and 14-21b show the respective skeletons of the "code" for the two original functions, while Figure 14-21c shows the skeleton of the combined function. Note that the functions are combined; they are not just called one after the other. Thus, the before-function can actually exit, in which case the inherited function would not be performed at all.

Before inheritance can be used for several purposes. The child function can serve as a monitor, reporting or recording data whenever the function is called. It can serve as a filter, checking whether the conditions are such that the general routine should be skipped. It can also serve as a preprocessor, modifying or adjusting values before supplying them to the general routine. Two different parameter sets were used for the two functions in the example for the sake of clarity; however, in practice a common set is often used.

Method Inheritance: After

After inheritance is so named because the function stored in the child's slot is applied *after* the inherited function from the parent has been applied. The situation is the same as depicted in Figure 14-20 and Figures 14-21a and 14-21b, but the functions are combined differently, as shown in Figure 14-21d.

After inheritance can also be used for several purposes. Again, the child function can serve as a monitor, reporting or recording the effects of the application of the parent routine. It can also serve as a post-proces-

```
Modified-Diagnostic-Function (Parameters-2, Parameters-1);
Special Function Code;
Call General-Diagnostic-Function (Parameters-1);
Return;
End;
```

Figure 14-21c Skeleton of the Modified Diagnostic Function with Before Inheritance

```
Modified-Diagnostic-Function (Parameters-2, Parameters-1);
Call General-Diagnostic-Function (Parameters-1);
Special Function Code;
Return;
End;
```

Figure 14-21d Skeleton of the Modified Diagnostic Function with After Inheritance

sor, modifying or adjusting values before they are returned from the function. Again, two different parameter sets were shown, but the child function usually uses the parent function's parameters.

Method Inheritance: Other

Inheritance can be defined and implemented in many other ways. For example, the parent function could be inherited into the "middle" of the child code. Rather than combining the functions to form a new function associated with the child, the knowledge crafter could achieve the equivalent processing by sending the child function up to be processed with the parent function. This type of inheritance is analogous to the "send to super" feature of SmallTalk(1).

Object-Oriented Programming

The development of programs on the basis of associating all data and programmed behavior (e.g., functions) with each object in the application system is known as *object-oriented programming*. Messages are sent to objects requesting that particular functions or services be performed. The object responds, relying on methods (functions) to provide the requested action. Necessary data are obtained from the requesting message, from data stored with the object, and from other objects as necessary.

Such message passing may appear similar to function or subroutine calls, and well it should. However, it differs in that the definition of the function is taken from the object *receiving* the message, not the object sending the message.

Each object can be represented as a frame, with the data about that object stored in slots in its frame. The various behaviors of the object are provided by methods that are also stored in the frame's slots. Messages are then exchanged between objects to provide a collection of behaviors that represent the purpose of the entire system.

Many people have concluded that object-oriented programming is nothing more than the development of programs using subroutine calls to a core set of subroutines. While technically true, that opinion misses the point that object-oriented programming represents a methodology for thinking about a problem, an approach to structuring a computer program. The modularization and the association of data with each object provides a number of benefits including error reduction and comparatively easy maintenance.

The simulation language Simula(2) was probably the first successful language to employ object-oriented programming techniques. More recently, object-oriented programming has been refined in the SmallTalk(1) programming language system. Under one name or another, various dialects of LISP offer facilities that support object-oriented programming. For example, ZetaLISP™(3), LUCID CommonLisp(4), and other LISP dialects offer an object-oriented programming capability through a system called FLAVORS.

Example

Consider a knowledge-based application dealing with failure diagnostics for automobiles. Objects would be constructed representing various kinds of automobiles. A frame-based representation, such as shown in Figure 14-9, would be a typical means for representing such a system. As was discussed previously in the subsection on procedures and function inheritance, various diagnostic routines could be provided at various levels of the knowledge taxonomy, with local modifications made to reflect differences between manufacturers' products, differences between models, and so forth.

The diagnostic routines would be called into play by a set of rules that analyzed symptoms exhibited by a car. A message to a particular automobile (object) would trigger the performance of the requested diagnostic function for that car. The inference mechanism would not need to perform tests to isolate which procedures should be applied given the identity of the particular car being examined. The appropriate diagnostic routines would already be associated with that car. The inference mechanism would only need to execute the function (perform the method).

Thus, in developing the diagnostic logic of the system, the knowledge crafter need not be concerned about providing the necessary tailoring each time a particular diagnostic procedure is to be used to produce additional information about the failure in the automobile. All such specialization will already be reflected in the methods for the diagnostics associated with each given automobile.

Obviously, this approach has several benefits in terms of development efficiency, ease of modification, simpler application logic, clarity of documentation, and reduction in number of errors. Further, development of a complete set of methods for "every" object is not as formidable a task as it might at first appear. Because of the hierarchical structure of the objects and the inheritance capabilities, much of the method development for individual objects (frames) is provided implicitly through inheritance rather than explicitly through separate coding.

The key observation to be made about object-oriented programming is how the benefits are derived from the integration of the approach with the various facilities of a frame-based representation.

Example Continued

Assume that the critical facts associated with a particular automobile undergoing a diagnostic test are to be printed out. This request may arise from the execution of a rule-set, or from a knowledge crafter or a user browsing the knowledge base and seeking to obtain certain information.

In this case, however, an extensive set of programs is not needed. A single message to the frame containing the automobile of interest, requesting that its critical data be displayed on the screen, will suffice. The "critical data" method for that particular automobile will assemble the necessary data for that car directly; an extensive set of tests to determine which types of data are considered critical for particular brands and models of automobiles is not needed. Next, this method sends a message to an "output" object that has routines for displaying a set of data on the screen. (If the data were to be sent to a printer or a disk file, the process would be similar except that the message would be sent to a different method. No local program code is involved in determining the way to package and transfer the data to any particular device.)

The benefits from such modularization are striking. A change in a diagnostic procedure for a particular model of automobile can be made directly to the appropriate method associated with that automobile. All changes would be localized to a single method. The knowledge crafter would not need to search for all sections of the entire program that referenced or were in some way involved with that particular diagnostic. Even scattered revisions can often be made in a single place, since the revision would be inherited downward in the representation hierarchy to all descendants.

If a developer modifies a printer driver (e.g., as a result of a change made to the printer actually attached to the computer system), only the one method that is responsible for displaying data on that printer need be changed. No other code fragments would be involved with the printer, eliminating the need for the knowledge crafter to search through the application looking for code fragments and then to examine that code to determine whether modifications would be required to reflect the change made to the equipment.

Where Is Object-Oriented Programming Useful?

The preceding paragraphs have focused on the maintenance advantages of object-oriented programming; however, the representational benefits are available in a wide variety of applications. Any time the application involves the behavioral representation of a set of objects, object-oriented programming is a candidate development style or approach. Similarly, the object-oriented approach should be considered any time the application logic involves such behavioral performance or triggering of a behavior from several locations. Keep in mind that the benefit of this means of structuring and applying knowledge derives from the structural characteristics of the application, not the particular domain knowledge to be associated with the system.

As a practical matter, object-oriented programming is inextricably intertwined with a frame-based representation and the organization of the knowledge base. Many of the benefits of the object-oriented approach will be lost if a frame-based representation is not used. This provides two hints for use during the design process in Chapter 6:

- Any time a frame-based representation appears to be appropriate, an object-oriented programming approach should be considered.

- Any time an object-oriented approach appears to be appropriate, based on expected behavioral characteristics of the application, employing a frame-based representation should be considered (though perhaps in conjunction with other representational forms as well).

Interestingly, despite the close relationship between frame-based organizations, rule-based systems, and object-oriented programming, a rule-based system operating with a frame-based representation generally represents a violation of object-oriented programming principles. Technically, in a pure object-oriented approach, data from a frame (e.g., slot definitions and values) must be kept within the object itself and are not accessible from outside. Only the functions operating within the object have free access to the data. This restriction enforces the modularity and independence required to achieve the benefits of object-oriented programming. However, this requirement, if enforced, would prevent a rule-based knowledge representation from accessing the information contained in a companion frame-based representation!

Advantages of Frame-Based Reasoning

The chief advantage of frame-based reasoning is that it provides a means for structuring a variety of types of data in the knowledge base and a framework whereby not only the data but also the structure of those data can be reasoned about. Thus, a frame-based representation:

- Greatly aids in structuring the design for a knowledge-based application

- Enables rules and procedures in an application to be more generic, thereby reducing rule-set or procedure size and making the knowledge base easier to understand and test

- Compartmentalizes the data in the knowledge base, oftentimes reducing the complexity so that an application can be built and tested in less time

- Permits greater understanding of knowledge structure and relationships through graphical displays of the structure
- Enhances the maintainability of the knowledge base
- Provides many of the essential characteristics of an object once the type of that object has been identified, eliminating the need to derive these properties individually.

Crafting a Knowledge-Based Application Using a Frame-Based Representation

An early step in studying frame-based reasoning is to examine various information taxonomies. Such taxonomies are interesting to manipulate. Soon the student has an opportunity to relate a taxonomy to a ruleset and to relate taxonomies to one another. Making these relations can also be enjoyable, but soon interest turns toward developing such taxonomies.

In a rule-based reasoning system, where rules or rule-sets are the only medium for representing and storing knowledge, getting started is (supposedly) easy. The student just starts "writing rules."

In a frame-based reasoning system many more issues need to be considered. First, the type of reasoning that will be necessary must be planned. Then the tasks to be performed by the rules have to be specified and the requirements to accomplish that processing must be determined. Only then can the developer start to sketch out a few rules, identify a small hierarchy of frames, and actually test that the structural concept performs as expected.

We have found that, in developing the beginnings of a frame-based representation for an application, blackboard and paper sessions held among the knowledge-crafting team members are best interspersed with sessions at the workstation to test the ideas. Frame-based application development systems are typically implemented for use with AI workstations and incorporate a considerable number of graphical aids for creating and testing the application. This hardware-software combination offers remarkable efficiency early in the development cycle; teams can often sketch out an implementation for two hours' worth of designing at the blackboard in about one hour at a workstation.

The consequences of this efficiency are significant. First, developers are much less reluctant to throw away a design that is only partially correct; second, it does not take very long to get the design correct. In addition, the success or failure of a given design can be determined in rather short order so that developers can usually find an opportunity to test and measure a pet design.

Problems with Frame-Based Reasoning

Perhaps the most detrimental aspects of frame-based reasoning systems are that frame-based and object-oriented programming techniques are not yet commonplace in the computer world and people need time and patience to master the techniques and use them both fluently and properly. These techniques are fundamentally simple, although at first they may seem complex. It is well worth the several months' time that it might take for a knowledge crafter to become highly proficient in their use.

Efficiency Considerations

One of the major dissatisfactions expressed with frame-based reasoning concerns efficiency. The structures and capabilities that have been described in this chapter offer a wide variety of benefits, but these benefits are achieved only at a price. The dynamic ability to modify the knowledge structure or to modify the facets associated with a slot during execution of the application system requires that a considerable amount of checking be performed at execution time. The computer cannot store a fact in a frame with the execution of a single store instruction. Instead, the various facets governing the slot must be referenced to verify that storage of this particular value is permitted, to check whether this action is to be trapped, and so forth. A simple store command that would involve a single computer instruction in systems using other forms of knowledge representation can easily explode into the tens and hundreds of instructions. This expansion, of course, is accompanied by a concomitant degradation in the application's execution speed.

Abuse of Frame-Based Reasoning

This chapter has focused on the advantages that a developer can gain using a frame-based approach for representing certain aspects of an application's knowledge base, but the process can also be abused. In a desire to build taxonomies, a new knowledge crafter can easily become overly enthusiastic and create inappropriate taxonomies. Such mistakes can lead to severe difficulties subsequently when the knowledge crafter must reason about the knowledge. We have labeled persons having this difficulty as having contracted *taxonomic fever*.

The other form of abuse is similarly insidious. Much of the advantage of a knowledge-based approach to problem solving arises from the use of nonprocedural representations of knowledge. However, the ability to store functions in frames provides the developer with the opportunity to convert an application into a conventional program, relying almost exclusively on procedural program representations. Like Pandora's box, once the lid is opened (i.e., a procedural program is permitted), procedural approaches (which are what most people have experienced with computers) can proliferate. Sometimes developers, particularly novices, must be prevented from doing procedural programming, which would force that person at least to think in the less familiar nonprocedural terms. In the previous chapter we termed this disease *procedural fever*.

"Taxonomic Fever"

A novice can easily succumb to taxonomic fever, which causes a taxonomy to be devised to represent every phenomena in sight. While most of the outward signs of this disease disappear after the first few days of exposure to object-oriented programming or frame-based reasoning, the inward vestiges of the disease can linger, with a wayward taxonomy creeping into a design every now and then. Therefore, a certain litmus test needs to be applied to each taxonomy in the design, namely:

- How does this taxonomy support the reasoning process?
- Does the taxonomy refine the reasoning concept, that is, does each unit of the taxonomy in the direction of the leaves represent a specialization of the root (most general) unit?

If the knowledge crafter has difficulty verifying these tests, the taxonomy and the rules that use it may not be well-designed.

An Example

Consider the automotive diagnostic application, for example. In such an application, the taxonomy and the rules should represent the order and structure of the automotive diagnostic process, which could easily have several taxonomies (with some, perhaps, containing only rules). Among these taxonomies, however, it would be surprising to find a car parts taxonomy that starts with the car as a whole and goes down through all the various assemblies and subassemblies to the final bolts and nuts. Why? Because the complete parts structure of a car is not used to diagnose an automotive malfunction; the mechanic does not selectively test each nut, bolt, and washer. He does not reason over the whole car, and his underlying reasoning in isolating a problem and diagnosing it is quite different from that described by the parts taxonomy.

A Taxonomic Mistake

One of the mistakes frequently made by novice knowledge crafters is the construction of an inconsistent taxonomy. If, for example, AUTOMO-BILES is the top frame in a taxonomy and if 4-CYLINDER is a leaf frame at the bottom of the taxonomy, then 4-CYLINDER should be a specialization of AUTOMOBILES. Although representing a more specialized object, 4-CYLINDER should still characterize something that would be known as an automobile. Since 4-CYLINDER is a more specialized engine rather than a more specialized automobile, the taxonomy is at least mislabeled if not in error. Such mislabeling can really confuse and obfuscate knowledge in a frame-based representation.

Unfortunately, the knowledge crafter can fairly easily fall into this type of trap. An example was shown in connection with Figure 14-11b, in which MY-FORD was depicted as an instance of both AUTOMOBILES and ENGINES. Another example is shown in Figure 14-22. The taxonomy is consistent until the class FORD is reached. At this point rather than the class being broken down into different types of Ford automobiles, the class is broken down by the components that go into a car. The fact that the remainder of the hierarchy is consistent with those components does not eliminate the problem. The switch in logical progression has already been made. The best procedure to test for such representational errors is

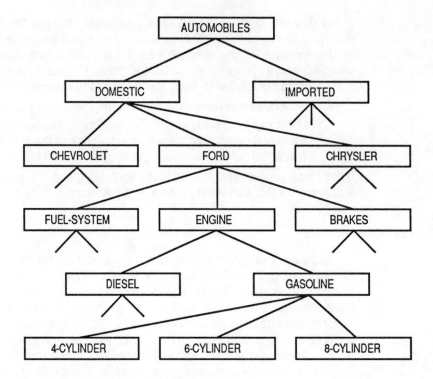

Figure 14-22 An Erroneous Taxonomy

to ask at each level whether those objects represent types of objects belonging to parent classes.

Fortunately, these problems diminish greatly as people become more accustomed to and familiar with frame-based reasoning and its capabilities.

"Procedural Fever"

A word of caution should be provided at this point. After knowledge crafters become familiar with the capabilities of frame-based reasoning systems, they develop an understanding of where and how to employ functions. Typically, functions are used rather sparingly in an application, being inserted only at points where their computational abilities are truly needed.

Functions, however, provide a mechanism to revert back to old and comfortable programming practices. They can thus provide a wonderful escape hatch for the novice: in frame-based reasoning a rule can invoke a function in which the novice is free to hack his way out of the problem. Yes, functions do make sense where computation is necessary, but the use of functions to handle fundamental reasoning problems may indicate that the application is improperly structured, that the developer has indeed caught procedural fever.

Summary

Frame-based reasoning offers an attractive range of techniques for structuring a knowledge-based application and for supporting very rapid prototype development. It can provide enormous benefits in knowledge representation and system modification. However, these tools do not replace the detailed analysis of the application necessary for it to be a success, and blind application of these tools can lead to problems.

A Warning

The rather broad range of frame-based capabilities described in this chapter does not imply that any particular knowledge-based application development tool has all of these capabilities. Some tools, of course, do not offer any frame-based representational capabilities; others offer subsets of the capabilities described herein. Part of the feasibility study and the early design work involves examining the problem's natural knowledge representations, comparing these requirements with the representational capabilities of eligible tools, and finally selecting a development tool and organizing the knowledge to fit within the representations available.

Rule of Thumb

Frame-based reasoning is in many ways like physics. In that domain, the behavior of the physical world generally has a simple explanation. Thus, if the researcher finds that the explanation of a particular phenomenon (or the solution of a particular problem) is becoming difficult or "messy," the difficulty is an indication that a different approach should be taken, that a different representation of the problem should be considered.

Similarly, reasoning with frame-based knowledge is generally a relatively straightforward process. If the knowledge crafter finds that working with a particular representation is becoming increasingly difficult, that difficulty is usually an indication that the representation is wrong. In our experience, stopping at this point and trying a different structure for the knowledge usually significantly reduces the logical complexity of the problem.

Because frame-based reasoning development tools are large and normally require large, specialized workstations, applications developed using them are difficult to move into environments where delivery versions of these tools may not exist. More and more delivery environments are being supported by the manufacturers of these software tools; as time progresses, this problem should become less critical. Also, new personal computer systems built around the Intel 80386 chip may provide a cost-effective delivery vehicle for many applications using frame-based reasoning tools.

References

1)   Goldberg, A. and D. Robson, *Smalltalk-80: The Language and Its Implementation,* Addison-Wesley, Reading, Mass., 1983.

2)   Dahl, O.J. and K. Nygaard, "SIMULA—An Algol-Based Simulation Language," *Communications of the ACM,* Vol. 9, No. 9, 1966.

3)   Symbolics, *Zetalisp,* Cambridge, Mass., 1985.

4)   Lucid, *LUCID CommonLisp*, Menlo Park, Calif., 1986.

CHAPTER 15

Knowledge Crafting
with Multiple Contexts

The yachts shown here at the dock are all identical, having come from the same mold. However, they will pass through a series of different contexts as their skippers attack the same problem—traversing the race course ahead of the other yachts. Each skipper will tackle the problem in a slightly different fashion, leading to a different set of decisions. At the conclusion of the race, each yacht will be in a terminal context, with one of those contexts—the one containing the winning yacht—being more favorable than the others. Similarly, a knowledge-based application can reason about the given problem data in a series of different contexts, with each series representing a different approach and a sequence of different decisions. At the conclusion of the analysis, the terminal solutions can be evaluated and the optimum one selected. Chapter 15 describes the various ways in which multiple contexts can be used in an application to facilitate the solution of a problem.

Introduction

The previous two chapters discussed forms of knowledge representation (rules and frames) that applied to a single *context*. That is, the context of a rule-set (or frame set) was depicted as being a single, all-encompassing universe. Anything that existed, existed in that universe; any changes that were made or conclusions that were drawn applied to that universe. A slot in a frame was described as containing a single value (or a set of values) that related to some aspect of the current universe; it did not contain sets of values, each set pertaining to a different universe or to the same universe at different points in time.

Yet, for many types of problems, knowledge can be represented in different contexts and reasoned about in its own context. For example, consider the problem of planning a route from your house to a friend's house at a time when a parade is moving through town. As you plan your route from street corner to street corner, several things will be changing. Obviously, your location (and the history of your past movements) will be different at each street corner. Unless you can move at the speed of light, however, traveling conditions will also change while you are moving from corner to corner; traffic flows and street closures will change over time as the parade moves through town. Thus, the environment (context, if you will) through which you are traveling will change during the course of the trip. Each decision to be made at a street corner (i.e., which corner to move to next) will be made in a different context. This context includes not only the sequence of decisions you previously made but also the routing alternatives open to you at that particular time.

Knowledge representations and reasoning mechanisms can be modified in several ways to permit a knowledge-based application to address problems characterized by multiple or changing contexts. In some cases each context is an extension of a previous context (i.e., knowledge is added to form new contexts). In other cases contexts are marked by the elimination of knowledge. For example, a context at 9 AM might offer crossing Main Street at 5th Avenue as an alternative, but this crossing would not be an alternative in a context at 9:15 AM as the parade would be passing through the intersection at that time.

The use of multiple contexts can raise a new problem for the knowledge crafter to address—searching. The web of possible contexts for a problem can be viewed as a search space. The context network contains all solutions; all that remains for the application is to find an appropriate solution. When the number of possibilities becomes so large that checking all paths through the network is impossible, some type of search strategy will be necessary to limit the number of possibilities explored to some smaller, computationally feasible amount.

All of these aspects can be implemented in several ways; the challenge to the knowledge crafter is to determine an appropriate set of contexts for the application and then to select the best mechanism to work with those contexts.

The Concept of Multiple Contexts

The parade example showed the desirability of using different contexts to represent the state of the universe at different points in time. However, multiple contexts are also desirable for representing different potential or possible states of the universe when the actual state is not known (or cannot be determined). The need to make decisions under conditions of uncertainty or inadequate information is often cited as a rationale for applying a knowledge-based system. These systems are supposed to operate with key information missing and still reach conclusions. How can this be done?

The knowledge-based reasoning discussed in earlier chapters has functioned on the basis of complete information availability. That is, only if the appropriate information is known will the indicated decisions be made, facts concluded, or procedures applied. The key point is information availability, not certainty. The rule structures described in Chapter 13 can handle uncertainty, as shown by the following rule:

IF   there is smoke (certainty greater than .8)
THEN   there is fire (with certainty greater than .7).

The problem arises in a situation where the information to fire a rule is insufficient but where a decision must be made so that further inferencing can take place. A "no conclusion because of insufficient data" type of response is not appropriate.

The solution is to use multiple contexts. One context would be used for each possible decision that could be drawn if appropriate information were available. Each context would be identical in all respects except for a different value for the decision that had to be made. Reasoning could then proceed in each context independently, determining the result (conclusions) that would follow if the assumed decision were the correct one (or were actually made). In other words, rather than stop the reasoning process because of the lack of necessary information, we have just substituted uncertainty about which context is correct. The outcome in each context (i.e., the implications of each decision) can then be determined. The lack of information now implies uncertainty about which context is correct, but it has not precluded determining the implications had that information been available.

An Example

Consider the problem of selecting what clothes to wear tomorrow when a key piece of information—the weather forecast—is missing. Clearly, the reasoning process could come to no conclusion because of the missing information, or it could resort to a catchall rule of the form:

IF   the information needed to decide what clothes to wear
            tomorrow is inadequate
THEN   wear the same type of clothes that were worn today.

A more appropriate alternative would be to establish a number of contexts. Each context would contain the same information about wardrobe, the same knowledge about clothing preferences, and so forth. That is, the knowledge base of each context would be identical to the current context. The new contexts would differ, however, in that each would contain a different assumption about tomorrow's actual weather conditions. Thus, one context might assume rain, another snow, another warm and sunny, and so on. The knowledge-based system could then determine what clothes should be selected in each context. As shown in Figure 15-1, a raincoat and umbrella might be selected in the rainy context, boots in the snowy context, and shorts in the sunny context. The only remaining task would be to determine the next day which context was applicable. The optimum set of clothes could then be worn, as selected in that context.

Another Example

The previous example used multiple contexts because a critical piece of information about the environment (namely, tomorrow's weather) was unknown. However, multiple contexts can also be used very effectively in situations where the inferencing mechanism or the user must make a decision. Lacking information about the implications of each alternative that might be selected, the decision maker needs to find out more about the consequences of the possible choices before actually making the decision. Thus, a set of contexts could be created, one for each possible alternative decision. The best context (i.e., decision) could then be selected, based on the consequences of each choice (as determined by reasoning in each context). Further inferencing could then proceed in the selected context in the same fashion as described previously in Chapters 13 and 14.

Consider, for example, a hiker in the woods coming to a fork in the trail. No sign is present to help the hiker decide which branch of the trail to take, but clearly one of the two paths must be taken. The natural action is to form two contexts, as shown in Figure 15-2a. Using a map, the hiker explores the implications of choosing the first context (taking the left fork),

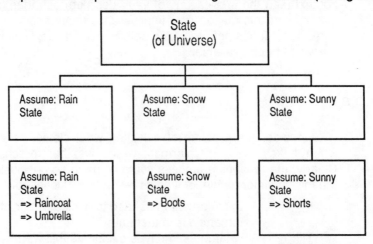

Figure 15-1 Clothes Selection

determining that the destination can be reached, that the distance would be eight miles, and that the terrain would be level. Then the second context (taking the right fork) could be similarly examined, determining that the destination can be reached, that the distance would be five miles, and that the terrain would be hilly. The hiker could then pick the most appropriate fork (e.g., the longer but flatter route) and proceed with the hike. As shown in Figure 15-2b, the added contexts can be discarded and reasoning can be resumed, using the new decision, from the point where it had previously been halted (when it had encountered the path selection issue).

The knowledge crafter thus has a variety of reasons for wanting to work with multiple contexts. In each case, a set of contexts is hypothesized, with each context containing an identical knowledge base except for the assumptions about a key decision. In principle, as many contexts would be created as there were alternatives for the decision to be made. However, in some cases, creating only a subset of the possible contexts may be permissible, thereby improving computational efficiency. For example, the person selecting tomorrow's clothes during the summer could eliminate the context for snowy weather.

Hierarchical Context Structure

The preceding examples have reflected a flat or one-layer context structure. Faced with a decision, the reasoning mechanism constructed

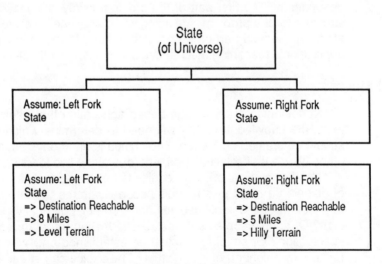

Figure 15-2a   Contexts for Hiker's Path Selection

State (of Universe)
Left Fork Taken

Figure 15-2b   Knowledge Structure after Path Selection

and explored a set of contexts reflecting the decision alternatives. However, the exploration of one of those contexts might in turn give rise to another decision that required the creation of another layer of contexts. Thus, the multiple-context concept should be viewed as a hierarchical or tree structure, with each context possibly spawning additional contexts at the next lower level of the hierarchy.

Terminology

A number of existing commercially available knowledge-based reasoning tools offer some form of multiple context capability. Unfortunately, the developers use a variety of terms in the sales and promotional literature for these products. Thus, for example, ART™ looks at each context as a "viewpoint" on the knowledge and hence offers a viewpoint mechanism. KEE™, on the other hand, terms its contexts "worlds" and hence offers a capability to reason about multiple worlds. Knowledge Craft™ relies on a truth maintenance mechanism embedded in its OPS5 forward-chaining mechanism.

Reasoning with Multiple Contexts

The problem of reasoning with multiple contexts can be divided into two parts, although decisions made for each part should not be made independently. The first part of the problem involves selecting the context structure for the problem—deciding when and where contexts will be created. The second part of the problem relates to the manner in which the application's reasoning mechanism should process those contexts.

Context Structure

In designing a knowledge-based application that uses multiple contexts, the knowledge crafter will need to determine which new contexts should be created and when. The choice is often obvious, as in the case of the hiker's trail selection problem (one of the two forks has to be taken).

In other applications, the choice is not so clear. The earlier example of planning a route to a friend's house illustrates the difficulty. Should a new context be established for each corner potentially reached in the plan? Or should contexts be established when the plan reaches a major intersection? Or should a context be established only when the plan enters a new neighborhood or district? The choice can affect more than just computational efficiency; it may make the problem more or less difficult to address with a knowledge-based system.

Similarly, the knowledge crafter will need to decide how long contexts should be maintained. If contexts are maintained for the duration of the problem solution, the result is a tree-structured set of contexts, as shown in Figure 15-3b. On the other hand, contexts may be spawned, reasoned about, and then discarded, as was done in the hiking example (see Figures 15-2a and b). Thus, a very flat structure could be maintained. The choice has implications for the types of reasoning that can be applied to the application.

The structuring of the knowledge in an application can be critical to the success of that system, regardless of which type or types of representations are used for the knowledge. Applications with hierarchical structures can be addressed particularly well with multiple contexts; this approach can provide considerable benefits in terms of solution speed and quality. Hierarchical problem solving is addressed at the end of this chapter and again in Chapter 17 in connection with blackboard representations.

Reasoning with Contexts

The second part of the multiple-context problem involves reasoning with the various contexts created during problem solution. A variety of mechanisms can process the knowledge contained in a context as well as in a structure of contexts. Although the choice of context structure is different from the selection of the reasoning mechanism to work with that structure, the decisions are not independent. One structure may fit the problem but be difficult to reason with. Conversely, an effective reasoning mechanism may not work well with the context structure that fits the problem. Thus, the best structure-mechanism *combination* must be selected. The knowledge crafter can employ the following three mechanisms to reason with the context structure that might be created:

1. Parallel reasoning
2. Pruning
3. Merging.

Illustrative Example

An example can serve as a framework to discuss each of these mechanisms. Assume that Jim has made two lists of activities for a warm Saturday afternoon, as shown in Figure 15-3a. The first list consists of the "work" he must do around the house, the second of the "fun" activities that he hopes to have time for.

A knowledge-based system attempting to select and order the activities to be performed could easily generate a huge context tree. In this example the activities could be performed in 5,040 possible sequences, and a total of 13,700 contexts could be generated. This tree is too large to reproduce in this book; Figure 15-3b presents only a section of this tree for illustrating each of the three approaches.

Work List	Fun List
TAKEOUT the garbage	WATCH the ball game on TV
MOW the lawn	RELAX with a cold beer
PAINT the shed	TALK with Susan on the phone
	READ the new issue of *Fishing* magazine

Figure 15-3a Activity Lists

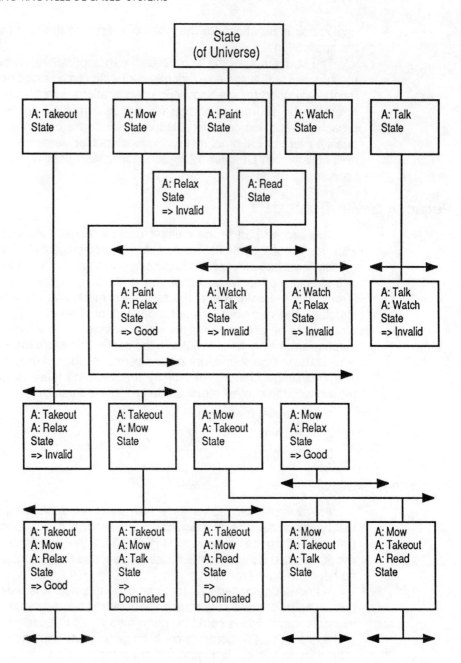

Figure 15-3b   Portion of Context Tree

Now, consider how a knowledge-based application might reason with these contexts. The context tree for the Saturday afternoon example is a conceptual structure that reflects all the contexts that potentially could be spawned. The figure's contents do not imply that all of these contexts would be spawned or even that all those that were spawned would coexist at one time. Part of the tree might never be grown (e.g., never explored) and part of it might be cut off (e.g., removed) so that it no longer existed. Thus, the actual context tree at any particular time would consist of some number of contexts (greater than or equal to one) distributed across a number of levels (again greater than or equal to one).

Parallel Reasoning

The ability to have multiple contexts in existence at the same time provides the opportunity to reason with those contexts in parallel. For example, consider the following rule that might be contained in the Saturday afternoon knowledge base:

IF   you are hot and sweaty
AND   RELAX with a cold beer is still on the fun list
THEN   RELAX with a cold beer would be a good next activity.

This rule has application in several contexts and could validly be tested in all contexts. Thus, it can logically be applied "everywhere" rather than being applied to selected contexts one by one. Such a global application of the rule considerably simplifies the logic for the knowledge crafter. In essence, the rule would appear as:

IF   *in any context* you are hot and sweaty
AND   RELAX with a cold beer is still on the fun list
THEN   RELAX with a cold beer would be a good next activity
          after this context.

In the case of the contexts shown in Figure 15-3b, the rule only fired in those contexts that followed one in which a MOW or PAINT activity was taking place. The resulting GOOD conclusion is shown for the three applicable contexts.

The preceding example involved the application of a rule to each context, but the use of a multiple-context representation is independent of other forms of knowledge representation that might be used. Thus, knowledge in a frame structure would be reproduced in each child frame, and that knowledge could be accessed in each context. Similarly, procedural knowledge could be replicated in frames, and so forth.

Pruning

If the inference mechanism seeks to generate all possible contexts, the computer system will rapidly grind to a halt. Even for our small problem involving the scheduling of seven activities, the number of contexts (13,700) can become unwieldly. Obviously, if the use of multiple contexts is to be feasible, mechanisms are needed to reduce the search space, to reduce the number of contexts generated and considered. One such mechanism is referred to as *pruning*, the trimming of the context tree analogously to the way a living tree in the garden might be pruned.

When a branch is trimmed, no further contexts are spawned from it. Thus, the higher up in the tree a branch can be trimmed, the greater the number of contexts that need not be generated and that need not be examined. Pruning can take place on a context-by-context basis. For example, if Jim believed that he should relax with a cold beer only after doing something that would make him hot and thirsty, then a context involving the RELAX activity would not be considered appropriate unless it also contained PAINT or MOW as previously scheduled activities (i.e., indicating that a more strenuous PAINT or MOW activity had been performed). Any schedule containing TAKEOUT and RELAX as the first two activities would be viewed as less favorable than other schedules that contained a different first pair of activities.

When evaluating the desirability of the TAKEOUT-RELAX context, the inference mechanism could therefore decide to prune the tree at this point, to block the generation of any further contexts from this one, thereby preventing the generation of any activity sequence beginning with TAKEOUT and RELAX as the initial activities. This pruning was shown in Figure 15-3b by the INVALID conclusion for the TAKEOUT-RELAX context and by the lack of any further contexts spawned from it.

Another way to prune the search space is through the use of constraints. Such constraints would be a set of conditions that all contexts must satisfy. These conditions might reflect the valid range that the values in a slot might take, the number of objects that might be permitted in a class, the state in which certain values would be valid, and so forth. Any context for which these conditions were not satisfied could immediately be marked INVALID, pruning the tree at that point. Consider a constraint of the form:

IF   the number of work activities remaining to be performed
            exceeds the number of fun activities to be performed
THEN   mark this context as invalid.

As shown in Figure 15-3b, this results in the pruning of three potential branches of the tree, as the context involving WATCH and RELAX and the two contexts involving WATCH and TALK have been marked as INVALID.

The previously expressed desire to prevent the RELAX activity unless preceded by a more strenuous activity could also have been established as a constraint as follows:

IF   the RELAX activity is contained in this context
AND   the MOW activity remains to be performed
AND   the PAINT activity remains to be performed
THEN   mark this context as invalid.

The application of this constraint would effectively mark the initial context containing RELAX as invalid, thereby preventing any further contexts from being spawned from it.

If a set of constraints can be developed that will eliminate a number of potential contexts near the top of the tree or that will eliminate a large percentage of the possible contexts, then an application may proceed as if it would generate all possible contexts. Otherwise, finding some other approach to limit the number of contexts considered will be necessary. This topic is treated further in the subsection on search mechanisms below.

Dominance provides yet another way to prune the search space. If the inference mechanism can determine that one of the developing solutions will necessarily be better than another one, then it can prune the dominated context, marking it invalid so that no further contexts will be spawned from it.

For example, Jim's preference to RELAX after a hot, sweaty activity can be used to prune the search tree in this manner. As shown in Figure 15-3b, the TAKEOUT-MOW-RELAX activity is rated GOOD. Hence, Jim will view TAKEOUT-MOW-RELAX as a better context than either the TAKEOUT-MOW-READ or TAKEOUT-MOW-TALK contexts, since the latter two contexts offer a less preferred fun activity after the hot and sweaty MOW activity. That is, any solution branch containing the TAKEOUT-MOW-RELAX context would be preferred over solutions containing the TAKEOUT-MOW-READ or TAKEOUT-MOW-TALK contexts, so no further contexts need be generated and evaluated from the two less preferred contexts. This pruning is indicated in Figure 15-3b by the dominated conclusion for the two less preferred contexts and by the lack of any further contexts spawned from them.

Merging

Another way to reduce the search space is through the use of context merges. When two contexts have identical sets of facts and assumptions, the context tree need not be extended further from both contexts. Anything that could be inferred or deduced in one context could be inferred or deduced in the other. Thus, the branches extending from each identical context would also be identical. The identical contexts can safely be merged into one, so that only one branch rather than two will be explored by the inference engine, working from the common context.

Consider the state of the household chores after the garbage has been taken out and the lawn mowed. If all of the activity selection rules are based on the identity of the activities that have been performed and that remain to be performed, then the order in which tasks have been performed is not important. The TAKEOUT-MOW context and the MOW-TAKEOUT context would be identical. Both of those tasks would have been performed, and the same set of five activities would remain to be performed. Thus, the activities that follow from the TAKEOUT-MOW context will be the same as those that follow from the MOW-TAKEOUT context. As can be seen in Figure 15-3b, TALK and READ are established as the next contexts, and these extend identically from both the MOW-TAKEOUT and the TAKEOUT-MOW contexts.

The merge of the TAKEOUT-MOW and MOW-TAKEOUT contexts is shown in Figure 15-3c. Not only have the two contexts been merged, but the number of subcontexts in the tree spawned from these contexts has been cut in half.

The use of multiple contexts can essentially provide sequence information, even though the scheduling rules are not sequence-dependent. That is, the rules that determine the activity to perform next are based solely on the identity of the activities that have been performed and that remain to be performed, the order of task performance being irrelevant. Yet, if one works from the top of the context tree down to a leaf, the sequence in which the activities were selected for performance will be identified.

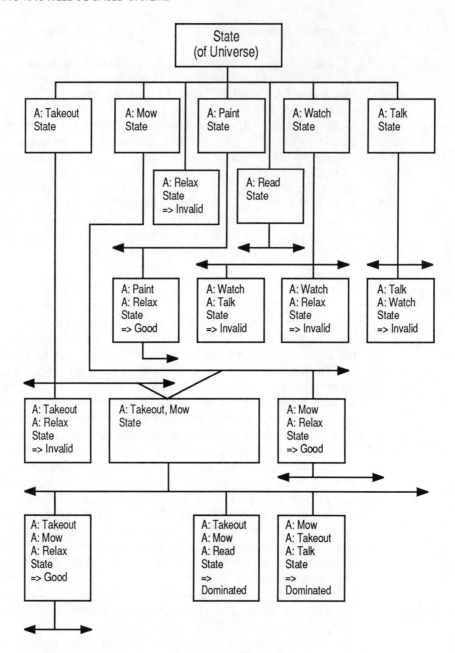

Figure 15-3c Portion of Context Tree with Merge

Truth Maintenance Systems

The discussion so far has focused on what is called *monotonic reasoning*. Because each new context adds to the assumptive base in the context, the assumptive base grows monotonically as contexts are added. However, nonmonotonic reasoning, when the addition of a new context may involve a reduction in the number of assumed facts, is sometimes appropriate. As soon as facts that are true in one context are permitted to be retracted in a subsequent context, a number of problems can arise.

An important function of a *truth maintenance system* or TMS is to address these problems, to maintain the truth or consistency of contexts with respect to their children. (For this reason, these systems are sometimes called "consistency management systems.") Thus, if one assumption is changed, all conclusions resulting from that assumption must be retracted. A brief example might make this statement clearer.

Nonmonotonic Reasoning

Consider a knowledge base consisting of two rules:

Rule 1:   IF   THE STOPLIGHT IS RED
            THEN   IT IS NOT SAFE TO CROSS
                    THE INTERSECTION

Rule 2:   IF   IT IS NOT SAFE TO CROSS
                    THE INTERSECTION
            THEN   APPLY THE BRAKES AND
                    STOP

As shown in Figure 15-4a, the assertion of the hypothesis THE STOPLIGHT IS RED leads to the derivation of IT IS NOT SAFE TO CROSS THE INTERSECTION, which in turn leads to the derivation of APPLY THE BRAKES AND STOP. If THE STOPLIGHT IS GREEN were to be assumed (i.e., THE STOPLIGHT IS RED were to be retracted) and if no further action were to be taken, the incorrect situation shown in Figure 15-4b would result. Clearly, IT IS NOT SAFE TO CROSS THE INTERSECTION would not have been inferred in the absence of THE STOPLIGHT IS RED fact. Thus, the facts inferred from an assumption in a context should be retracted when the assumption is retracted, as shown in Figure 15-4c.

The process can become a bit more complicated. First, the process needs to trace through all the implications. If retracting THE STOPLIGHT IS RED leads to the retraction of IT IS NOT SAFE TO CROSS THE INTERSECTION, then the same reasoning should lead to the subsequent retraction of APPLY THE BRAKES AND STOP (which would not have been concluded without IT IS NOT SAFE TO CROSS THE INTERSECTION). The situation shown in Figure 15-4d would result.

Although the preceding may seem fairly straightforward, more complications can arise. Consider the presence of a third rule:

Rule 3:   IF   A BIG TRUCK IS RAPIDLY
                    APPROACHING ON THE
                    CROSS STREET

            THEN   IT IS NOT SAFE TO CROSS
                    THE INTERSECTION

If indeed a big truck were approaching on the cross street, then the retraction of THE STOPLIGHT IS RED should not lead to the retraction of IT IS NOT SAFE TO CROSS THE INTERSECTION, since a means (pre-

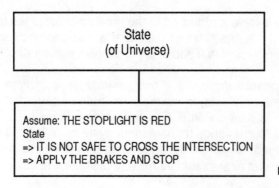

Figure 15-4a Initial Conditions

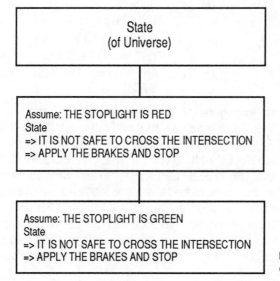

Figure 15-4b Retraction of an Assumption

viously unused) would still exist to derive IT IS NOT SAFE TO CROSS THE INTERSECTION (i.e., from A BIG TRUCK IS RAPIDLY APPROACHING ON THE CROSS STREET).

The Dark Room

A second complication arises in that some types of inferences are irreversible. That is, for some types of reasoning, the states that have been passed through are important, not just the final state. Thus, it would be undesirable for the retraction of an assumption to lead to the retraction of an inference based on that assumption, since it would be important to know that the inference had at one time been made. The following example should clarify the distinction being made, as it shows one situation in which reversibility is desired and another situation in which reversibility is not desired.

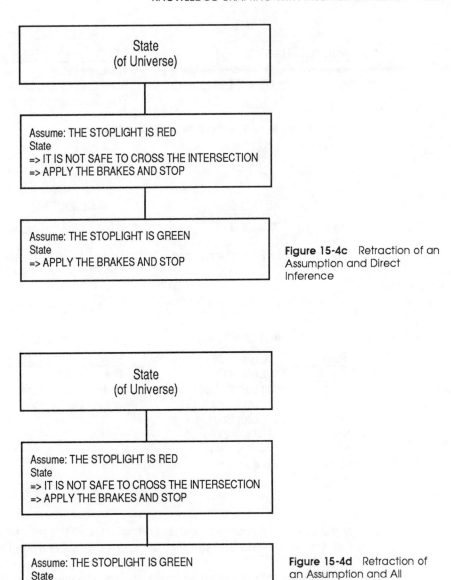

Figure 15-4c Retraction of an Assumption and Direct Inference

Figure 15-4d Retraction of an Assumption and All Inferences

Consider a closed room that contains a light, two people, and an opened roll of film on a table. Let us assume initially that the light is off and the room dark. From this information we can derive that the two individuals cannot see each other and that the film is unexposed. This situation, termed State 1, is shown in Figure 15-5a. The left side of the figure displays the assumption and derived facts; the right side displays the resulting state of the room.

Next the light is turned on, yielding the fairly obvious result shown in Figure 15-5b. The previously existing facts that Doug cannot see Marie

	ACTIONS	RESULTING
Assume:	The Light Is Off	STATE OF UNIVERSE
=>	Doug Cannot See Marie	The Light Is Off
=>	The Film Is Unexposed	Doug Cannot See Marie
		The Film Is Unexposed

Figure 15-5a State 1: Room with Light Turned Off

	ACTIONS	RESULTING
Assume:	The Light Is Off	STATE OF UNIVERSE
=>	Doug Cannot See Marie	The Light Is Off
=>	The Film Is Unexposed	Doug Cannot See Marie
		The Film Is Unexposed

- -

	ACTIONS	RESULTING
Retract:	The Light Is Off	STATE OF UNIVERSE
Assume:	The Light Is On	The Light Is On
<=	Doug Cannot See Marie	Doug Can See Marie
<=	The Film Is Unexposed	The Film Is Exposed
=>	Doug Can See Marie	
=>	The Film Is Exposed	

Figure 15-5b State 2: Room with Light Turned On

and that the film is unexposed are retracted, and the new facts that Doug can see Marie and that the film is exposed are inferred. This produces State 2.

Next the light is turned off again, leaving the situation shown in Figure 15-5c. State 3 is exactly like State 1 *except* that the room has passed through State 2. The fact that Doug can see Marie has been retracted, but the fact that the film is exposed is not retracted since it is an irreversible change.

As might be suspected, the truth maintenance process can be handled in a variety of ways. Three of the major types of TMS are:

1.   Justification TMS (JTMS)

2.   Logic-based TMS (LTMS)

3.   Assumption-based TMS (ATMS).

A complete description of each of these TMSs is beyond the scope of this book; see Doyle(1), McAllester(2), and de Kleer(3) for further information. The following three subsections briefly illustrate the major differences between these alternative forms of TMS.

ACTIONS		RESULTING
Assume:	The Light Is Off	STATE OF UNIVERSE
=>	Doug Cannot See Marie	The Light Is Off
=>	The Film Is Unexposed	Doug Cannot See Marie
		The Film Is Unexposed

- -

ACTIONS		RESULTING
Retract:	The Light Is Off	STATE OF UNIVERSE
Assume:	The Light Is On	The Light Is On
<=	Doug Cannot See Marie	Doug Can See Marie
<=	The Film Is Unexposed	The Film Is Exposed
=>	Doug Can See Marie	
=>	The Film Is Exposed	

- -

ACTIONS		RESULTING
Retract:	The Light Is On	STATE OF UNIVERSE
Assume:	The Light Is Off	The Light Is Off
<=	Doug Can See Marie	Doug Cannot See Marie
=>	Doug Cannot See Marie	The Film Is Exposed

Figure 15-5c   State 3: Room with Light Turned Off Again

Justification TMS

In the basic justification TMS (JTMS), the set of beliefs in the assumptive basis can only grow. It never shrinks. This "moving in one direction only" reflects what is called *monotonic* behavior. The JTMS is the simplest type of TMS. Each fact (predicate) is either in the assumptive base or out of it. If it is in, then it is BELIEVED; if out, it is NOT BELIEVED. Note, however, that not believing something is not the same as believing that thing to be false. In terms of the example about crossing the intersection, NOT BELIEVING that THE STOPLIGHT IS RED does not imply BELIEVING that THE STOPLIGHT IS NOT RED.

The key characteristic of the JTMS is that each fact has only one support item. The preceding example about crossing the intersection had three rules:

Rule 1:	IF	THE STOPLIGHT IS RED
	THEN	IT IS NOT·SAFE TO CROSS
		THE INTERSECTION

Rule 2:	IF	IT IS NOT SAFE TO CROSS THE INTERSECTION
	THEN	APPLY THE BRAKES AND STOP
Rule 3:	IF	A BIG TRUCK IS RAPIDLY APPROACHING ON THE CROSS STREET
	THEN	IT IS NOT SAFE TO CROSS THE INTERSECTION

Assuming that THE STOPLIGHT IS RED and that A BIG TRUCK IS RAPIDLY APPROACHING ON THE CROSS STREET are true, the conclusion IT IS NOT SAFE TO CROSS THE INTERSECTION is potentially supportable by both facts and thus by Rules 1 and 3. However, in the JTMS, there would never be more than one supporting fact. The inferencing process goes only so far as to find the first support for a conclusion. Thus, IT IS NOT SAFE TO CROSS THE INTERSECTION would be supported by either THE STOPLIGHT IS RED or by A BIG TRUCK IS RAPIDLY APPROACHING ON THE CROSS STREET, depending on whether Rule 1 or Rule 3 happened to be fired first.

One version of the JTMS employs nonmonotonic reasoning, in which the beliefs in the assumptive base can grow and shrink. This considerably more complex system uses dependency-directed backtracking to maintain consistency. In this case the system backtracks by retracting the item that caused the inconsistency rather than the last item to be inferred. However, this type of reasoning can lead to looping behavior for some types of problems, creating a nonterminating condition for the inferencing process.

Logic-Based TMS

The logic-based TMS (LTMS) is built on a clause structure in which each predicate has one of three values: TRUE, FALSE, or UNKNOWN. That is, the knowledge is stored as a set of logical clauses, with the clauses being interpreted on the basis of whether or not an inference might be made from them. The LTMS has a particular advantage in that contradictions can be detected without having to calculate the particular contradiction. Thus, the LTMS tends to be very efficient, requiring less justification and hence less calculation than does the JTMS. On the other hand, the LTMS has some theoretical gaps. Fortunately, because the conditions under which the LTMS fails are rarely encountered in actual problems, this approach is generally an effective one for practical application.

The approach of the LTMS is quite different from any of the approaches previously discussed, as the following example will illustrate. Assume that the climate at a particular ski resort in the winter is either cold or snowy (or perhaps both). This knowledge can be represented by requiring that at least one of the predicates IT IS COLD and IT IS SNOWY evaluate to TRUE. This situation could be represented by a weather clause, W, as follows:

W = ((IT IS COLD, TRUE) (IT IS SNOWY, TRUE))

The LTMS then tries to infer facts from this clause. If, for example, either of the predicates evaluates to TRUE, nothing can be inferred about the truth of the other predicate. But, if one of the predicates evaluates to FALSE, then the truth of the other predicate can be inferred, as shown below on lines 2 and 4 of Figure 15-6.

The LTMS proceeds by calculating a measure called Potential Satisfiers (PS), which is a count of the predicates that are not unsatisfied. If PS = 2, no inferences are possible. If PS = 1, an inference might be possible. If PS = 0, a contradiction exists. Thus, if IT IS SNOWY evaluates to TRUE and IT IS COLD evaluates to UNKNOWN, PS will equal 2 and no inference can be made about the truth of IT IS COLD. On the other hand, if IT IS SNOWY evaluates to FALSE while IT IS COLD evaluates to UNKNOWN, PS will equal 1 and it will be possible to infer the truth of IT IS COLD. However, a PS value of 1 does not guarantee that an inference can be made. For example, if IT IS SNOWY evaluates to TRUE and IT IS COLD evaluates to FALSE, PS will have a value of 1 (the IT IS COLD predicate is not satisfied), but no inference can be made about either predicate as both already have values. Given a clause with two predicates, nine possible combinations of predicate values might occur. These are summarized in Figure 15-6.

Assumption-Based TMS

The assumption-based TMS (ATMS) works in a considerably different fashion than either the JTMS or the LTMS. The ATMS operates with multiple contexts in parallel, much as was done in the preceding example that selected the chores and leisure activities to be performed. In theory, the ATMS creates all possible contexts and reasons with all of them.

IT IS SNOWY	IT IS COLD	PS Value	Inference
UNKNOWN	UNKNOWN	2	None
UNKNOWN	FALSE	1	IT IS SNOWY = TRUE
UNKNOWN	TRUE	1	None
FALSE	UNKNOWN	1	IT IS COLD = TRUE
FALSE	FALSE	0	Contradiction
FALSE	TRUE	1	None
TRUE	UNKNOWN	1	None
TRUE	FALSE	1	None
TRUE	TRUE	2	None

Figure 15-6 LTMS Reasoning for Two-Predicate Clause

However, in actuality all the contexts need not be created; the minimal set of supporting contexts is calculated and reasoning proceeds from this base.

The ATMS basically operates in parallel to find all solutions to the problem (i.e., every context that satisfies the constraints). The user must then select the best solution (i.e., an evaluation function must be applied to each context, permitting the "best" one to be selected). The JTMS, on the other hand, proceeds to find solutions serially. Thus, the user must evaluate each acceptable context and determine whether to terminate the solution process or to examine the next acceptable context. Depending on the problem being attacked by the knowledge crafter, one approach may be more appropriate than the other.

The TMS Dilemma

Because the differences between the different TMS approaches are significant, the knowledge crafter must select the proper mechanism for his problem. Yet, the knowledge crafter's freedom of choice is significantly restricted by the availability of tools embodying these systems. At present, the commercial knowledge-based tools that provide a multiple-context capability use ATMS-like inferencing mechanisms. The knowledge crafter desiring to use a JTMS or an LTMS system therefore must construct that system as part of the application development activity. However, most of the work on TMS has been restricted to the research laboratory, and the implementation of such a system for a particular application would be very complicated, raising questions of practicality. Yet, as we have seen, the issue cannot really be ignored, nor can an unsuitable TMS be used. Given the current state of TMS development, the knowledge crafter faces a real dilemma if the design of an application calls for the use of multiple contexts in a fashion not supported by an existing development tool.

Search Mechanisms

A knowledge-based system with a multiple-context capability can (at least conceptually) form a tree of all possible contexts. Each parent spawns a set of children containing all possible values for a particular assumption or set of assumptions. Each child in turn spawns all possible grandchildren, and so forth. The leaf contexts of this tree then contain all possible contexts that can be generated that might contain a solution to the problem. Conceptually, then, the knowledge-based system need only evaluate the quality of the leaf contexts (e.g., the quality of each potential solution) and select the best one.

As a practical matter, however, all possible contexts cannot be generated, for the potential number of contexts for realistic problems far exceeds the capability of today's computer systems to generate, store, and test those contexts. The problem, then, shifts to one of finding an efficient method to search the tree without having to generate and examine every possible context. A good search strategy will minimize two measures:

1.   The number of contexts needlessly examined (e.g., contexts that do not lie on a path from the top context to the optimum leaf context)

2.   The number of "good" leaf contexts overlooked.

As with many things in the real world, these criteria are somewhat contradictory. That is, mechanisms that perform favorably according to the first measure do so at the expense of their performance according to the second measure, and vice versa. Fortunately, the performance of a mechanism is not independent of the structure and characteristics of an application. Hence, the knowledge crafter can improve the process of searching the application's solution space by selecting an appropriate mechanism for that particular application from among the following three general types of search strategies:

1.   Breadth-first search

2.   Depth-first search

3.   Controlled search.

The example of selecting Saturday's activities will again be used as an illustration.

Breadth First

The *breadth-first* search begins at the top of the tree. All contexts are generated for the next level. These are then evaluated, all contexts for the next level generated, and so forth. Only after the full breadth of the tree has been explored on a particular level will the next level deeper in the tree be explored—hence the term breadth-first.

Beginning at the root or top node, all possible contexts are spawned. Each is examined in turn for feasibility (no constraint violations or contradictions). In addition, each context may be evaluated for desirability. A decision can be made to terminate (prune) the tree at any point, so that no further consideration would be given to a particular context (and all its potential subordinate contexts) that appeared to contain a much less favorable solution than other contexts. Then the search moves one level lower in the tree. All the children of each context are generated, and each child is examined, all grandchild contexts spawned and examined, and so forth. The process of examining a context and spawning further contexts continues level by level until:

•   An inconsistency is found, in which case the branch is pruned and no further contexts will be generated.

•   The context is unfavorably evaluated, in which case the branch is pruned and no further contexts will be generated.

•   The context is found to duplicate another context, in which case the contexts are merged.

•   A terminal or leaf node is found (a solution), which can then be evaluated for quality.

This type of search will derive all possible solutions to the problem, from which the best can be selected. This search strategy is reflected in Figure 15-3b. From the root context, seven contexts are spawned, each containing one of the seven possible activities. One of these (RELAX) is immediately marked INVALID as a constraint is violated. Then, the six possible next contexts are spawned, making a total of 36 contexts at the second level of the tree (although only eight are shown in Figure 15-3b). Of these, three are invalidated and two are merged, as shown in Figure 15-3c. (There would be additional invalidations and merges among the second-level contexts not shown in the figure.) Then third-level contexts would be spawned, of which only three are shown in Figure 15-3c. When this process terminated, each leaf context would either be marked as INVALID or would contain an acceptable set of activities.

If all the paths from root context to the leaf context are approximately the same length (which they would be in this example), then the breadth-first search will produce no solutions for "a long time" and will then produce all the solutions "all at once." Thus, the process cannot be interrupted during the calculations to see "how it is doing." No early solutions are generated to permit an estimation of the quality of solutions being produced.

If a good constraint set for an application can be generated, many potential branches of the context tree can be pruned early in the process (i.e., near the top of the tree), making this search procedure an effective one for the application. Computational requirements can be made reasonable, and the breadth-first search has the nice property of producing all solutions. This property permits the application to select the optimum solution.

However, this approach is only effective for situations that are heavily constrained (i.e., for which there are few valid solutions). In many applications the constraints will not be sufficiently limiting to permit heavy pruning near the top of the tree. As a consequence, the number of nodes to be considered will grow exponentially, and dimensionality characteristics will result in the application becoming computationally infeasible.

Depth First

The *depth-first* search is essentially the opposite of the breadth-first search. From the root context, a particular (single) context is selected and spawned. (This selection may be based on an evaluation of all the contexts that could be spawned at the next level, picking the one that appeared "most promising," or it could be made somewhat arbitrarily, such as by randomly selecting from among the possible next contexts to spawn.)

The process continues, working deeper and deeper down the tree of contexts until:

- An inconsistency is found, in which case the branch is pruned and no further contexts will be generated.
- The context is unfavorably evaluated, in which case the branch is pruned and no further contexts will be generated.

- The context is found to duplicate another context, in which case the contexts are merged.
- A terminal or leaf node is found (a solution), which can then be evaluated for quality.

At this point the search strategy *backtracks* up the tree to a higher level and then repeats the process. That is, long strings of contexts are pursued from "top to bottom" or from root to leaf. Thus, a context is explored downwards in the tree to a leaf context before any other contexts at its same level are considered—hence the term "depth-first." After reaching a leaf context, the search strategy must determine whether to terminate the process (a "good enough" solution has been found) or to what higher level to backtrack.

Figure 15-7 shows a portion of a depth-first search. From the root context a series of contexts have been spawned, reflecting a particular sequence in which the activities could be performed. Note that at the bottom of the tree the inference mechanism has backtracked, producing two more paths. Notice also that since each context is sequence-independent, there is but a single leaf solution into which all valid solutions will be merged. In addition, as shown for the breadth-first search, constraints can result in the termination of a particular search before a complete solution is reached. Thus, two of the contexts violated the constraint about performing work activities before fun activities and were marked invalid.

The depth-first search essentially produces solutions linearly over time. If a good evaluation function of partial solutions can be developed for an application, the "most promising" paths to pursue down through the tree can be picked early in the search. The search would thus discover a large portion of the "good" solutions early in the search process and thus terminate before all solutions had been considered, thereby eliminating the need to generate and test many of the contexts.

Even if the contexts to pursue are being selected randomly, the depth-first approach can be advantageous. Since results are being produced over time, these can be monitored. As soon as an acceptable solution is found (or as soon as the rate of producing better solutions declines), the search can be terminated.

Depth-first search has an additional advantage in that it can be applied in environments that do not permit multiple contexts to be generated. Since the inference mechanism never backtracks until consideration of a particular branch has been terminated and since only one context is considered at any one time, all evaluations can be performed in a single context. However, to make use of a single context, the inference mechanism needs to be able to "undo" any inference that was previously made. That is, when moving back up a level, from level n to level n-1 in the conceptual context tree, the inference mechanism must remove each inference made at level n and thus restore the context to that which existed at level n-1 previously. (Thus, while backtracking can be performed in a single-context environment, it can be handled much more efficiently with some of the multiple-context environments.)

Depth-first search is not without its drawbacks, however. If a particular path is basically a bad one, then this approach will spend considerable

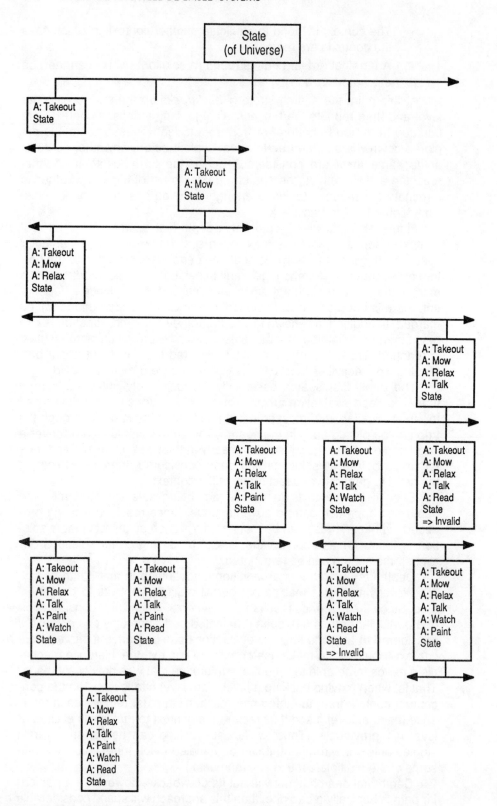

Figure 15-7 Depth-First Search

time evaluating many branches near the bottom of the tree that are all bad. To avoid this inefficiency, the system must have a good predictive function that will predict the likelihood of a context leading to good or bad (or infeasible) solutions. The knowledge crafter's ability to produce such a predictive evaluation function for partial solutions will depend on the characteristics of the application. One way to overcome this difficulty is to try to decompose the problem into smaller pieces, each of which might be tackled independently. Such hierarchical problem solving is addressed below and again in Chapter 17.

Controlled

The *controlled* search is a composite of the breadth-first and depth-first approaches, being essentially an attempt to obtain the advantages of both search strategies without incurring the disadvantages of either. The search of the context tree is initiated at the top or root context and works down the tree to leaf contexts. However, at each level, the search mechanism has the option of exploring in breadth (i.e., evaluating a number of contexts at that level) or proceeding in depth (i.,e., proceeding to the next lower level). Further, because contexts are preserved, the inference mechanism can skip from one context to another without having to perform all the logical operations to retract and remake inferences. That is, the inference mechanism can skip from a context at level 5 to a context at level 4 on a different branch of the tree without having to backtrack to a common context at level 2 and then make additional inferences to move back down to level 4.

As illustrated in Figure 15-8, the inference mechanism can skip directly from the shaded node at level 5 (assumptive base of TAKEOUT-MOW-RELAX-TALK-WATCH) to the shaded node at level 4 (assumptive base of TAKEOUT-MOW-WATCH-PAINT) without having to move up the context tree from level 5 to the shaded context at level 2 (assumptive base of TAKEOUT-MOW) that is common to both branches and then moving back down to level 4.

Thus, unlike either the breadth-first or depth-first search approaches, a controlled search can be set aside at any particular point to pursue a new branch or to resume exploration of an old branch that had previously been set aside. If the partial solution evaluator comes up with an unfavorable value at any context, the search need not terminate consideration of that particular branch of the context tree, but rather set that context aside and either:

- Begin to explore a new branch, working from a context at a higher level on the same branch of the tree
- Continue to explore an old branch that had previously been set aside.

If a particular branch of the tree looks unpromising, attention can be shifted to a different branch. However, should the exploration of that branch appear even less promising after a few contexts have been explored, search on the previous branch can be resumed.

Many methods can be used to control the search. For example, a branch-and-bound approach may be used to control context selection, or

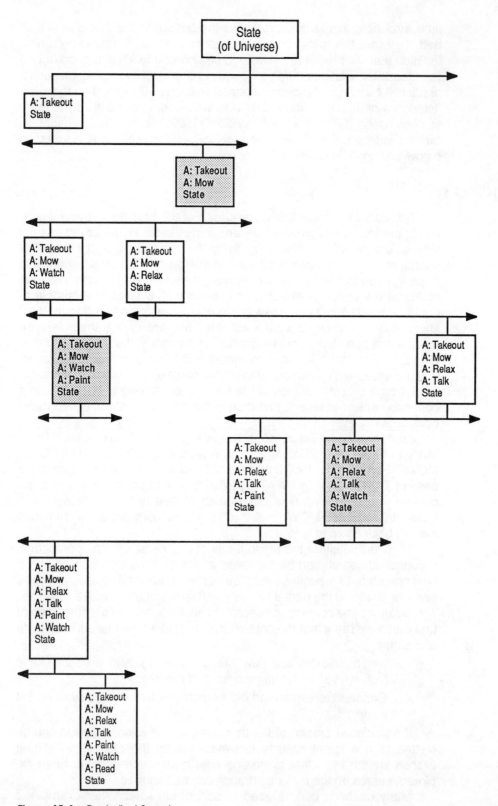

Figure 15-8   Controlled Search

a heuristic of a human domain expert may be captured and used. The approach that might be most effective for any particular application will depend on the characteristics of that application's context tree (i.e., search space).

Although the controlled-search approach appears to offer a significant advantage, two rather substantial requirements must be met if it is to be used effectively:

1. A good evaluation function for partial solutions is needed, for not only must promising branches of the tree be picked, but efficient decisions must also be made about when a particular branch is not likely to yield a better solution than another and should temporarily be set aside.

2. An effective function is needed to select the next context (from among the set of all previously visited contexts) from which the search should proceed.

A controlled search approach is often advantageous when the knowledge crafter is trying to capture the decision-making approach of a human expert. For example, a human scheduler often will note that a particular schedule sequence being developed looks unpromising, set it aside, pick up another sequence, and so forth. This type of behavior can be reflected in a controlled-search strategy, incorporating the scheduler's heuristics, whereas this behavior could not be reflected in either the breadth-first or depth-first searches.

Deciding How to Use Multiple Contexts

Given the many ways of using the capabilities afforded by multiple contexts, how can the knowledge crafter decide which style of usage is most appropriate? The first consideration is the type of application being crafted. The use of multiple contexts is particularly helpful for search, planning, scheduling, or design types of problems. Such problems often have a very broad range of solution alternatives, so broad in fact that, unlike a diagnostic problem, enumeration or analysis of all solution candidates is not possible.

Further, information about the implications of a design or schedule as it is being constructed is generally not available. That is, without exploring the implications of a particular choice (by pursuing further schedule construction), the inference mechanism cannot determine whether that choice is a good one. In terms of setting up Saturday's schedule of activities, Jim does not know whether taking out the garbage before mowing the lawn will result in a better or worse schedule of activities until he knows what this choice implies about the rest of the schedule. Consequently, a form of trial-and-error must be used in the development of a schedule; a multiple-context type of representation provides a good fit to the problem.

Dimensionality

Although the multiple-context form of representation offers a number of advantages, it does suffer from a major liability—dimensionality. Consequently, this factor should influence the design of any application using multiple-context representation. The designer must not only be aware of dimensionality, but also take steps to counteract its impact. Despite the ease with which new contexts can be spawned by currently available development tools, and despite the efficiency with which a particular context might be able to be evaluated, the knowledge crafter still has to consider the computational implications of exploring a branch (along with all its subbranches) that might emanate downward from a particular context. The number of contexts to be considered can easily grow explosively, leading to computational infeasibility regardless of how efficiently the system might be able to process any particular context. Thus, the preeminent design consideration when using multiple contexts is the reduction of dimensionality, finding ways to prune the search space so that fewer contexts will need to be generated and considered.

If the solution space for a problem is tightly constrained, then generating a constraint set that will prune many of the branches near the top of the tree may be relatively easy. Thus, a breadth-first search could be used effectively. Not only could the number of contexts to be evaluated be sufficiently reduced to permit efficient computation, but this approach would provide a complete set of feasible solutions to the problem, from which the optimum or best solution could be selected.

On the other hand, if the type of problem to be addressed is loosely constrained, most of the contexts at the top of the tree will satisfy the constraints. This situation could result in an explosive growth in the number of contexts to be considered. Hence, if very many alternatives are to be considered at the top of the tree, use of the breadth-first search strategy may not be feasible.

In such a case, a depth-first search strategy might be more effective. Given an appropriate partial-solution evaluator, the quality of the solutions being produced could be monitored as execution proceeds and the search stopped after a few good ones had been found. The degree to which this will be possible for an application, however, depends on the characteristics of that application. If a good partial-solution evaluator can be provided, then most of the "good" solutions will be discovered early in the search, permitting early termination.

Even if the evaluator is not adept at picking out good branches to pursue, the depth-first approach may still prove effective. If the characteristics of the application are such that a number of solutions are of approximately equal quality and *the* best solution need not be found, then even a "random" evaluator will enable solutions to be examined at random. Like any stochastic process, the user can watch the solution process, terminating it when a sufficiently good solution has been found or when the rate of finding better solutions declines below a cutoff threshold.

On the other hand, the use of a partial-solution evaluator that cannot detect unpromising branches will cause the depth-first approach to expend a needless amount of computation pursuing infeasible sub-branches. If a branch is basically infeasible, then all of the subbranches will be infeasible (or undesirable), and the depth-first search will consider the basic path and all its variants, determining that indeed each is infeasible for the same reason.

In such situations a hierarchical approach may be appropriate. Such an approach often enables many of the poor solutions to be eliminated at a high level. With fewer considerations, fewer contexts are to be evaluated, which reduces the dimensionality problem. Then each high-level solution can be examined in more detail at the next level, again with fewer alternatives left to be considered in detail. By reducing dimensionality problems through a hierarchical approach to the problem, a multiple-context representation might effectively be used at each level of the analysis, whereas it might be ineffective if the problem were approached without decomposition.

A controlled-search approach can effectively be used when a good partial-solution evaluator can be constructed. Although the controlled search is less sensitive to algorithm quality than depth first, high-quality algorithms are needed to attack dimensionality effectively. If such algorithms are not available or cannot easily be generated, the knowledge crafter should consider whether:

- The domain expert has sufficient expertise to develop a knowledge-based system using a multicontext representation.
- The problem is too big and complex to be approached as represented (e.g., in its entirety). (In this case the problem should be decomposed into smaller pieces, each of which might be solved more effectively, and then a global solution assembled from the pieces.)

Hierarchical Problem Solving

One approach to problem decomposition is to view the problem at different levels of abstraction. First, the knowledge crafter should seek to solve the problem when it is represented in a high-level or abstract form. Then, for each of the "good" solutions found at this coarse level, the knowledge crafter should attempt to determine if the next lower or more detailed level has any solutions, and so forth. The number of levels of abstraction needed to solve the problem efficiently with the tools and knowledge available will depend on the characteristics of the specific problem. In many cases, however, two levels will suffice.

Human experts frequently decompose problems by abstraction, thereby reducing the degree of problem complexity closer to the level that can be understood and treated by the human brain. Consequently, the knowledge crafter may find that a number of guidelines already exist for decomposing the problem. Further, existing knowledge-based system development tools can be used effectively with such a multilayered structure of the problem. The following example of a planning problem illustrates the approach.

An Example

A couple is planning a visit to the San Francisco Bay Area. The man is interested in architecture and would like to see the Golden Gate Bridge, the Transamerica Pyramid building, Stanford University, and the University of California at Berkeley. The woman would like to see Sausalito, Ghirardelli Square, Jack London Square, and the deYoung Museum. Both would like to visit Fisherman's Wharf and Coit Tower as well as ride a cable car. Their task is to find a route that will minimize transportation time between the various sites they wish to see. (This is a variant of the classical traveling salesman problem.)

Rather than attempting to solve the problem directly (producing a list of destinations in the order to be visited), they abstract the problem. First the destinations are clustered into four groups, depending on their general geographical location, as shown in Figure 15-9a. The sightseeing problem can now be restated as finding the best route between the four geographical areas. This problem is small enough that a good solution can be found fairly easily. Our tourist couple decide to visit the Peninsula first, then move around the Bay to the East Bay, then cross the Bay Bridge to San Francisco, and finally cross the Golden Gate Bridge to Marin County.

At the next level, a plan must be devised for each cluster in the more abstract plan. Thus, each cluster is taken individually and a visiting plan developed for the destinations within that cluster. In some cases, because of constraints, there may be no path through the cluster that will satisfy the abstract plan. In other cases, the best solutions may be poor, necessitating a return to the more abstract level to develop a different plan. In the

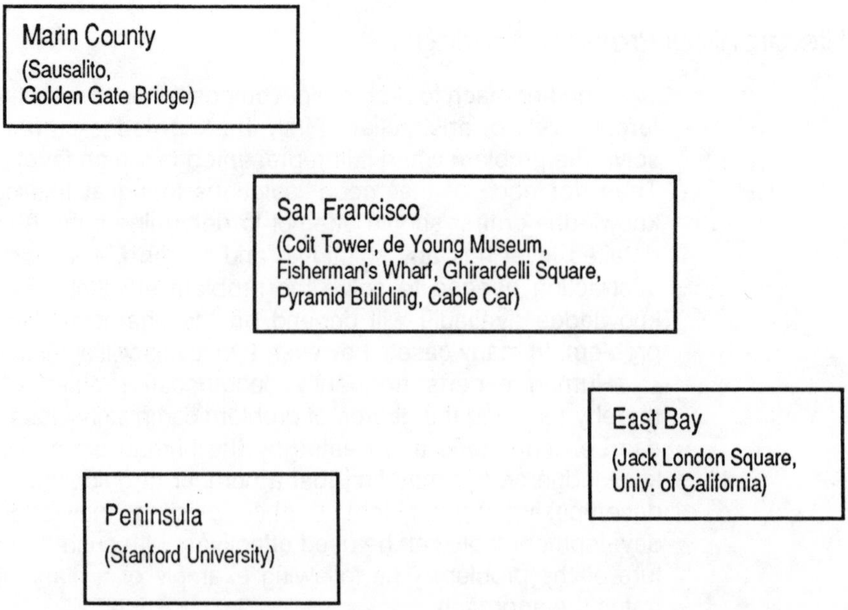

Marin County
(Sausalito,
Golden Gate Bridge)

San Francisco
(Coit Tower, de Young Museum,
Fisherman's Wharf, Ghirardelli Square,
Pyramid Building, Cable Car)

East Bay
(Jack London Square,
Univ. of California)

Peninsula
(Stanford University)

Figure 15-9a Geographic Destinations (First Level)

example, three of the four clusters can be scheduled easily. The Peninsula cluster consists of only a single location. Arriving in the East Bay from the south, the tourists select a plan that takes the freeway directly to Berkeley and then stops by Jack London Square in Oakland just before crossing the bridge to San Francisco. From San Francisco, the easiest way to Sausalito is over the Golden Gate Bridge, so the sequence for the Marin County cluster is easily selected.

The San Francisco cluster is more difficult, however, so the six sights in this cluster can be further grouped into three zones, as shown in Figure 15-9b. Now a route can be planned between these zones.

Central San Francisco, being located near the western end of the Bay Bridge, can be visited immediately after arriving in San Francisco from the East Bay. Because West San Francisco is located near the terminus of the Golden Gate Bridge, that should be the last of the San Francisco zones visited, since the San Francisco cluster of sights is to be exited via the Golden Gate Bridge. Thus, the visit order is Central San Francisco, North San Francisco, and then West San Francisco.

Our tourists then drop down to the third level of abstraction and solve the scheduling problem for each zone. This task is fairly straightforward because the two sights in Central San Francisco fall in a line between the entry and exit points for the zone, as do the three sights in the North San Francisco zone.

Thus, what at first was an apparently complex scheduling problem turned out to be a series of solutions to a set of much smaller, simpler problems. The same type of simplification can be used just as effectively when more realistic problems are involved. Although the knowledge-based system might have to consider all the pieces of several abstract solutions, the solution of each problem at each level will likely be vastly less complex and more likely to have feasible solution approaches. The net result should be a more effective computational approach to the global problem to be solved.

Usage with Other Representations

The solution of problems through the techniques of abstraction and decomposition was discussed in this chapter in connection with the use of multiple contexts as a knowledge representation mechanism to support a

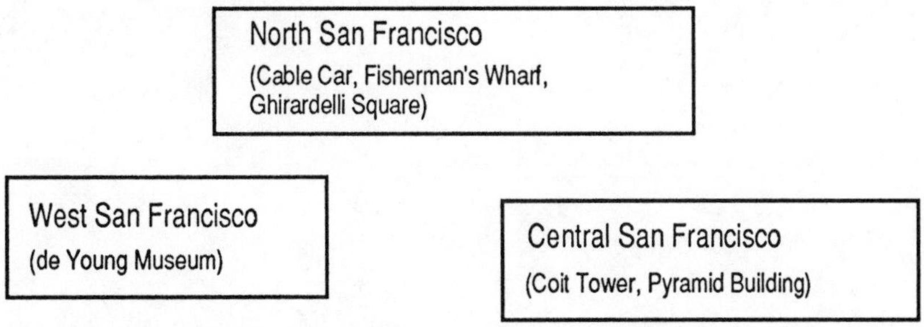

North San Francisco
(Cable Car, Fisherman's Wharf, Ghirardelli Square)

West San Francisco
(de Young Museum)

Central San Francisco
(Coit Tower, Pyramid Building)

Figure 15-9b Geographic Destinations (Second Level)

search strategy. However, these techniques also have value when used with many forms of knowledge representation and reasoning. Any time the complexity of a problem can be reduced, the power and efficiency of the available problem-solving tools are enhanced, be those tools the human mind, a conventional analysis program, or a knowledge-based system. Accordingly, hierarchical problem structuring should be seriously considered whenever the solution of a problem begins to become computationally unwieldly. The application of this technique is further discussed in Chapter 17 in connection with blackboard representations.

References

1) Doyle, J., "A Truth Maintenance System," *Artificial Intelligence*, Vol. 24, 1979.

2) McAllester, D., "A Widely Used Truth Maintenance System," unpublished, 1985.

3) de Kleer, J., "An Assumption-Based Truth Maintenance System," *Artificial Intelligence*, Vol. 28, 1986.

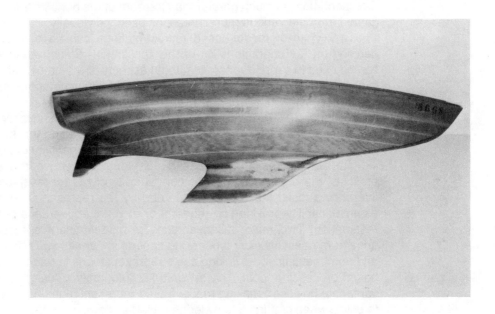

CHAPTER 16

Knowledge Crafting with Model-Based Representations

Certain problems, such as the tank testing of a hull design, are prohibitively expensive to perform with an actual yacht hull. Hence, designers perform the tests using a model of the hull. Similarly, knowledge about a system (e.g., an electronic circuit) can be represented as a model, and the knowledge-based application can reason about that model. Chapter 16 describes various types of model-based representations and the use of these models by a knowledge-based application.

Generally speaking, model-based representations are not used in isolation but are combined with other techniques to bring a more powerful technology to bear on the problem. In this case the whole is definitely greater than the sum of its parts; that is, the benefit from a combination of representations is much greater than the sum of the benefits that might be gained from the various representations used individually.

Two types of model-based representations can be employed, depending on the characteristics of the application. *Static representations* can be used to support reasoning about aspects of a system that are relatively constant, such as the interconnections between components. Thus, static representations are often used with diagnostic or failure isolation applications. *Dynamic representations* can be used to investigate the time-varying characteristics of systems, often substituting for the system itself when experimental use or behavioral measurement is not possible.

The advantages of model-based representations derive from the generality of the representation, the compatibility of the representation with inferencing tools, the economy afforded by the representation, and the communicability provided by the form or external appearance of the representation. Two major disadvantages of model-based representations arise from relatively slow processing speeds in certain types of situations and from the difficulty in linking these representations to traditional model-based processing tools. The advantages frequently outweigh the disadvantages, however, making model-based representations a powerful tool to utilize when crafting a knowledge-based system.

Model-Based Representations

Some types of knowledge can best be represented as a loose unstructured collection of facts. Thus, in the example on eating in Chapter 13, I AM AT HOME and I EAT SWEDISH PANCAKES are facts that could be placed on a simple "list of knowledge." Other types of knowledge can best be expressed as rules, as frames in a hierarchical structure, as procedures, or in some other representational form.

These forms cannot easily be used to represent certain types of knowledge, however. Consider a model of a business organization as an example. The description of the behavior of the corporation's components (e.g., departments, facilities, staff, workload) and of the manner in which those components are interconnected (i.e., how they relate to each other), form the essence of a model. It would be very difficult to represent this type of information as a set of rules and very inefficient to represent the data as a collection of facts. It would be much more straightforward to represent the information simply as a model of the firm and to work with the knowledge in that form.

An Example

A diagram of an electronic circuit illustrates what might be included in the knowledge base to provide information about the circuit and permit the inference mechanism to reason about the behavior of that circuit. Such a circuit could be represented in a traditional hierarchical knowledge taxonomy, along the lines described in Chapter 14. Such a taxonomy, representing the various circuits, is illustrated in Figure 16-1.

Circuit Taxonomy

The frame at the top, labeled CIRCUIT-COMPONENTS, represents the complete set of components from which a circuit could be constructed. Children of this frame, such as GATES and CONNECTORS, represent various subclasses of components from which a circuit could be constructed, while the descendants of those frames in turn represent types of gates and connectors (e.g., AND-GATE, NAND-GATE). The descendants of these latter frames would in turn represent more specific forms of each of the basic component types (e.g., F3 representing a three-way fan-out connector).

Circuit Taxonomy with Instances

But the taxonomy shown in Figure 16-1 merely describes the material from which a circuit can be constructed. It does not describe or represent any particular circuit. This shortcoming can be remedied, however, by extending the illustration of Figure 16-1 to include specific instances of components. The totality of component instances shown at the bottom of the hierarchy would depict a particular circuit. Thus, a circuit consisting of

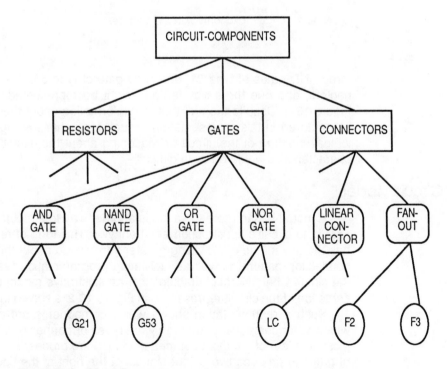

Figure 16-1 Circuit Taxonomy

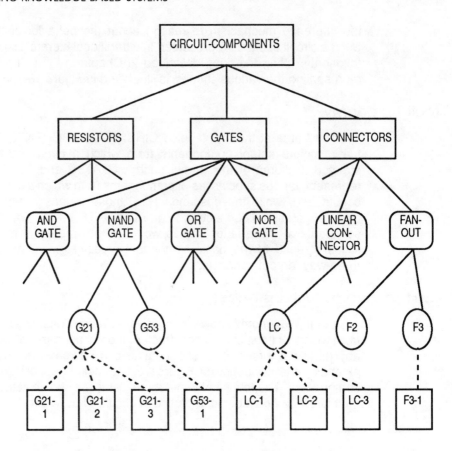

Figure 16-2 Circuit Taxonomy with All Instances

three AND gates of type 21, one AND gate of type 53, three linear connectors, and one three-way fan-out might be represented as shown in
Figure 16-2. Despite the fact that "all" information about the circuit could
be captured in this representation, visualizing either the logical or topo-
logical structure of the circuit or reasoning about the circuit's behavioral
characteristics would be quite difficult.

Circuit Model

A model-based representation is another way to structure knowledge
about the circuit's construction and behavior. This form of representation
has the advantage of providing greater information about the component
connection pattern as well as facilitating programmatic reasoning about
the circuit's behavioral characteristics. An illustrative model-based representation of the circuit represented in Figure 16-2 is shown in Figure 16-3.

Such a representation shows which components are connected to
which other components through what types of connectors. It readily depicts how four of the input sources at the left are processed through a set
of gates to produce two output signals at the right of the figure. The fifth
input can be seen to connect with the feedback loop. This type of repre-

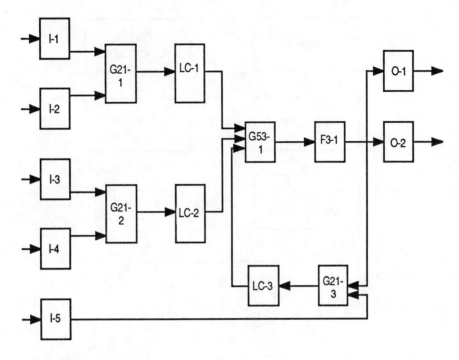

Figure 16-3 Circuit Model

sentation facilitates reasoning about which gates will be open or closed in response to particular input signal combinations, and hence about the state of every gate and the extent of current flow on every connector.

Types of Model Representations

A model can be represented in a variety of ways, with the knowledge crafter's choice depending on the characteristics of the problem and the manner in which the inference engine is to operate on the knowledge represented in the model. However, the two basic ways a knowledge-based system operates on the knowledge represented in a model are statically and dynamically. Each class of representation has different implications for how the knowledge about the model might be organized and represented, as we will show below.

Static Model Representations

The static representation of a model can be viewed as a collection of nodes and arcs. These may be represented by specialized icons or symbols, as in Figure 16-3, or simply by generic node and arc symbols that bear labels. For example, the model shown in Figure 16-4 uses generic nodes and arcs to represent the process of generating a purchase order in a large company.

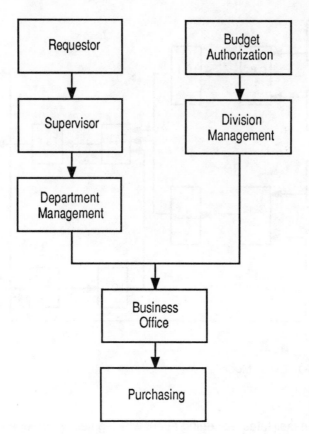

Figure 16-4 A Model of Purchase-Order Issuance

Purchase-Order Model

A staff member needing an item of equipment initiates a request, which passes up the administrative hierarchy through the cognizant supervisor to the department manager. The approved request then moves to the business office where it is matched against another paperwork stream, this one representing the budget approval for the expenditure. Following business office approval, the request moves to purchasing where the purchase order is issued. The nodes in the model variously represent people or functions, while the arcs represent the paths of paperwork flows.

Hydraulic Model

Similarly, this type of representation could be used to model a hydraulic system. The nodes would represent the pumps and valves in the system, while the arcs would represent the pipes connecting the various pieces of equipment. Such a system is illustrated in Figure 16-5. The rather straightforward connection patterns shown in Figures 16-4 and

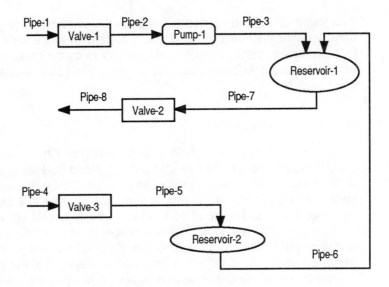

Figure 16-5 A Model of a Hydraulic System

16-5 are not a requirement of the representation, however. The connection pattern could be tangled; it might contain loops or circular patterns, such as the loop between G53-1 and G21-3 via connectors LC-3 and F3-1 depicted in Figure 16-3.

A Comparison of Model-Based and Rule-Based Usage

A static model is analogous to a set of production rules. In each case, a set of data is provided as input (to the model or to the rule-set) and another set of data is returned. Providing a set of input data values to the model is analogous to providing a set of conditions to a rule-set (for the IF part of production rules). The set of output data derived from the model would be analogous to the consequents produced by the THEN part of the rules whose conditions were satisfied. This mode of model usage is conceptually analogous to forward-chaining with a set of production rules.

Similarly, supplying a set of system output data (actual or hypothesized) to the model would be analogous to supplying consequent data to a rule-set (for the THEN part of production rules). The derivation from the model of the input data that could have given rise to those outputs would be analogous to deriving necessary conditions from the IF parts of rules having the given consequents. This mode of model usage is conceptually analogous to backward-chaining through a set of production rules.

Use of Static Representations

Static, model-based representations of knowledge are particularly useful for reasoning about the connection paths between components. Such an activity is frequently a part of failure analysis. The inference engine might attempt to reason either from cause to effect (e.g., to determine whether the failure of component A could produce the observed effect at measurement point B) or from effect to cause (e.g., to determine what component failures could produce the observed values at measurement point B).

Illustrative Use of the Circuit Model

As an illustration, the static representation of Figure 16-3 could be used to determine whether input signal I-5 could potentially reach Gate G53-1 if Gate G21-3 failed in the open position. That is, the system could trace the connections in the model and infer whether any physical path extended from the source of I-5 to G53-1, given that G21-3 was permanently open. (The system could not, however, infer whether the pattern and timing of inputs I-1 through I-4 would actually permit [or prevent] the existence of a path to G53-1. The transient behavior of the circuit in response to the failure or to changes in input signals cannot be determined from the static model; only steady-state conditions for constant input can be considered.)

Illustrative Use of the Hydraulic Model

Another example of static model usage involves reasoning about the cause of failure in a hydraulic system. If no fluid were detected flowing in Pipe P-5 in Figure 16-5, the system could resort to basic fluid-flow principles as they apply to the model in order to determine the possible causes of the lack of fluid flow in P-5. Typically, the inference mechanism would first refer to a set of cases representing common failure modes for the particular hydraulic system in question. Then, if the problem were not one of the common cases, the system might resort to a set of heuristics (represented as rules or procedures) to identify the problem. If the cause of the failure still could not be identified, then the system might resort to applying basic physics principles to the model.

In that case, the following set of principles about fluid flow would be applied to the model:

- There must be fluid in a connected reservoir in order to have fluid that can be made to flow in a pipe.
- Fluid will not flow unless there is pressure in the system.
- An elevated reservoir will provide pressure if it contains fluid.
- A pump will supply pressure if there is fluid at its intake.
- Fluid will not flow through a closed valve.
- Pressure cannot be transmitted through a closed valve.

The inference mechanism could then work along the pipe network represented in the model to determine the point of system failure, utilizing information from sensors about fluid flows in various pipes, about the status of valves and pumps, about reservoir conditions, and so forth. This approach is not the fastest nor most efficient means to isolate many types of problems, but it is effective when no specific case and no specific rules exist to address the particular problem at hand.

This type of model-based reasoning, working from general principles, is often called *qualitative reasoning* or deep reasoning. Its attractiveness results from the robustness of the problem solution capability it provides. This topic is addressed below in the subsection on generality of representation.

Benefits of a Static Representation

The use of the static form of model-based representation can provide the knowledge crafter with a number of benefits relating to:

- Clarity
- Familiarity
- Maintenance
- Simplification
- Efficiency
- Application.

Benefits of a Static Representation: Clarity

When used appropriately, the static form of model-based representation offers a distinct advantage over other forms of representation in terms of clarity of presentation. The knowledge crafter can more easily understand the system being modeled because visual examination is possible. The logic is not lost in a tangled web of specific rules, nor is it hidden in many lines of procedural code. The connections between components are not submerged beneath a hierarchical structure of component knowledge. Human beings are much better at picking out errors and omissions from a graphical or visual representation than from listings of code or tables of numbers.

Benefits of a Static Representation: Familiarity

The representational form for the model may also turn out to be similar to the way in which the information is actually represented and used by employees currently working in the problem domain. The circuit diagram shown in Figure 16-3 probably closely resembles circuit diagrams that an electrical engineer might use. Thus, working with a more familiar representation, the expert can more easily identify errors or misrepresentations in the knowledge base. The user may find it more comfortable to work with this type of representation too.

Benefits of a Static Representation: Maintenance

A static, model-based form of representation can also improve the maintainability of a knowledge-based system. Configuration or other changes to the model are straightforward, involving merely a change in component connections or component parameters. Since the structure of the model is not embedded in a program, a series of complex changes to, for example, a set of production rules or a collection of procedural code would not be needed. Further, the visual identification of locations to be changed and the visual confirmation of those changes will reduce errors. Thus, not only can the knowledge crafter make changes faster, but fewer errors are likely be introduced in the process of making those changes.

Benefits of a Static Representation: Simplification

The static, model-based form of representation also provides such benefits as simplification of other representations that either are related to or work with the model-based knowledge. For example, a few general rules might suffice to reason about the model, in place of a much larger number of very specific rules in which the model knowledge was implicitly embedded. Similarly, a few general procedures might be substituted for a number of procedures referring to a collection of less structured knowledge about the modeled system. Use of a higher level representation generally results in the use of fewer but more general constructs, thereby contributing to clarity and conceptual understanding.

Benefits of a Static Representation: Efficiency

Although the characteristics of model-based representations do provide a certain comprehension efficiency for people trying to understand a model, the more common view of efficiency focuses on the computer system that would execute or process a knowledge-based application. Use of a model-based representation can contribute to processing efficiency in three ways:

- Storage size
- Memory usage
- Processing performance.

The model-based representation of the static knowledge about a system is fairly compact, which reduces the volume of storage needed for the knowledge base. Further, with a more compact representation, the execution of the application exhibits a greater storage locality of reference, thereby reducing the amount of paging or swapping activity and hence improving the processing performance of the computer system. In addition, the reduction in the number of rules or procedures that might be required to work with the model-based representation further reduces the amount of storage space required. The smaller number of rules also implies faster compilation times, if not faster processing times.

Benefits of a Static Representation: Application

Static, model-based representations can be used to considerable advantage, particularly when used to extend or enhance other forms of knowledge representation. For example, we have seen this type of representation used very effectively in knowledge-based diagnostic applications oriented toward production equipment in factories. The various mechanical and electrical components of the equipment, and the respective linkages or interactions between them, were represented in the form of a model. Both procedural and rule-based knowledge were used for reasoning with the model-based knowledge.

Dynamic Model Representations

The dynamic representation of a model may similarly be viewed as a collection of nodes and arcs. In this case, however, the analyst's concern is about the system's dynamic behavior, about the effects of changing inputs over time, and about the propagation of those changes through the system.

In contrast to the static representation, the dynamic representation may be viewed more like a collection of procedures that, taken together, reflect the behavior of the system through time. In either case, some knowledge about the dynamics or time-based behavior of the system must be associated with its representation. A traditional (discrete or continuous) simulation model would be an example of a dynamic model-based representation, permitting the dynamic behavior of the system to be observed and measured over time and hence to be reasoned about. Some of the better model-based representation techniques can be found in such languages as Simula(1), which permit an object-oriented structuring of the model.

A Comparison of Model-Based and Rule-Based Usage

Like the static model, the dynamic model can also be viewed as a set of (very complicated) IF-THEN rules. Given a set of conditions, actual or hypothesized, the model provides a set of consequents (output). However, in this case, the output is based on the simulated dynamic behavior of the system rather than on the firing of a particular rule or set of rules. This type of dynamic use of a model-based representation can therefore be viewed as a forward-chaining application.

Use of Dynamic Representations

Dynamic, model-based representations are particularly useful in situations where hypotheses about system behavior cannot be tested or verified using the actual system, either because that system does not exist or because it is not available for test purposes. In such situations, actual system measurements cannot be used as input to support the knowledge-based system's reasoning; however, output from the dynamic model can be used instead. An inability to reason with actual system data might occur, for example, when the real system had failed, when instrumentation was not available, when test operation of the system would be very expensive, or when experimental use of the system might produce catastrophic results. In all of these cases, use of the system in an experimental mode to test the consequences of hypothesized situations would be precluded. Hence, just as a traditional analysis must rely on a simulation in such circumstances, so must a knowledge-based system rely on a model in similar circumstances.

A similar inability to rely on data from the actual system can arise when the system is in production use. Such a system cannot be manipulated to obtain measurements relating to particular system states. A safety valve in the hydraulic system of a power plant could not be opened, for example, to determine the resultant behavior, as interference with power production is unlikely to be tolerated. Thus, measurements from the actual system can only be used for those states that happen to occur in the course of regular operation; measurements from all other states must be obtained from a knowledge-based representation such as a dynamic model.

A Circuit-Based Illustration

Consider, as an example, the diagnosis of a failure in the circuit depicted in Figure 16-3. Assume that, contrary to specification, an oscillating signal was detected on connector LC-3. The inference mechanism might hypothesize that Gate G53-1 had failed and use a dynamic model of the circuit to test whether such a failure would produce a system state similar to the one being observed. This determination could not be made using measurements from the actual system, since the as-yet unisolated failure could interfere with the system's performance in an unknown fashion.

Improved Inferencing Performance

The primary advantage offered by a dynamic, model-based representation is the improved inferencing capability that the knowledge-based system can provide. Because information in many cases could not be measured or determined were it not for the dynamic model, the inference mechanism would have to work with values of UNKNOWN rather than modeled estimates. As a consequence, the knowledge-based system's inferencing would be much less effective. For example, the ranges associated with recommended parameter values might be wider, or the solution set of possible failures might contain a larger number of possibilities.

Application

Despite the advantages of applying a dynamic model-based reasoning capability, few tools are available to assist in this process. SIMKIT™(2) is a knowledge-based modeling tool that provides many of the needed capabilities, but its developers have focused primarily on the simulation aspect of the problem. Although this tool does rely heavily on the underlying object-oriented programming and representational capabilities of KEE™(3), the availability of KEE™'s inferencing capabilities has yet to be exploited. Thus, SIMKIT™ might be viewed as a simulation tool with a compatible knowledge-based reasoning capability that the knowledge crafter can use.

A much more integrated capability is planned for Simulation Craft™(4). This product will utilize an underlying knowledge-based system to aid the analyst with a variety of modeling tasks ranging from experimental design to result analysis. This product is still under development, however, and the capabilities that will ultimately be incorporated into that product are not yet known.

CACI is taking a different approach with its SIMSCRIPT II.5™(5) product. The firm is considering whether to add a knowledge-based reasoning capability to this conventional simulation language. In the meantime, the paper by Andes(6) illustrates how some knowledge-based reasoning capabilities can be represented using current SIMSCRIPT II.5™ constructs.

Advantages of a Model-Based Representation

The advantages to be derived from use of a model-based knowledge representation depend to some degree on the specific problem and on the characteristics of the knowledge to be represented. However, all applications can accrue four general types of advantages from the use of this form of representation. These benefits derive from the *generality* of the representation, the *compatibility* of the representation with inferencing tools, the *economy* afforded by the representation, and the *communicability* provided by the form or external appearance of the representation.

Generality of Representation

A knowledge-based system that relies entirely on specific rules or heuristic procedures for representing knowledge has a very serious weakness. When the system faces a situation that is not addressed by one of the specific heuristics (whether represented by rules or procedures), the system cannot handle that case. In a sense, the system can treat only those specific cases that it has been "taught." Even though the number of such cases might be very large, this flaw still remains.

Yet, many domains exist in which a knowledge-based system would be very helpful, but in which the number of possible situations or cases is far too numerous to treat individually. Even if only specific symptoms rather than complete cases are treated, the number of individual items to be addressed is still enormous.

The model-based representation provides the "safety net," the "else clause" in a programming statement, the procedure to be used when "everything else fails." The model representation can be viewed as providing the complete specification of the system being investigated. If no specific procedures or heuristic rules apply, then the inference mechanism can reason about the system's behavior by applying some general principles to the model's representation.

A considerable body of research has been undertaken on this subject under the name of qualitative reasoning. The papers by Hamscher(7) and by Fink, Lusth, and Duran(8) are illustrative and provide an introduction to the topic of qualitative reasoning as well as a number of additional references.

The advantage to be gained from representation generality is very real; the application should be able to respond reasonably to a broader range of inputs and situations. However, the knowledge crafter will not achieve such robustness automatically or without planning. General principles for reasoning about the model must be provided. For example, a model of a mechanical system would need to include some basic laws of physics regarding forces and motion. Developing the set of relevant principles, putting them in a form in which they can be applied efficiently, and ensuring completeness of the representation are not easy. These are nontrivial problems, and further research is needed.

Compatibility of the Representation

Many of the ways in which knowledge might be represented in a model-based structure are compatible with the use of variables in rule systems and with various types of pattern-matching algorithms that are provided in commercially available inference engines. These very powerful techniques are quite useful when applied to model-based representations.

Economy of Representation

Generally, a model-based representation of knowledge can be relatively compact; yet, that knowledge can be accessed and used quickly without much additional processing or transformation. Thus, storage space, paging, and processing power are used more efficiently.

Communicability of the Representation

The model-based representation offers other advantages for communicating or sharing knowledge. As discussed previously in connection with static model-based representations, the form of the knowledge can facilitate greater understanding of that knowledge, minimize errors, and facilitate maintenance by staff members. Familiarity with the representation's form can aid experts and users alike in assessing the knowledge. Knowledge-crafting sessions can become much more productive, because the experts can deal with the knowledge representations directly rather than trying to understand something quite foreign to them or having to rely on the knowledge crafters for "translation." Users can operate more productively, because they are already comfortable with and accustomed to working with information expressed in the same type of representation.

A model-based representation, especially a static model, provides a valuable mechanism to share knowledge about system structure between different applications that address a common system. For example, the model-based representation of a piece of machinery provides an excellent communication mechanism to share structural information between an application advising on component selection (i.e., parts, materials) during the design of the machine and an application analyzing the failure possibilities of that design.

Disadvantages of Incorporating Model-Based Structures

Although the advantages of a model-based knowledge representation are both real and significant, a price must be paid. The benefits are neither automatic nor free. For example, being able to reason from basic principles about a system by applying those principles to a model-based representation of the knowledge will enable a more robust application system to be developed. Yet, developing and representing the appropriate set of basic principles is a nontrivial task, as is the problem of developing a model representation that is complete (perhaps in an unexpected dimension).

Again, the degree to which particular disadvantages of a model-based form of knowledge representation are encountered by a knowledge crafter depends on the specific problem and on the solution approach being attempted. However, two general types of disadvantages, currently associated with model-based forms of representation, must be considered. These relate to the *speed* with which an inference mechanism can reason about a model and the relatively poor *linkage* of the knowledge-based system with more traditional mechanisms for processing model-based knowledge (e.g., discrete-event simulations).

Speed

Although model-based knowledge can generally be accessed efficiently, the use of qualitative reasoning can result in a relatively slow processing rate. Because the system is working from basic principles rather than with higher level concepts (e.g., theorems) or short-cut heuristics, the system must derive much more information and hence must perform much more processing.

Remember how much easier it was in high school physics to select and apply a formula to solve a problem than it was to derive that formula before applying it? Similarly, it is much easier for a knowledge-based system to apply a heuristic than it is to do qualitative reasoning. For example, consider the need to determine the time it will take the family car to accelerate from rest to 50 miles/hour. It is far faster to use a heuristic of the form

IF   the accelerator of a family car at rest is depressed hard

THEN   the car will accelerate to a velocity of **x** miles/hour in **x**/4 seconds

than it is to derive the time at which the car's velocity will be 50 miles/hour by calculating accelerations and positions from the basic physical laws of motion.

Some aspects of model-based reasoning are akin to theorem proving. Consequently, many false starts and many trips down unproductive paths can occur. Because of the number of steps likely to be involved, the necessary processing can be slow and tedious. Fortunately, a properly designed system does not totally rely on a model-based representation of knowledge. Other forms of knowledge are often used with or applied to the model-based knowledge. Only when other knowledge, rules, and procedures are inadequate to address a particular case directly would search-type approaches be used.

The knowledge crafter is cautioned not to confuse search strategies or reasoning from basic principles with other types of reasoning that heuristic rules can perform on a model-based representation. The speed disadvantage lies with the former approaches, not with the latter; in fact, the use of heuristic rules with a model-based representation can often provide results very rapidly.

Linkage

As was discussed above, nonprocedural, model-based knowledge representations fit very well into knowledge-based reasoning systems. Tools and techniques are available today to work with these types of representations quickly and efficiently, but some situations, particularly involving dynamic models, lend themselves to a more traditional, procedurally oriented representation. Because these conventional simulation techniques have been developed and used over a number of years by thousands of researchers, fairly powerful tools are available. It would be beneficial to be able to take advantage of such developments. A conventional discrete-event simulation model, for example, could be used to represent the knowledge, and the simulator rather than a rule could be executed with various parameter values to determine the resulting behavioral characteristics of the system under study.

Unfortunately, taking advantage of the body of tools and procedures that have accumulated over the years is generally very difficult. In many cases, the knowledge-based system is written in a language whose representation structure is incompatible with the structure of a traditional modeling tool. In other cases, the knowledge-based system runs on a computer system that does not provide for the execution of traditional tools or that does not interface with a system that could run those tools.

Thus, with current technology, we cannot link together or develop synergy between knowledge-based representational forms that have evolved from the AI culture and the processing mechanisms that have evolved from the modeling or simulation culture. Additional research should permit tools from these two areas to be merged so that the developer can take advantage of the relative strengths of each.

There are encouraging signs that this is beginning to happen. SIMKIT™ already provides the dynamic modeling capability, and IntelliCorp is expected to exploit the underlying knowledge-based capabilities of KEE™. The Carnegie Group is developing such capabilities for Simulation Craft™, although that product has yet to be introduced commercially. On the conventional side, CACI is planning to add some knowledge-based capabilities to Simscript II.5™. Furthermore, customers as well as vendors are involved, seeking to tie their conventional and knowledge-based systems together, to permit communication between representations using either technology, and ultimately to be able to convert from one technology to the other to take advantage of their relative strengths.

Summary

Although static representations provide many benefits, the real power of a model-based representation is only realized when it is combined with other knowledge representations and inferencing mechanisms. The benefits that result from compactness and clarity of the representation are generally the easiest to obtain, and by themselves these benefits are sufficient to warrant consideration of this form of representation. A number of inferencing tools can process model-based representations efficiently, leading to further economies. Thus, significant benefits are currently achievable from the use of knowledge-based representations.

On the other hand, some of the characteristics offering the greatest potential are only a promise at the present time. They largely reside in the research laboratory rather than in the commercial world of practical application. Thus, the use of model-based representations to support qualitative reasoning offers tremendous promise, but more research is needed before such a capability can be routinely used. Similarly, the ability to interface knowledge-based dynamic models with traditional model-based processing tools offers great promise for economies in application development. Again, however, the interfaces that do exist today are poorly developed, and further research is needed.

References

1) Dahl, O. J. and K. Nygaard, "SIMULA— An Algol-Based Simulation Language," *Communications of the ACM*, Vol. 9, No. 9, 1966.

2) IntelliCorp, *The Simkit System: Knowledge-Based Simulation-Tools in KEE*, IntelliCorp, Mountain View, Calif., 1985.

3) Fikes, R. and T. Kehler, "The Role of Frame-Based Representation in Reasoning," *Communications of the ACM*, Vol. 28, No. 9, 1985.

4) Sathi, N., M. Fox, V. Baskaran, and J. Bouer, "Simulation Craft™: An Artificial Intelligence Approach to the Simulation Cycle," *Proceedings of the SCS Summer Simulation Conference*, SCS, San Diego, Calif., 1986.

5) Kiviat, P. J., R. Villanueva, and H. M. Markowitz, edited by A. Mullarney, *The Simscript II.5 Programming Language*, CACI, Los Angeles, Calif., 1983.

6) Andes, D. K., *Artificial Intelligence in SIMSCRIPT II.5*, CACI, La Jolla, Calif., 1986.

7) Hamscher, W., "Using Structural and Functional Information in Diagnostic Design," *Proceedings of the 2nd AAAI Conference*, AAAI, Menlo Park, Calif., 1983.

8) Fink, P. K., J. C. Lusth, and J. W. Duran, "A General Expert System Design for Diagnostic Problem Solving," *IEEE Transactions on Pattern Analysis and Machine Intelligence*, Vol. PAMI-7, No. 5, September 1985.

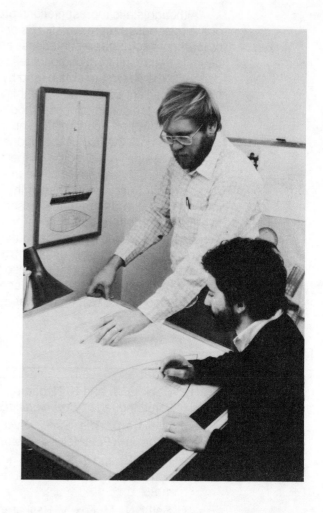

Members of the design team are using the drafting table as a blackboard, working out a series of interdependent subproblems and communicating the solutions with each other by changing the design sketched out on the table. Similarly, a knowledge-based system can use this type of cooperative approach to solve problems. Intelligent knowledge sources substitute for the yacht designers, and an electronic blackboard substitutes for the drafting table. However, the solution methodology is the same. Chapter 17 discusses the use of the blackboard approach to knowledge representation and problem solution.

Knowledge Crafting with Blackboard Representations

Blackboard systems are so named because they organize and process knowledge in a fashion analogous to a group of people working around a blackboard. The *blackboard* is used as a repository for the knowledge being assembled by the group. Each person represents a *knowledge source*, a specialized source of knowledge about some aspect of the problem. A leader provides a *control* function, guiding or focusing the activities of the knowledge sources as well as sequencing their access to the blackboard.

Knowledge can be represented on the blackboard and in the knowledge sources in various ways. A blackboard system is not so much a particular form of knowledge representation as it is a way of organizing and processing knowledge represented in other forms. Thus, a blackboard approach can be thought of as a problem solution process.

The Blackboard Concept

The blackboard concept was the basis for the HEARSAY II speech recognition system developed by Reddy and his colleagues(1,2) at Carnegie-Mellon University, which in turn has served as a guide for a number of other blackboard-based applications. The first system for building blackboard systems (AGE) was constructed by Nii and Aiello(3) at Stanford University. A very good description of the blackboard methodology, the history of its development, and the use of this technology in several applications is contained in a two-part article by Nii(4,5) in *The AI Magazine.*

A blackboard system can be thought of as a framework in which knowledge can be arranged so that it can be distributed and yet shared among a number of cooperating processes. That is, the knowledge about a problem can be distributed to a set of specialists called *knowledge sources*, each of which has a particular area of expertise. Part of the knowledge is encoded on the blackboard, which is the shared portion of the knowledge base through which the specialists communicate. The remainder of the knowledge resides with the individual specialists who operate independently of each other (except for the implicit communication that takes place through the knowledge placed on the blackboard).

Most of these specialists can be viewed as domain experts who deal with the subject matter of the application. Each works to further the state of collective knowledge as represented on the blackboard, thereby contributing to the problem's solution. However, in addition to the domain specialists, at least one specialist must have expertise relating to the solution process. This specialist (or cooperating set of specialists) performs a *control* function, guiding the activities of the other specialists and sequencing their access to the blackboard to make modifications. Thus, an application using a blackboard structure can be viewed schematically as shown in Figure 17-1.

Like the multiple-context form of representation described in Chapter 15, the blackboard representation is not a complete form of representation; it is only a structure within which knowledge can be placed using

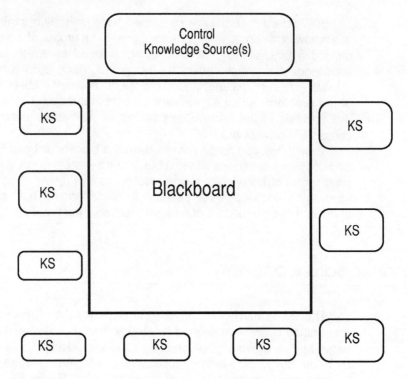

Figure 17-1   Schematic of a Blackboard System

other forms of representation. Because the structure of the knowledge within the framework is not part of the blackboard specification, a variety of knowledge representations are compatible with, and thus can be used with, a blackboard structure.

The blackboard thus serves a dual role in a knowledge-based application. Like other forms of knowledge representation, the blackboard structure governs access to and modification of the knowledge represented on the blackboard. However, the blackboard also serves as a solution methodology, setting forth an approach to developing a solution to the problem at hand. Like the structure aspect of the blackboard, the methodology aspect is only partially specified. Thus, a blackboard structure provides room for many different solution approaches. The blackboard approach can be viewed more as a philosophy or a set of guidelines than as a carefully specified process.

Components

As shown in Figure 17-1, a blackboard knowledge representation is constructed from three major components:

1.   Knowledge sources (expertise)
2.   Blackboard (knowledge storage and communication)
3.   Control (problem-solving strategy).

Because the three types of components play different roles, each offers different facilities to the knowledge crafter.

Knowledge Sources

The knowledge sources represent expertise that is captured in the overall knowledge-based system. Each knowledge source represents some particular specialized knowledge pertaining to the problem being solved. This knowledge may be represented in different ways, for example, as a collection of logical relationships or rules, or as a subroutine or function programmed in a conventional procedural programming language. Whatever form of representation is used within a knowledge source, however, the knowledge reflects an action (i.e., a change to the blackboard) under appropriate circumstances.

A knowledge source is itself made up of a number of subcomponents. For example, a knowledge source in BB1(6), the blackboard system developed at the Stanford Knowledge Systems Laboratory, has 16 different subcomponents. Conceptually, however, two major subcomponents need to be recognized—the knowledge to be applied and the knowledge about when that knowledge should be applied. These are referred to as the *action* part and the *condition* part of the knowledge source. Like a specialist, the knowledge source consists of some expertise as well as a knowledge of when that expertise is applicable.

Knowledge Sources: Condition

The condition part of the knowledge source specifies when the knowledge source would have something to contribute. That is, when the specified conditions are satisfied, the knowledge source can appropriately be fired or executed. Until those conditions are satisfied, the knowledge source can be ignored.

Consider a group of experts gathered together to determine whether a newly discovered manuscript was indeed written by Shakespeare or whether it is a forgery. As long as the conversation among the experts focuses on the text of the manuscript (e.g., word frequencies, grammatical constructions), the chemist can sit back and relax. When the subject turns to the composition of the ink on the paper and the age of the paper, however, the chemist must be alert and contribute to the discussion.

Knowledge Sources: Action

The other major part of the knowledge source specifies the actions that are to be taken based on the data (situation) presented on the blackboard. Such actions can involve the placement of new facts on the blackboard, the modification of data on the blackboard, or even the deletion of data from the blackboard (the housecleaning function).

Note that conditions can also be represented within the action part of the knowledge source. The conditions specified in the condition part of the knowledge source specify the conditions under which the expertise or knowledge contained in the knowledge source is relevant. The conditions in the action part of the knowledge source specify which pieces of knowledge are applicable to the particular situation being considered.

In terms of the previous example, the chemist's knowledge becomes applicable when the conversation turns to the materials used to record the text. If the focus of the conversation at a particular moment is on the spectrographic analysis of the ink, however, then the chemist will apply only that part of the specialized chemical knowledge that relates to ink composition, temporarily ignoring the expertise related to the chemical composition of the paper.

The Blackboard

The operation of a blackboard system can be likened to a collection of specialists that have gathered together to tackle a problem. However, if the specialists are allowed to talk directly to each other, a number of side conversations will develop. As a result, some of the specialists would not know some of the information or conclusions being developed or contributed by the other specialists. To prevent this from happening, everyone must be included in all conversations. Each expert must work alone and then share all conclusions with the others by writing them on the blackboard for all to see. These characteristics of independent operation and globally shared information are fundamental to the blackboard approach to problem solving.

The blackboard thus represents the communication medium through which the knowledge sources (e.g., specialists) communicate their findings to each other. The blackboard is the:

- Source of all data on which a knowledge source operates
- Destination for all conclusions from a knowledge source.

The Blackboard: Types of Knowledge

The blackboard contains two types of knowledge: static and dynamic. The static knowledge is typically the domain-specific knowledge that is relevant to the problem and that will have a relatively long life during the solution process. Static knowledge generally consists of factual data relating to initial conditions, parameter values, relationships, and the like. In terms of the Shakespearean manuscript, the text of the manuscript, the size of the paper, and a count of word frequencies would be represented on the blackboard as static knowledge.

Dynamic knowledge is typically the knowledge that is generated during the execution of the application system. It will consist not only of new facts but also of short-term communications such as hypotheses, goals to be pursued, requests for data (from other sources), and suggestions. The dynamic data will frequently be modified or deleted after a short period of time.

The Blackboard: Multiple Blackboards

The discussion thus far has referred to "the blackboard" as if there were only a single blackboard. However, since knowledge crafters often want to characterize knowledge in structured relationships, the blackboard can be similarly "divided." Whether a knowledge crafter chooses to view one blackboard containing a set of subareas or to view several individual blackboards is irrelevant. The concept is the same.

For the Shakespearean manuscript problem, a blackboard might be placed on one wall of the room for communication and data regarding the text of the manuscript, while a blackboard on another wall might be reserved for data on paper and ink.

The blackboard form of representation is often used in problems where the knowledge has a hierarchical structure. In such a case, the blackboard can be divided into subblackboards, with each representing a horizontal slice through the hierarchy. Raw data might be placed at the lowest level of the blackboard. Knowledge sources acting at this level would produce intermediate results that are placed at a higher level on the blackboard. Other knowledge sources, operating on the partially processed data, would leave their results at the same or a higher level, and so forth.

The Blackboard: Housekeeping

In analyzing one particular problem, given one set of facts, the knowledge crafter may reasonably permit the blackboard to contain a complete record of the data and communications related to the solution of the problem. That is, the blackboard is not erased. However, for real-time systems that involve continuing analysis of a problem, such as the monitoring of input signals about a refinery production process over a period of hours or days, the blackboard can become quite cluttered. Even if the blackboard is "very large," so that it is not "filled up," it can become filled to the point where analysis becomes quite difficult, where it takes too long for a knowledge source to find a relevant piece of data on the blackboard.

Thus, a specialized knowledge source responsible for "cleaning" the blackboard is needed. In some cases sufficiently "old" information is merely deleted. In other cases, selected information must be copied down (archived in a history file) before being erased from the blackboard. The particular mechanism used and the conditions under which information will be deleted are a function of the particular problem being addressed by the application. Nevertheless, the knowledge crafter should consider the blackboard clean-up problem during the design stage of the application.

Control

A group of experts left in a room without direction will likely wander around somewhat aimlessly in their search for a solution to the problem. The solution process needs to be guided or controlled. Consider the approach to the Shakespearean manuscript problem if a forgery were suspected. Initially word frequencies might be examined in an attempt to quickly disqualify the manuscript. If this fails, it might be much more productive to shift the focus of the inquiry to the age of the paper than proceed with a long series of quibbles about sentence construction. Such a shift in focus is part of the control function.

Control: Provision

Knowledge sources are used to provide the required control functions within the context of the blackboard system. Structurally, these knowledge sources are the same as the domain-related knowledge sources discussed previously, but they focus on the control of the problem-solving process rather than on the domain knowledge.

The control knowledge sources provide control functions in two ways—by placing information on the blackboard that will influence the knowledge sources and by selecting the knowledge sources to be fired (executed) from among those that qualify. Control knowledge sources can place a variety of information on the blackboard. For example, information about goals might be disseminated in this way, guiding the individual knowledge sources on the conclusions they should work toward or on the direction they should pursue. In the Shakespearean manuscript problem, the task of disproving authenticity (as opposed to proving authenticity) would represent such a goal.

Similarly, state information can be used to influence the knowledge sources, since certain knowledge sources might be applicable only in certain states. In the Shakespearean manuscript problem, changing the state from "words" to "ink" would suffice to activate the chemist knowledge source and to inactivate some of the grammar-related knowledge sources.

Control: Strategy

The mechanics of the control function are fairly straightforward, as described in the previous subsection. The real issue concerns the approach that the knowledge crafter should embed in the control function. This approach will be a function of the application and the solution strategy used by the expert(s). However, the following examples of control strategies should illustrate the possibilities:

- **Event-driven**—The control function reacts to the occurrence of particular events. Thus, for example, a monitoring application might react to the event "a new data item has arrived" by selecting those knowledge sources that can process newly arrived data. Similarly, it might react to the event "alarm condition" by selecting those knowledge sources that can process alarms.

- **Expectation-driven**—The control function operates from a model of the solution process. Based on the available knowledge, it can develop expectations about the character of the solution or at least about the next appropriate steps to be taken. The control function can select as firing candidates those knowledge sources that might corroborate the expected information. Thus, for example, in a diagnostic system the failure pattern may be such that an electrical failure is more likely than a hydraulic failure. The control function would then select those knowledge sources that might either confirm or refute this expectation.

- **Request-driven**—The control function selects knowledge sources that are likely to provide information that has been requested by other knowledge sources. Thus, in the case of the Shakespearean manuscript, were the chemist to request information about the spectral analysis of the ink, the moderator of the discussion would turn the floor over to those individuals who could comment on the findings of that analysis.

- **Goal-directed**—The control function selects knowledge sources likely to contribute to a particular goal it is working toward. Goals may be established to attempt to prove a hypothesis, triggering backward reasoning. They may be established to try to generate hypotheses, triggering forward reasoning. In the case of the Shakespearean manuscript, the initial goal was to attempt to prove a forgery. However, if little progress is made toward reaching this goal, the control function might switch to another goal, such as trying to prove the manuscript authentic.

Strategies may focus on objects on the blackboard or on knowledge sources (or on a combination of these). For example, in trying to identify the cause of equipment failure, the control function could focus on an object, the electrical system. In this case, any knowledge source dealing with the electrical system would be favored. Alternatively, the control function could focus on a knowledge source, the circuit resistance tester. This knowledge source would then be applied to all objects on the blackboard having the property of electrical circuits.

Control: Other Dimensions

Several other dimensions to the control function may be relevant to a particular application. In a truly parallel system, for example, all of the eligible knowledge sources could proceed to act simultaneously. However, most systems are actually executed on serial processors. Thus, control is not just choosing those knowledge sources to execute that will tend to make the best contributions to the solution of the problem, but it is also picking the single knowledge source to execute next. Consequently, some type of tie-breaker, such as the following, may be necessary:

- Priority of knowledge source
- Alphabetical order of knowledge source name
- Number of other knowledge sources whose execution might be enabled as a result of a knowledge source's contribution
- Likelihood that a knowledge source would contribute to removing a key bottleneck.

Following the execution of the selected knowledge source, the control knowledge source must perform two functions:

- Requalifying all previously ready-to-execute knowledge sources to make sure that the actions of the one knowledge source that was executed did not render any of these no longer executable
- Identifying all other knowledge sources that might now have become executable as a result of the actions taken by the knowledge source that was executed.

Note that a given knowledge source may appear on the executable list more than once. That is, for each object or set of conditions appearing on the blackboard for which a knowledge source is applicable, that knowledge source can be placed on the executable list with an indication to apply itself to the particular target object or situation. The variables in a knowledge source are bound to particular values for each situation in which the knowledge source was instantiated.

An example may clarify this point. Consider an older brother, George, whose expertise is putting on his younger brothers' and sister's boots on snowy winter days. The condition for activating George is the existence of the proper state (snowy winter day) and the proper object (child wanting to go outside). Thus, if Mary, Peter, and Jeff want to go outside on a snowy day, George would be placed on the executable list three times—once for Mary, once for Peter, and once for Jeff. A particular instance of George would then be selected for application from among the candidates. If the selection were performed with the criterion of females first, then the instance of George bound to Mary would be activated. This particular instantiation of George would check Mary's feet for the presence of boots (i.e., to see if his expertise could be applied) and, if lacking, would proceed to assist Mary in putting her boots on.

Another specialized control requirement arises in real-time environments. In this situation the knowledge source selection problem is a bit more complex. Rather than just sequencing the candidate knowledge sources, the system may need to determine which instantiated knowledge sources shall be executed at all. If processing is beginning to fall behind real time (i.e., more computation is to be performed than there is time to perform it), then some candidate knowledge sources will have to be "ignored," or dropped from consideration, because of the lack of processing power. Thus, part of the control function is to select the knowledge sources to be applied so that the more critical ones are processed in real time and the less critical ones are processed only as time is available. This process is not straightforward, however, as the criticality of a knowledge source may change as a function of how much time has passed since it was last executed.

The discussion thus far has been directed toward the ideal case, with each knowledge source operating independently of all the rest, communicating only via the blackboard. Practical applications often depart from the ideal, however. For example, the knowledge crafter may not be able to eliminate all dependence between knowledge sources. The control knowledge sources will therefore need to provide some type of sequential control in order to prevent sequence-dependent errors from arising.

An Analogy

To illustrate the blackboard process in terms that may be more familiar, consider a noncomputer-based problem solved using a blackboard methodology. One we particularly like was described by Barbara Hayes-

Roth(7) and serves to illustrate how the various parts of the blackboard operate and relate to each other.

The problem is the assembly of a jigsaw puzzle, with hundreds of disoriented pieces to be assembled into a picture. Putting the puzzle together is being undertaken as a family project.

Knowledge Sources

The various family members represent the knowledge sources, each bringing some particular expertise to the problem of assembling the puzzle. Little brother Peter specializes in turning all the pieces right side up. Mary performs the discrimination function, sorting the pieces according to their likely subject (e.g., sky, buildings, vegetation). Other family members specialize in assembly tasks. Jeff specializes in edges, assembling the border of the puzzle. Bob specializes in sky, being very good at distinguishing fine differences in shading and thus able to reduce the set of blue pieces to a very small subset that could possibly fit at any particular position in the puzzle. George specializes in buildings, and so forth.

Blackboard

The family room table serves as the main blackboard, holding the partially assembled puzzle as the pieces are put together. Several other blackboards are used in this exercise. The box contains all the "unprocessed" pieces. All the adjoining countertops display additional pieces that are partially processed (i.e., that have been turned picture side up and are grouped in terms of picture content or piece geometry). The use made of these other blackboards depends on how the control function has determined the problem should be attacked.

The content of the various blackboards changes during the problem solution process. The box of disorganized pieces is gradually depleted. Information is built up on other blackboards, and the completed puzzle gradually emerges on the table.

Some of the blackboard communication takes place verbally. Thus, the plaintive shout, "Has anyone seen a small green edge piece?" is the analog of the suggested goal, to inform other knowledge sources that the identification of a green edge piece is an important task and that, control permitting, they should apply any expertise they might have toward solving this subproblem.

Other types of communication are theoretically redundant. For example, the statement, "Bob, here is a piece of sky for you," is merely shorthand for, "Bob, don't forget to look on the blackboard for new sky pieces because one has just been put there." Because all knowledge sources are by definition triggered by the appearance of any relevant information, the placing of an additional piece in the collection of sky pieces should be sufficient communication to cause Bob to examine that piece.

Control

Clearly, the puzzle could be assembled by each family member performing his or her function independently and randomly. Thus, Bob could continually scan the blackboard looking for sky pieces. Any time he found one with the proper shading, he would try to place it in the puzzle. This approach involves considerable wasted effort, however; the puzzle could be assembled more efficiently if the family members worked together according to a plan.

Any of several strategies might be used to speed the assembly process. One strategy would be to reduce the number of pieces that need to be considered at any one time by a family member. This strategy might be implemented by a series of goals. For example, the first goal might be to turn all the pieces picture side up. Then a search might be made for all the edge pieces, then all the sky pieces, then all the green pieces, and so forth. As soon as a set of pieces had been sorted, the appropriate family member could begin to work with that set. Communication would still be required through various blackboards in connection with the pieces that are invariably misclassified on the blackboard (e.g., the blue piece that represents a part of a boy's shirt rather than part of the sky).

This strategy could also be implemented through a different set of goals. For example, the pieces might be categorized by geometry rather than color. There would be a blackboard for pieces with a single tab on each side, for two tabs on opposite sides, for two tabs on adjoining sides, and so forth.

Mother might be viewed as the control knowledge source. She might make initial decisions about the solution strategy. Thus, if the puzzle were a landscape, she might suggest that pieces be grouped in six categories: sky, mountain, tree, lake, building, and everything else. On the other hand, if the puzzle had large areas of an indistinguishable pattern (e.g., a picture of a thousand gumballs in a bowl), she might select a strategy of grouping pieces by geometry.

Later, as the assembled puzzle began to take shape, Mother would act as the traffic cop. Not everyone could approach a particular area of the puzzle at the same time to see if a particular piece (or set of pieces) might fit. Therefore, she would select who should be permitted to try a few pieces in a particular place. This strategy is analogous to selecting the next knowledge source to activate.

Assumptions

The operational characteristics of a blackboard system depend on a set of assumptions that underlie its design. In many cases, these assumptions will be met by an application, so that a blackboard representation will be appropriate. In other cases, however, these assumptions may not be satisfied, and using a blackboard representation will be difficult. Therefore, in considering whether to use a blackboard representation, the knowledge crafter should explicitly consider the degree to which the application fits the blackboard requirements. If a system is built on an inappropriate foundation, then the developer should not be surprised by unexpected results or strange system behaviors.

The knowledge crafter needs to consider three assumptions that generally underlie a blackboard system:

1. Static knowledge sources
2. Decomposable knowledge
3. Independence.

Static Knowledge Sources

The knowledge that resides on the blackboard itself has both static and dynamic components, but the knowledge represented in the knowledge sources is generally assumed to be static. That is, the knowledge sources are not modified during the course of problem solution; only the knowledge represented on the blackboard, the knowledge available to all knowledge sources, is modifiable. Thus, in considering the development of a knowledge-based system using a blackboard form of representation, the knowledge crafter should ascertain that the essence of the expertise to be represented in the system can be structured so that only static expertise can be placed in the knowledge sources.

Decomposable Knowledge

The expertise to be represented in the system should be of such a nature or have such a structure that it can be decomposed into a number of separable pieces. Knowledge with a complex interlocking structure is difficult to decompose into separate knowledge sources. The result is a small number of complex knowledge sources, which partially defeats the purpose of selecting a blackboard representation in the first place. Further, if procedural knowledge is being represented in the knowledge sources, the small number of complex routines begins to resemble a conventional program, further reducing the advantage that the selection of the blackboard paradigm can be expected to provide.

Knowledge Source Independence

Ideally, each knowledge source should be able to run independently of all the others. That is, the only input to the knowledge source is from the blackboard, and the only output from the knowledge source is to the blackboard. The knowledge source should not have to call other knowledge sources to perform its function. (It may do this implicitly by leaving a request for information on the blackboard at the completion of execution. Later, if the other knowledge source places the desired information on the blackboard, that action should trigger the original knowledge source to reperform its analysis using the new information.) In other words, whenever the right conditions prevail (the necessary type of input data is found on the blackboard), the eligible knowledge source can proceed to process those data. This independence minimizes the need for additional control logic to perform *required* sequencing, since logically the eligible knowledge sources can be applied in any order. It does, however, require the control logic to perform the *desired* sequencing to implement the chosen solution strategy, to try to reach a problem solution as quickly as possible.

Problem knowledge cannot always be divided into completely independent knowledge sources. Thus, interactions between knowledge sources cannot always be avoided. In some cases the necessary intercommunication can be forced into the blackboard framework, using state variables that are placed on the blackboard. In other cases more specialized mechanisms, such as specialized control knowledge sources, must be developed. In the extreme, two knowledge sources could be permitted to communicate directly. However, the fewer exceptions, the cleaner the design and the easier it will be for the knowledge crafter to work with that design.

Blackboard Dependencies

Unlike the knowledge sources, the knowledge or objects represented on the blackboard frequently exhibit dependence rather than independence. Various items are generally related to each other by one or more relations such as:

- Has a
- Is a
- Connected to
- Associated with.

Thus, the blackboard itself can be viewed as a "tangle" of knowledge. Some of the relations are hierarchical, pointing to specializations (e.g., has a) or generalizations (e.g., is a) while other relations (e.g., connected to) relate to problem-dependent relationships. The critical point to recognize is that part of the power of the methodology arises from the relationships between the knowledge on the blackboard, for the knowledge sources often reason about or contribute to these relationships.

Hierarchical Structure

A blackboard form of knowledge representation can be used most effectively for problems that can be decomposed hierarchically; that is, the knowledge sources can be arranged in a hierarchical fashion. Each knowledge source can be viewed as taking data from one level of the blackboard and putting information back on the same or a higher level. Data on the lowest level can be thought of as raw data, while the data at higher and higher levels of the blackboard represent more highly processed information. Similarly, the knowledge sources that work at each level can be thought of as representing progressively more abstract or general knowledge.

Bottom-Up Layering

As mentioned previously, addressing a problem at progressively finer levels of detail can be a very effective way to tackle large, complex problems. The blackboard form of representation can easily be adapted to this type of knowledge representation and problem solving. Such a knowledge source structure is reflected in Figure 17-2.

The input dependencies of knowledge sources on the outputs of other knowledge sources have been used to construct a hierarchy. Thus, the knowledge source to attach assembled chunks of the puzzle to pieces that are already anchored in the puzzle can only operate when puzzle chunks are available. Similarly, the various chunk formation knowledge sources can operate only when pieces are available in the identified collections for them to act upon, and the knowledge sources to collect those pieces can operate only when there are turned-up pieces on which to work. Thus, the lower level knowledge sources summarize the raw data (individual puzzle pieces), while the higher level knowledge sources deal in broader terms producing more general concepts (collections of related pieces, chunks of attached pieces).

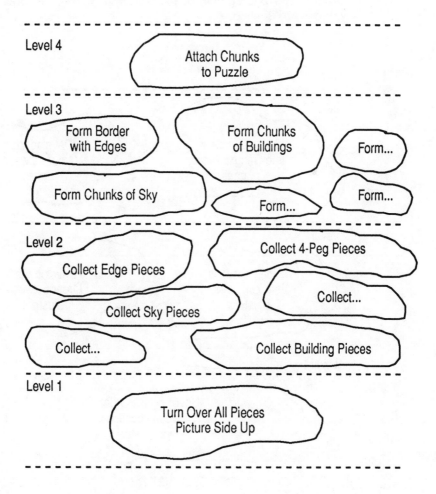

Figure 17-2 Hierarchical Knowledge Source Structure for Puzzle Assembly

Top-Down Layering

The examples given have used the blackboard to implement a bottom-up process, and many blackboard applications have been bottom-up types of processing where raw data are converted into more and more highly structured information. The blackboard methodology is not inherently a bottom-up process, however. For example, in a scheduling problem such as is outlined in Figure 17-3, a high level or coarse overall plan is prepared, then more specialized planning is applied to various pieces of the general plan. This problem was previously discussed in Chapter 15, and its solution was shown in Figures 15-9a and 15-9b for a multiple-context paradigm.

The lower knowledge sources cannot operate until the higher level knowledge sources have acted. Thus, a route between locations in a cluster cannot be found until the clusters have been defined, and a route between clusters in a zone cannot be found until the zones have been defined. The progression from zone to cluster to location is very natural in terms of the aggregation of the data with which the routing knowledge sources are dealing.

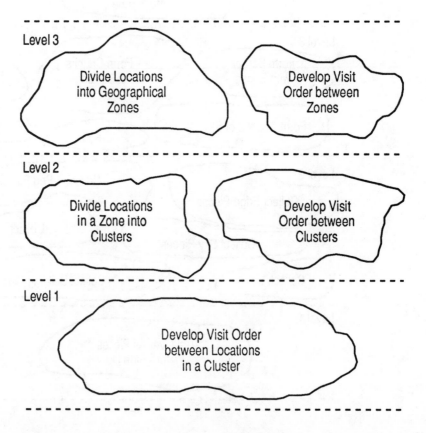

Figure 17-3   Hierarchical Knowledge Source Structure for Planning

Figure 17-3 also illustrates two other aspects of the blackboard. First, because dependency relationships can exist within a level as well as between levels, the knowledge source at the top level to plan a route between zones cannot operate until the zones have been defined. Yet, both knowledge sources are operating at the same level. Second, because some of the knowledge sources will be instantiated multiple times, the knowledge source to break a zone down into clusters will potentially be instantiated once for each zone.

Such a structuring or layering of expertise is well suited to the human technique of reasoning at different levels of abstraction. Higher level knowledge sources are employed to deal with more general concepts, while the lower level knowledge sources are used to deal with much more detailed operations applied to much narrower domains. Depending on the characteristics of the application, data may be passed up or down through the hierarchy of blackboards. Thus, the blackboard framework is conducive to the representation of problem-solving knowledge used by humans in solving problems. Such a straightforward mapping of the human representation of the knowledge to the application representation can greatly facilitate the knowledge-crafting problem.

When to Use a Blackboard Representation

Blackboard representations have a variety of uses. Early applications involved real-time data processing domains, including speech processing and signal processing. However, the blackboard representational form is also appropriate for certain types of scheduling or planning applications, although a level of procedural control may have to be placed over the entire blackboard process in such cases.

Applicability

The clues for the possible applicability of a blackboard knowledge representation for an application relate to the characteristics of this methodology. Thus, a blackboard representation might routinely be considered for problems that naturally decompose into a number of smaller, independent structures. Similarly, if aspects of the knowledge base (e.g., factual knowledge, expertise) have a clearly recognizable variation in level of detail or if the human experts use a hierarchical solution methodology for the problem, a blackboard system would be an appropriate representational candidate to consider.

Although the blackboard structure can accommodate a wide variety of representations (e.g., frames, rules), it probably offers the best means of representing procedural knowledge. Hence, if a knowledge crafter encounters difficulty in converting domain expertise to a nonprocedural form, that knowledge might be represented procedurally in a set of knowledge sources.

Although these characteristics indicate situations where a blackboard representation might be desirable or appropriate, in the case of decomposability and independence, these characteristics are also necessary ones. The absence of some of the other characteristics (e.g., procedural knowledge, hierarchical knowledge structure), however, does not imply that the use of a blackboard would be inappropriate. For example, a good blackboard system can be built that has a *flat* structure (i.e., a hierarchy with only a single level). The power of the representation can, however, be exploited to a much higher degree if the knowledge does permit a hierarchical application structure.

Risks

A major characteristic (and advantage) of a blackboard system, namely, the application of procedural knowledge in a much more structured manner, is also the greatest weakness of this representational form. Most knowledge crafters today have computing backgrounds that have emphasized procedural programming. By training and by experience, these individuals tend to think in procedural terms. This trait causes a common failing found in rule-based applications—the incursion of procedural knowledge in what should be a nonprocedural representation.

In other words, without prior experience with nonprocedural thinking and nonprocedural knowledge representations, a knowledge crafter can very easily slip into organizing knowledge in procedural terms. The blackboard model's ready accommodation of such thinking is tempting. It entices the novice to think in "comfortable" procedural terms, perhaps to represent certain aspects of the domain knowledge in procedural terms that might best be represented in some nonprocedural form. Thus, the blackboard form of representation aids and abets the spread of "procedural fever."

References

1) Reddy, D. R., L. D. Erman, and R. B. Neeley, "A Model and a System for Machine Recognition of Speech," *IEEE Transactions on Audio and Electroacoustics*, Vol. AU-21, 1973, pp. 229-238.

2) Erman, L. D., F. Hayes-Roth, V. R. Lesser, and D. R. Reddy, "The Hearsay-II Speech Understanding System: Integrating Knowledge to Resolve Uncertainty," *ACM Computing Surveys*, Vol. 12, 1980, pp. 213-253.

3) Nii, H. P. and N. Aiello, "AGE: A Knowledge-Based 'Program for Building Knowledge-Based Programs'," *Proceedings of the 6th International Joint Conference on Artificial Intelligence*, William Kaufmann, Inc., Los Altos, Calif., 1979, pp. 645-655.

4) Nii, H. P., "Blackboard Systems: The Blackboard Model of Problem Solving and the Evolution of Blackboard Architectures," *The AI Magazine*, Vol. 7, No. 2, Summer 1986, pp. 38-53.

5) Nii, H. P., "Blackboard Systems: Blackboard Application Systems, Blackboard Systems from a Knowledge Engineering Perspective," *The AI Magazine*, Vol. 7, No. 3, August 1986, pp. 82-106.

6) Garvey. A., M. Hewett, M. Johnson, Jr., R. Schulman, and B. Hayes-Roth, *BB1 User Manual: How to Implement a System in BB1*, Knowledge Systems Laboratory, Stanford University, Stanford, Calif., October 1986.

7) Shurkin, J., "Can a Machine Be Taught to Categorize and Organize Knowledge?" *The Stanford Observer*, Stanford University, Stanford, Calif., May 1986, p. 7.

A variety of technologies go into a completed yacht. If properly combined, the result is a high-quality, well-crafted sailing vessel that will provide years of good service to its owner. Similarly, a variety of knowledge representations go into a completed knowledge-based application. If properly combined, the result is a high-quality, well-crafted application that will provide years of good service to its users. Chapter 18 discusses how the knowledge crafter should select from among the various knowledge representations when crafting an application.

Selecting Appropriate Knowledge Representation Techniques

Each of the knowledge representation techniques described in the preceding five chapters has relevance to particular types of knowledge; none is applicable to all forms of knowledge. Yet, choosing the appropriate representations for each portion of an application's knowledge base is still something of an art (hence our use of the term "crafting" in this book). We have not found an algorithm that produces the best decomposition of a problem and most appropriate set of representations of the knowledge. Consequently, we cannot provide a set of rules or procedures that the crafter should follow in conducting this task, but we can offer a set of six guidelines that have proven to be very useful:

1. Select the representation to fit the problem.
2. Decompose the problem.
3. Plan for the needed representations.
4. Work to the strengths of the representations.
5. Keep the problem structure visible.
6. Understand the system being used.

The relevance and importance of a particular guideline to a particular application development effort will, of course, depend on the characteristics of the system being crafted. Not every guideline will apply in every situation. Each guideline should be carefully considered, however, for it could make the evolving knowledge-based system much more efficient, more powerful, more understandable, and less costly to maintain.

Select the Representation to Fit the Problem

The form(s) of representation chosen for the knowledge must match the inherent structure of the problem. This rule appears to be so obvious as not to require a formal statement. Although no one would likely dispute this statement, many ignore it.

At first, the task appears quite simple. The knowledge crafter has only to look at the natural forms of the knowledge and the inferencing procedures being used and then find representations (and tools having those representations) that match these forms. Unfortunately, the structures of real-world problems often differ from the most common structures in use today in knowledge-based systems.

We have been told of a number of systems that have become unnecessarily complex simply because an inappropriate form of knowledge representation was used. For example, in one system, the basic application involved diagnosing an equipment failure. The essence of the problem was one of selection or categorization. Initially, the developers chose a knowledge structure in which domain knowledge and control knowledge were intertwined. The resulting system was workable, but complex. Subsequently, a different knowledge-crafting team recast the system in a structure that exclusively used backward-chaining rules with a fact list; the switch in representation reduced the number of rules by a factor of seven. Because control was provided by the backward-reasoning inference mechanism, a new control code section was not required. Thus, the rule-count reduction was not diluted by having to add new control rules. Not only was the execution of the resulting application much faster, but the diagnosis logic was also much easier to understand.

But Our System Only Does . . .

Perhaps the most common failing stems from knowledge crafters trying to force a body of knowledge into a particular representational form that a previously acquired system development tool can handle. The fact that the tool was suitable for an earlier application does not necessarily make it appropriate for later ones. Yet, because some software is relatively expensive, organizations frequently pressure their staff to use "what's available" rather than acquire "yet another" piece of software. Unfortunately, the resulting damage in terms of complexity, development difficulty, and maintainability can far exceed the acquisition costs involved.

Multiple Representations Often Needed

Many problems do not fit neatly into a single representation. Rather than picking the "least misfitting" representation as the one to be applied to all aspects of the problem, the knowledge crafter should divide the knowledge associated with the problem into pieces or sections. One section might best be captured in a frame representation, while another might best be captured in a rule representation, and so forth.

The model form of representation is a case in point. In generating a system for circuit failure diagnosis, the knowledge crafter should not rely solely on a circuit model and the physical principles governing the movement of electrical currents. Instead, the model and physical principles should be augmented with some degree of knowledge categorization, some heuristics about diagnosing circuit problems, and some files of system characteristics associated with higher frequency failure conditions. Thus, concerns about the slow speed with which model-based reasoning can be performed have less relevance, since the application would only rely on the model-based representation for part of the solution process.

Similar arguments can be made concerning overreliance on production rules, which is a common failing of applications constructed using some of the less expensive, microcomputer-based development tools.

Sometimes the tasks of subdividing problem knowledge and assigning representations are straightforward; the appropriate subdivisions and their representations are obvious. Other times, however, the knowledge crafter may need to go through a considerable process of trial and error to accomplish these tasks. In general, encountering difficulty in putting the knowledge into a particular representation or in working or reasoning with that knowledge is a signal to reorganize the knowledge or use different representations.

Look Beyond the Current Problem

In selecting the representations to use for an application, knowledge crafters should also consider the ways in which the application might change in the future. In what directions might it be expanded? What additional capabilities might be desired? What initial functions might be modified or extended? The answers to these types of questions can indicate where flexibility is required in the application and hence in the knowledge structure being developed. Such flexibility needs should be considered by the knowledge crafters as they select the knowledge representation(s) to be used for an application.

Decompose the Problem

Complexity tends to increase exponentially with problem size, with a parallel increase in the development and maintenance resources required, as well as in the error count and debugging effort involved. Because the ability of the knowledge crafter to understand the entire application decreases with increasing complexity, the problem should be decomposed into a larger number of smaller problems whenever possible. In general, the simplicity afforded by the smaller problems significantly outweighs the increase in number of problems to be addressed. As a result, not only is each component of the decomposed application easier to construct, understand, and maintain, but the entire application becomes more manageable.

Decomposition Alternatives

Just as knowledge can be represented in many ways, so too can a problem be decomposed in many ways. The type of decomposition used is not as important (as long as it makes sense within the context of the problem) as is the act of decomposing. Whatever the mechanism, the result will be a more efficient system that facilitates the application of intelligent reasoning to the problem.

Consider an application that provides construction advice on excavating and pouring the foundation, building the frame, roofing the building, and painting the interior and exterior. The problem may be broken down into independent segments without those segments being required to be used in a particular sequence. Thus, the problem might be structured as a blackboard system with knowledge sources as shown in Figure 18-1.

Each knowledge source (e.g., PAINTING) could be applied independently and repeatedly in many different situations as the house is built. Thus, the knowledge contained in PAINTING would be applied to the exterior of the house, to the interior walls, and to cabinetry. A complicated web would result if the sequence of control links between these knowledge sources were to be traced during a construction advising session.

The problem may also be broken down hierarchically as shown in Figure 18-2. In such a breakdown, the PLANNING segment might cover planning for the construction of the entire house. Thus, it might allow a specific two-week period for the pouring of the foundation and basement floor. On the other hand, the CONTRACTOR COORDINATION segment might be trying to establish the work flow on specific days during that two-

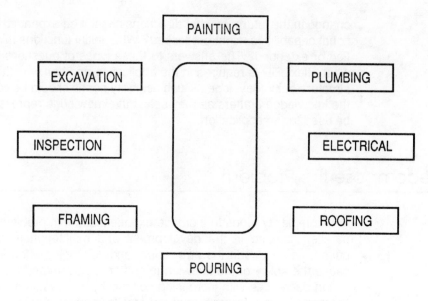

Figure 18-1   Blackboard Construction System

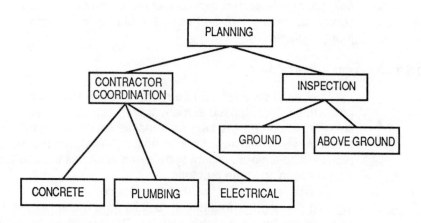

Figurre 18-2   Hierarchical Construction System

week period since the plumbing, electrical, and concrete subcontractors would have to interact during that period.

Efficiency Improvement

Not only does decomposition encourage simplification of the problem, but it also fosters efficiency. Consider a 1,000-rule system that can logically be divided into 20 sets of 50 rules. Because the inferencing mechanism, whether using forward- or backward-chaining, must consider all the rules in the set (either at run time or at compile time, depending on the inference mechanism), a set of 50 rules is clearly much more efficient to handle than a set of 1,000 rules. This decomposition technique is particularly useful for applications to be run on personal computers. A 1,000-rule knowledge base will overwhelm many systems, while a knowledge base of 20 rule-sets having 50 rules each can be processed quite rapidly.

Dimensionality Problems of Multiple Environments

The number of multiple environments being considered at any step must be kept as small as possible. Since each environment can spawn multiple new ones, the number can grow exponentially. The amount of available computing capacity can easily be swamped.

Clearly, the knowledge crafter can establish constraints that can be applied at every level to prune the search space. Further, various evaluation functions can be used to rank partial solutions according to their likelihood of being part of a "good" solution. Yet, while these factors help, they still operate within the basic structure of the problem. A major reduction in the computational requirements requires a reduction in the dimensionality of the problem.

Such a reduction can be achieved using a decomposition mechanism. Thus, fewer dimensions are considered when a planning problem is solved at an abstract level than at a more detailed level. The omitted dimensions will, of course, have to be considered at a lower level of detail. However, the number of environments to be considered with this approach is additive between levels in the search space, not multiplicative.

Plan for the Needed Representations

Unfortunately, the representations that a knowledge crafter might like to use for a particular knowledge-based application do not always form a proper subset of the representations afforded by the tools available for use in constructing that application. That is, the availability of tools to work with particular representational forms (or the development effort required to develop such tools) will influence the design of the knowledge-based system. Thus, a development tool should not be chosen before the design has been completed. Otherwise, the system design may be unnecessarily constrained.

Under these circumstances, the knowledge crafter must first define the most appropriate set of knowledge representations and then identify the best tool kit that will permit use of those representations. In many cases, none of the available tools will provide just what is desired. An iterative cycle then follows, with the knowledge crafter reviewing the "next best" design choice and comparing its needs with available tool kit offerings, and so on as necessary. In this way, an "as-good-as-possible" system design can be prepared. Otherwise, the knowledge crafter is likely to turn out an "as-good-as-possible-when-using-tool-x" design, one that might not be nearly as powerful or provide as nice a match to the characteristics of the problem.

Work to the Strengths of the Representations

Having selected a set of representational forms for the knowledge to be incorporated within the system, the knowledge crafter should try to structure or organize the system so as to take maximum advantage of the strengths of those representational forms. (The opposite advice is valid also: try to avoid the weaknesses of each representation. Knowledge crafters are generally much more alert to this recommendation, however.)

Pattern Matching with Rules

Some inferencing systems have a very efficient pattern matcher built into their rule-based inferencing mechanism. If such a system is being used, the knowledge crafter should take advantage of that capability whenever possible. For example, rather than just detecting whether a particular slot in a frame contains a set of specified values, the matcher can determine whether those values occurred in a particular order. The knowledge crafter can thus make a specific test (e.g., whether three events took place between two particular values) or a more general test (e.g., whether any events took place between the two specified values).

This pattern-matching capability opens up many alternatives for dealing with state variables, state sequences, and the like. For example, every rule in a rule-set could have an applicable state designation included. Because a change in the value of the current state would in effect tailor the rule-set for the current state, the knowledge crafter would not have to develop a complete rule-set for each application state. These pattern-matching capabilities can also be used to locate or identify particular conditions across multiple environments.

Multiple Levels of Abstraction with Blackboards

The power of the blackboard mechanism comes from the hierarchical structure that can be given to the knowledge sources. Thus, in a planning situation, the knowledge crafter can take advantage of the structure in a top-down manner. High-level knowledge sources (working at the highest level of abstraction) can be used to suggest solution strategies, provide an outline of potential plans, and so forth. Lower-level knowledge sources, working at increasingly detailed levels, can then fill in the details of the plan.

In a data analysis situation, the structure can be used in the reverse direction, working bottom up. Thus, knowledge sources at the lowest level refine the data and structure it. Other knowledge sources, working at increasingly higher levels of abstraction, process this information in turn, providing further generalizations at each step.

A "flat" or nonhierarchical blackboard (e.g., where every knowledge source operates at the same level, where data are not distributed in terms of generality or level of abstraction) should not necessarily be avoided.

However, the power of knowledge-based reasoning systems is their ability to work at different levels of abstraction, just as human experts do. Organizing the blackboard portion of a system in this way exploits the inherent power of the representation.

Procedural Knowledge in Rules

A typical failing of novice knowledge crafters is attempting to use a representation for other than its intended purpose. A rule-based system, for example, is by premise a nonprocedural form of representation, yet most knowledge crafters working today have always programmed using procedural languages. Hence, they tend to conceptualize a problem to some degree in procedural terms, and the procedural element becomes part of the perceived problem structure.

The effects of representing procedural information in the rule base are not surprising. Many more rules are required to represent the knowledge (particularly in comparison with use of a procedural representation). Sequencing is much more difficult to perceive in a rule representation, making development more difficult, debugging more tedious, and maintenance a more error-prone process. The resulting application does not appear to be very robust, for new cases stress it unexpectedly, revealing previously undetected sequence-dependent characteristics embedded in the rules.

Mixed Taxonomies

Similarly, the knowledge taxonomy in a frame-based knowledge representation must be used in the way that is consistent with its structure. That is, the children at each level in the hierarchy must be logical members of their parentage. The example provided in Figure14-22 and reproduced here as Figure 18-3 is illustrative. The top part of the taxonomy reflects a more and more detailed breakdown of the concept AUTOMOBILES. However, at the level of FORD this changes. FORD is broken down into its various components. Although such a subdivision is correct (a Ford does indeed have a fuel system, an engine, and brakes), it is erroneous in the context of the knowledge taxonomy that has already been established. This shift in context, which might be termed the "consistency trap," must be avoided at any level below the top of the hierarchy. A simple way for the knowledge crafter to avoid this problem is to ask if each level of the hierarchy reflects a specialization of the top or root class (not just of the class directly above since the definition of that class can be skewed to permit situations such as shown in Figure 18-3 to occur).

When the taxonomy is mixed, the knowledge crafter will likely encounter considerable difficulty in working with it in the future. Processes do not work conveniently; they break down in places. Some things become much more complex to represent. Working with a clean taxonomy will aid the knowledge crafter in taking advantage of the power of a taxonomic knowledge representation.

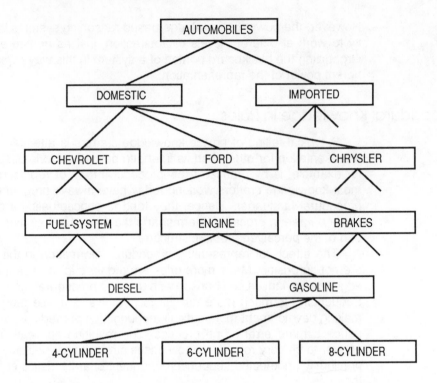

Figure 18-3   An Erroneous Taxonomy

Keep the Problem Structure Visible

One major purpose of using a knowledge-based approach to problem solving is to take advantage of the knowledge structuring that is afforded and of the mechanisms that exist for reasoning about knowledge in those structures. Having taken the step of using a knowledge-based approach, the knowledge crafter should make sure that those advantages are not lost by subsequent actions that tend to hide that structure. For example, a rule-based representation might have been selected for a portion of the knowledge base. Yet, if the knowledge is structured so that no rule depends on any other rule (i.e., a flat structure), little advantage comes from using this form of representation.

As an extreme example, consider a loan advisory system. All of the analysis might be performed with a series of functions programmed in C, Pascal, or Fortran. Each function would evaluate part of the data and return a value of TRUE or FALSE. Functions might be provided for:

- Return on investment (ROI)
- Socioeconomic factors (SE)
- Residual value analysis (RVA)
- Property considerations (PC)
- Country considerations (CC).

Then a rule-based loan-advisory application could be reduced to the following rule:

Rule 1:	<u>IF</u>	ROI
	<u>AND</u>	SE
	<u>AND</u>	RVA
	<u>AND</u>	PC
	<u>AND</u>	CC
	<u>THEN</u>	ADVISE MAKING THE LOAN

Rule 1 is not wrong, for it will work properly. The application will produce the desired answers. However, this approach has completely obscured the operation of the rule-based system. If the rule mechanism is important, then it should be used (and used explicitly). If use of a rule system is not important, then the knowledge crafter should not pretend to use it.

Understand the System Being Used

The advice "Understand the system being used" sounds so obvious as to be trite. Surprisingly, however, many people are using systems they do not understand, in part due to the helpful or friendly interfaces of some tools being offered commercially. Because these systems can be used without much study or understanding of theory, the many subtle characteristics that can affect solutions are not recognized. No wonder these systems are sometimes accused of providing "strange" results. The following examples illustrate some problems that are often glossed over in the knowledge crafter's desire to be a "user" of the technology rather than an "expert" in it.

Rule Evaluation Frequencies

The knowledge crafter should know something about the efficiency and side effects of rule evaluation. Consider the following example:

A forward-chaining system consists of the three rules shown in Figure 18-4.

Rule 1:	<u>IF</u>	I WILL TAKE THE BUS TO WORK
	<u>THEN</u>	I WILL NEED TO PUT ON BOOTS
Rule 2:	<u>IF</u>	THE STREETS WILL BE SLIPPERY
	<u>THEN</u>	I WILL TAKE THE BUS TO WORK
Rule 3:	<u>IF</u>	IT IS SNOWING
	<u>THEN</u>	THE STREETS WILL BE SLIPPERY

Figure 18-4   Rule-Set Execution Frequency Example

If the premise IT IS SNOWING is asserted to be true, then obviously the truth of the conclusion I WILL NEED TO PUT ON BOOTS can be derived. Various forward-chaining inference mechanisms would produce the same conclusion. The differences arise in how the different implementations might arrive at that conclusion:

- How many passes would be made through the rule-set—one, two, or three?
- Would listing the rules in the order Rule 3, Rule 2, and then Rule 1 make any difference in the number of premise evaluations?
- How many times would the premise I WILL TAKE THE BUS TO WORK be evaluated?

To increase application efficiency, the developer needs to know the number of premise evaluations and the feasible steps that can be taken to reduce this number. To ensure application correctness, the developer needs to know the number of times a particular premise will be evaluated and the existence of any side effects associated with that evaluation. Consider the five-rule backward-chaining example shown in Figure 18-5.

Assuming that one wishes to try to prove that I WILL NEED TO PUT ON BOOTS is true, and that nothing is known about the other four clauses (I WILL TAKE THE BUS TO WORK, THE STREETS WILL BE SLIPPERY, THE WALKS MAY BE SLUSHY, or IT IS SNOWING), a backward-chaining inference engine will not be able to derive I WILL NEED TO PUT ON BOOTS. The more important but subtle issue, however, concerns the number of times that the premise THE STREETS WILL BE SLIPPERY will be evaluated. Some systems will do it once, others twice. The implications are obvious if the evaluation of the premise requires extensive computational resources or produces any side effects.

Rule 1:	IF	I WILL TAKE THE BUS TO WORK
	THEN	I WILL NEED TO PUT ON BOOTS
Rule 2:	IF	THE STREETS WILL BE SLIPPERY
	THEN	I WILL TAKE THE BUS TO WORK
Rule 3:	IF	THE WALKS MAY BE SLUSHY
	THEN	I WILL NEED TO PUT ON BOOTS
Rule 4:	IF	THE STREETS WILL BE SLIPPERY
	THEN	THE WALKS MAY BE SLUSHY
Rule 5:	IF	IT IS SNOWING
	THEN	THE STREETS WILL BE SLIPPERY

Figure 18-5 Backward-Chaining Example

Rule Evaluation Side Effects

Simple rules of the form "IF fact THEN action" pose no evaluation problems. The inference mechanism need only look in the knowledge base to determine the logical truth (TRUE, FALSE, UNKNOWN) of the fact. Thus, a rule of the form:

Rule: IF   THE PACKAGE IS MAILABLE
         THEN   DETERMINE THE AMOUNT OF
                     POSTAGE NEEDED

would be evaluated by looking in the knowledge base (e.g., in a "fact list," in a slot of a frame) to determine whether the fact, THE PACKAGE IS MAILABLE, is TRUE. However, if the rule calculates the truth value rather than merely checking its existence, the situation becomes more complex. Consider the implications of the following rule:

Rule: IF   THE HEIGHT OF THE PACKAGE
                     PLUS TWICE THE LENGTH AND
                     WIDTH IS LESS THAN 96 INCHES
         THEN   DETERMINE THE AMOUNT OF
                     POSTAGE NEEDED

In this case, premise evaluation involves the referencing of three facts in the knowledge base (HEIGHT, LENGTH, WIDTH) and the performing of a calculation [$H + 2 (L + W) < 96$]. Although more calculation is now involved in the evaluation of the premise, no side effects (other than evaluation time) are involved.

Now let us consider a slightly more complex case where the size computation function not only determines whether the package is small enough to be mailed but also keeps a tally of the number of packages "measured."

Rule: IF   MAILABLE
         THEN   DETERMINE THE AMOUNT OF
                     POSTAGE NEEDED

where MAILABLE is a function that adds 1 to a counter of packages measured and returns TRUE if $H + 2 (L + W) < 96$.

Now the evaluation of the premise creates a side effect. Should this premise be evaluated three times for the same package, the figures being collected for number of packages measured would obviously be in error. Hence, the knowledge crafter must understand the operation of the inference mechanism being used and perhaps avoid the problem through a simple redesign (e.g., isolating the side effect and using a state variable to ensure that the computation is performed but once for each case).

Implications of Different Certainty Mechanisms

Consider a rule such as the following:

Rule: IF   IT WILL RAIN TODAY
         AND   I WILL HAVE TO WALK BETWEEN
                     BUILDINGS
         THEN   I WILL NEED AN UMBRELLA

This rule has a very clear meaning, offering little room for misunderstanding or confusion. If IT WILL RAIN TODAY and I WILL HAVE TO WALK BETWEEN BUILDINGS are two facts that are known to be TRUE, then the fact that I WILL NEED AN UMBRELLA will consequently be known to be TRUE. Now, however, let us add the further dimension of uncertainty.

Assume that IT WILL RAIN TODAY and I WILL HAVE TO WALK BETWEEN BUILDINGS are not known with certainty, but have certainty values of .6 and .3 respectively (e.g., there is only a 60% certainty that it will rain today). What certainty should be assigned to the fact that I WILL NEED AN UMBRELLA?

- .00 (i.e., FALSE) because neither of the required conditions are known with certainty
- .18 because this is the product of the two certainty factors for the two premises
- .3 because the conclusion cannot have greater certainty than any of its logical requirements
- .5 because this is the Baysian combination of the certainties of IT WILL RAIN TODAY and I WILL HAVE TO WALK BETWEEN BUILDINGS with the prior expectation of I WILL NEED AN UMBRELLA.

Clearly, the interpretation to be used depends on the particular problem being addressed. However, because of the widely varying interpretations possible, the knowledge crafter must understand the interpretation that will be given by the inference mechanism being used.

Summary

At the conclusion of Part II we provided a one-word summary (*planning*) of our advice for constructing a knowledge-based system. If Part III were to have a similar one-word summary, it would be *decomposition*. Whenever possible, the knowledge crafter should try to decompose the problem into smaller pieces—not only to make it easier to fit representations to each piece, but also to make the system easier to understand and maintain and more efficient to use.

Clearly, decomposition is not a panacea; it will not overcome a poor system design. However, if a problem is decomposed properly, a variety of limitations and constraints can generally be overcome.

BIBLIOGRAPHY

Andes, D.K., *Artificial Intelligence in SIMSCRIPT II.5*, CACI, La Jolla, Calif., 1986.

Dahl, O.J. and Nygaard, K., "SIMULA—An Algol-Based Simulation Language," *Communications of the ACM,* Vol. 9, No. 9, 1966.

de Kleer, J., "An Assumption-Based Truth Maintenance System," *Artificial Intelligence,* Vol. 28, 1986.

Dempster, A.P., "A Generalization of Bayesian Inference," *Journal of the Royal Statistical Society,* Volume 30, 1968.

Doyle, J., "A Truth Maintenance System," *Artificial Intelligence,* Vol. 24, 1979.

Duda, R.O., Hart, P.E., and Nilsson, N.J., "Subjective Bayesian Methods for Rule-Based Inference Systems," in *Readings in Artificial Intelligence,* Webber, B.J., and Nilsson, N.J., editors, Tioga Publishing Company, Palo Alto, Calif., 1981.

Erman, L.D., Hayes-Roth, F., Lesser, V.R., and Reddy, D.R., "The Hearsay-II Speech Understanding System: Integrating Knowledge to Resolve Uncertainty," *ACM Computing Surveys,* Vol. 12, 1980, pp. 213-253.

Fikes, R. and Kehler, T., "The Role of Frame-Based Representation in Reasoning," *Communications of the ACM,* Vol. 28, No. 9, 1985.

Fink, P.K., Lusth, J.C., and Duran, J.W., "A General Expert System Design for Diagnostic Problem Solving," *IEEE Transactions on Pattern Analysis and Machine Intelligence,* Vol. PAMI-7, No. 5, September 1985.

Fried, L., *Commercial Use of Expert Systems: A Survey of U.S. Corporations,* Report # BIP 86-1068, SRI International, Menlo Park, Calif., 1986.

Garvey. A., Hewett, M., Johnson, Jr., M., Schulman, R., and Hayes-Roth, B., *BB1 User Manual: How to Implement a System in BB1,* Knowledge Systems Laboratory, Stanford University, Stanford, Calif., October 1986.

Goldberg, A. and Robson, D., *Smalltalk-80: The Language and Its Implementation,* Addison-Wesley, Reading, Mass.,1983.

Hamscher, W., "Using Structural and Functional Information in Diagnostic Design," *Proceedings of the 2nd AAAI Conference,* AAAI, Menlo Park, Calif., 1983.

IntelliCorp, *The Simkit System: Knowledge-Based Simulation Tools in KEE,* IntelliCorp, Mountain View, Calif., 1985.

Kiviat, P.J., Villanueva, R., and Markowitz, H.M., edited by Mullarney, A., *The Simscript II.5 Programming Language,* CACI, Los Angeles, Calif., 1983.

Lowrance, J.D., *Evidential Reasoning with Gister: A Manual,* SRI International, Menlo Park, Calif., April 1987.

Lowrance, J.D., Garvey, T.D., and Strat, T.M., "A Framework for Evidential-Reasoning Systems," *Proceedings of the Fifth National Conference on Artificial Intelligence,* AAAI, Menlo Park, Calif., 1986.

Lucid, *LUCID CommonLisp,* Menlo Park, Calif., 1986.

McAllester, D., "A Widely Used Truth Maintenance System," unpublished, 1985.

Nii, H.P., "Blackboard Systems: Blackboard Application Systems, Blackboard Systems from a Knowledge Engineering Perspective," *The AI Magazine,* Vol. 7, No. 3, August 1986, pp. 82-106.

Nii, H.P., "Blackboard Systems: The Blackboard Model of Problem Solving and the Evolution of Blackboard Architectures," *The AI Magazine,* Vol. 7, No. 2, Summer 1986, pp. 38-53.

Nii, H.P. and Aiello, N., "AGE: A Knowledge-Based 'Program for Building Knowledge-Based Programs'," *Proceedings of the 6th International Joint Conference on Artificial Intelligence,* William Kaufmann, Inc., Los Altos, Calif., 1979, pp. 645-655.

Reboh, R., *Knowledge Engineering Techniques and Tools in the Prospector Environment,* Technical Note 243, Artificial Intelligence Center, SRI International, Menlo Park, Calif., June 1981.

Reddy, D.R., Erman, L.D., and Neeley, R.B., "A Model and a System for Machine Recognition of Speech," *IEEE Transactions on Audio and Electroacoustics,* Vol. AU-21, 1973, pp. 229-238.

Sathi, N., Fox, M., Baskaran, V., and Bouer, J., "Simulation Craft™: An Artificial Intelligence Approach to the Simulation Cycle," *Proceedings of the SCS Summer Simulation Conference,* SCS, San Diego, Calif., 1986.

Shafer, G., *A Mathematical Theory of Evidence,* Princeton University Press, Princeton, N.J., 1976.

Shortliffe, E.E., *Computer-Based Medical Consultations: MYCIN,* Elsevier, New York, N.Y., 1976.

Shurkin, J., "Can a Machine Be Taught to Categorize and Organize Knowledge?" *The Stanford Observer,* Stanford University, Stanford, Calif., May 1986, p. 7.

Symbolics, *Zetalisp,* Cambridge, Mass., 1985.

I N D E X

Abstraction, 83, 182, 314, 317
  levels of, 281–283
  multiple levels, 326–327
Acquisition. *See* Knowledge acquisition
Action, knowledge sources, blackboard
  representations, 304–305
Active value, 138
Activity selection problem, multiple
  contexts, 259–264, 273–279
Advisory systems, 4
Alarm condition, 308
Apollo, 16, 89
Appliance diagnostic system, 146–147,
  151
Application, 6, 7
  context, rule-based representation,
    207
  design, prototyping, 111
  domain boundaries, 51
  embedded, 98–99
  environment, 103, 104
  incompleteness, 147
  pilot, 145, 147–149, 151, 155
  reasoning capability, 131
  rewrite, 96–98
  size, 64
  skeleton, 117
  structure, initial, 103
Application requirements, 46–56
  developers, 50, 52
  environment, understanding, 48, 53
  experts, 50, 51
  feasibility study, 58
  issues addressed, 53
  management, 50–51
  priorities, 53
  realism, 54
  redesigning as requirements are
    clarified, 55
  shifting, 55
  solidity, 54–55
  specifications, 49
  cf. traditional software, 53–54
  unstated, 51
  users, 50–52
    education/training, 51–52
Apprentice knowledge crafters, 28–29,
  30–33, 114, 186
  interviewing expert, 35, 45
  local, 111
  schedules/scheduling, 167, 174
Architectural advisor, example, 146,
  147
Arcs, 289, 290, 295
ART, 16, 33, 90, 258
Arthur D. Little, 30
Artificial intelligence, 3–4
  workstation, 147, 150, 151
Assertion, hypothesis, 265
Assumed independence, knowledge
  sources, blackboard representations, 313–314
Assumed static, knowledge sources,
  blackboard representations, 313
Assumption, retraction, 265, 266, 267
Assumptive basis, 269
Attributes, 211; *see also* Slots
Authority, prototype evaluation,
  141–142

Automatic teller machines, 76
Automobile diagnostics, 244

Backtracking, 275
  dependency-directed, 270
Backward chaining. *See* Chaining,
  backward
Bandwidth, 93, 148
Bank loan officer, example, 146,
  148–149
Bayesian logic, 204
Behavioral knowledge, 84, 237, 240
Behavior, monotonic, 269
Behaviors, 211; *see also* Slots
Benchmark tests, 125
Benefits
  estimating, feasibility study, 72–73,
    77–78
  received, vs. expectations, pilot
    operation evaluation, 158–159
Bias, question, 40–41, 188
Blackboard representations, 19, 82, 84,
  85, 87, 88, 302–318
  assumptions, 312–314
  blackboard structure, 303, 304,
    306–307, 311
  boot problem, 310
  as communications medium, 303,
    306, 311
  components, 304–310
  concept, 303–304
  dependencies, 314, 315, 317
  example, 310–312
  hierarchical structure, 307, 314–318
    bottom–up, 314–316, 326
    top-down, 316–317
  housekeeping, 307
  knowledge crafter apprentice
    training, 33
  manuscript problem, 305–309
  multiple, 306–307
  puzzle problem, 310–312
  risks, 318
  technique selection, 326–327
  when to use, 317–318
Blank paper problem, 186
Boot problem, 310
Branch-and-bound approach, 277
Breadth-first search, 273–275

CADEUCES, 21
Call path, restricted, 70
Carnegie Group Inc., 90
  Knowledge Craft, 16, 33, 90, 258
  training courses, 31
Carnegie-Mellon University, 31, 32
Categorizing, 321
  frames, 217
Certainty
  rule-based representation, 203–204
  technique selection, 331–332
  uncertainty about, 205–206
Chaining, backward, 85, 91, 113, 117,
  202, 291, 321
  inference engines, 196–197, 199,
    201, 202, 207
    rule-based representation,
      196–197, 199, 202, 207
  rule evaluation, 330

Chaining, forward, 85, 91, 113, 117,
  136, 202, 295
  inference engines, 196, 197,
    199–202, 207
    rule-based representation,
      196–197, 199–202, 207
  rule evaluation, 329
Checkpoint and restart, application
  interface, 86
Circuit model, model-based
  representations, 288–289, 292,
  293, 295
Circuit taxonomy, model-based
  representations, 287–288
  with instance, 287–288
Clarity, static model-based
  representation, 293, 301
Class, 210, 228
  hierarchy, 218
  -instance relationship, 220
  relationships, 211
  rules, 238–239
  structure, frame-based reasoning,
    218–220, 222–224
  subclass, relationship, 220
Client meetings, introductory, feasibility
  study, 59
Closed-world mode, 202
Clothes selection problem, multiple
  contexts, 255–256
Clustering, 282
  frames, 217, 218
Color, man-machine interace, 100
Common-sense reasoning, expertise,
  62–63
Communicability, model-based
  representation, 297, 298
Communication, written, 20
Compactness, static model-based
  representation, 294, 301
Comparability, model-based
  representation, 297, 298
Compartmentalization. *See*
  Decomposition
Compatibility, feasibility study and
  prototype evaluation, 141
Competitive problems, 23
Complementary relation, 234
Completeness
  scheduling prototype development,
    174
  testing in prototype evaluation,
    125–126, 134
Complexity, 182
  feasibility study, technical issues,
    64–65
Computational infeasibility, 280
Computer system interfaces, 102
Concepts, 210, 218
Condition, knowledge sources,
  blackboard representations, 304
Configuration, 150
  changes, static model-based
    representation, 293
Connections, 222, 223
  paths, 291
  see also Linkage
Consequents, 196, 197, 199, 200
  matching with predicates, 200

Consistency, testing in prototype evaluation, 125, 126, 134–135
Constraints, 325
  design, 81
  pruning, 262
  search mechanisms in mulitple contexts, 274, 275, 280
  violation, 274, 275
Construction example, technique selection, 323–324
Consultants, independent, knowledge-crafting team, 29, 30
Context, 254
  generation (spawning), 260, 272, 273, 274, 280
  identical, 263
  switching, 277
  see also Multiple contexts
Context tree, 261
Contradictions, detected, 270
Control code, 117, 322
Control function, blackboard representations, 303, 304, 307–312
Control knowledge source, 312
Control language, 201
Controlled search, 273, 277–279
Control logic, 113
Control/management, project, 20–21
Control mechanism, 103
Conversion
  prototype-to-delivery, 145, 147, 148, 151
  prototype-to-pilot, 176–178
Corporate culture, 75
Cost
  -benefit analysis, feasibility study, 171
  estimating, 73–74
  feasibility study, 77–78
Cross-compilation, 96
Cultural issues
  delivery environment, 98
  feasibility study, 75–76

Daemons, 137, 138
Dark room problem, 266–269
Data acqusition and expertise, 61–62
Databases
  external, 69, 70, 93
  initial design, 104
  interface, 6, 101, 103
  mainframe, 88–89
Data collection, 154, 191
Data gathering, retrofitting, 190
Data interfaces, 103
Data order, permutations, 128
Debugger, dynamic, 138
Debugging, 327
  active values, 217
  prototype evaluation, 122, 133, 136–140
Decision, alternative, 256
Decomposition, 83, 188, 227, 277, 281–383
  blackboard representation, 317
  design, 182–183
  rule-based representation, 205
  technique selection, 321, 323–325, 332
Deep reasoning, 184, 293
Delivery
  considerations, design, 91–102
    environment, 83, 96–99
    interfaces, 99–102

environment, 103, 104
  design considerations, 83, 96–99
  feasibility study, scheduling, 170
  hardware, pilot operation, evaluation, 153
  pilot phase, 117
  support software, pilot operation, evaluation, 153
  vehicles, 92
  and design, 47
  version, cf. development, 149
Delivery system, 17–18, 50, 54, 91
  combination, 92, 95–97
  microprocessor-based, 92, 94–95
  terminal-based, 92–93
  workstation-based, 92, 93–94
Dependency-directed backtracking, 270
Depth-first search, mulitple contexts, 273, 274–277
Description, hierarchical structure, frame-based reasoning, 218, 219
Design, 9–10, 14, 15, 47–48, 79–105
  constraints, 21–22
  content, initial, 103
  crafting, 80–81
  decomposition of problem. See Decomposition
  delivery considerations, 91–102
    environment, 83, 96–99
    interfaces, 99–102
  development tools, 87–91
    hardware, 88–89
    software, 90–91
  documentation, 10
    scheduling pilot testing, 178
  feasibility study, 58–59, 77–78
  fitting structure to problem, 183
  initial, 102–105
    completion, 104
    confirmation, 104–105
  and initial prototyping, 113
  key principles, 181–184
  knowledge representation, 82–87
  overdesign, avoiding, 81
  rapid prototyping, 181–182, 191
  resource commitment, 181–184
    user interface, 183–184, 191, 192
  review and confirmation, 80
  schedules/scheduling, 171–173
  system building, key principles, 181–184
  team, communication, 80
  technique selection, 325
  tentative, 170, 171
  traditional, 81
Detail, multiple levels, 227
Deteriorating input, 126
Developers, application requirements, 50, 52
Development
  cycle, knowledge-based system, 14–16
    delivery, 17–18
    maintenance, 18
    pilot, 14, 17–18
    prototypes, 14, 16–17, 20
  environment, 103, 104
    feasibility study, scheduling, 170
  hardware, 16
  iterative, 88

parallel, 111, 112
  phase, 10
  resources, 53
  system, 92
    overview, 2–10
  time, feasibility study, technical issues, 63
  tools, 16, 17, 19–20
Development team, 25–33
  knowledge crafters, 26, 28–29
    apprentices, 28–29, 30–33
    interviewing, 28, 33
  management, 26–27
  project champion, 8, 22, 26, 27, 190
  project leader, 26–28
    assistant, 28
    qualifications, 27–28
  staffing, 28–30
  see also Knowledge-crafting team
Development tools, 16, 17, 19–20, 47, 182
  cf. delivery, 148
  design, 47, 87–91
    hardware, 88–89
    software, 90–91
  microcomputer-based, 322
Diagnostic applications
  automobiles, 244
  kitchen appliance, 146–147, 151
  static model-based representation, 294
Digital Equipment Corporation (DEC), 17, 89
  training courses, 32
Dimensionality, 325
  reduction, 280
Discrete-event simulation, 300
DNA molecule, 100, 101
Documentation, 20, 105
  adequacy, 159–160
  design, 10, 172–173
    revisions, 175
  operational phase, 163
  prototyping, 113
  scheduling pilot testing, 178
  self-, 163
  tools, 113
  user, 184, 190
Domain boundaries, application, 51
Dominance, 262–263
Dynamic model-based representations, 286, 295–297, 300, 301
  changing inputs, 295
  hypothesized situations, 295
  improved inferencing, 296

Economic issues, feasibility study, 72–75
  benefits, estimating, 72–73
  costs, estimating, 73–74
  pioneering considerations, 74–75
  risk assessment, 74
Economy, model-based representation, 297, 298
Education, knowledge-crafting team, 186, 191
Effectiveness, feasibility study and prototype evaluation, 141
Efficiency
  man-machine interface, 155–156
  representation, 237
  rule evaluation, 329, 330
  static model-based representation, 294, 301
  technique selection, 324–325

Embedded application, 98–99
End-user
    developmental role, 8
    prototyping, 110–111
Engineering workstation, 89, 147
Enhancement, 190
Entities, 210
Environment, multiple, 19, 113, 326
    dimensionality problems, 325
Epitec AB, 90
Epitool, 16, 90
    knowledge crafter apprentice
        training, 33
Errors
    batching vs. serial approach, 116
    detection cf. identification, 136
    identification, static model-based
representation, 293
    representation, 249
    sequence-dependent, blackboard
        representations, 310
Evaluation
    partial solutions, 275, 277, 279, 280
    plan, 189–190
    see also Pilot operation evaluation
Event-driven blackboard
    representations, 308
Evidential reasoning, 204
Execution, inefficient, 205
Expectation-driven blackboard
    representations, 308
Expectations, user, 54, 161
    cf. benefits, 158–159
Expert
    active vs. passive, 184
    application requirements, 50, 51
    articulateness, 67–68
    availability, 53, 67
    developmental role, 8
    feasibility study, 66–68
    interest, 67
        generating, 184–185, 191
    interviewing, 35–39, 42–45, 111,
        167, 170
    involvement in solution process, 85
    motivation, 68
    observation, 169
    problems with, 39–42
    support from, 22–23
Expert-Ease, 90
Expertise
    feasibility study, technical issues,
        61–63, 69
    multiple areas, 174
    representability, 61
    technical aspects, feasibility study,
        61–63, 69
    types of, 4–5
Explanation, application interface, 86
Exponential growth, 323, 325
EXSYS, 90
Extensions, operational phase, 164
External linkages, 70

Facets, 215–217, 236
Facilitated interaction, 156
Fact list, 321
Failure analysis, 292
False information, 40
Familiarity, 298
    static model-based representation,
        293
Feasibility of operation, roll-out
    evaluation, 162
Feasibility study, 14, 15, 48, 49, 57–78,

182, 227
    application requirements,
        preliminary, 58
    client meetings, introductory, 59
    constraints, 76–77
    cultural issues, 59, 75–76
    design, tentative, 58, 59
    economic issues, 59, 72–75
    expertise, technical aspects, 61–63,
        69
    interfaces, technical aspects, 69–71
    interviews with management, 59
    knowledge representation issues,
        82
    prototype evaluation, 140, 141
    report, 171
    schedules/scheduling, 167–171
    study team, 59
Feasibility study, technical issues,
    59–71
    bounds of problem, 60–61
    complexity, 64–65
    development time, 63
    expertise, 61–63, 69
    experts, characteristics of, 66–68
    input stability, 65–66
    interfaces, 69–71
    knowledge, characteristics of, 64,
        65
    management commitment, 69
    size, 64
    validation/testing, 71
Flat structure, 318
    blackboard representation, 326
Flavors, 91
Flexibility, 323
Force fitting, 183
Forward chaining. See Chaining,
    forward
Frame, 19, 210–218, 228, 229, 244
    categorizing, 217
    clustering, 217, 218
    creation, 235
    definition, 210
    destruction, 235
    facets, 215–217, 236
    instance, 228
    restrictions, 213–215, 236
        relation restriction, 214, 236
        representation restrictions, 213
        value restrictions, 214
    slots. See Slots
    structures, 217–228
    usefulness, 217–218
    value forms, 213
    values, active, 216–217
    see also Inheritance
Frame-based reasoning, 84, 209–251
    advantages, 246–247
        maintenance, 247
    frames, 210–218
    inheritance, 222, 228–233
    knowledge crafter apprentice
        training, 33
    problems, 247–250
    procedures (methods) as slot
        contents, 240–243
    relationship knowledge, 233–237
    rule-sets as slot contents, 237–240
    skeleton prototyping, 118
    structure, 218–228
Function call, object-oriented
    programming, 243
Functions, 250
    slot contents, 240–243

Future cases, testing for robustness,
    127
Fuzzy logic, 204

Garbage collection, 150
Generality, model-based
    representation, 297–298
Goal-directed blackboard
    representations, 309
Goal information, 308
The Gods Must Be Crazy, 185
Graphic representation, static model-
    based representation, 293
Graphics, 88, 95
    man-machine interace, 100, 101
    workstation, 94, 148

Hardware
    delivery, pilot operation, evaluation,
        153
    development, 16
    tools, 88–89
Heuristics, 4–5, 87, 279, 292, 299, 300,
    322
Hewlett-Packard, 17, 89
Hierarchical structure
    blackboard representations, 307,
        314–318, 326
        bottom-up, 314–316, 326
        top-down, 316–317
    frame-based reasoning, 218, 219,
        226–228
    knowledge sources, blackboard
        representations, 315, 316
    rule references, inheritance, 238
Hierarchies, 218
    flat, 318
    intersecting, frame-based
        reasoning, 221–224
    object-oriented programming, 245
    visual representation, static model-
        based representation, 293
Hooks, 122
Host-based computing, 94
Host processor, connection with
    microprocessor, 95–96
Host system migration, 165
Hydraulic system model, model-based
    representations, 290–293
Hypotheses
    assertion, 265
    rule-based representation, 196,
        198, 199

IBM, 17
    PC series, 89
    training courses, 32
Icons, 88, 100, 289
Identical contexts, 263
IF/THEN statements, rule-based
    representation, 196, 197, 199, 200
    consequent, 196, 197, 199, 200
    matching, 200
    predicate, 196, 197, 199, 200
Image, man-machine interface, 100
Inappropriate taxonomies, 248
Inconsistencies
    pilot delivery environment, 177
    scheduling prototype development,
        173
    testing in prototype evaluation, 125,
        126, 129, 134–135
Inconsistent taxonomies, 249
Independent consultants, knowledge-
    crafting team, 29, 30

Independent reasoning, 255
Induction, 90
Inefficent execution, 205
Inference Corp., 90
    training courses, 32
Inference engine, 5, 6, 182, 210
    backward chaining, 196–197, 199,
        201, 202, 207
    forward chaining, 196, 197,
        199–202, 207
    unsophisticated, 204
Inference mechanism, 82, 103,
    261–262, 279, 292
Information
    false, 40
    sources, application requirements,
        52
    taxonomies, skeleton prototyping,
        118
Inheritance, 33, 84, 228–233
    multiple, 231–233
    object-oriented programming, 245
    passing properties, 228
    procedures, 240–243
    rules, 238, 239
    types, 228–231
Initial design, 102–105
    completion, 104
    confirmation, 104–105
Input
    deteriorating, 126
    stability, feasibility study, technical
        issues, 65–66
    test, 130
Instances, 210
    frame, 228
    relationship knowledge,
        frame-based reasoning,
        234–236
    structure, frame-based reasoning,
        220, 221
Instantiation, 202–203, 210, 220, 226,
    310, 317
Intel 80386, 17, 89, 146, 149, 251
IntelliCorp, 90
    KEE, 16, 33, 90, 258, 296
    training courses, 32
Interaction, facilitated, 156
Interactive development, 19
Interface, 5, 6, 86
    as component in larger application,
        98
    computer system, 102
    database, 6, 101, 103
    design considerations, 99–102
    feasibility study, technical issues,
        69–71
    man-machine/user. See User (man-
        machine) interface
    model-based representations, 301
    real-time, 101–102
Interface Corp., ART, 16, 33, 90, 258
Interruptions, 42
Intersecting hierarchies, structure,
    frame-based reasoning, 221–224
Intersection, 232, 233
Interview, 115
    expert, 35–39, 42–45, 111
    feasibility study, 170
    management, 59, 170
Iteration, 102
Iterative development, 88
Iterative series, and initial prototyping,
    114–115

Jeffrey Perrone and Associates, 90
Justification, application interface, 86

KEE, 16, 33, 90, 258, 296
Keyboard skills, users, 75
Kitchen appliance diagnostic system,
    146–147, 151
Knowledge
    behavioral, 84, 237, 240
    compartmentalization/decomposi
        tion, 64
    decomposition. See
        Decomposition
    dynamic, 63
    and feasibility study, 63–66
    form, 66
    generation, 128
    nonprocedural, 128, 206, 248
    pattern, 66
    permanent, 63
    procedural, 210, 240, 300, 313,
        317–318
        cf. nonprocedural, 82, 84, 137,
            318, 327
    sharing, application interface, 86
    sources, lower cf. higher level, 317
    spurious, 128, 187–188, 191
    stability, 65
    static, 63
        cf. dynamic, blackboard
            representation, 306
    structure, 82, 103, 251
        initial prototyping, 113
    testing, 112
    types of, 4–5
    see also Relationship knowledge,
        frame-based reasoning
Knowledge acquisition, 5, 34–45
    expert, problems with, 39–42
    interviewing expert, 35–39, 42–45
    literature review, 35
Knowledge base, 5–6
    restructuring, 177, 183
    size, 64
Knowledge-based system
    applications, 6, 7
    criteria, 7–8
    definition, 4
    development cycle, 14–16, 18–20
        delivery, 17–18
        maintenance, 18
        pilot, 14, 17–18
        prototypes, 14, 16–17, 20
    in existing systems, 21–22
    interfaces, feasibility study, 69, 70
    life cycle, 9–10
    migration, 165
    sample problem areas, listed, 8
    structure, 5–6
Knowledge Craft, 16, 33, 90, 258
Knowledge crafters
    apprentice. See Apprentice
knowledge crafters
    developmental role, 8
        apprentice, 8–9
    development team, 26, 28–29
        interviewing, 28, 33
    feasibility study, technical aspects,
        67–68
Knowledge crafting, 321
    decomposition of testing process,
        188
    expert, generating intereste,
        184–185, 191

key principles, 181, 184–189
    shortcuts, avoiding, 186, 191
    spurious knowledge, avoid,
        187–188, 191
    staged completion, 189, 191
    system building, key principles,
        181, 184–189
    testing/debugging, planning ahead,
        187, 191
Knowledge-Crafting Bootcamp, 32
Knowledge-crafting team, 29–30, 184,
    191
    education, 186, 191
    experience, 185–186, 191
    schedules/scheduling, 167–169
    see also Development team
Knowledge representation
    appropriate, 185
    and design, 82–87
        application interface, 84, 86
        condition of knowledge, 84, 87
        control, 84–86
        domain knowledge, 84, 87
    efficiency, 237, 246–248
    errors, 249
    higher-level, 294
    modification, 248
    natural, 251
    technique selection, 327
    see also Frame-based reasoning;
Rule-based representation
Knowledge representation, technique
    selection, 320–332
    decomposition, 321, 323–325, 332
    fit to problem, 183, 321–323
    keep problem structures visible,
        328–329
    multiple representations, 322
    plan for needed representation,
        325, 332
    system, understanding, 329–332
    taxonomies, mixed, 327–328
    work to strengths of
        representations, 326–327
Knowledge sources, blackboard
    representations, 303–306, 308,
        310, 311–317, 326
    action, 304–305
    assumed independence, 313–314
    assumed static, 313
    condition, 304
    hierarchical structures, 315, 316
Knowledge structures, design process,
    47

Leaf contexts, search mechanisms in
    mulitple contexts, 272, 273
Legal issues, 23–24
Life cycle, knowledge-based system,
    9–10
Line testing, prototype evaluation, 142,
    143
Linkage, 224
    model-based representations, 299,
        300
Linking problem, multiple contexts,
    256–257
LISP, 16, 21, 91
    knowledge crafter apprentice
        training, 33
    mainframe, 150
LISP machine, 17, 33, 89
Lists, unordered, 84
Loan technique selection, 328–329

Logic
  Bayesian, 204
  fuzzy, 204
Logical testing, pilot application,
  crafting, 149
Loops, 91

M.1, 90
Mainframes, 88–89, 150
  garbage collection constraints, 150
  time-sharing system, 148
Maintenance, 18
  application requirements, 53
  documentation, scheduling pilot
    testing, 178
  as knowledge domain evolves, 190
  operational phase, 164
  static model-based representation,
    293–294
  unmaintainable rule-sets, 205
Management
  application requirements, 50–51
  in development team, 8, 26–27
  feasibility study, 69, 170
  style/philosophy, 75
Man-machine interface. See User
  (man-machine) interface
Manuscript problem, blackboard
  representations, 305–309
Matching scheme, 201
Merging multiple contexts, 258,
  263–264, 273, 275
Messages, object-oriented
  programming, 243, 244
Meta rules, 201, 204
Methods, 113
Microcomputers, 17, 89, 94, 95, 148,
  322
Microprocessor, 17, 88, 89
  delivery systems, 92, 94–95
  host processor, connection, 95–96
  Intel 80386, 17, 89, 146, 149, 251
  Motorola 60820, 17, 146
Migration, operational phase, 165
Milestones
  iterative prototyping, 114, 115
  prototype evaluation, 123
  skeleton, 118
Mistakes, man-machine interface, 156
Misunderstandings, 40, 41
MIT, 31, 32
Model-based representations, 33, 82,
  83, 85, 285–301, 322
  advantages, 297–298
  circuit model, 288–289, 292, 293,
    295
  circuit taxonomy, 287–288
    with instance, 287–288
  disadvantages, 299–300
  dynamic, 286, 295–297, 300, 301
    changing inputs, 295
    hypothesized situations, 295
    improved infeencing, 296
  example, 286–287
  cf. rule-based systems, 291, 295
  static, 286, 289–294, 298, 301
    benefits, 293–294
    hydraulic system, 290–293
    purchase order model, 290
Modification, 190
  roll-out evaluation, 161
Modularization, 244–246
Monitoring active values, 216
Monotonic reasoning, 264, 269

Motorola 68020, 17, 146
MS-DOS, 149
Multilevel prototype evaluation,
  122–123
Multiple contexts, 253–284
  activity selection problem, 259–264,
    273–279
  clothes selection, 255–256
  concept, 255–257
  context structure, 257–259
    hierarchical (tree), 257–259
  dark room problem, 266–269
  examples, 255–257
  how to use, 279–284
    dimensionality, 280–281
    hierarchical problem-solving,
      281–284
  linking problem, 256–257
  reasoning, 258–264
    merging, 258, 263–264, 273,
      275
    parallel reasoning, 258, 261
    pruning context tree, 258,
      261–263, 273, 274
  terminology, 258
  tourist problem, 282–283
  truth maintenance systems,
    264–272
  see also Search mechanisms,
    mulitple contexts
Multiple environment, 19, 113, 326
  dimensionality problems, 325
  knowledge crafter apprentice
    training, 33
  representations, 82, 83, 85, 87
Multiple representations, 322
MYCIN, 21

National culture, 75
New hires, knowledge-crafting team, 30
Nodes, 289, 290, 295
Nonmonotonic reasoning, 264–270
n-tuples, 84
Null inheritance, 230–231
Numeric cf. symbolic processing, 3

Object, 210, 218
Object data, 243–244
Object-oriented programming, 134,
  138, 210, 237, 240, 243–246, 249,
  296
  frames, 244
  function call, 243
  functions (services), 243
  hierarchy, 245
  inheritance, 245
  knowledge crafter apprentice
    training, 33
  messages, 243, 244
    passing, 243
  object data, 243–244
  slots, 244
Operating environment, pilot operation,
  evaluation, 153
Operational phase, 162–165
  evolution from pilot, 163
  see also Pilot operation evaluation
Operations, key principles, 181,
  189–192
  evaluation plan, 189–190
  opinion leaders, support from,
    190–191
  support services, 190–192
Opinion leaders, 190–191

OPS5, 16, 33, 91, 258
Organizational constraints, 22–24
Organization-related problems, 23
Output, test, 130
Overdesign, avoiding, design, 81
Oversimplification, 185

Package problem, rule evaluation, 331
Paging, 294
Parallel development, 175
Parallel processing, 188
Parallel prototyping, 112, 119–120
Parallel reasoning, 258, 261
Parallel system, blackboard
  representation, control function,
  309
Parameters, 211; see also Slots
Partial solutions, evaluation, 275, 277,
  279, 280
Particularization, 222, 223, 231
Pascal, 91
Pattern
  detection, 188
  knowledge, 66
  matching, 33
    rule-based representation,
      201–202, 205, 207
    technique selection, 326
PC-DOS, 149
Performance, rule-based
  representation, 207
Personal computers, 17, 89, 94, 95,
  148, 322
Pilot , 9, 10, 14, 17–18
  evolution to operational phase, 163
  schedules/scheduling, 176–179
  strategy, 117
  testing, 18
Pilot application, 155
  logical testing, 149
  prototype-delivery environment
    conversion, 145, 147, 148, 151
Pilot operation evaluation, 153–162
  benefits received, vs. expectations,
    158–159
  productivity, 157–158
  roll-out evaluation, 161–162
  solution quality, 158
  support, adequacy, 159–160
  user attitudes, 160–161
  user-interface, 154–157
Pioneering considerations, economic
  issues, feasibility study, 74–75
Potential Satisfiers (PS), 271
Predicate, 196, 197, 199, 200, 270
  evaluation, 201–202
    multiple, 204–205
  matching with consequents, 200
Predictive function, 277
Premise evaluations, rule evaluation,
  330, 331
Priorities, application requirements, 53
Private knowledge, 4, 5
Problem-dependent monitoring,
  debugging, 137, 139–140
Problem, subdivision of, 64–65
Procedural approach, 85
Procedural fever, 206, 248, 250
Procedural knowledge, 210, 240, 300,
  313, 317–318
  cf. nonprocedural, 82, 84, 137, 318,
    327
Procedures, slot contents, 240–243
Processing, symbolic cf. numeric, 3

Production rules, 291, 322
Production version, 17
Productivity
    feasibility study and prototype
        evaluation, 141
    pilot operation evaluation, 157–158
Programming
    practices, good, 20–21
    procedural, 248
Project champion, 22, 190
    developmental role, 8, 26, 27
Project control/management, 20–21
Project leader, development team,
    26–28
    assistant, 28
    qualifications, 27–28
Project scheduling. *See* Schedules/
    scheduling
Prolog, 21, 91
Prototype, 9, 10, 14, 16–17, 20, 91
    cycles, 116
    delivery environment conversion,
        145, 147, 148, 151
    errors, batching vs. serial approach,
        116
    final, 116–117
        review, 175
    initial, 102
        review, 114–116
    intermediate levels, 115
    -to-pilot translation, 176–178
Prototype development, 173–176
    first, 173–174
    intermediate, 173
    second, 174
Prototype evaluation, 121–143
    authority, 141–142
    debugging, 122, 133, 136–140
    feasibility study, 140, 141
    line testing, 142, 143
    milestones, 123
    multilevel, 122–123
    planned, 122
    scheduling, 174
    test cases, 142–143
    validation, 122, 123, 140–143
        coverage, 140–141
    see also Testing in prototype
        evaluation
Prototyping, 14, 16–17, 109–120
    documentation, 113
    evaluation, 111, 120
    general considerations, 110–111
    initial, 110, 112, 113–117
    parallel, 112, 119–120
        independent disciplines, 119
        synthesizing, 120
        sections, developing and
            integration, 120
    rapid, 17, 18, 19, 55, 80, 81,
        181–182, 191
    schedules/scheduling, 173–176
    separate pieces, 112, 119–120
    skeletal, 112, 117–119
    strategies, 112–113
    testing, 16
    tools, 16–17
    validating, 16
Public knowledge, 4
Purchase order model, model-based
    representations, 290
Puzzle problem, blackboard
    representations, 310–312

Qualitative reasoning, 293, 297, 299
Question

bias, 40–41, 188
    interviewing expert, 37
Questioner-scribe role switching,
    interviewing expert, 36–38

R1, 21
Radian Systems, 90
Rapid prototyping, 17, 18, 19, 55, 80,
    81, 181–182, 191
Real-time systems, 66, 104, 307, 310,
    317
    interfaces, 101–102
Reasoning
    from basic principles, 299, 300
    capability, application, 131
    deep, 184, 293
    hierarchical, frame-based
        reasoning, 226–228
    independent, 255
    mechanism, 47, 186
    monotonic, 264, 269
    multiple contexts, 258–264
        merging, 258, 263–264, 273,
            275
        parallel reasoning, 258, 261
        pruning context tree, 258,
            261–263, 273, 274
    nonmonotonic, 264–270
    parallel, 258, 261
    qualitative, 293, 297, 299
    under uncertainty, 185–186
Recording interview, 38
Refinement, 218
Regression testing, 162
    testing in prototype evaluation, 129,
        136
Relation
    complementary, 234
    restrictions, 214, 236
Relationship, 222, 224
    proper cf. improper, 225
    structured, 224
    taxonomies, 234, 235
    visual relationship, 224
Relationship knowledge, frame-based
    reasoning, 233–237
    facets, 236
    groups, 235
    instances, 234–236
    usefulness, 236–237
Representability, expertise, 61
Representation. *See* Knowledge
    representation
Requalifying, blackboard
    representation, control function,
        309
Request-driven blackboard
    representations, 308–309
Requirements
    design, 81
    feasibility study, 77–78, 170
Resource centers, knowledge-crafting
    team, 29–30
Resource commitment, design,
    181–184
    user interface, 183–184, 191, 192
Resources, development, 53
Restrictions
    frames, 213–215, 236
        representation restrictions, 213
        value restrictions, 214
        relation restriction, 214, 236
    inheritance, 230
Retrofitting, data gathering, 190
Reversibility, 266
Risk assessment, economic issues,

feasibility study, 74, 77–78
Robustness, 298, 299
    future cases, testing for, 127
    testing in prototype evaluation, 125,
        126–128
Roll-out evaluation, pilot operation
    evaluation, 161–162
Rule(s), 19, 113
    class, 238–239
    debugging, 137–138
    evaluation, 329–331
    formats, 117, 196, 201
    inheritance, 238, 239
    production, 322
    rule-based representation, 198
    structure, 240
    taxonomies, 237–239
Rule-based representation, 33, 87,
    117, 195–207, 237
    application context, 207
    backward chaining inference
        engines, 196–197, 199, 202, 202,
        207
    certainty factors, 203–204
    closed-world mode, 202
    decomposition, 205
    example, 197–200
    forward chaining inference engines,
        196–197, 199–202, 207
    hypotheses, 196, 198, 199
    IF/THEN statements, 196, 197,
        199, 200
        consequent, 196, 197, 199, 200
        matching, 200
        predicate, 196, 197, 199, 200
    cf. model-based representations,
        291, 295
    pattern matching, 201–202, 205,
        207, 326
    performance, 207
    problems with, 204–206
    rules, 198
        format, 196, 201
    rule sets, 199–202
        execution, 201
    segmentation, 202, 205
    terminal predicates, 196–199
    tie-breaking, 135
    variables, 202–203
Rule firing
    monitoring, 134
    -order variation, testing in prototype
        evaluation, 128, 129, 135–136
    permutations, 128, 135–136
RuleMaster, 90
Rule-sets, 117, 113
    execution, rule-based
        representation, 201
    inheritance, 239
    large, overloads, 205
    rule-based representation, 199–202
    slot contents, 237–240
        multiple, 237
    unmaintainable, 205

S.1, 16, 33, 91
Scaling up, 183
Schedules/scheduling, 166–179
    apprentices, 167, 174
    design, 171–173
    expert interviews, 167
    feasibility study, 167–171
    knowledge-crafting team, 167–169
    pilot version, 176–179
    prototyping, 173–176
    roll-out evaluation, 162

selection study from candidate
applications, 167–169
Schema, 210
Scope, feasibility study and prototype
evaluation, 141
Scribe, interviewing expert, 36–38
Scripts, 130
initial design, 104
Search algorithms, 135
Search mechanisms in mulitple
contexts, 254, 262, 272–279
breadth-first search, 273–275
constraints, 274, 275, 280
violation, 274, 275
controlled search, 273, 277–279
depth-first search, 273, 274–277
leaf contexts, 272, 273
search space, 261, 263
search tree, 272–273
Search strategies, 300
Securities analysis, 127
Security, 147
application interface, 86
interfaces, feasibility study, 69–71
Segmentation, rule-based
representation, 202, 205; see also
Decomposition
Selection, 321
Self-documentation, 163
Sensors, 103, 104
Sequence
dependence, 135, 136, 310, 327
independence, testing in prototype
evaluation, 125, 135, 136
representation, slots, 212
Sequencing, required cf. desired, 313
Sequential control, blackboard
representations, 310
Serial processors, blackboard
representation, control function,
309
Shared system, design considerations,
97
Shells, 71
Shortcuts, avoiding, knowledge
crafting, 186, 191
Side-effect problems, 202
rule evaluation, 329–331
Signal processing, 317
SIMKIT, 296
Simplification, 283, 324
static model-based representation,
294
Simula(1), 295
Simulation Craft, 296
Simulation, discrete-event, 300
Simulation model, 295, 296
Simulators, 104
Size, feasibility study, technical issues,
64
Skeleton, prototyping stratgy, 117
Skill level, users, 141
Slots, 138, 211, 212, 213, 215, 216,
225
contents, 237–243
procedures, 240–243
rule-sets, 237–240
inheritance, 228–229
object-oriented programming, 244
values, 228, 229
see also Inheritance; Relationship
knowledge, frame-based
reasoning
Software
delivery support, pilot operation,
evaluation, 153

specification, 96
tools, 90, 91
Solution
methodology, blackboard
representation, 304, 317
partial, evaluation, 275, 277, 279,
280
process, 85–86
quality, pilot operation evaluation,
158
Specialists, cooperating, 303
Specialization, 220, 227, 249
Specification, software, 49, 96
Speech processing, 317
Speed, 322
model-based representations,
299–300
Spurious knowledge, 128, 187–188,
191
SRI International, 30, 32, 69
Staffing development team, 28–30
Staged completion, knowledge crafting,
189, 191
Stanford University, 31, 32
State information, 308
State variables, 326
Static model-based representations,
286, 289–294, 298, 301
benefits, 293–294
hydraulic system, 290–293
purchase order model, 290
Storage management, 150
Storage space, model-based
representation, 294, 298
Structured relationship, 224
Structures, frames, 217–228
Study team, feasibility study, 59
Subclass, 210, 228
-class, relationship, 220
structure, frame-based reasoning,
219–220, 222, 223
Subdivision of problem, 64–65
Sun Microsystems, 17, 89
Support, 191
adequacy, pilot operation
evaluation, 159–160
materials, scheduling pilot testing,
178
services, 190–192
user, adequacy, 159–160
Swapping, 294
Switching contexts, 277
Symbolic cf. numeric processing, 3
Symbolics, 16, 89
Symbols, 289; see also Icons
System building, key principles,
180–192
design, 181–184
knowledge crafting, 181, 184–189
operations, 181, 189–192
summary, 191–192
System development, overview, 2–10
System modification, 323
System outputs, application
requirements, 53

Taxonomic fever, 248–249
Taxonomies, 113, 228, 233, 234,
247–250
inappropriate, 248
inconsistent, 249
information, skeleton prototyping,
118
mixed, knowledge representation,
technique selection, 327–328
relationships, 234, 235

rule, 237–239
structure, frame-based reasoning,
220–224, 226, 227
multiple, 221
tree structure, 220, 222, 227
Technology, hidden, 185
Teknowledge, 90, 91
M.1, 91
S.1, 16, 33, 91
Tektronix, 17, 89
Terminal, 54
-based delivery systems, 82–93
Terminal predicates, rule-based
representation, 196–199
Terminology
expert, 41
multiple contexts, 258
Test cases, prototype evaluation,
142–143
Testing
automating, 130
benchmark, 125
facilities, 122, 130
future cases, robustness, 127
interviewing expert, 44–45
pilot, 18, 149, 178–179
planning ahead, knowledge
crafting, 187, 191
regression, 162
user, scheduling pilot testing, 178
see also Debugging
Testing in prototype evaluation, 16,
122–136
completeness, 125–126, 134
consistency, 125, 126, 129,
134–135
as continuous process, 124
objectives, 125–129
regression testing, 129, 136
robustness, 125, 126–128
rule firing-order variation, 128, 129,
135–136
sequence independence, 125, 135,
136
techniques, 129–136
test cases, 122–132
sources, 132–133
tracing, 129, 133–134, 137
user interface, 123, 130
Texas Instruments, 16, 89
Text, man-machine interface, 100
Tie-breaking, 135, 309
Time-sharing system, 148
Tools
debugging, 137
delivery version, 148
cf. development, 149
development. See Development
tools
documentation, 113
prototyping, 16–17
software, 90, 91
technique selection, 325
usage, 186
Tourist problem, multiple contexts,
282–283
Tracing
debugging, 133, 137, 139
testing in prototype evaluation, 129,
133–134, 137
Trade-offs, 88
feasibility study, 78
Traditional software, 53–54
Training, 191
adequacy, 159
feasibility study and prototype

evaluation, 141
man-machine interface, 156–157
operational phase, 163–164
support personnel, 164
scheduling pilot testing, 178
user, 54, 76
vendors, 32
Transaction validator example, 146, 150
Tree, context, 261
pruning, 258, 261–263, 273, 274
Tree structure, frame-based reasoning, 220, 222
Truth, 196
Truth maintenance systems, 264–272
assumption-based, 268, 271–272
justification, 268–272
logic-based, 268, 270–272

Uncertainty, 203–204; *see also* Certainty
Union, 232, 233
Units, 210
Universe, 254, 255
state of, 255–257
University of Michigan, 31
University of Sweden, 31, 32
University of Tokyo, 31
UNIX, 149
Unordered lists, 84
Updates, operational phase, 164
Usability, man-machine interface, 156

Usage pattern, 155
User
application requirements, 50–52
education/training, 51–52
attitudes, pilot operation evaluation, 160–161
cultural issues, 75, 76
documentation, 105, 184, 190
initial design, 104
interview, feasibility study, 170
keyboard skills, 75
-related problems, 23
skill level, feasibility study and prototype evaluation, 141
support
adequacy, 159–160
operational phase, 164–165
training, 54
cultural issues, 76
untrained, 98
User (man-machine) interface, 6, 99–101, 103, 110
application requirements, 52, 53
design, 172, 183–184, 191, 192
parallel prototyping, 119
pilot operation evaluation, 154–157
testing in prototype evaluation, 123, 130

Validation, 10
feasibility study, technical issues, 71

prototype evaluation, 16, 122, 123, 140–143
coverage, 140–141
Value
active, frames, 216–217
inheritance, 229–230
restrictions, 214
Value forms, frames, 213
Variables, 226
rule-based representation, 202–203
state, 326
Vendors
hardware and software, 16–17
knowledge-crafting team, 29, 30
training, 32
Viewpoints, 258
Visual representation, relationships, 224

Weather problem, rule evaluation, 330
Windowing environment, 88
Work environment, cultural issues, 76
Workstations, 88, 89
AI, 147, 150, 151
-based delivery systems, 92–94
engineering, 89, 147
Worlds, 258
Written communication, 20

Xerox, 16, 17, 89
Loops, 91